Understanding
Twice-
Exceptional
Learners

Understanding Twice-Exceptional Learners

Connecting Research to Practice

Edited by

C. Matthew Fugate, Ph.D.,
Wendy A. Behrens, M.A. Ed.,
and Cecelia Boswell, Ed.D.

Routledge
Taylor & Francis Group

NEW YORK AND LONDON

Library of Congress Cataloging-in-Publication Data

Names: Fugate, C. Matthew, editor. | Behrens, Wendy A., editor. | Boswell,
   Cecelia A., 1949- editor.
Title: Understanding twice-exceptional learners : connecting research to
   practice / C. Matthew Fugate, Wendy A. Behrens, and Cecelia Boswell.
Description: Waco, TX : Prufrock Press Inc., 2020. | Includes
   bibliographical references. | Summary: ""Understanding Twice-Exceptional
   Learners" offers an in-depth look at the needs and lived experiences of
   students who are twice-exceptional"-- Provided by publisher.
Identifiers: LCCN 2020025953 (print) | LCCN 2020025954 (ebook) | ISBN
   9781646320776 (paperback) | ISBN 9781646320783 (ebook) | ISBN
   9781646320790 (epub)
Subjects: LCSH: Twice exceptional children--Education. | Learning disabled
   children--Education. | Children with autism spectrum
   disorders--Education. | Gifted children--Education.
Classification: LCC LC3965 .U64 2020 (print) | LCC LC3965 (ebook) | DDC
   371.94--dc23
LC record available at https://lccn.loc.gov/2020025953
LC ebook record available at https://lccn.loc.gov/2020025954

First published in 2020 by Prufrock.Press Inc.

Published in 2021 by Routledge
605 Third Avenue, New York, NY 10017
2 Park Square, Milton Park, Abingdon, Oxon OX14 4RN

Routledge is an imprint of the Taylor & Francis Group, an informa business.

© 2020 by Taylor & Francis Group

Cover and layout design by Allegra Denbo

ISBN: 9781032144542 (hbk)
ISBN: 9781646320776 (pbk)

DOI: 10.4324/9781003239345

Dedication

To Rob, Bob, and Kent for their unwavering
support of us throughout this project.

Table of Contents

Acknowledgements

WE would like to express our sincere appreciation to the chapter authors for their tireless work and contributions to this project. We would also like to thank Joel McIntosh, Katy McDowall, and the entire team at Prufrock Press for their belief in the importance of this project from the very beginning. Additionally, we would like to express our sincere gratitude to Cheryll M. Adams, Ph.D., Lynette Breedlove, Ph.D., Jeff Danielian, Megan Foley-Nicpon, Ph.D., Mary L. Slade, Ph.D., and Debbie A. Troxclair, Ph.D., for their thoughtful feedback and reviews on this project. Finally, thank you to our families and friends for their unconditional support and unwavering belief in our work. This book is for the twice-exceptional among us.

—Matt, Wendy, and Cecelia

Introduction

Messages From the Editors

I HAVE reflected a lot on my journey as an educator as we have prepared this book. One of the reasons that this project is so important to me was realizing the lack of preparation that I had when I first entered the classroom. Do not get me wrong; I received a wonderful education from a nationally recognized educator preparation program. However, upon reflection I realized that, contrary to what is stressed to preservice teachers, my preparation involved a "teach-to-the-middle" model—the student population was presented as primarily homogenous in their developmental needs. When differentiation was discussed, the conversation was primarily from a deficit perspective, focusing on what teachers can do to "fix" the student who is struggling. What was missing is what is lacking in many programs—adequate preparation for when gifted students walk into your classroom expecting that you will advance their understanding of the world. And what was *never* discussed was what to do if those gifted students also have special education needs.

Educators often think of gifted students as those who hang on the teacher's every word, turn in their work on time, and are always perfect, requiring

1

little, if any, correction. Those that work in the field of gifted education know that these students are a myth. Gifted students challenge educators every day. Gifted students look at the world through critical eyes and come armed with an endless barrage of questions. They seek out new ways to address problems that often contradict the way that they have been taught. In short, there is no such thing as ideal gifted students. This challenge is compounded when gifted students are also identified with learning and behavioral differences that require special education services.

For many educators, the idea of a student being twice-exceptional (2e) is an oxymoron. How can a student be identified as gifted and also have a learning disability? Conversely, how can a student who has a learning disability also be gifted? Yet, there are an estimated 385,000 twice-exceptional students sitting in our classrooms (Assouline et al., 2015), and more likely than not, that number is much larger. These children live with each of their feet in a different world, and educators have to understand what those two worlds look like in order to help these students grow and develop.

When I worked as a classroom teacher and gifted coordinator, I was always on the lookout for resources and tools that would benefit my students. All too often, I would find classroom materials that sounded "cute" but had little evidence of being anything more than that. When I would turn to research journals, the results described in the articles would often sound interesting, but I would find myself asking, "So what? How does this help my students?" Since moving into academia, I have made it a priority to answer those questions in my work. This book provides readers with an in-depth look at the needs and lived experiences of students who are twice-exceptional. Each chapter includes an in-depth literature review of disabilities and learning challenges that teachers commonly see in classrooms and are often seen in twice-exceptional students. These literature reviews are followed by vignettes that describe the experiences of gifted students with the disability covered in that chapter, along with questions that ask the reader to think about these students on a deeper level.

This book is a resource for preservice and inservice teachers in undergraduate and graduate programs—as well as for professional development—that addresses how teachers teach and work with students in this population. I hope that you find this book to be a valuable resource for your own professional growth and that it helps you better understand the experiences of the students you serve.

In closing, I would like to thank my dear friends Wendy and Cecelia for taking this journey with me. I learn so much from them every day, and I look forward to many more years of collaboration and fellowship.

—Matt

EVERY child is entitled to a challenging and appropriate education. Does the concept change with the child, the setting, or the severity of need? The answer can vary. Although educators' obligation to provide an appropriate education is unquestionable, unique student needs require modification to content and instruction. For students with either significant skill deficits or extraordinary talents, the answer is often clear. However, twice-exceptional students, with remarkable strengths as well as significant challenges, require a different approach. Educators must provide both an intellectually stimulating curriculum and the necessary accommodations to meet special education needs.

As a district coordinator of services, my discovery of twice-exceptional learners often followed conversations with a special education teacher, sharing news of a student labeled "LD" or "EBD" who was also "really smart." A closer look revealed, on several occasions, a twice-exceptional learner. Although the discovery was welcomed, the understanding necessary to address the student's gifted and special education needs was often missing. An Individualized Education Program (IEP) detailing accommodations was required by law; however, guidance for concurrently addressing gifted education needs was conspicuously absent. Special education needs, protected by the Individuals With Disabilities Education Act (IDEA, 1990), prevailed in every case. IDEA requires schools to find and evaluate students with learning challenges at no cost to families. Gifted learners in the United States have no such protection.

I delved into the research, hoping to satisfy my growing need to understand disabilities and their impact on gifted learners. Strategies to address student behaviors were interesting but did nothing to help me understand the "why" and "what." My research continued when I became a state director of gifted education. My new position afforded me countless opportunities to speak with parents anxious to support twice-exceptional learners, as well as educators seeking advice on identification and effective models of service. My knowledge increased, but I still felt something was missing.

I was hopeful but unable to find a thorough review of the literature with recommendations that put a "human face" on the issues that twice-exceptional students encounter. I wondered how to relate the stories of the students whose needs were unmet. Could a publication of research and recommendations with vignettes help bridge the gap? I decided it was time to share the idea with my friend Matt Fugate, a well-known 2e researcher and scholar. Matt immediately saw a need for the project and agreed to help me pitch the idea to Joel McIntosh at Prufrock Press. My dear friend and frequent coauthor Cecelia Boswell was also "all in" from the beginning. Cecelia's vast experience and perspective as an administrator, teacher, and consultant have been a great contribution to this project. I've thoroughly enjoyed Friday morning "Book Club"—our weekly, 2-hour editing conversations. Fortunately, our next project on culturally responsive teaching in gifted education has begun.

—Wendy

WHEN Wendy called to tell me about the concept that she and Matt had developed for a book addressing twice-exceptional students' nature and needs, I said, "I want in." The concept for this book was one that I could not bypass. Wendy's experience as state director and Matt's expertise in the field of 2e make perfect partners for this educational endeavor. I considered myself lucky to add to the harmony of this duo. A book for professionals looking to further their knowledge and career on topics at the forefront of education and to hear from experts in the field, explore vignettes about learners, and have professional resources was a rare prospect. This book provides all that and more.

The search for experts in each of the fields presented in this book brought us into contact with passionate researchers and practitioners. The expertise they share in this book gives insight into their thinking about children and young adults who, while gifted, experience learning challenges that are hidden because of their abilities. These authors show both sides of learning abilities and differences. For example, in Chapter 1, Baum and Schader provide historical references that impact the current field of twice-exceptionality. For the practitioner, this book gives insight and concrete examples of students who seem to be a mystery. Each chapter offers ways to determine the best course of action to develop any child's full potential.

Each chapter offers the depth of research that comes from the authors' passion for their subject. Research and practice have been fully explored by each author. The field of twice-exceptionality recognizes each of these contributors for their expertise in the selected fields. Matt, Wendy, and I are indebted to each author for what they have given us on this journey and what we offer to readers for their own journeys.

The vignettes in each area of exceptionality were written by the editors in an effort to illustrate students whom educators might see in real-world settings. The vignettes and the questions to further readers' understanding of each exceptionality were designed with educators in mind. My hope is that the vignettes bring the chapters' research and descriptions to life.

I envision this book for educators of children, young adults, and even adults. This book is for those who wonder why their learning is or was not experienced in same way as their peers. As you explore dyslexia and dyscalculia, executive function, autism spectrum disorders, Attention Deficit/Hyperactivity Disorder, and anxiety through the eyes of these professionals, the vignettes, or subsequent discussions, think of those who will be helped because you took the time for this book—I do.

—*Cecelia*

References

Assouline, S. G., Colangelo, N., VanTassel-Baska, J., & Lupkowski-Shoplik, A. (Eds.). (2015). *A nation empowered: Evidence trumps the excuses holding back America's brightest students* (Vol. 2). The University of Iowa, The Connie Belin & Jacqueline N. Blank International Center for Gifted Education and Talent Development.

Individuals With Disabilities Education Act, 20 U.S.C. §1401 *et seq.* (1990). https://sites.ed.gov/idea/statuteregulations

CHAPTER 1

Twice-Exceptionality
A Field Whose Time Has Come

Susan M. Baum and Robin M. Schader

Over the past 3 decades, worldwide interest in a special population of students has caught the attention of scholars, practitioners, and parents. Known as the twice-exceptional, or 2e, this group of learners is characterized by advanced abilities as well as learning difficulties that include deficits in areas such as reading, writing, focusing attention, and/or understanding social cues. These deficits are often associated with disability diagnoses and special education accommodations. Students' strengths, however, may find a home in the field of gifted education. Figure 1.1 shows possible combinations constituting twice-exceptionality.

Although 2e students have high, even exceptional, abilities in some domains, their challenges (which can include academic, social, emotional, and behavioral issues) can hold them back. Their educational journeys are often filled with detours and roadblocks, as their learning and behavior profiles are frequently at odds with traditional methods of schooling (Assouline & Whiteman, 2011; Baum et al., 2014; Foley-Nicpon et al., 2011; Reis et al., 2014).

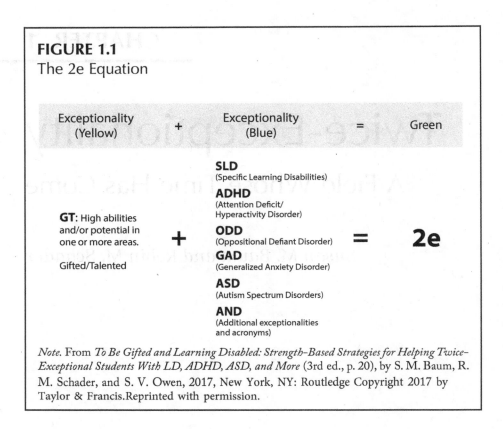

FIGURE 1.1
The 2e Equation

Exceptionality (Yellow)	+	Exceptionality (Blue)	=	Green

GT: High abilities and/or potential in one or more areas. Gifted/Talented	**+**	**SLD** (Specific Learning Disabilities) **ADHD** (Attention Deficit/ Hyperactivity Disorder) **ODD** (Oppositional Defiant Disorder) **GAD** (Generalized Anxiety Disorder) **ASD** (Autism Spectrum Disorders) **AND** (Additional exceptionalities and acronyms)	**=**	**2e**

Note. From *To Be Gifted and Learning Disabled: Strength-Based Strategies for Helping Twice-Exceptional Students With LD, ADHD, ASD, and More* (3rd ed., p. 20), by S. M. Baum, R. M. Schader, and S. V. Owen, 2017, New York, NY: Routledge Copyright 2017 by Taylor & Francis.Reprinted with permission.

The concept of twice-exceptionality is difficult because the two distinct needs of 2e students cannot be segregated. This means that addressing one aspect in isolation of the other is not optimal and may, in fact, be detrimental to successful learning.

Consider 2e students in this way: Each 2e student has distinguishing strengths usually associated with "giftedness" (think yellow) and complex challenges usually associated with "special education" (think blue). As with painting, when yellows and blues mix, variations of green result. Neither the yellow nor the blue can be taken out of the mix and still result in green. Think of twice-exceptional students as green. They will always be green, living with their incongruous combination of gifts and disabilities (see Figure 1.2).

The arrows in Figure 1.2 are a two-dimensional representation of green, one that risks implying that students are a static blend or type, but the reality is that each student moves across the spectrum from yellow to blue at different times, within different environments, and in response to changing conditions. When stakeholders understand their supporting roles, they can help 2e students maximize and develop their strengths while discovering ways to minimize and accommodate for their challenges.

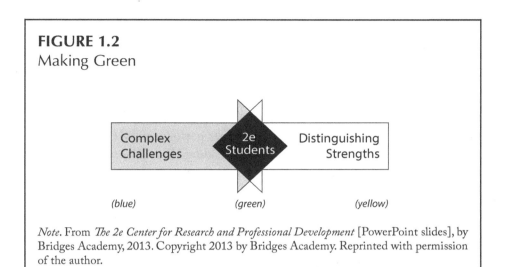

FIGURE 1.2
Making Green

Complex Challenges | 2e Students | Distinguishing Strengths

(blue)   (green)   (yellow)

Note. From *The 2e Center for Research and Professional Development* [PowerPoint slides], by Bridges Academy, 2013. Copyright 2013 by Bridges Academy. Reprinted with permission of the author.

Unfortunately, even today some professionals continue to argue that gifted students cannot also have disabilities or special needs. Others claim that the 2e population is too amorphous. Increasing evidence suggests that these students not only exist, but also have remarkable minds (Foley-Nicpon et al., 2011). In fact, many believe that these students represent future creators and leaders in a world that requires innovation and talent.

This chapter provides an overview of the origins of the field of twice-exceptionality, the characteristics of 2e students, clear definitions that guide practice, and an educational approach that can support their needs.

The Origins of the Field

The relatively new field of twice-exceptionality results from a marriage between two branches of education: gifted education (with a focus on identifying advanced abilities and providing enrichment and talent development opportunities) and special education (with a focus on identifying deficits and remediating those deficits). Each of these educational specializations addresses human differences. Long before these two fields were firmly established individually, psychologists referenced the still-argued idea that individuals could be both exceptionally able and display concurrent learning, behavioral, and social issues. Hollingworth (1923) wrote about students with superior intelligence and limiting deficiencies. She began her work at the Clearinghouse for Mental

Defectives, but also led the work at the Speyer School for rapid learners in New York City, as she was fascinated with highly gifted students. Through her study of seven nonreaders with IQs ranging from 94 to 130, Hollingworth noted that some of them also had difficulty learning in specific areas. She also wrote, "Occasionally, a very intelligent child is found who does not readily learn arithmetic and on the other hand there exists children whose ability at calculations far exceeds expectation from other performances" (p. 114).

Similarly, Orton (1925), who studied reading disorders, recognized that learning issues were not necessarily due to below-average intelligence scores as measured by the Stanford Binet IQ test. This finding was later confirmed in studies conducted by Asperger (1944), who was looking at children who exhibited sets of behaviors that seemed incongruous—excellent logical abstract thinking and isolated areas of high knowledge and/or intense interest, but also pedantic speech, impairment of two-way interactions, repetitive and stereotyped play, and unawareness of and inability to deal with environmental demands. He later pointed out that some of these individuals had high levels of intelligence (Asperger, 1979).

However, these observations went no further. No effort was made to distinguish students who may have had both high abilities and disabilities from those students with disabilities and average or less-than-average abilities. In fact, in all cases, attention was drawn to the disability regardless of the levels of cognitive abilities. For example, Cruickshank et al. (1961) investigated students who exhibited neurological deficits, such as:

- increased motor activity,
- poor organization of behavior,
- distractibility of more than ordinary degree under ordinary conditions,
- persistent faulty perceptions,
- persistent hyperactivity, and
- awkwardness and consistently poor motor performance.

These deficits resulted in students' failure to read, write, and spell. In their work on teaching methods for children who are brain-injured and hyperactive, Cruickshank et al. noted that many of the children also possessed superior intelligence. However, their study focused on the need for a structured environment in which distractions were minimized within an individualized curriculum for their sample of students. Although it was apparent that the students were often scoring in the superior range on an intelligence test, there were no specific strategies for accommodating their advanced abilities.

Interestingly, Cruickshank (1977) later hypothesized that hyperactivity and distractibility may actually describe the way some high-ability students absorb information, suggesting that attention to all stimuli in their environment actually may have enhanced their knowledge acquisition. But, in reality, although special education expanded to include students with superior intellectual abilities, the focus remained on what students could *not* do, what their learning and attention issues were, and how to remediate their deficits.

This deficit-based approach took on a life of its own when Kirk and Bateman (1962) offered an alternative hypothesis as to why students with at least average ability were having difficulties in school. They argued that the etiology of the problem resulted from underlying language and learning deficits, which stemmed from perceptual and cognitive processing difficulties. Kirk and Bateman coined the term "learning disabilities," which steered away from the concomitant behaviors of hyperactivity and distractibility. Interestingly, the intellectual profiles of those they observed showed peaks and valleys that distinguished the group from below-average students who presented a more even pattern of abilities.

In 1966, Gallagher, an educational psychologist who was interested in both gifted students and students with learning challenges, pointed out that some students with learning disabilities had considerable strengths in comparison to their areas of weakness. Gallagher (1986) later referred to these students as *twice-exceptional*—the first mention of that term to describe students who were gifted and displayed learning disabilities at the same time. This new label, however, still focused on "fixing" as the primary approach to addressing learning differences, without regard to students' ability potential.

During this period, interest in gifted and talented students was also gaining momentum. Psychologists sought to understand the characteristics of individuals who scored in the top 2% of the population on measures of intelligence. Around the same period, Hollingworth (1923) presented a contrasting view. She saw a great need for this group of students to have a learning environment especially designed to meet their "brilliance" and introduced the idea of enrichment as a way to meet the needs of gifted students.

In short, the fields of special education and gifted education were taking different paths. Giftedness was narrowly defined to include students who demonstrated high cognitive abilities, without any nod to those who may have concurrent learning challenges. Gifted students received advanced curriculum and enrichment, while those students identified as requiring special education services were supported through a remedial approach, regardless of their intellectual profiles. In the United States, the separation was reinforced by the passage of two federal laws. The first, the Education for All Handicapped Children Act of 1975, mandated a free and appropriate public education for all children with disabilities, ensured due process rights, and mandated Individualized

Education Programs (IEPs) and placement of students in the least restrictive environment. There was no mention of students with gifts and talents. The second law, the Gifted and Talented Children's Education Act of 1978, included the establishment of the National Leadership Training Institute, Office of Gifted and Talented, and defined *gifted and talented* as follows:

> Children, and where applicable youth, who are identified at the preschool, elementary, or secondary level as possessing demonstrated or potential abilities that give evidence of high-performance capability in areas such as
> - intellectual domains
> - creativity
> - specific academic areas
> - leadership ability
> - performing and visual arts
>
> and who by reason thereof require services or activities not ordinarily provided by the school.

Note that the definition of giftedness was expanded to include specific domains, as opposed to the more conservative notion of the top 2% of the population indicated through IQ testing. Unfortunately, unlike the special education legislation, this act neither mandated nor funded identification of, or programs for, gifted students.

A Merging of Two Fields

Professionals from both gifted education and special education ultimately began to acknowledge that a portion of the students with whom they were working required a dual diagnosis. Some students being served in special education were indeed creative, talented, or gifted in certain areas. Likewise, there were students in gifted programs who were struggling in specific areas and underachieving. Many were having difficulty producing work, maintaining focus during class, and organizing their world. In addition, new theories of intelligence (e.g., Gardner, 1983/2011; Sternberg, 1985) challenged the idea that abilities can be represented by a single score on a traditional intelligence test. Broadened definitions of giftedness opened the door to the possibility of dual diagnosis. Renzulli's (1978) definition of giftedness as a set of three behaviors—above-average ability, creativity, and task commitment occurring in certain people, at certain times, and under certain conditions—laid the groundwork for students with learning or behavior challenges to also be recognized as having the potential for gifted behaviors. Publications began to provide information about gifted individuals with disabilities and how their issues confound educators' understanding of their unique needs (e.g., Maker, 1977; Meisgeier et al., 1978). Researchers began noting that those who were then called the "gifted handicapped" had need for enrichment and talent development, as well as special educational support—academically, socially, and emotionally.

During the next 2 decades, scholars began conducting research on the characteristics of students who were noted to be twice-exceptional, piloting programs to identify and address their needs. Baum and Owen (1988) found that students with learning disabilities and high intellectual ability (GT/LD) were creative, had more intense interests than their gifted peers (GT) without learning disabilities or peers with learning disabilities (LD) and average intelligence. But, at the same time, the GT/LD experienced low self-efficacy, saw themselves as academic failures, and exhibited the most disruptive behaviors in school out of the three groups studied. In 1997, Brody and Mills conducted a review of literature on GT/LD and suggested that these students could be considered the most misunderstood of all exceptionalities: "They are often not identified and continue to be a severely misunderstood and underserved population" (p. 292). They also argued that these students should have access to both gifted and special education services.

In 1988, the Jacob K. Javits Gifted and Talented Students Education Act (now the Jacob K. Javits Gifted and Talented Students Education Program, 2015) began providing research and program development grants for the purpose of addressing the needs of underserved students, including gifted students with disabilities. As a result, model programs have appeared, and systematic studies have looked at identification and educational approaches suitable for these dually-diagnosed youngsters.

A growing body of evidence from the Javits initiative has revealed that the twice-exceptional population is composed of not only gifted students who have also been identified with specific learning disabilities, but also populations of high-ability students from most areas of special education. Technically, 2e refers to students who are identified as gifted and talented and also diagnosed with one or more of the special education categories as defined by the Individuals With Disabilities Education Act (IDEA, 1990), with the exception of those students with cognitive disabilities. Accounting for most of this population are high-ability students with one or more of the following: specific learning disabilities (SLD), Attention Deficit/Hyperactivity Disorder (ADHD), and autism spectrum disorders (ASD; Assouline & Whiteman, 2011).

Operational Definitions of Twice-Exceptionality

The need emerged for a comprehensive definition of twice-exceptionality with specific criteria for identification and services. In 2009, a national Joint Commission on Twice-Exceptional Students was formed to discuss the state of research related to 2e students and to adopt a new definition based on available research and scholarly discourse. The commission included researchers, practitioners, clinical psychologists, and educational therapists with extensive experience with twice-exceptional students. Two versions of the definition coming from this meeting have been published: (1) An operational definition with guidelines for identification and programming was published in *Gifted Child Quarterly* (Reis et al., 2014), and (2) a more pragmatic definition, intended to be used across disciplines by different practicing professionals, was published in a special issue of *Gifted Child Today* (Baldwin et al., 2015) devoted to explaining how the definition can be used by professionals.

First, here is the 2014 definition:

> Twice-exceptional learners are students who demonstrate the potential for high achievement or creative productivity in one or more domains such as math, science, technology, the social arts, the visual, spatial, or performing arts or other areas of human productivity AND who manifest one or more disabilities as defined by federal or state eligibility criteria. These disabilities include specific learning disabilities, speech and language disorders, emotional/behavioral disorders, physical disabilities, Autism Spectrum Disorders (ASD), or other health impairments, such as Attention Deficit/Hyperactivity Disorder (ADHD). These disabilities and high abilities combine to produce a unique population of students who may fail to demonstrate either high academic performance or specific disabilities. Their gifts may mask their disabilities and their disabilities may mask their gifts. Identification of twice-exceptional students requires comprehensive assessment in both the areas of giftedness and disabilities, as one does not preclude the other. Identification, when possible, should be conducted by professionals from both disciplines and, when at all possible, by those with knowledge about twice-exceptionality

in order to address the impact of co-incidence/co-morbidity of both areas on diagnostic assessments and eligibility requirements for services.

Educational services must identify and serve both the high achievement potential and the academic and social-emotional deficits of this population of students. Twice-exceptional students require differentiated instruction, curricular and instructional accommodations and/or modifications, direct services, specialized instruction, acceleration options, and opportunities for talent development that incorporate the effects of their dual diagnosis.

Twice-exceptional students require an individual education plan (IEP) or a 504 accommodation plan with goals and strategies that enable them to achieve at a level and rate commensurate with their abilities. This comprehensive education plan must include talent development goals, as well as compensation skills and strategies to address their disabilities and their social and emotional needs. (Reis et al., 2014, pp. 222–223)

This is the 2015 definition:

Twice-exceptional individuals evidence exceptional ability and disability, which results in a unique set of circumstances. Their exceptional ability may dominate, hiding their disability; their disability may dominate, hiding their exceptional ability; each may mask the other so that neither is recognized or addressed. 2e students, who may perform below, at, or above grade level, require the following:

- Specialized methods of identification that consider the possible interaction of the exceptionalities,
- Enriched/advanced educational opportunities that develop the child's interests, gifts, and talents while also meeting the child's learning needs,
- Simultaneous supports that ensure the child's academic success and social-emotional well-being, such as accommodations, therapeutic interventions, and specialized instruction, and
- Working successfully with this unique population requires specialized academic training and ongoing

professional development. (Baldwin et al., 2015, pp. 212–213)

Recognizing the Twice-Exceptional Learner

Twice-exceptional students have two seemingly paradoxical sets of behaviors: those aligned to their high cognitive and creative abilities, and those associated with their particular challenge area. Typical gifted behaviors include (Baum et al., 2017; Renzulli & Reis, 2014; Webb et al., 2007):

- unusual alertness early in life;
- rapid learning and quick thinking;
- strong memories and retention of information;
- large vocabularies and complex sentence structure for their age;
- understanding of advanced word nuances, metaphors, and abstract ideas;
- enjoyment of solving problems involving numbers and puzzles;
- self-teaching in reading and writing;
- unusual emotional depth, intense feelings, and reactions;
- abstract, complex, logical, and insightful thinking;
- sense of idealism and justice at an early age;
- concern with social and political issues and injustices;
- longer attention spans, persistence, and intense concentration;
- preoccupation with one's own thoughts and daydreaming;
- impatience with self or others' inabilities or slowness;
- learning of basic skills more quickly and with less practice;
- asking probing questions, going beyond what is being taught;
- wide ranges of interests (sometimes extreme interest in only one area);
- highly developed curiosity and asking of limitless questions;
- experimentation and doing things differently;
- putting ideas or things together in ways that are unusual or not obvious (divergent thinking);
- keen and sometimes unusual senses of humor, particularly with puns;
- organizing things and people through games or complex schemas;
- imaginary playmates (in preschool) and vivid imaginations; and/or
- talents in distinct domains, such as the arts, engineering and design, technology, and robotics, writing, mathematics, etc.

Although twice-exceptional students can exhibit many of these traits, they also demonstrate traits that are often associated with dyslexia, specific learning disabilities, and/or autism spectrum disorders. These traits include anxiety, oppositional and defiant behaviors, hyperactivity, issues in social understandings and behavior, and lack of productivity. Some have poor reading and math skills, problems in spelling and handwriting, difficulties with expressive language, lack of organizational skills, inability to focus and sustain attention, limited capacity for social interaction, and poor self-efficacy and esteem (Assouline & Whiteman, 2011; Baum et al., 2014; Reis et al., 1995).

A major review of empirical studies conducted by Foley-Nicpon et al. (2011) acknowledged that twice-exceptional students are set apart from other populations of exceptional students (cognitively, socially, and emotionally). Foley-Nicpon et al. emphatically declared there could no longer be an argument denying that students with high abilities or gifts and talents in specific domains could be simultaneously academically challenged and diagnosed with one or more other exceptionalities as defined by IDEA. Twice-exceptional students may present a host of conundrums, including:

- high-level comprehension (need for sophisticated content) *but* with reading limitations,
- creative and sophisticated ideas *but* difficulty putting them down on paper,
- task commitment and flow time *but* difficulty attending to tasks when things are auditory,
- potential for expertise *but* difficulty learning novice skills with automaticity, and/or
- desire to fit in *but* little social awareness.

In addition, this population of students is often highly asynchronous in development (Baum & Schader, 2018a), for they are uneven in the development of their intellectual, social, emotional, and physical skills. This means that their intellectual development may exceed that of their age-mates, while their social, emotional, and physical development lags behind. As described by one twice-exceptional student:

> Mentally I'm probably 2 or 3 years ahead of most kids my age, but socially I'm 3 years behind. So, I'm stuck in this sort of weird time warp thing where I'm at the same time, younger and older than kids my age. (Baum et al., 2017, p. 61)

Complexity of Dual Diagnosis

Complex 2e profiles require nontraditional approaches for developing abilities and simultaneously addressing any academic and behavioral challenges. The uniqueness of individual cognitive, social, emotional, and physical attributes creates issues in identification as well as in best meeting students' individual needs. Traditional methods used to identify and support these students' gifts and talents and/or their special education needs can lead to both misdiagnosis and missed diagnosis (Baum et al., 2017; Webb et al., 2016).

Identification of Gifts and Talents

Because of the existence of concurrent learning difficulties, twice-exceptional students might not be recognized as gifted and talented by standard identification procedures. With intellectual profiles that are jagged, superior scores in some areas are neutralized or depressed by challenging weaknesses. This results in a lower full-scale score that may not meet the arbitrary requirements set by district policies for identifying gifted students. Likewise, using classroom performances as criteria for being labeled gifted and talented can be problematic. For example, even though a 2e student may reveal a remarkable depth of knowledge, advanced vocabulary, and skill in arguing any theory when questioned verbally, they may struggle when required to put their ideas on paper and can be nonproductive, sullen, and obstinate. Teachers, without knowledge of this profile, may label students like this as lazy and oppositional defiant. As a result, rather than recognizing a student's need for enrichment and respecting their advanced abilities, the focus becomes remedial and/or punitive. In fact, Baum (1985) found that up to 33% of students receiving special education services had IQs in the superior range in either verbal or performance areas on the Wechsler Intelligence Scale. None of the students in this study were identified as gifted or talented, nor did they receive services allocated to gifted students without disabilities.

Identification for Special Education Services

Likewise, students who have been identified as gifted but never meet academic expectations may have learning disabilities. However, their high abilities prevent them from falling far enough behind to warrant a special education evaluation. These students can remain on grade level and even earn high grades in some subjects by spending considerable time getting their work done, often with the support of their parents or tutors (which, in actuality, masks the problem). By the time the difficulties are recognized and properly identified, these students may have fallen behind, become highly anxious and depressed, and/ or dropped out. They frequently feel like failures, not understanding why they are not able to keep up with their gifted classmates. These feelings can lead to a downward spiral causing them to shut down, act out, or give up (Baum et al., 2014, 2017; Webb et al., 2016).

Further Complications

Another difficulty in recognizing twice-exceptional students is that gifts and learning challenges can mask each other. In this case, a student is not identified as gifted nor receiving special services to support their learning challenges. In an ongoing tug of war, the intellectual abilities hide the disabilities, and the disabilities disguise the gifts and talents. Children like this are hard to identify because their performance is not remarkable. However, if they are fortunate in finding a teacher whose methods align to how they learn best, moments of brilliance may appear. This often occurs in arts-integrated classrooms or courses in science, engineering, and technology. In classrooms such as these, reading and writing are often replaced by experiential learning and creative productivity is encouraged, which are more appropriate approaches for some 2e students.

Finally, because of the complex combination of high abilities and disabilities, behaviors can be easily misinterpreted. For instance, when high-ability students are not intellectually challenged, they may have a difficult time attending to tasks and waiting their turn to respond, especially when they already know the information. They can refuse to do assignments that are too easy and can display behavior problems when asked to hide their abilities or put them on hold—behaviors that can lead to the false impression that they have attention deficits or are oppositional defiant.

Meeting Their Needs: A Paradigm Shift

The definitions of twice-exceptionality underscore a critical need for professionals to work with the full complexities of these students in order to provide appropriate services. Such students require enrichment and remediation, as well as special counseling. A dual diagnosis of advanced abilities with disabilities is more complex than may be seen on the surface, and the complexity impacts the kinds of programs that can support these students for success.

Understanding the Complexities of the 2e Learner

Working with 2e students requires careful consideration of whether traditional enrichment/talent development and remedial approaches are appropriate. Bright minds require intellectual challenge to stay focused and attend to the tasks at hand. Therefore, watering down the curriculum to an appropriate reading level for a gifted student with dyslexia may cause embarrassment or boredom because of the low-level content—leaving the student with nothing new or interesting to comprehend. Likewise, using advanced reading material to engage the student's intellect may be equally as frustrating if they cannot decode the words.

Consider gifted students with ADHD who crave intellectual stimulation to focus and attend, but who are required to engage in a curriculum that is neither novel nor complex. For these students, the pace at which lessons are taught may be too slow to hold their interest. Critical factors like these are often overlooked when designing educational programs.

The dilemmas of dual diagnosis also relate to expectations for engaging students in the social environment. Socialization requires that "an individual acquires a personal identity and learns the norms, values, behavior, and social skills appropriate to his or her social position" (Dictionary.com, n.d.). In other words, socialization requires interactions with others who have some things in common. When a highly verbally gifted child with ASD is placed in a social skills class with students who do not share that student's intellectual prowess nor the intensity with which they pursue their interests, there may be little common ground for authentic socialization to develop.

It behooves professionals not to think of twice-exceptional students as simply needing gifted services and remedial accommodations—as though they are separate entities—but rather understand that these students bring their gifts with them to the remedial setting and their challenges to enriched settings. This concept is what led to the metaphor of green described in the opening paragraphs of this chapter.

Dual Differentiation and the "Green" Student

Using the idea of "green" gives professionals a way to understand and discuss the need for experiences in which students' high abilities and talents are considered along with their challenges when planning learning activities (see Figure 1.3). For instance, students with dyslexia or poor decoding skills may participate more fully in literature discussions by using poetry. Often the greatest poets use the simplest diction in presenting metaphors colorfully and succinctly. Discovering the meaning of a poem will certainly engage a mind that seeks complexity and, at the same time, ease the cognitive demand when decoding. Consider Robert Frost's poem "Stopping by Woods on a Snowy Evening," as illustrated by Susan Jeffers (Frost, 1978). The words within the piece are easy to decode. The metaphor is open to rich interpretation, making the educational experience simultaneously simple and complex:

> The woods are lovely, dark and deep.
> But I have promises to keep,
> And miles to go before I sleep,
> And miles to go before I sleep.

In short, using an illustrated book of classic poetry is a prime example of dual differentiation. It satisfies the needs of a 2e learner with reading challenges because the student can cognitively engage and participate fully in discussion because they are able to decode the words (Baum et al., 2001).

Strength-Based, Talent-Focused, Dually Differentiated Learning

Looking at what students can do is in contrast to the traditional assumption that 2e students' deficits must be remediated before attention can be given to their abilities and interests. Remediation with little or inappropriate attention to students' gifts or talents can lead to feelings of inadequacy and low self-efficacy (Baum & Owen, 1988). Moreover, because remediation techniques usually lack the very characteristics high-ability students require for successful learning, educational plans using this approach are limiting (Baum et al., 2017). In addition, 2e students who are eligible for—and invited to—advanced classes may discover that there is little tolerance for their learning differences (Schultz, 2011).

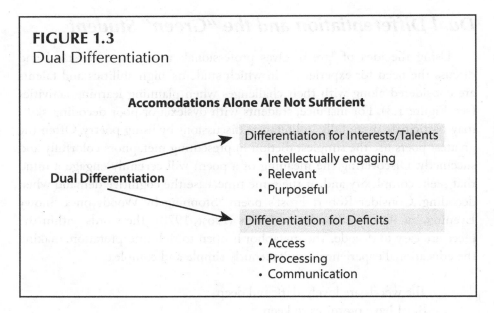

FIGURE 1.3
Dual Differentiation

Accomodations Alone Are Not Sufficient

Dual Differentiation

Differentiation for Interests/Talents

- Intellectually engaging
- Relevant
- Purposeful

Differentiation for Deficits

- Access
- Processing
- Communication

Even when a particular student's dual set of needs is acknowledged, meeting those needs in productive ways is complicated. However, a strength-based, talent-focused approach can provide entry points that have proven to be successful in helping 2e students reach academic, social, and behavioral goals (Baum et al., 2014; Baum & Schader, 2018b).

Baum et al. (2014) defined a strength-based, talent-focused approach as using the knowledge of students' strengths, cognitive profiles, learning preferences, interests, and talents to engage them in the curriculum. The strengths and interests can be leveraged for skill development—including academic skills, self-regulation skills, executive function, and emotional regulation. The term *talent focus* is used for ongoing identification and recognition of students' talents, budding interests, curiosities, and passions, and provides opportunities for enrichment that build on and expand possible areas of talent or interest. Embedded in this approach is the idea of *talent development*, which involves providing opportunities (both within and outside of the curriculum) to develop students' advanced abilities and interests in their own right, not as a means to other ends or as a reward. Talent development must be regarded as an essential, nonnegotiable component of any program designed for twice-exceptional learners.

The idea that diagnoses such as dyslexia or ADHD are also associated with particular strengths is relevant when considering programs for 2e learners (Archer, 2015; Armstrong, 2012; Eide & Eide, 2011; Grandin & Panek, 2013). This growing awareness comes from the acknowledgement that neurodiverse minds are assets to be nurtured, not disabilities to be "fixed." Individuals who do not think or see the world in mainstream ways are said to be "wired differently." These different kinds of minds can give rise to extraordinary abilities and talents (one exception) that accompany learning and/or behavioral challenges (also an exception). Table 1.1 provides a condensed look at some of the challenges and associated strengths for those with ADHD, dyslexia, and ASD.

In short, evidence suggests that twice-exceptional students are best served when the potential benefits of their particular "wiring" are considered. The following story of Riley (adapted from Kennedy et al., 2018) provides a glimpse into the importance of identifying and addressing strengths, abilities, interests, and talents within an educational program.

A Strength-Based, Talent-Focused Approach in Action

Riley is a friendly, energetic eighth-grade girl who exhibits many of the qualities one might expect from a bright student with ADHD wiring. For example:

- She's quite disorganized and has difficulty completing tasks.
- When required to sit still in class for an extended period of time, she can become talkative and disruptive.
- She tends to miss details and frequently fails to follow directions, which results in difficulty with math procedures, calculations, and spelling.

On the other hand, Riley has many strengths. In particular, she has a superior ability to recognize patterns and find innovative solutions to problems. She is a good writer, and her acting performances consistently demonstrate creativity. In addition, she has a collaborative spirit, which makes her well-liked by other students.

Riley was diagnosed with ADHD when she was 8 years old. Both her father and her older brother also have ADHD diagnoses. After years of unsuccessful learning, she moved to a school for 2e learners. In recounting her elementary school years, Riley said, "Teachers would tell me to just focus; that's like telling someone with asthma to just breathe . . . I had bad grades and couldn't do anything about it." A different Riley emerged after just a year at the new school: "They really get me. I don't doze off or look into space anymore

TABLE 1.1

Challenges and Benefits of Differently-Wired Brains

	ADHD Wiring	
Type	"Simply put, ADHD can be best understood as a brain with a very low boredom threshold. People who have it chafe against the mundane and routine, and yet they excel in chaotic situations" (Archer, 2015, p. xv1).	
Challenges	■ Easily distracted, selectively attentive, difficulty completing tasks ■ Hyperactive, needs stimulation and movement ■ Impulsive and disorganized	
Benefits	■ Often creative, intuitive, thinkers with a flair for innovation and out-of-the-box thinking ■ Can have high energy ■ Often willing to take a risk, engage in adventure, seek novelty, and show curiosity	
	Dyslexic Wiring	
Type	"Dyslexia is an ability within the sensory mechanism of the nervous system to perceive the world with a multidimensional view. When properly trained and informed, dyslexics can use their natural abilities to shift percep- tions, enhance creativity, refine thinking, and improve physical performance" (Judah, n.d., para. 3).	
Challenges	■ Difficulty decoding written language ■ May be poor in spelling and handwriting ■ Problems with rote memorization of facts and details	
Benefits	■ May be metaphorical thinkers, can see things that others miss ■ Often can visualize things in 3-D spatial perspectives; can think like an architect, engineer, or filmmaker ■ Can use narrative reasoning by recalling stories, episodes, and concepts	
	Autism Spectrum Wiring	
Type	"Children with Autism Spectrum Disorder (ASD) often also have some unique challenges to overcome in building routines and relationships that are functional and fulfilling. While much of current research and therapeutic intervention focuses on addressing those challenges, more and more research is showing that people living with ASD may also benefit from unique strengths previously unnoticed by the general population" (Panzano, 2018, para. 1).	
Challenges	■ Often unable to grasp the big picture or concept ■ May show social awkwardness and social unawareness ■ Inflexible with thinking and require predictability and routine	
Benefits	■ May be knowledgeable, skilled, and passionate in a particular area of interest and highly motivated to pursue it ■ Have the ability to focus intently on details and procedures ■ Tend to use logic in decision making with no regard for the emotional, is able to see the world in black and white and with unfettered honesty	

Note. Adapted from Baum & Schader, 2018a.

because I like my classes. I never thought I was good at math, but now I can actually help my classmates in math class!"

Keys to Change

Riley's educational transformation appears to be linked to the school's strength-based, talent-focused approach to learning. Teachers are encouraged to document and use their knowledge of students' learning attributes, interests, and background experiences to provide necessary support in skill development. Careful consideration is given to creating a positive classroom environment. Specifically, the school aims to:

1. provide a psychologically safe environment,
2. offer strength-based choices,
3. connect the curriculum to the real world,
4. help students become self-aware, and
5. engage students in talent development opportunities.

Providing a Psychologically Safe Environment. According to Maslow (1958), a psychologically safe environment is one in which students experience a sense of belonging. That sense of belonging develops when teachers make a concerted effort to get to know their students—their hopes and dreams for the school year (and the future), what puts light in their eyes, and the challenges that make it difficult for them to succeed. Riley quickly felt that her teachers believed she could succeed. She felt valued and respected. Classroom work, as well as homework, was dually differentiated to take advantage of her high cognitive abilities, specific interests, and talents, as well as her learning challenges.

Offering Strength-Based Choices. Teachers collect and use student information to differentiate and personalize the learning experience (e.g., Riley's teachers noticed that she enjoyed being in front of a crowd, making people laugh using irony and wit). With this information, teachers can then empower their students through options within the core curriculum that engage and encourage students to build skills, knowledge, and strengthen their areas of weakness. For humanities, the teachers designed four different approaches for students to choose among. It was no surprise that Riley chose a humanities class that focused on mysteries that changed history, giving her a chance to imagine herself as an FBI agent researching a case. The plethora of possibilities that came from solving a mystery kept her interested and engaged in the diverse curricular topics.

Making Real-World Connections. Teachers can help students make real-world connections with successful role models. Riley was asked to research a famous person with whom she could identify. Because one of her dreams is to become a successful comedienne, she selected Lucille Ball, who was one of the first women in the television industry, the first public figure in a biracial relationship both on and off screen, and the first to openly show a pregnancy on TV in her show *I Love Lucy*. This research led to many conversations about girls with ADHD.

Helping Students Become Self-Aware. Teachers aim to help students become productive and effective architects of their own lives. As with any typical middle school student, Riley has challenges with self-regulation. On one occasion, when feeling "hyper," she requested a classroom break, only to realize that the break did not help. As she returned, the middle school director asked if running some laps might help get her energy out. The on-the-spot experiment worked, which gave the director and Riley an opportunity to talk about differences between physical breaks and mental breaks. The discussion included how Riley might communicate her needs when she felt dysregulated but previously used strategies were not working.

Engaging Students in Talent Development. Electives to discover and develop strengths and talents are treated as essential components of the educational program. During the year, project-based, weeklong learning experiences are planned regularly in which students, with the support and guidance of teachers, collaborate to solve problems and become creative producers. During one project period, students were asked to select a cause important to them and to explore ways they might make a difference for this cause. Riley chose the group interested in improving education. Working within her group, she wrote, acted in, and directed a powerful performance about a dystopian society. Riley was able to show her ability to write, create, and be in charge of a performance. Her classmates had an opportunity to see Riley shine.

What Was Learned

In many ways Riley represents a typical gifted student with ADHD. Table 1.2 outlines some evidence-based strategies that were used to help Riley become a productive learner.

TABLE 1.2
Strategies for Working With Gifted Students With ADHD

ADHD Challenge	Suggested Strategy	How It Applied to Riley
Difficulty sustaining attention during a task.	Incorporate opportunities for movement.	Establish guidelines for Riley to run when she needed to burn off energy and refocus.
Lack of ability to initiate tasks.	Present stimulating and/or novel content.	Options for Riley (and other students) to select topics in humanities class.
Difficulty with production.	Include opportunities that value student strengths.	Riley's project choice allowed her to: ■ collaborate with peers; ■ write, direct, and produce scripts in dráma and humanities classes; and ■ show her talents.
Need for emotional support.	Develop positive relationships with teachers and administrative staff.	The teachers and support staff developed rapport with Riley to help her identify successful learning strategies. Frequent and regular teacher check-ins with Riley helped cement caring relationships.
Mismatched learning environment.	Provide a program that is sensitive to all aspects (intellectual, physical, social, emotional, and creative needs).	Riley was accelerated in performing arts class. She was given support with missing math skills.

Let Strengths Take the Lead

The field of twice-exceptionality has come a long way since its tentative beginnings. Practitioners now have information to help recognize these students and to understand the sets of often contradictory needs that must be met. Researchers continue to provide evidence of supportive learning options.

Schools and programs for 2e students are appearing worldwide, both in the private and public sectors, and publications and materials provide guidelines for students whose bright minds work in unique ways. All point to the success of an approach that honors what a student can do, as opposed to beginning with the remediation of deficits, as seductive as "fixing" might appear.

In the words of Hallowell (2005), a renowned psychologist with expertise in learning differences, dyslexia, and ADHD:

> I have learned first and foremost to look for interests, talents, strengths, shades of strengths, or the mere suggestion of a talent. Knowing that a person builds a happy and successful life not on remediated weaknesses but on developed strengths, I have learned to put those strengths at the top of what matters. (p. 34)

References

Archer, D. (2015). *The ADHD advantage: What you thought was a diagnosis may be your greatest strength.* Avery.

Armstrong, T. (2012). *Neurodiversity in the classroom: Strength-based strategies to help students with special needs succeed in school and life.* ASCD.

Asperger, H. (1944). Die autistischen Psychopathen im Kindesalter. *European Archives of Psychiatry and Clinical Neuroscience, 117*(1), 76–136.

Asperger, H. (1979). Problems of infantile autism. *Communication, 13,* 45–52.

Assouline, S. G., & Whiteman, C. S. (2011). Twice-exceptionality: Implications for school psychologists in the post–IDEA 2004 era. *Journal of Applied School Psychology, 27*(4), 380–402. https://doi.org/10.1080/15377903.2011.616576

Baldwin, L., Baum, S., Perles, D. & Hughes, C. (2015). Twice-exceptional learners: The journey toward a shared vision. *Gifted Child Today, 38*(4), 206–214. https://doi.org/10.1177/1076217515597277

Baum, S. (1985). *Learning disabled students with superior cognitive abilities: A validation study of description behaviors* [Unpublished doctoral dissertation]. University of Connecticut.

Baum, S., & Schader, R. (2018a). *2e2: Teaching the twice exceptional viewer's guide.* Child of Giants LLC.

Baum, S., & Schader, R. (2018b). Using a positive lens: 2e students as engaged learners In S. B. Kaufman (Ed.), *Twice exceptional: Supporting and educating bright and creative students with learning difficulties.* Oxford University Press. https://doi.org/10.1093/oso/9780190645472.003.0003

Baum, S. M., Cooper, C. R., & Neu, T. (2001). Dual differentiation: An approach for meeting the curricular needs of gifted students with learning disabilities. *Psychology in the Schools, 38*(5), 477–490.

Baum, S. M., & Owen, S. V. (1988). High ability/learning disabled students: How are they different? *Gifted Child Quarterly, 32*(3), 321–326. https://doi.org/10.1177/001698628803200305

Baum, S. M., Schader, R. M., & Hébert, T. P. (2014). Through a different lens: Reflecting on a strength-based, talent-focused approach for twice-exceptional learners. *Gifted Child Quarterly, 58*(4), 311–327. https://doi.org/10.1177/0016986214547632

Baum, S. M., Schader, R. M., & Owen, S. V. (2017). *To be gifted and learning disabled: Strength-based strategies for helping twice-exceptional students with LD, ADHD, ASD, and more* (3rd ed.). Prufrock Press.

Bridges Academy. (2013). *Bridges 2e Center for Research and Professional Development* [PowerPoint slides].

Brody, L. E., & Mills, C. J. (1997). Gifted children with learning disabilities: A review of the issues. *Journal of Learning Disabilities 30*(3), 282–296. https://doi.org/10.1177/002221949703000304

Cruickshank, W. M. (1977). Myths and realities in learning disabilities. *Journal of Learning Disabilities, 10*(1), 51–58. https://doi.org/10.1177/002221947701000112

Cruickshank, W. M., Bentzen, F. A., Ratzeburg, G. H., & Tannhauser, M. T. (1961). *A training method for hyperactive children.* Syracuse University Press.

Dictionary.com. (n.d.). *Socialization.* https://www.dictionary.com/browse/socialization

Education for All Handicapped Children Act of 1975, Pub. L. No. 94-142 (1975). https://www.govinfo.gov/content/pkg/STATUTE-89/pdf/STATUTE-89-Pg773.pdf

Eide, B. L., & Eide, F. F. (2011). *The dyslexic advantage: Unlocking the hidden potential of the dyslexic brain.* Penguin Group.

Foley-Nicpon, M., Allmon, A., Sieck, R., & Stinson, R. D. (2011). Empirical investigation of twice-exceptionality: Where have we been and where are we going? *Gifted Child Quarterly, 55*(1), 3–17. https://doi.org/10.1177/0016986210382575

Frost, R. (with Jeffers, S.). (1978). *Stopping by woods on a snowy evening.* Dutton.

Gallagher, J. J. (1966). Children with developmental imbalances: A psychoeducational definition. In W. Cruickshank (Ed.), *The teacher of brain-injured children* (pp. 23–43). Syracuse University Press.

Gallagher, J. J. (1986). The conservation of intellectual resources. In A. Copely, K. Urban, H. Wagner, & W. Wieczerkowski (Eds.), *Giftedness: A continuing worldwide challenge.* Trillium Press.

Gardner, H. (2011). *Frames of mind: The theory of multiple intelligences.* Basic Books. (Original work published 1983)

Gifted and Talented Children's Education Act of 1978, 20 U.S.C. § 3311 *et seq.* (1978). https://www.govinfo.gov/content/pkg/STATUTE-92/pdf/STATUTE-92-Pg2143.pdf

Grandin, T., & Panek, R. (2013). *The autistic brain: Thinking across the spectrum.* Houghton Mifflin Harcourt.

Hallowell, E. (2005). The problem with problems. *Independent School, 65*(1), 30–38.

Hollingworth, L. S. (1923). *Special talents and defects: Their significance for education.* Macmillan. https://doi.org/10.1037/13549-000

Individuals With Disabilities Education Act, 20 U.S.C. §1401 *et seq.* (1990). https://sites.ed.gov/idea/statuteregulations

Jacob K. Javits Gifted and Talented Students Education Program, 20 U.S.C. § 7294 (2015). https://congress.gov/114/plaws/publ95/PLAW-114publ95.pdf

Judah, B. A. (n.d.). *Disability or talent? Our definition of dyslexia.* Dyslexia & Learning Disability Center. https://dyslexiacenter.com/disability-or-talent

Kennedy, M., Sevilla, C., & Vargas, K. (2018, August 14). *Brains wired differently: Students with ADHD.* 2e News. https://www.2enews.com/teaching-learning/brains-wired-differently-students-with-adhd

Kirk, S. A., & Bateman, B. (1962). Diagnosis and remediation of learning disabilities. *Exceptional Children, 29*(2), 73–78. https://doi.org/10.1177/001440296202900204

Maker, C. (1977). *Providing programs for the gifted handicapped.* Council for Exceptional Children.

Maslow, A. H. (1958). A dynamic theory of human motivation. In C. L. Stacey & M. F. DeMartino (Eds.), *Understanding human motivation* (pp. 26–47). Allen.

Meisgeier, C., Meisgeier, C., & Werblo, D. (1978). Factors compounding the handicapping of some gifted children. *Gifted Child Quarterly, 22*(3), 325–331. https://doi.org/10.1177/001698627802200316

Orton, S. T. (1925). "Word-blindness" in school children. *Archives of Neurology and Psychiatry, 14*, 581–515. https://doi.org/10.1001/archneurpsyc.1925.02200170002001

Panzano, L. (2018). *Five research-based strengths associated with autism.* http://blog.stageslearning.com/blog/five-research-based-strengths-associated-with-autism

Reis, S. M., Baum, S. M., & Burke, E. (2014). An operational definition of twice-exceptional learners: Implications and applications. *Gifted Child Quarterly, 58*(3), 217–230. https://doi.org/10.1177/0016986214534976

Reis, S. M., Neu, T .W. & McGuire, J. (1995). *Talent in two places: Case studies of high-ability students with learning disabilities who have achieved* (RM95114). University of Connecticut, National Research Center on the Gifted and Talented.

Renzulli, J. S. (1978). What makes giftedness: Reexamining a definition. *Phi Delta Kappan, 60*(3), 180–184, 261.

Renzulli, J. S., & Reis, S. M. (2014). *The Schoolwide Enrichment Model: A how-to guide for talent development* (3rd ed.). Prufrock Press.

Schultz, J. (2011). *Nowhere to hide: Why kids with ADHD and LD hate school and what we can do about it.* Wiley.

Sternberg, R. J. (1985). *Beyond IQ: A triarchic theory of human intelligence.* Cambridge University Press.

Webb, J. T., Amend, E. R., Webb, N. E., Goerss, J., Beljan, P., & Olenchak, F. R. (2016). *Misdiagnosis and dual diagnoses of gifted children and adults: ADHD, bipolar, OCD, Asperger's, depression, and other disorders.* Great Potential Press.

Webb, J. T., Gore, J. L., Amend, E. R., & DeVries, A. R. (2007). *A parent's guide to gifted children.* Great Potential Press.

Author's Note. This chapter is adapted with permission from our chapter in *Handbuch der Begabungs- und Begabtenfoerderung,* by Victor Mueller-Oppliger and Gabriele Weigan (Eds.), 2020, Beltz Verlag.

CHAPTER 2

Executive Functions, Executive Skills, and Gifted Learners

Eleonoor van Gerven

This chapter explores how executive function influences gifted students' learning processes. Rather than describing all neuropsychological aspects of executive function in depth, this chapter focuses on the elements and processes that are relevant for teachers to understand how learning and executive function are intertwined. This information is related, in particular, to the education of gifted students and those who are twice-exceptional.

Executive function does not refer to a learning disability. Everyone needs executive function, and gifted students are no exception. The concept of executive function was first defined in the 1970s, referring to the ability to control and direct one's behavior. The idea of a system that regulates behavior was not entirely new. Interest in the concept of self-regulated control of human behavior goes back as far as the 1840s, when Phineas Gage, after an accident wherein an iron rod pierced his frontal lobe, became unable to inhibit his responses (Ratiu & Talos, 2004). In the second half of the 20th century, scientists became more interested in understanding the role of the prefrontal cortex in intelligent behavior (Goldstein et al., 2014). The prefrontal cortex functions as the control panel of the brain and controls one's thinking and behavior. Executive functions are located in this part of the brain.

These first descriptions of executive functions focused on the ability to orchestrate basic cognitive processes during problem-solving situations. These first research projects were not focused on education and classroom situations (Flavell et al., 1970). It was not until the 1980s that the concept of executive functions was extended to education (Meltzer, 2018). By that time, it became clear that the ability to control behavior affects learning and that problems in this domain lead to problems in education and upbringing.

In education, problems with executive functions are often associated with Attention Deficit/Hyperactivity Disorder (ADHD) and autism spectrum disorders (ASD). ADHD refers to a persistent pattern of inattention and/or hyperactivity-impulsivity that interferes with functioning or development, as characterized by inattention and/or hyperactivity and impulsivity (see also Chapter 3, this volume). ASD refers to persistent deficits in social communication and social interaction across contexts not accounted for by general developmental delays and to restricted, repetitive patterns of behavior, interests, or activities (see also Chapter 7, this volume). The strong association between these disorders and executive functions is understandable when the core concepts of the various definitions of executive functions are taken into consideration. Executive functions refer to the cognitive processes that are necessary to direct and control a person's actions (Friedman et al., 2006). The inability to control one's executive functions affects a person's daily life. Students with ADHD or ASD experience problems controlling their behavior, although their problems may be very different. In education, functioning in the social environment at school and a student's academic development may be at risk when a student experiences problems with executive functions. However, it is a misconception that only students with ADHD or ASD experience problems with executive functions. These problems may occur amongst other students as well, and again, gifted students are no exception.

In education, executive function has become a hot topic. The number of books and articles addressing executive function has increased fivefold since the turn of the century (Zelazo & Carlson, 2012). This applies specifically to publications that involve gifted learners (Kroesbergen et al., 2017). This may suggest that most gifted learners have difficulties with executive function; however, that suggestion is highly questionable. There is no prevalence rate for the number of gifted students who cope with executive functioning problems. In general, gifted students have the potential to become successful learners and high achievers. Their intellectual capacities form a solid foundation to obtain and process information. Their high learning potential often sets the standards for high expectations regarding student development.

However, not all gifted students achieve as highly as educators expect them to, and not all gifted students are fully equipped for learning despite their high intellectual capacities (van Gerven, 2017c). When a gifted student does not achieve as expected, teachers become alarmed, either by test results, the student's behavior, or worried parents. What often follows is a process of "structured tinkering" with the student as the main object of concern and action. First observations and responses often refer to the student's lack of concentration, limited ability exercising sustained attention, lack of planning and organization skills, lack of time management, or difficulties regulating emotions and task initiation. Problems with flexibility and metacognition are often mentioned as well. As a result, teachers, parents, and caretakers may conclude that there is something wrong with the gifted student's executive functioning skills, especially when other students in the classroom do no show similar problems. These symptoms are often interpreted as the student having a learning or developmental disability, such as ADHD or ASD, and not being gifted. Sometimes, it is assumed that the student displaying these symptoms might be twice-exceptional, and based on this interpretation, interventions may be misaligned. Gifted students displaying these symptoms may be twice-exceptional, but it is relevant to explore how education contributes to the development and use of executive functions, as well as how systemic influences determine what gifted students experience in this matter. To be absolutely clear, this chapter is not about diagnoses or misdiagnoses. This chapter is about understanding the effect of education on executive function and, based on that understanding, options for meaningful interventions.

Teachers who have worked with multiple students who are gifted and have problems with executive functions may think that all gifted learners have similar challenges. As a result, a misconception regarding metacognition (i.e., thinking about thinking) may occur. Although training (coaching) executive function can have an influence on (gifted) students, that does not imply that a solution has been found. Systemic or ecological influences are equally important for that success (Jolles, 2011; van Gerven, 2015; van Meersbergen & Jeninga, 2012; Ziegler et al., 2017). That means that the process of "structured tinkering" should have a broader perspective and should, therefore, include both the student as an object for change and the other factors in the student's ecology. The word *gifted* is in brackets to signify that strategies used for developing executive skills for gifted students may be beneficial for all students.

A Brief Overview of the Chapter

This chapter first describes what executive functions are, why they are important, and how they relate to executive skills. There is some proof that gifted students have better executive functions than other students (Arffa, 2007; Geake, 2009; Sastre-Riba & Viana-Saenz, 2016), suggesting that they are better equipped than other students for learning. Although their executive function might be better, the achievements of gifted students are not always commensurate with their intellectual potential, so the distinction between executive functions and executive skills must be made clear.

Second, this chapter provides a brief overview of the development of executive function, focusing on 0- to 12-year-olds. Research shows that executive functions develop most rapidly during preschool years (V. Anderson et al., 2014; Meuwissen & Zelazo, 2014), but the brain develops as a result of individual experience. When particular parts of neural networks are activated and used, these networks become stronger. Connections between unused neurons are pruned away (Jolles, 2011). That does not imply that executive functions are fully developed at the age of 12. It merely shows a central developmental line that gradually proceeds during adolescence and early adulthood. During adolescence, there are no "new" executive functions developed, but human beings become more in control of their executive function compared to the early years of their development. The increasing level of control represents the biggest difference between the age groups.

Third, this chapter describes the interplay between the development of executive skills and students' ecological systems. Students' ecological systems consists of five components in a direct interplay with student development: the teacher, a student's family, peers, the curriculum, and the physical learning environment (van Gerven, 2015; van Meersbergen & Jeninga, 2012). As interplay suggests mutuality between two or more components, not only do these components influence the student, but also the student influences these components.

Fourth, this chapter explains why executive function has become such an important topic in education. The understanding of the notion of executive function and executive skills is conditional to understand the answer to this question. At this point it will become clear that executive function itself is not a "new" notion or a "new" disability. Executive function has likely always been there and has always been important for people to direct their thinking and behavior (Goldstein et al., 2014). However, educational beliefs and strategies that are implemented in society today differ in terms of the age, scope of the impact on daily life, and student performance. A paradigm shift in education toward a social-constructivist approach urged the need for effective executive function (Bambs et al., 2016; Onderwijsraad, 2014). Problem solving, self-regulation, and social collaboration have become key aspects in educational strategies. The focus on a social-constructivist approach has increasingly led to a demand for effective high-level executive functioning skills at a relatively young age (Jolles, 2011; Kroesbergen et al., 2017).

Fifth, this chapter explores how learning affects executive skills. The examination of the underpinning concepts of Marzano and Kendall's (2007) new taxonomy of learning objectives provides an understanding of how the complexity of learning content ignites the need to develop and use effective executive skills. This context shifts from the notion of underachievement to the notion of underlearning. Underlearning refers to a situation in which a student's developmental potential is not actualized as a result of a mismatch between the educational opportunities provided and the student's educational needs.

Finally, this chapter stresses the need for a systemic approach to help gifted children to overcome difficulties in applying executive skills. In a prediagnostic stage, a systematically implemented intervention can help to explore if the lack of the effective use of executive skills is the result of a systemic influence or a child factor.

Executive Functions and Executive Skills

Students need executive functions to focus and sustain their attention, plan and organize their behavior, prioritize information, control their emotions, initiate working on assignments, and check if they are doing the appropriate things at the appropriate time and in the appropriate manner. Executive function can be compared with a "traffic control center" for human behavior. Executive functions are located in the frontal lobe (P. Anderson, 2014) and can be described at a cognitive level, referring directly to a student's innate abilities, as they control thinking and behavior (Friedman et al., 2006).

At a behavioral level, executive skills demonstrate what a student can do with the innate abilities of their executive functions (Dawson & Guare, 2009). Behavior can be defined as the result of the interplay between a person's innate abilities and inabilities implemented and exploited in different contexts and under multiple circumstances (van Meersbergen & de Vries, 2017). Qualifying executive skills as behavior clarifies where upbringing, learning, and education come in regarding the development of executive skills. Executive skills are the result of a developmental process. Learning, upbringing, and education influence that process.

At a cognitive level, three different domains of executive function can be distinguished: inhibition, shifting, and updating. Inhibition is the ability to control and suppress dominant responses. Shifting is the ability to switch between tasks and optional responses. Updating refers to the process of storing and adjusting information in one's working memory. Working memory is considered to be an integral component of executive functioning (P. Anderson, 2014). Working memory is the part of the brain where incoming information is temporarily stored and processed. Friedman et al. (2006) suggested that the relation between the domains of executive function are differentially related to intelligence. Their research suggests that working memory seems to have a close relation with intelligence, but inhibition and flexibility (shifting) do not correlate as highly with intelligence. However, there is also research that shows that gifted learners have better executive functions than nongifted students (Bracken & Brown, 2006; Sastre-Riba & Viana-Saenz, 2016). They should be able to perform well, especially on tasks calling on flexibility and inhibition (Sastre-Riba & Viana-Saenz, 2016). Further, Geake (2009) stated that there is research that suggests that gifted learners have very good working memory. Their neurological networks seem to work more efficiently, and that contributes to a higher level of information processing. As their neurological networks contribute to the quality of information processing, they also contribute to a higher level of executive function. Thus, gifted learners seem to be equipped with higher executive functions (Kroesbergen et al., 2017).

Learning requires all three domains of executive function equally (Kroesbergen et al., 2017). In the classroom, one can recognize simple examples of the daily use of executive function through students' abilities to regulate their behavior. Self-regulation incorporates most of the executive functions (Barkley, 2012). Having a group conversation with students requires the use of communication rules. Students waiting for their turn to talk, listening to others, not running off, or not screaming when someone does not agree with them all require students' abilities to control dominant responses. In that same group conversation, the need for shifting becomes clear. To follow and understand what is said, students have to shift their attention from one person to another. They have to shift their perspective on what is said, as updating existing information takes place by listening to what is said. Response inhibition might be relevant because updating with new information requires the flexibility to weigh if an intended response is still appropriate.

Students also need their response inhibition to prevent being distracted when doing their coursework. A car passing by, another student walking through the classroom, two classmates next to each other having a whispered conversation, or students exchanging notes—remaining focused under these circumstances requires the ability to inhibit dominant responses, such as looking around or joining conversations among classmates. Shifting is required when doing coursework, for example, when different mathematical calculations are required. Shifting between addition, subtraction, or division requires moving from one skill set to another to complete the current task. If various shifts are sequentially required while handling one specific mathematical problem, the need for flexibility increases. In this same context, a student has to be able to update results mentally before taking the next step in solving the mathematical problem. Updating is also needed for comprehensive reading. While reading, the student is required to adjust their understanding of theme, plot, and characters. Updating, therefore, places the highest call on one's working memory (Benedek et al., 2014).

Although one cannot observe executive function because it is a cognitive activity that takes place in a student's brain, one can observe behavior as a result of cognitive activity. That is the type of behavior that is referred to as executive skills. To develop good executive skills, executive functions are necessary, as these functions provide the necessary neurological network. The influence between functions and skills is reciprocal. That means that although executive functions are required for developing the skills, the application of the skills is required to develop stronger executive function (Kroesbergen et al., 2017). In laymen's terms, even if one is properly wired, if the wires are not being called on, one will not develop the necessary skills. If one does not develop the skills, the wiring does not become stronger. If the wiring does not become stronger, it becomes less likely that one will be able to develop more effective skills.

Research shows that for each executive function, there are clusters of interrelated behavior, but differences for clustering amongst authors can be recognized. When one considers three publications aimed at teachers and parents, for example, Dawson and Guare (2009), Cooper-Kahn and Foster (2013), and Morraine (2012), one can see differences in their clustering (see Table 2.1). Dawson and Guare described 11 types of behavior matching the executive function. Cooper-Kahn and Foster described eight different types of behavior, just like Morraine, although they organize the clusters slightly differently from each other. These behavioral clusters of executive skills are relevant for teachers. As the clusters describe concrete behavior, the skills become observable. Once

TABLE 2.1

Comparison of Three Different Ways of Clustering Executive Skills

Dawson & Guare (2009)	Cooper-Kahn & Foster (2013)	Morraine (2012)
Sustained attention		Attention
Working memory	Working memory	Memory
Organization	Planning and organizing	Organization
Planning and prioritizing		Planning
Response inhibition	Inhibition	Inhibition and initiative
Task initiation	Taking initiative	
Emotion regulation	Emotion regulation	Control of behavior and emotion
Flexibility	Flexibility	Flexibility
Goal-directed persistence	Process monitoring	Goals
Metacognition	Evaluating one's behavior	
Time management		

Note. From *Les 3. Executieve Functies En Dubbel-Bijzondere Leerlingen: Post-HBO registeropleiding tot Specialist Dubel-Bijzondere Leerlingen,* by. E. van Gerven and A. Weterings-Helmons, 2014, Slim! Educatief. Copyright 2014 by Slim! Educatief. Reprinted with permission of the author.

one can observe what is going on, it becomes easier to understand how one can influence the development and the use of these skills.

Every student has a personal profile of relative strengths and weakness regarding the application of executive skills (van der Donk et al., 2015; Ylvisaker & Feeney, 2014). These strengths and weaknesses may change under different circumstances (van Gerven & Weterings-Helmons, 2014). If students are allowed to work in their domain of personal interest, they may show a different profile in the application of executive skills compared to situations in which tasks are mandatory and outside their domain of interest. As a result of these systemic influences, it is possible for two people who observe the student in different circumstances and conditions to have different observations and conclusions. This is an important indicator that profiling a student's functioning provides only useful information if the results of the observations are interpreted contextually.

As the use of executive functions are intertwined, it is understandable that all executive skills are somehow interrelated. They all influence the learning process. To ascertain if specific deficits in executive functioning hinder a student and how this affects their learning process, neuropsychological assessment is needed. However, when a teacher is confronted with a student having problems applying executive skills, these test results are often not available. Hence, a strategy that helps teachers to assess executive skills in a prediagnostic stage may be helpful. Lezak's (1995) approach of executive functioning can provide a further understanding for educational practice. She divided executive function into four domains: volition, planning, purposive action, and effective performance. These four domains show similarities with the learning process in general. Looking at learning through Marzano and Kendall's (2007) behavioral model can help teachers to understand where in the learning process a student may benefit from additional support to develop and apply executive skills.

Volition is the process in which a student consciously decides to take up a task (Lezak, 1995). In other words, there is an intention to carry out goal-directed behavior. This intention forms the point of departure for intended behavior. In order to do that, the student has to plan their behavior. Leading questions at this stage are: "What am I going to do to reach my goals, and what is a good way to do this?" Thus, planning requires the ability to divide the entire process into manageable steps in a logical sequence. Once the process is planned, it has to be put into action. This requires the initiation and maintenance of intended behavior. This is the part when the student has to find their personal "on-and-off switch." The ability to control the use of this switch effectively contributes to failure and success. Keep in mind that this part of the process is about not only how to get into action, but also when and how to slow down and stop on time. During the implementation of the intended behavior, it is important for a student to self-monitor their actions to achieve the desired results. Monitoring and evaluating a process is only effective if actions and results are seen as interrelated. In other words, "Are my plan and my actions truly contributing to reaching the intended goals?" There are no reasons to assume that, based on their intelligence, these domains would function differently for gifted learners when compared to nongifted learners. So there may not be a difference in executive function, but under specific circumstances, there may be a difference in applying and developing executive skills (Kroesbergen et al., 2017).

Developing Executive Functions

The development of executive function and the transfer from function to skills starts from the day a child is born. The word *development* implies that although the brain structure may be there, this infrastructure is relatively immature. Consider it a work in progress. Four major developmental periods identified are: 0–1 year, 1–3 years, 3–7 years, and 7 years and up (V. Anderson et al., 2014). Each period has specific physical characteristics regarding the development of the brain. Each growth spurt of the brain comes with different developmental tasks. During these developmental stages, there are so-called sensitive periods. During a sensitive period, a behavioral function may experience major growth.

Making use of the concept of sensitive periods is not new in education. Montessori (1993) already used the generic concept of sensitive periods in the design of her educational theory. She explained it as a window in time wherein a child benefits the most from education being trained in specific skills matching that specific sensitive period. Montessori considered this the best time to teach and exercise skills in the domain of the child's spontaneously displayed interests. The sensitive periods regarding the development of executive skills are basically underpinned with the same notion of the most effective time to learn and consolidate new behavior.

When it comes to executive function, new behavior is developed and consolidated during these sensitive periods. The system involved in this new behavior can establish and adjust interconnections with the other parts of the brain. As noted previously, this process involves the continuous interplay between executive function and executive skills.

In the first developmental period (0–1 year), babies receive stimuli and respond to them. They store and process information. To do this, the ability to inhibit dominant responses is relevant. The practice of effectively storing and processing information is needed to learn how to become and stay focused (Dawson & Guare, 2009). Attention control is the first executive function that emerges and is conditional for goal setting and cognitive flexibility (V. Anderson et al., 2014).

As young children experience loads of stimuli, they have to develop the ability to shift their attention to new things when new stimuli occur. Dawson and Guare (2009) described that behavior showing flexibility (the ability of to shift) becomes more and more visible between 12 and 24 months. Prioritizing stimuli and excluding stimuli require the ability to suppress primary responses. In their first 4 years, children learn to sustain attention and how to manage information needed for a specific task. During that process, updating becomes relevant, as it helps them to get a better understanding of the world around them. The connection between what is known and what is new may lead to an understanding of what is unknown, and therefore, what could be explored. This is how curiosity is fed by regular experiences. From this perspective, updating will also lead to new learning (spontaneous) questions. Most children are relatively successful explorers when it comes to the world around them. Gifted students are often characterized as curious and eager to learn from a very young age (Kieboom & Venderickx, 2017; Kreger-Silverman, 2013). They can be so intrigued by their discoveries that they seem to be completely absorbed in new experiences. At a relatively young age, they show their ability to stay focused, integrate exciting and new information, and shift their attention when relevant.

People need executive functions to control their thinking and behavior, such as social behavior (Dick & Overton, 2010). Young children often respond physically toward each other. They often exercise new behaviors enthusiastically. Parents and educators have taught children that "hugging is a good thing" when saying goodbye, so a child may start hugging all of the children on the playground without making any distinction if hugging is the appropriate thing to do at that time. Young children are then taught how to inhibit the response to hug all of the children and only hug another person when it is appropriate. Similar to this process, parents and educators also teach children "not to use their hands" to get what they want, but rather to ask for what they want. They need to learn to suppress the response to hit another child and shift to a more accepted type of behavior. When children are taught new and relevant behavior, they update the information on what is appropriate under specific circumstances. They exercise their ability to suppress the primary response to hit another child and shift to a more appropriate response. However, this is where one can see how difficult this process of inhibition, updating, and shifting is, as young children often experience difficulties with cognitive flexibility. Once they have been taught the rule, they know they are not supposed to hit another child. However, they may find it difficult to live up to this rule and replace the primary behavior with new behavior.

At school, a similar response can be observed during group conversations. Before they enter school, children are taught that if asked a question, it is a good to answer. If the teacher leads a group conversation, they often ask questions. However, with 30 students in a classroom, conversation rules apply. So, the teacher teaches the students to raise hands if they want to answer the question and wait until the teacher addresses them. With young children, one can observe that even though they raise their hands, they start talking at the same time. Consequently, they demonstrate that they understand the new rule, but at the same time, they show that it is still difficult for them to shift from former behaviors. Selecting and applying new rules is equally important as the ability to inhibit the tendency of applying former rules or behavior (Zelazo et al., 2003).

Around the age of 6, children become relatively able to resist distractions (P. Anderson, 2014). Educators use that ability once they start lengthening the tasks students have to do. Educators set up specific rules in their classrooms to help students stay on task. Educators do not teach children to stay focused by telling them to stay focused, but educators teach them how to ignore and exclude distractions. Teachers do this in an environment in which the level of distractions is as low as possible. Students are taught to select between stimuli relevant for the task or not relevant for the task, and as a result of a good selection process, sustained attention develops. Simultaneously, educators start offering students more complex tasks based on piled instructions. In doing so educators offer students insight into the bigger picture of the task, instead of only offering information about the next smallest step in the learning process. Young children who benefit from visual stimuli may no longer rely solely on these cues as the use of auditory stimuli to process information develops (P. Anderson, 2014).

Getting a broader perspective by extending a task depends on the use of macro-procedures and students' working memory. Gradually tasks become more complex. The higher the complexity level of a task, the more intense the call is on planning and monitoring. Children are taught how to plan their actions and how to monitor if they are still on the right track. In time, the level of control by the teacher gradually decreases. Responsibility for planning and organizing a task, time management, and reflecting if the results match the intended objectives is incrementally transferred to students.

Most executive functions are still a work in progress when children enter adolescence. The developmental pace is different for each function. For this age group, external factors become a greater influence if the developing skill is transferred into an applied skill of concrete behavior.

Zelazo and Carlson (2012) made a distinction between "cool" and "hot" executive function. "Cool" aspects of executive function refer to the cognitive aspects and are usually related to the lateral prefrontal cortex. "Hot" aspects of executive function refer to behavioral aspects that involve motivation and emotional control. Cool and hot executive aspects of executive function often work together, but there seems to be a difference in the developmental pace and level of complexity to acquire both aspects. Young children seem to be able to make rational decisions based on the ability to understand the consequences of actions as long as a decision involves somebody else's behavior and not their own. They can give "sensible advice," showing that they understand that if the other person controls their behavior, the result will be better (Meuwissen & Zelazo, 2014). However, when a decision involves young children personally, and motivation and emotion become involved, controlling behavior and dealing with delayed rewards turn out to be really difficult. This is why young children on the playground can tell another child that it is not good to take away somebody else's toys, but almost simultaneously they can take away another child's toy because they are not yet able to inhibit their own desires. According to Zelazo and Carlson (2012), similar distinctions can be observed in more challenging situations with older children and adolescents. This distinction between cold and hot executive functions is helpful to understand how executive function influences gifted learners at school. As the ability to control hot executive function comes with age, it is understandable that relatively young children and adolescents may have a problem with taking on tasks that are not directly rewarding or that they do not value as much as educators do. Although students may be perfectly capable to explain rationally why a task is important, they may not have the self-control yet to overcome any negative emotions or a lack of motivation.

The Influences of the Ecological System

Students are part of a broader ecological system (van Gerven, 2015; van Meersbergen & Jeninga, 2012; Ziegler et al., 2017). This system includes socioeconomic influences, such as governmental policies, poverty, or war. These factors are often hard to change. Other influencers that are easier to effect include the role of the teacher, the curriculum that is offered, the physical learning environment, the role of peers, and the role of the family. Four of the components in the system are human beings and can act independently (i.e., students, teacher, peers, family). These aspects are called "actors." Two aspects in the system cannot act independently (i.e., curriculum, learning environment); they influence the student but only as a result of an action of one of the actors. Therefore, they are called "factors." When two or more components are addressed in the following section, they are referred to as "(f)actors."

In the concept of the student's ecological system, the student is placed in the center of action (Pameijer & van Beukering, 2007; Robertson & Pfeiffer, 2016; van Gerven, 2015; van Meersbergen & de Vries, 2017). The interplay between the (f)actors in the system determines the result of a student's development (see Figure 2.1). For example, if a teacher offers students a curriculum in their zone of actual development instead of their zone of proximal development, the student likely does not feel sufficiently challenged and maybe even

FIGURE 2.1
The Student's Ecological System

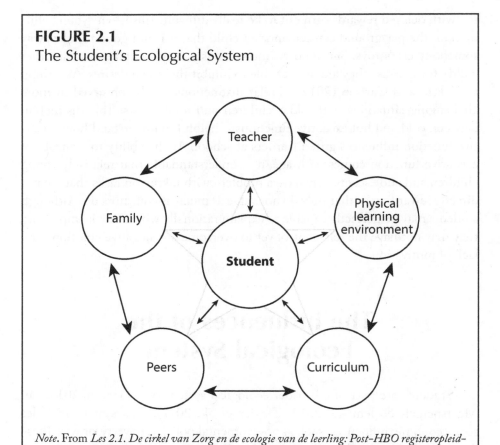

Note. From *Les 2.1. De cirkel van Zorg en de ecologie van de leerling: Post–HBO registeropleiding tot Specialist Begaafdheid*, by E. van Gerven, 2014, Slim! Educatief. Copyright 2014 by E. van Gerven. Reprinted with permission of the author.

feels bored. The zone of actual development is when a student can complete a task without any help. The learning steps are relatively small, and most knowledge and skills are previously developed. The zone of proximal development refers to when the student needs the help of a teacher or a peer with a higher skill set to complete a task. The learning steps are bigger, and knowledge and skills that are needed to complete the task are not yet acquired. When a student feels bored due to a curriculum that focuses on the zone of actual development, they may respond negatively toward the teacher, complain at home about school, or even disrupt home life as a way to air feelings regarding their lack of well-being at school. The student's response may lead to new action by the teacher and parents or caretakers. In theoretical constructs of giftedness, the systemic influences are often referred to as catalysts (Gagné, 2010; Kieboom & Venderickx, 2017; Sternberg, 2002; Subotnik et al., 2011; Ziegler et al., 2017).

Seen through this lens, the ecological system influences the development of executive skills (Cooper-Kahn & Foster, 2013; Dawson & Guare, 2009; Jolles, 2011; Morraine, 2012). The higher the demand on executive skills, the more likely it will be that these skills will develop. The more support the ecological system provides in developing the skills, the more likely it will be that the student's skills will be of a higher quality and more effectively applied.

Imagine the following situation. During a professional development course, a teacher was taught that gifted students prefer top-down learning strategies and learning autonomously. The teacher decides to apply their new understanding of how gifted students learn to their classroom situation. For their only gifted student, the teacher provides an enriched curriculum based on the concept of top-down learning and their assumption of the student's ability and preference to learn independently. The teacher falsely translates the need for autonomy to the idea that the student does not need nor want help. Once at home, the student complains about their day. The student chooses to tell their parents that the task they were assigned was utterly boring and that it was "no fun at all," so they chose not to complete it. In reality, the student's enriched coursework was really difficult because the content was complex, and they did not possess all of the knowledge and skills needed for the assignment. There were no other students working on the same or a similar assignment. As the student previously had only experienced successes in learning, this current experience was new, and they did not know how to deal with it. The student showed no volition to start the assignment and was not able to see the value of the task. Having a low self-efficacy regarding this task and experiencing hardly any effective support, the student did not start to plan their work or take any other actions. Instead of asking directly for help, the student fell into passive behavior. At the end of the day, they did not turn in the assignment. In these cases, if the parents pave their child's way, stress that going to school should be the equivalence of "having fun," and inform the teacher that their child is excused from enriched tasks that supplement the regular curriculum, this student may never learn how to persevere. If these parents, on the other hand, explore what was really going on, they may call on the teacher to set up a parent-teacher-student conference in order to discuss how all (f)actors in the student's ecological system could contribute to an optimization of the learning process. The first solution may affect the development of executive skills negatively. The second solution may affect the development of executive skills positively. This example not only explains how different actors influence the development of executive skills, but also indicates that educational and instructional strategies influence the development of executive skills.

The Paradigm Shift in Education Related to Executive Function

Since the turn of the century, a shift in educational didactics and strategies has become noticeable. A traditional approach to education is no longer seen as sufficient (Unesco, 2015). The high-speed development of knowledge and skills, and the increasing emphasis on technology, requires that people can adjust themselves at the same pace (Onderwijsraad, 2014; Vlaams Ministerie van Onderwijs en Vorming, n.d.). Therefore, education needs modifications by adjusting the traditional didactics to modern requirements (De Bie, 2016). This means a shift from a knowledge-transfer-based didactic and instructional strategy toward a knowledge-construction based didactic and instructional strategy, also referred to as social constructivism. This shift is complex. Knowledge transfer can be a straightforward process. Educators know what knowledge and skills to be taught. They also know to assess the results of the learning process. Knowledge construction, however, is not always straightforward. Process and results can vary enormously. Educational objectives are not always easy to stipulate because often new knowledge is constructed, and qualitative criteria to assess this new knowledge are difficult to predict (Marzano & Kendall, 2007).

While learning, the use of this modern didactic approach requires the student's application of different skills from the traditional way that teaching used to require. These skills are often referred to as 21st-century skills. For daily practice in education, the shift means that educators have to teach children how to become self-regulating, creative, and critical thinkers. Educators must expect students to become high-functioning problem solvers and to learn and work in a social context that requires them to be active participants and effective team players. On top of that, educators expect students to develop the ability to reflect on their behavior as the trigger for processes and results (Bambs et al., 2016; Vermeulen & Vrieling, n.d.).

This clarifies that 21st-century skills require the application of higher order thinking skills. Automated and memorized responses while working on the task are no longer sufficient (Marzano & Kendall, 2007). These tasks require a high level of deliberate attention. The higher the level of deliberated attention, the more the task calls on a student's executive function (P. Anderson, 2014). This implies that modern educational didactics and strategies call highly on students' executive skills. When this modern didactical approach is introduced from the first day the student enters the school, the immediate emphasis on executive function becomes higher than under previous educational paradigms.

The necessary executive skills cannot be taught by working from a booklet on Monday mornings between 9 and 10 o'clock, so to speak (Cooper-Kahn & Foster, 2013; Dawson & Guare, 2009; Morraine, 2012). Students develop these skills over a long period by taking on all kinds of assignments and projects in various educational contexts (Kroesbergen et al., 2017). These educational contexts not only refer to learning at school, but also include formal and informal learning in an out of the school environment, such as at home, a sports club, a music club, a youth orchestra, or a workplace (Subotnik et al., 2011). An executive-function-friendly environment both at home and at school contributes positively to students' development (Cooper-Kahn & Foster, 2013; Dawson & Guare, 2009; Meuwissen & Zelazo, 2014; Morraine, 2012).

The emphasis on the social-constructivist approach and 21st-century skills forms an important explanation for the increasing interest for executive function both in research and in daily classroom practices. However, just like executive function, 21st-century skills are not new, not even in education (Mol Lous, 2011; Thijs et al., 2014). What is new is the fact that these 21st-century skills are valued as important for everybody and not only for the higher educated (Unesco, 2015). By broadening and stressing the necessity of the effective use of executive skills, it becomes understandable that teachers working from a social-constructivist approach observe how children without the effective use of their executive skill lag behind their peers in their educational successes. Executive function turns out to be a valid predictor of school success (Zelazo & Carlson, 2012). According to Gathercole and Alloway (2013) and Veenman (2013), executive function is an even better predictor than intelligence. Students who show good executive skills while working on assignments achieve highly and are more likely to be recognized as gifted than students with an identical learning potential but who do not achieve highly as a result of the lack of effective use of their executive skills (Kornmann et al., 2015; Zelazo & Carlson, 2012).

Executive Skills, Learning, and Achievement

Learning is not just something that mysteriously happens to students. Good education means that the teacher intervenes purposely in a way that makes it possible for a student to develop their potential by working hard and putting in much effort in a well-prepared educational environment (Claxton & Meadows, 2009; Hattie, 2013; Marzano & Kendall, 2007). In this context, the student goes through four stages of development: (1) unconscious incompetence, (2) conscious incompetence, (3) conscious competence, and (4) unconscious competence.

Learning takes place during the period of transfer between conscious incompetence and conscious competence (Maslow, 1954; see also Figure 2.2). The application of newly acquired knowledge and skills in the stage between conscious competence and unconscious competence is to be seen as practicing in the zone of proximal development (Vygotsky, 1978). The student is able to perform the task as long as the teacher or a peer with a higher skill set is there to provide support if needed. What happens in both stages, is that the teacher intentionally intervenes in a way that changes the student's knowledge, skills, and behavior (van Gerven, 2017c). Hence, learning requires a healthy tension between what is known and what is unknown. As a result, a student who is learning will make mistakes, ask questions, and experience uncertainty. The teacher accepts that when the student starts working on the assignment, they are not yet fully competent. In order to help the student in this process of mastery and becoming competent, the teacher instructs the student, supports them, and offers on a daily basis "Vitamin T" for Trying, "Vitamin F" for coping with Failure, "Vitamin D" for coping with Disappointment, "Vitamin P" for Perseverance, and "Vitamin C" for Celebrating successes (van Gerven, 2014).

As long as the balance between incompetence and competence is healthy, learning can take place. Learning is a state of mind that is needed during childhood to provide a person with the opportunity to develop the necessary skills they need in order to become a successful, intelligent adult (Dweck, 2006/2016). Each learning activity calls upon a student's executive functions to operate effectively; the interplay between all of the different skills is conditional (P. Anderson, 2014). The need for the use of executive skills increases when the following circumstances occur (Kroesbergen et al., 2017):

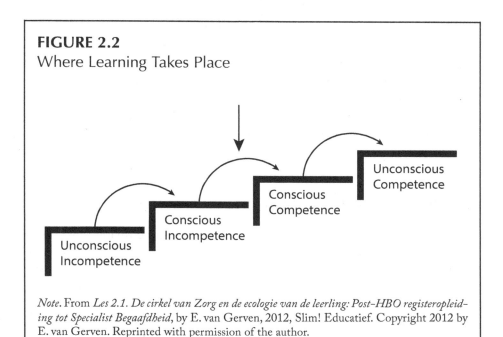

FIGURE 2.2
Where Learning Takes Place

Note. From *Les 2.1. De cirkel van Zorg en de ecologie van de leerling: Post–HBO registeropleiding tot Specialist Begaafdheid*, by E. van Gerven, 2012, Slim! Educatief. Copyright 2012 by E. van Gerven. Reprinted with permission of the author.

- The less familiar a student is with the task and objectives, the more the student will experience the task as complex and the higher the need for executive skills. This implies that notions of words like *difficult*, *challenging*, and *complex* are affected by learning (P. Anderson, 2014; V. Anderson et al., 2014). Thus, different students may have a different experience or rely differently on their executive functions while performing an identical task.

- The notion of a "learning step" refers to the domain of not yet existing knowledge or not yet acquired skills that have to be acquired to meet the learning objectives. The size of the steps that are needed to bridge the gap between what is known and unknown contributes to the complexity of the task. Therefore, large learning steps require higher executive skills. Learning steps that are not a match for the distance an individual student has to bridge based on previous knowledge and skills and in regard to learning objectives call either too highly on executive skills or only from a negative perspective. For instance, they may place an unrealistic demand on the will to persevere when the knowledge and skills that are needed to be successful are not yet fully acquired. Or they may demand too much of a student's resiliency while coping with failure and therefore only offer negative emotions during the learning process.

- The more complex the mental procedure that is required for the task, the higher the requirements on executive skills. Therefore, lower level thinking skills, such as remembering, recalling, and applying, no longer call highly on executive skills once they are acquired. They can be memorized relatively easily, and once that process has taken place, the student can apply this information almost automatically.

Familiarity With the Task and Objectives

The process of acquiring knowledge and skills can be divided into three phases: the cognitive phase, the associative phase, and the autonomous phase (Marzano & Kendall, 2007). Each phase calls differently on executive skills. With the increase of competencies regarding the learning objectives, the call on the student's working memory becomes less stringent. However, being familiar with a task and the learning objectives does not mean that the task no longer requires response inhibition, updating, and shifting. On the contrary, this call may even increase, especially when the student's level of competency implies that the task is not challenging at all. Response inhibition under these circumstances is needed to prevent the student from quitting before the task is completed. Updating may become more difficult, as there is hardly any sustained attention necessary, and as a result, the student may miss relevant information during the process of working on the task (Kroesbergen et al., 2017).

- **The cognitive phase:** The student needs to verbalize each step of the procedure that is required to complete the task. During this phase, the student can apply the procedure but is not yet able to pay attention to various details that may come along. Internal speech is important for a student's success. This phase calls highly on all three executive functions: inhibition, shifting, and updating. The student has to take things step by step (inhibition). The student has to adjust knowledge and understanding as a result of integrating existing and new knowledge and skills (updating). The student has to replace current behavior with new behavior as understanding grows, and an increase of skills requires different actions (shifting).
- **The associative phase:** The student has become competent in manipulating knowledge and skills needed to apply the procedure on global contours. Mistakes occur less and less. As a result of the knowledge and skills being internalized, the call on the student's working memory

decreases. Internal speech is less necessary but may be used to correct mistakes once they are noticed by the student. A flowchart symbolizing the logic sequence of the actions that should be applied at the detail level can be helpful at this stage to support the student's ability to self-monitor. In this phase, the ability to inhibit responses stays relevant. Sustained attention and goal-persistent behavior are important contributors to success. The ability for shifting stays relevant, as does the ability to shift between strategies at the required pace.

- **The autonomous phase:** At this stage, knowledge and skills are internalized at such a level that their use hardly calls on the working memory at all. In this phase, inhibition becomes important to help the student to ignore feelings of boredom, dullness, and routine.

Gifted students are often offered classroom assignments that are a match for most students calling on their zone of proximal development but that are below the learning potential of the gifted learner. In situations like this, gifted learners may discover they are able to achieve at high levels without completing assignments. So although most students in a classroom have a true learning experience while doing their coursework (being consciously incompetent and becoming consciously competent), gifted students will associate these success moments of high achievements based on unconsciously acquired competences with "learning." They were unconsciously competent and became conscious of their competence by doing the assignment (van Gerven, 2017c). The model used in Figure 2.3 changes in this perspective compared to the model shown in Figure 2.2.

The Complexity of the Required Thinking Skills

Learning is about the acquisition of knowledge and mental procedures. Combined knowledge and skills create a cognitive system. In this system, relatively simple and more complex thinking skills can be distinguished. These thinking skills can hierarchically be presented. Bloom's (1956) taxonomy, Marzano and Kendall's (2007) new taxonomy of educational objectives, and Tarricone's (2011) taxonomy of metacognition are good examples. The higher the thinking process takes place in the hierarchy, the more intensely the skill calls on the executive functions.

Acquiring and Using Knowledge. Acquiring knowledge is a less complex mental capacity than internalizing mental procedures (L. Anderson & Krathwohl, 2001). Knowledge and knowledge application form the bottom

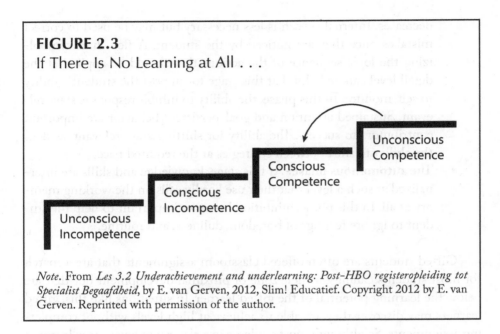

FIGURE 2.3
If There Is No Learning at All . . .

Unconscious
Competence

Conscious
Competence

Conscious
Incompetence

Unconscious
Incompetence

Note. From *Les 3.2 Underachievement and underlearning: Post-HBO registeropleiding tot Specialist Begaafdheid*, by E. van Gerven, 2012, Slim! Educatief. Copyright 2012 by E. van Gerven. Reprinted with permission of the author.

layer of the hierarchy and consists of four aspects. These four aspects can be hierarchically classified as well:

- **Vocabulary:** Vocabulary forms a base level of knowledge. There are domain-specific concepts represented in vocabulary. Having access to these concepts and this vocabulary is conditional for developing the knowledge domain. Hence, language is conditional for understanding. However, the fact that a student has developed the right vocabulary does not automatically imply that the student has acquired an in-depth understanding of the knowledge in that specific domain.

- **Facts:** The second level in the hierarchy of knowledge is represented in facts. Domain-specific facts refer to information about people, events, timelines, and characteristics of product. Domain-specific vocabulary is needed to describe domain-specific facts.

- **Generalizations:** The third level of the hierarchy refers to the notion of generalizations. The ability to recognize concepts and facts outside the original context and to apply them correctly in a new context is called generalization. One can only generalize information based on a broad vocabulary and the knowledge of facts.

- **Principles:** Principles refer to the ability to recognize and understand causal relations and relations wherein a certain interplay between facts becomes clear without a direct causal relation. The ability to recognize and apply principles is the highest level of knowledge application.

Acquiring and Using Mental Processes. Learning involves just as much the "how" (skills) as the "what" (knowledge; J. R. Anderson, 1983; Snow & Lowman, 1989). The "how" refers to mental procedures, and again these can be classified hierarchically. In order to do that, they need to be divided into skills and processes:

Skills include:

- **Single rules:** These are simple if/then statements and are often represented in a small set of steps that do not require accompanying steps. For example, "If I write a sentence, then I start with a capitalization of the first character." Or, "If I finish a sentence, then I use a period to make the reader aware that my sentence is finished."
- **Algorithms:** These refer to a set of rules applied in a specific sequence. Algorithms have specific predictable outcomes and specific steps. Algorithms are used when doing math or when programming a computer.
- **Tactics:** These represent a strategy to solve a problem or to do a task. This strategy may differ depending on the context and the person that uses the tactic. For example, there are several strategies that can be used to make a summary. Based on the intention of how to use the summary, a student may use a different tactic to summarize content.

Identical to knowledge, skills can be internalized. Once they are internalized, they are acquired at an automated level and require hardly any conscious mental processes to apply. Seen through this lens, skills can be qualified as lower order thinking activities (Marzano & Kendall, 2007). Therefore, internalized skills are independent of executive skills in the development of executive functions.

Processes are macroprocedures. Macroprocedures require a combination of different skills in changing orders and in different combinations. Problem solving, researching, experimenting, and decision making are all macroprocedures. Macroprocedures cannot be done without the conscious use of different skills. They require constant self-monitoring of behavior. Hence, macroprocedures call highly on executive functions. The complexity of macroprocedures qualifies them as higher order thinking skills (Marzano & Kendall, 2007).

Using Executive Skills. Based on the previous information, it becomes clear that the complexity of a task is determined by the combination of two factors: (1) the number of steps a student has to take from start to finish and (2) the student's level of familiarity with the application of the mental process that is required for the task. The complexity of the mental process itself is not variable. The required number of steps for a specific procedure and the way these steps are related to each other stay the same. Familiarity with the process grows with experience. The more familiar a student is with the required procedure, the faster a task can be done. Therefore, the complexity of a task has a twofold effect on applied executive skills.

First, when taking on a new task, executive functions are important because of the unfamiliarity with the required steps of the mental procedure itself. Becoming familiar with new procedures depends on a student's ability to inhibit dominant responses. In order to achieve success, sustained attention, goal-persistent behavior, and the regulation of emotions are necessary when not successful on the first attempt (Dawson & Guare, 2009). The ability to cope with failure and disappointment and persevere has to be learned. A new task or a new curricular content calls highly on the student's working memory. The student must be able to keep the information about the necessary steps on hand in order to apply them in the required sequence. Shifting is essential to determine the relevance of the next steps and the sequence of these steps. Planning, organizing, prioritizing mental procedures, and flexibly using strategies during this process are required.

Additionally, the complexity of the process influences the execution of a task once knowledge and skills are acquired at an autonomous level. In those cases, the task hardly calls on the student's working memory (Marzano & Kendall, 2007). The task will still rely on the student's ability to inhibit dominant responses, even though this is measurably different compared to a situation in which all knowledge and skills are still new. Because the novelty of the application of the knowledge and skills decreases over time, sustained attention becomes important, especially when the task is considered less engaging. The more steps the procedure requires, the more important it is for a student to stay focused. If at this point the students loses their attention, the chance for mistakes increases. Having automated the knowledge and skills does not negate that, under these circumstances, mistakes can occur easily. The same applies for emotion regulation. If a task does not rely on the student's zone of proximal development, it is likely that the student becomes bored (van Gerven, 2013). Emotions and behavior that accompany boredom have to be suppressed in order to end the task as requested, within the given amount of time, and at the required level. Shifting remains relevant; without the ability to shift, the student may forget to switch between actions, resulting in unnecessary mistakes.

Executive Functions and Gifted Learners

Educators might assume that gifted students have well-developed executive functions as long as they are not hindered by a specific learning disability or a behavioral disability (Kroesbergen et al., 2017). If a gifted student is educationally challenged, the student will be able to put these well-developed executive functions to use and transform them to well-used executive skills. However, in daily practice, educators might observe that not every gifted child has well-developed executive skills. This raises the question about the origin of the problem. If there is no neurobiological explanation for the less developed skills, the answer should be sought in the student's educational context. The development of executive functions on the cognitive and behavioral level is hindered in the following educational settings:

- The gifted student is, from an early age, placed in an educational context wherein they are most familiar with the mental procedures that are required, and as a result, they are unprepared to cope with complex emotions that occur during a learning process;
- The gap between formerly developed competencies and the competencies to be acquired is too small to create true learning experiences.
- Only lower order thinking skills are trained, and no complex mental procedures were required.
- The student is frequently allowed to withdraw from learning experiences because they do not qualify the experiences as "fun."

Consequently, good executive functioning does not necessarily transfer to good executive skills. As a result, the domino effect applies. Without appropriate skills, achievement will not increase. Lack of achievement may result in access to fewer enrichment activities. Without the enrichment activities aiming for the student's zone of proximal development, the opportunity for the gifted student to develop executive skills decreases (Kroesbergen et al., 2017). This domino effect refers to an educational situation in which underlearning and underperforming is (unconsciously) encouraged. Underlearning refers to a process during which the student's developmental potential is not called on as possible. As a result, the student's achievements represent a learning process that is insufficiently tuned to the student's educational needs. Therefore, the student's self-actualization of their developmental potential lags behind compared to what it could have been. Thus, underlearning is not a qualification of the student or their achievements, but a qualification of an ineffective learning process being influenced by the (f)actors in the student's ecological system (van Gerven, 2013).

It is likely that underachievers and underlearners have not developed the executive skills that are needed to perform in their zone of proximal development. On this new challenging level, a student is confronted with assignments that make them feel consciously incompetent. This student has not experienced this before and is now forced to take on the challenge by themselves ("You are such a good student; you can do this on your own."). Under these circumstances, it is only reasonable that the student experiences anxiety, making it unlikely that they take on the challenge they are confronted with. The emotions the student experiences are a fear of the unknown and of failing (Whitley, 2001). Marzano and Kendall's (2007) behavioral model explains the process that takes place. Once a task is started, the self-system is activated, and the student will explore his motivation (Csikszentmihalyi, 1999). According to Deci and Ryan's (2000) triad of relationship, competence, and autonomy, the student may consider: "Do I relate positively to the learning objectives of this task? Am I competent enough to take this task on? Am I in a position that offers just enough autonomy to make personal choices during the learning process?" At this metacognitive level, the student estimates their chances for success by checking if their knowledge and skills are developed so that they will be successful. If the student concludes that they will not achieve as anticipated by themselves or others, their motivation to become engaged in the task will decrease. As a result of this, the student may be reluctant to complete the assignment. Once started, the student is not able to sustain their attention for fear of failing. This adds to the level of anxiety that already has been raised by being confronted with the feeling of being consciously incompetent. The student may then opt for a less challenging task and be deprived of the opportunity to develop executive skills (e.g., time management, organization). When faced with another challenge, the cycle starts again.

Twice-exceptional students are an exception when it comes to the development of their executive functions. Having ADHD or ASD provides the neurobiological explanation for the lack of executive function, and thus the problems twice-exceptional students experience in developing effective executive skills (van Gerven, 2017a, 2017b). The problems these students experience influence almost every developmental domain (Trail, 2011). Twice-exceptional students with a specific learning disability, such as dyslexia or dyscalculia, may also experience problems with the application of executive skills. Although the learning disability does not automatically imply that the development of executive functions is disturbed by the disability itself, the executive skills may be under pressure. The problems that occur often relate to the domains that are directly affected by the learning disability. Suppose a student has dyslexia. Now keep in mind the steps of Marzano and Kendall's (2007) behavioral model described previously. A student's motivation may be affected for tasks in which the student either has a low level of self-efficacy or does not experience a real value of the learning objectives (Siegle & McCoach, 2017). If the assignment requires reading, writing, and spelling, a gifted student with dyslexia may conclude that they possess the required knowledge but that they lack the skills to complete the work. This lack of self-efficacy may negatively influence the student's motivation. If the student's motivation is low, they may experience difficulties sustaining attention and remaining on task. Repeated failure may influence the student's emotional self-regulation (Baum et al., 2017; Trail, 2011). The discrepancy between understanding and the ability to produce in the required way and at the required level may result in task avoidance, and the ability to suppress dominant responses may become more difficult over time. If the student has not yet been identified as twice-exceptional, they may be seen as underachieving. In this scenario, strategies that are focused on underachievement fail to attend to the undiagnosed disability.

The Opportunities of a Systemic Approach

When it comes to interventions and solutions that are easily applicable in the classroom, there is no evidence that specific interventions to develop executive skills are successful for all gifted learners or only for gifted learners. The success of interventions depends on the combination of a student's individual educational needs and executive challenges. Believing that there is one ideal solution is a fallacy. Rather, personalized interventions have a higher success rate (van Gerven, 2019).

Teachers may need to ascertain if lack of executive skills are related to ecological (f)actors. If so, interventions may be relatively easy to implement. van Gerven and Weterings-Helmons (2014) developed a pedagogical-didactical strategy for teachers as the first step in this process. Their strategy does not exclude the possibility of a neurobiological explanation. It merely offers the option to optimize the educational placement before determining if further assessment is necessary. The underpinning concept is the change- and solution-focused approach. This approach does not imply that at a certain point in time a classifying diagnosis cannot become important. A classifying diagnosis can provide access to educational opportunities that may not be otherwise available. The change- and solution-focused approach may lead to improvements for students before a classifying diagnosis is made, due to their ecological system. In this approach, a diagnosis becomes important if it leads directly to an improvement of the student's situation. If that is not the case, and one can realize similar improvements, then seeking a classifying diagnosis may not be necessary (van Gerven, 2018). The strategy developed by van Gerven and Weterings-Helmons (2014) is based upon the following assumptions:

- There is no evidence that all gifted students have problems with executive function.
- There is evidence that gifted students have better executive function than nongifted students.
- Under the right conditions, gifted students are capable of developing and applying effective executive skills.
- Twice-exceptional students may experience difficulties with executive function. These students may have difficulties with the development and use of effective executive skills.
- Executive skills may only develop when the curriculum offered requires that students work within their zone of proximal development. Without learning, the need for executive skills does not occur.
- The ecological system affects the development and use of executive skills. Hence a student's use of executive skills may be situational.
- If the ecological system influences the development and use of executive skills, both gifted students and twice-exceptional students may benefit from an optimization of the system.
- Executive functioning is malleable, and due to neurobiological differences, twice-exceptional students may not benefit as much from these system optimizations as other gifted students.
- All interventions should be based on StiCoREx strategies (van Gerven, 2018): stimulate, compensate, remediate, and exempt:
  - *Stimulate* the use of both strengths and challenges (van Gerven & Troxclair, 2017). Remember that doing something in a context that confronts them with a relative weakness might be something a student avoids. Encourage the student to take on challenges and develop strengths. See abilities as well as disabilities.
  - Teach students to use their ability to *compensate* for their challenges. Teach them that their ability to compensate may be affected by differing circumstances.
  - Use *remediation* to help students develop skills.

○   An *exemption* is justifiable when stimulation, compensation, and remediation have not helped students develop.

■   Once a student has developed strategies for the use of an executive skill and these strategies are internalized at an age-sufficient level, the scaffolds and resources for supporting the use of these strategies become less necessary and may be gradually dismantled.

Van Gerven and Weterings-Helmon's (2014) strategy combines the need for responding meaningfully to educational needs. By intervening, the persistency of problem(s) becomes clear. This distinction is helpful to determine if stimulation, compensation, and remediation strategies are effective and, therefore, require exemption. The problems' level of persistence, combined with the level of support, indicates if the problems were caused by ecological or by child factors. If, within a relatively short time (twice in 6 weeks) and with limited interventions, the student develops their executive skills to a higher level or uses these skills more effectively, there seems to be a relatively low level of persistence. Under these circumstances, it is likely that systemic influences were the cause. If, in a similar time, intensive interventions are applied and the results stay limited or show little progress, the problems seem to be more persistent and may call for further diagnosis. However, if intensive interventions are applied and the results are limited, further diagnosis may be required.

The systemic approach can best be compared with a set of interconnected gear wheels. Turning one wheel means that the other wheels turn as well. The problem that one wants to address is called "the need for change." The need for change is determined in collaboration with the student, and preferably also the parents, through a series of steps:

1.   Determine the need for change. If the need for change is stipulated as a learning objective for the student, it becomes future-focused. Just like with other learning objectives, SMART (strategic, measurable, attainable, realistic, time-bound) goals are important.

2.   Create a profile of the student's strengths and challenges regarding the problem that is to be addressed. This is when focus becomes important. All aspects that are not directly related to the need for change are set aside. That does not mean that they are not important, but it means that considering the need for change, their priority is not high enough.

3.   Determine how the (f)actors in the ecological system affect these strengths and challenges. What influences in the student's life may impact their learning process?

4. Go on a "treasure hunt." Start by looking for and analyzing exceptions to the situation. Just like in Step 2, this is done by profiling strengths and challenges, but now they are related to the positive moments. Identical to step three, an inventory of influences of the ecological system is made.

5. Compare performance and expectation. How do they differ? Once these differences are found, they are a very strong indicator to identify what interventions may be successful. At this point, it is relevant to realize that these successful moments indicate that all (f)actors are competent in applying the strategy. This means that the need to develop completely new behavior may not be as necessary as previously thought. Often small changes prove to be very effective.

6. Stipulate "golden sentences," starting with, "I think things will improve if. . . ." These sentences are deduced from the results of the treasure hunt, and each actor can contribute one sentence.

7. Determine collaboratively what the suggestions for solutions named by all actors share. Based on the similarities, a final intervention is described.

8. All of the actors stipulate three things they each can realistically contribute to the intervention. Additionally, the teacher and the student stipulate three possible changes for the curriculum and the physical learning environment. Keep it small and simple. Keep in mind that various actors will contribute to the intervention daily. A contribution can be something small that one does (e.g., giving a daily compliment for a job well done) but can also be something that one does not do any longer (e.g., reducing complaints).

9. Create ownership for the student. The student selects from all of the contributions suggested for the intervention one contribution that each (f)actor will implement. This way the intervention becomes realistic and has a reasonable chance for success.

10. Document the need for change, the design of the intervention, and the intended outcome.

It Is Better to Prevent Than to Cure

There is evidence that gifted learners may have better executive functions than nongifted learners, but this does not imply that they have better executive skills. The lack of effective executive skills is not always due to a disability or to a neurodiverse aptitude.

The connection between the development of executive functions and executive skills is reciprocal and requires a context wherein learning takes place. Learning is conditional for the development of executive skills. Seen through this lens, gifted learners are similar to other learners. However, for most students, there are ample opportunities for learning, and those may be different for gifted learners. Coursework mostly calling on a lower order thinking level will not be sufficient for gifted learners. Gifted students who are potential or even notorious underlearners are not likely to develop effective executive skills in this environment. Without these skills, it becomes harder to develop commensurate with their potential, and this may legitimize the interventions preventing underlearning and underachievement.

The shift in education toward social-constructivist learning is a two-edged sword. It provides lots of challenging opportunities for all learners and thus also for gifted learners. But it also requires a different role of the teacher, requiring different competencies and a different attitude. This change may or may not be easy to achieve on short-term notice; that depends on the system where these changes may be needed.

The social-constructivist approach relies on the use of executive skills. This can be seen as an opportunity, but it can also clarify why some gifted students experience more problems applying effective executive skills than others. If executive skills were not needed previously, the student cannot be expected to acquire these skills overnight with a swift change of the curriculum. For most students, educators provided support while learning. Instruction, scaffolding, and feed forward are required for their success. Gifted students need the same level of support.

Every student needs a teacher. This teacher shows them how to plan, organize, and prioritize. The teacher helps them to sustain their attention and to stay focused. The teacher is there to help them regulate emotions when things do not go directly as planned. In order for gifted students to learn, educators may need to adjust assumptions on learning behavior of gifted students so that their executive function and executive skills are developed commensurate with their potential.

FROM THE EDITORS

Student Vignettes

Ethan

Ethan is a middle school student who has been identified as gifted since third grade. Elementary classes worked for him. The regular classes were easy, and gifted classes were all about competitions. He could choose the ones he wanted. Ethan often chose group competitions so that the other members of the group could do all of the planning. He contributed ideas.

Ethan's Point of View. Okay, if I am gifted, why can't I seem to get anywhere with my projects? I see this huge task in front of me and see the most amazing outcome you can imagine, but I don't know how to get there. I want to do the project, but the work seems overwhelming. I will tell the teacher that this is too easy and boring. She'll let me do whatever I want. I can finish reading my book or just draw.

Ethan's Teacher's Point of View. Ethan needs to develop areas of executive function. I don't know where to start. He has many good ideas for individual projects but can never quite get started and rarely finishes. I've noticed that in group projects, he gives ideas, and the others in the group do the work. He and Wyatt get along well because Ethan has the ideas and Wyatt does the work. Ethan likes projects much better than drill and practice, even though he always does well with any short paper.

Discussion Questions

1. Are Ethan's issues in the classroom his problem, his teacher's problem, or both? Why, or why not?
2. What is the first step the teacher should take to help Ethan with his executive function?
3. Do you think Wyatt should be involved in the teacher's efforts with Ethan? If so, in what way?
4. Does Ethan's lack of executive function skills suggest a label of twice-exceptionality?

FROM THE EDITORS, *continued*

Claire

Claire is in the third grade. Her parents and her teachers believe she might be gifted, but they are not quite sure. Some call her flighty. Claire wonders what flighty means.

Claire's Teacher's Point of View. Claire has dozens of good ideas when presented with a problem, but she never follows through with her ideas. She just likes having the idea and someone else actually doing the work. Claire seems to know a great deal about many subjects if, and only if, they are of interest to her. Even then, she wants to play with the information. She rarely completes a project that she indicated she wanted to do. Until she decides to settle down and to quit flitting from project to project, idea to idea, without reaching a goal or even setting a goal, I don't think she should be identified for gifted services.

Claire's Mother's Point of View. What a mind Claire has! She is always coming up with odd solutions to family problems or creating ideas for the family to do together. As long as we finish out her idea, everyone (Claire) is happy. If we ask her to plan, organize, and initiate one of her ideas, she says, "Oh, never mind." We never know what she is going to do next. She may be studying something new online, go outside to jump on the trampoline, or play with the dog, and then she is back in with an idea for creating a new way to get dressed in the morning. My mother, her grandmother, calls her flighty. We call her delightful.

Discussion Questions

1. What executive function skills, if any, is Claire struggling with?
2. Should she be referred for gifted identification?
3. In what ways should the teacher help Claire develop her executive function skills?
4. In what ways may Claire be twice-exceptional?

References

Anderson, J. R. (1983). *The architecture of cognition*. Harvard University Press.

Anderson, L., & Krathwohl, D. R. (Eds.). (2001). *A taxonomy for learning, teaching, and assessing: A revision of Bloom's taxonomy of educational objectives* (Complete ed.). Longman.

Anderson, P. (2014). Towards a developmental model of executive functioning. In V. Anderson, R. Jacobs, & P. J. Anderson (Eds.), *Executive functions and the frontal lobes: A lifespan perspective* (pp. 3–22). Psychology Press.

Anderson, V., Anderson, P., Jacobs, R., & Spencer Smith, M. (2014). Development and assessment of executive functioning: from preschool to adolescence. In V. Anderson, R. Jacobs, & P. J. Anderson (Eds.), *Executive functions and the frontal lobes* (pp. 123–154). Psychology Press.

Arffa, S. (2007). The relationship of intelligence to executive function and non-executive function measures in a sample of average, above average, and gifted youth. *Archives of Clinical Neuropsychology, 22*(8), 969–978. https://doi.org/10.1016/j.acn.2007.08.001

Barkley, R. A. (2012). *Executive functions: What they are, how they work, and why they evolved*. Guilford Press.

Bambs, H., Steyaert, S., Van Respaille, L., Steyaert, J., Nuytemans, M., & Berghmans, E. (2016). *Van lerensbelang*. https://onderwijs.vlaanderen.be/sites/default/files/atoms/files/Van-Lerensbelang-eindrapport.pdf

Baum, S. M., Schader, R. M., & Owen, S. V. (2017). *To be gifted and learning disabled: Strength-based strategies for helping twice-exceptional students with LD, ADHD, ASD, and more* (3rd ed.). Prufrock Press.

Benedek, M., Jauk, E., Sommer, M., Arendasy, M., & Neubauer, A. C. (2014). Intelligence, creativity, and cognitive control: The common and differential involvement of executive functions in intelligence and creativity. *Intelligence, 46*, 73–83. https://doi.org/10.1016/j.intell.2014.05.007

Bloom, B. (Ed.). (1956). *Taxonomy of educational objectives: The classification of educational goals. Handbook I: Cognitive domain*. Longmans Green.

Bracken, B. A., & Brown, E. F. (2006). Behavioral identification and assessment of gifted and talented students. *Journal of Psychoeducational Assessment, 24*(2), 112–122. https://doi.org/10.1177/0734282905285246

Claxton, G., & Meadows, S. (2009). Brightening up: How children learn to be gifted. In T. Balchin, B. Hymer, & D. Matthews (Eds.), *The Routledge international companion to gifted education* (pp. 3–9). Routledge.

Cooper-Kahn, J., & Foster, M. (2013). *Boosting executive skills in the classroom: A practical guide for educators*. Jossey-Bass.

Csikszentmihalyi, M. (1999). *De weg naar flow*. Boom.

Dawson, P., & Guare, R. (2009). *Smart but scattered: The revolutionary "executive skills" approach to helping kids reach their potential*. Guilford Press.

De Bie, B. (2016). *Ontwikkeling van een Zelfevaluatietool voor de Implementatie van 21ste-eeuwvaardigheden in Vlaamse basisscholen* [Master's thesis]. Open Universiteit Nederland.

Deci, E. L., & Ryan, R. M. (2000). The "what" and "why" of goal pursuits: Human needs and the self-determination of behavior. *Psychology Inquiry, 11*(4), 227–268. https://doi.org/10.1207/S15327965PLI1104_01

Dick, A., & Overton, W. (2010). Executive function: Description and explanation. In B. Sokol, U. Müller, J. Carpendale, A. Young, & G. Iarocci (Eds.), *Self and social regulation. Social interaction and the development of social understanding and executive functions* (pp. 7–34). Oxford University Press.

Dweck, C. S. (2016). *Mindset: The new psychology of success*. Ballantine Books. (Original work published 2006)

Flavell, J. H., Friedrichs, A. G., & Hoyt, J. D. (1970). Developmental changes in memorization processes. *Cognitive Psychology, 1*(4), 324–340. https://doi.org/10.1016/0010-0285(70)90019-8

Friedman, N. P., Miyake, A., Corley, R. P., Young, S. E., Defries, J. C., & Hewitt, J. K. (2006). Not all executive functions are related to intelligence. *Psychological Science, 17*(2), 172–179. https://doi.org/10.1111/j.1467-9280.2006.01681.x

Gagné, F. (2010). *Building gifts into talents: Brief overview of the DMGT 2.0*. Université du Québec à Montréal.

Gathercole, S., & Alloway, T. (2013). *De invloed van het werkgeheugen op het leren: handelingsgerichte adviezen voor het basisonderwijs*. SWP.

Geake, J. G. (2009). *The brain at school: Educational neuroscience in the classroom*. Open University Press.

Goldstein, S., Naglieri, J. A., Princiciotta, D., & Otero, T. M. (2014). Introduction: A history of executive functioning as a theoretical and clinical construct. In S. Goldstein & J. Naglieri (Eds.), *Handbook of executive functioning*. Springer.

Hattie, J. (2013). *Leren zichtbaar maken*. Bazalt Educatieve Uitgaven 2013.

Jolles, J. (2011). *Ellis en het verbreinen*. Neuropsych Publishers.

Kieboom, T., & Venderickx, K. (2017). *Meer dan intelligent alleen*. Lannoo.

Kornmann, J., Zettler, I., Kammerer, Y., Gerjets, P., & Trautwein, U. (2015). What characterizes children nominated as gifted by teachers? A closer consideration of working memory and intelligence. *High Ability Studies, 26*(1), 75–92. https://doi.org/10.1080/13598139.2015.1033513

Kreger-Silverman, L. K. (2013). *Giftedness 101*. Springer.

Kroesbergen, E., Verkaik, D., & van Gerven, E. (2017). Executieve functies en begaafdheid. In E. van Gerven (Ed.), *De Gids: Over begaafdheid in het basisonderwijs* (2nd ed., pp. 223–240). Leuker.nu.

Lezak, M. (1995). *Neuropsychological assessment* (3rd ed.). Oxford University Press.

Marzano, R. J., & Kendall, J. S. (2007). *The new taxonomy of educational objectives* (2nd ed.). Corwin.

Maslow, A. (1954). *Motivation and personality*. Harper & Brothers.

Meltzer, L. (Ed.). (2018). *Executive function in education. From theory to practice* (2nd ed.). Guilford Press.

Meuwissen, A. S., & Zelazo, P. D. (2014, November). Hot and cool executive function: Foundations for learning and healthy development. *Zero to Three*, 18–23.

Mol Lous, A. (2011). *Passend Onderwijs: Haute couture of Zeeman? Inaugurele rede bij de installatie van het lectoraat Passend Onderwijs/Inclusive Education*. Hogeschool Leiden. https://www.hsleiden.nl/binaries/content/assets/hsl/lectoraten/passend-onderwijs/publicaties/lr.passendow.pdf

Montessori, M. (1993). *De methode*. Nederlandse Montessori Vereniging.

Morraine, P. (2012). *Helping students take control of everyday executive functions: The attention fix*. Kingsley.

Onderwijsraad. (2014). *Een eigentijds curriculum*. https://www.onderwijsraad.nl/publicaties/adviezen/2014/05/19/een-eigentijds-curriculum

Pameijer, N., & van Beukering, T. (2007). *Handelingsgericht werken: een handreiking voor de intern begeleider*. Acco.

Ratiu, P., & Talos, I. F. (2004). Images in clinical medicine: The tale of Phineas Gage, digitally remastered. *New England Journal for medicine, 351*(23), e21.

Robertson, S., & Pfeiffer, S. (2016). Development of a procedural guide to implement response to intervention (RtI) with high-ability learners. *Roeper Review, 38*(1), 9–23. https://doi.org/10.1080/02783193.2015.1112863

Sastre-Riba, S., & Viana-Saenz, L. (2016). Executive functions and high intellectual capacity. *Revista de Neurologica, 62*(S01), S65–S71. https://doi.org/10.33588/rn.62S01.2016025

Siegle, D., & McCoach, D. B. (2017). Underachievement and the gifted child. In S. I. Pfeiffer, E. Shaunessy-Dedrick, & M. Foley-Nicpon (Eds.), *APA handbook of giftedness and talent* (pp. 559–573). American Psychological Association. https://doi.org/10.1037/0000038-036

Snow, R. E., & Lowman, D. F. (1989). Implications of cognitive psychology for educational measurement. In R. L. Linn (Ed.), *Educational measurement* (pp. 263–331). American Council on Education.

Sternberg, R. J. (2002). *Succescolle intelligentie*. Lisse: Swets & Zeitlinger.

Subotnik, R. F., Olszewski-Kubilius, P., & Worrell, F. C. (2011). Rethinking giftedness and gifted education: a proposed direction forward based on psychological science. *Psychological Science in the Public Interest, 12*(1), 3–54. https://doi.org/10.1177/1529100611418056

Tarricone, P. (2011). *The taxonomy of metacognition*. Psychology Press.

Thijs, A., Fisser, P., & van der Hoeven, M. (2014). *21e eeuwse vaardigheden in het curriculum van het funderend onderwijs: een conceptueel kader*. SLO.

Trail, B. A. (2011). *Twice-exceptional gifted children. Understanding, teaching, and counselling gifted students*. Prufrock Press.

Unesco. (2015). *Rethinking education. Towards a global common good?* https://unesdoc.unesco.org/ark:/48223/pf0000232555

van der Donk, M., Tjeenk-Kalff, A., & Hiemstra-Beernink, A. (2015). *Beter bij de les. Training executieve functies*. Lannoo.

van Gerven, E. (2012a). *Les 2.1. De cirkel van zorg en de ecologie van de leerling: Post-HBO registeropleiding tot specialist begaafdheid*. Slim! Educatief.

van Gerven, E. (2012b). *Les 3.2. Underachievement and underlearning: Post-HBO registeropleiding tot specialist begaafdheid*. Slim! Educatief.

van Gerven, E. (2013). *Knapzak praktijkgidsen: Begaafde onderpresteerders*. Leuker.nu.

van Gerven, E. (2014). *Knapzak praktijkgidsen: Uitdagend Onderwijs*. Leuker.nu.

van Gerven, E. (2015). *Knapzak praktijkgids: De cirkel van zorg voor de intern begeleider*. Leuker.nu.

van Gerven, E. (2017a). Begaafde leerlingen met ADHD. In E. van Gerven (Ed.), *De Gids: Over begaafdheid in het basisonderwijs* (2nd ed., pp. 279–296). Leuker.nu.

van Gerven, E. (2017b). Begaafde leerlingen met een autismespectrum stoornis. In E. Van Gerven (Ed.), *De Gids: Over begaafdheid in het basisonderwijs* (2nd ed., pp. 199–224). Leuker.nu.

van Gerven, E. (2017c). Preventing and overcoming underachievement in primary gifted school students. *TEMPO, 38*(3), 28–35.

van Gerven, E. (2018). *Addressing the needs of twice-exceptional students in the classroom*. Slim! Educatief. https://www.slimeducatief.nl/artikelen/download/29

van Gerven, E. (2019). Het begeleiden van dubbel-bijzondere leerlingen: Houd interventies passend en klein. *Tijdschrift voor Remedial Teaching, 27*(4), 22–24.

van Gerven, E., & Troxclair, D. (2017). *Theory to practice: classroom strategies to support gifted students with ADHD* [Conference session]. CEC-TAG Conference 2017, Boston, MA, United States.

van Gerven, E., & Weterings-Helmons, A. (2014). *Les 3. Executieve functies en dubbel-bijzondere leerlingen: Post–HBO registeropleiding tot Specialist Dubel-Bijzondere Leerlinge*n. Slim! Educatief.

van Meersbergen, E., & de Vries, P. (2017). *Handelingsgericht werken in passend onderwijs*. Perspectief uitgevers.

van Meersbergen, E., & Jeninga, J. (2012). De ecologie van de leerling. Een systeemgericht model voor het onderwijs. *Tijdschrift voor Orthopedagogiek, 51*(4), 175–185.

Veenman, M. (2013). *Metacognitie bepaalt leerresultaat*. http://www.didactief online.nl/blog-blonz/11701-metacognitie-bepaalt-leerresultaat

Vermeulen, M., & Vrieling, E. (n.d.). *21e-eeuwse vaardigheden: achtergronden en onderwijsimplicaties*. Welten-instituut, Open Universiteit.

Vlaams Ministerie van Onderwijs en Vorming. (n.d.). *Pre-ambule Eindtermen voor de 21ste eeuw: "Een baken met een vliegwiel"*. Vlaams Ministerie van Onderwijs en Vorming. http://docs.vlaamsparlement.be/pfile?id=1140369

Vygotsky, L. (1978). *Mind in society. The development of higher psychological processes*. Harvard University Press.

Ylvisaker, M., & Feeney, T. (2014). Helping children without making them helpless: Facilitating development of executive self-regulation in children and adolescents. In V. Anderson, R. Jacobs, & P. J. Anderson (Eds.), *Executive functions and the frontal lobes: A lifespan perspective* (pp. 409–438). Psychology Press.

Whitley, M. D. (2001). *Bright minds, poor grades: Understanding and motivating your underachieving child*. Perigee Books.

Zelazo, P. D., & Carlson, S. M. (2012). Hot and cool executive function in childhood and adolescence: Development and plasticity. *Child Development Perspectives, 6*(4), 354–360.

Zelazo, P. D., Müller, U., Frye, D., & Marcovitch, S. (2003). The development of executive function in early childhood: VI. The development of executive function: Cognitive complexity and control—revised. *Monographs of the Society for Research in Child Development, 68*(3), 93–119. https://doi.org/10.1111/j.0037-976X.2003.00266.x

Ziegler, A., Stoeger, H., & Balestrini, D. P. (2017). Systemic gifted education. In J. Riedl Cross, C. O'Reilly, & T. L. Cross (Eds.), *Providing for the special needs of students with gifts and talents: Shared perspectives from international researchers* (pp. 15–56). CTYI Press.

CHAPTER 3

To Be Gifted and ADHD

Understanding the Unique Challenges

C. Matthew Fugate

The Oxford Dictionary defines *exceptionality* as something that is unusual or not typical. As giftedness is outside the norm, it is, by definition, an exceptionality (Moon & Reis, 2004). Subotnik et al. (2011) noted that varying definitions of giftedness are often built around the principles of high IQ, emotional fragility, creative productive giftedness, talent development in specific domains, unequal access, and practice (p. 6). When a student presents a combination of characteristics of giftedness (e.g., advanced academic ability, creativity, leadership) and a learning and/or behavioral deficiency like Attention Deficit/Hyperactivity Disorder (ADHD), they are said to be twice-exceptional (2e).

According to the fifth edition of the *Diagnostic and Statistical Manual of Mental Disorders* (DSM-5; American Psychiatric Association [APA], 2013), ADHD can be diagnosed based upon the level of inattentiveness and/or hyperactivity-impulsivity exhibited within an individual in more than one setting, resulting in one of three subtypes—ADHD, predominately inattentive presentation; ADHD, predominately hyperactive-impulsive presentation; or ADHD, combined presentation. Further, the DSM-5 estimated prevalence rates for ADHD diagnoses requiring special services in the United States to be between 5% and 13% of school-aged children. Additionally, reports have estimated worldwide-pooled prevalence rates to be 5.2%–7.2% (e.g., Polanczyk et al., 2007; Thomas et al., 2015). Finally, clinic-referred samples are more likely to represent children with co-occurring disabilities and lower IQ (Zentall, 2006); who are 3–7 times more likely to be suspended or expelled, retained, and/or provided with special education services (LeFever et al., 2002); and who have significantly higher dropout rates and chances for failure in school (Barron et al., 2006) than nonclinical, school-based samples.

Historical Overview of ADHD

The first known mention of symptomologies related to inattention occurred in 1798 by Scottish physician Sir Alexander Crichton (Lange et al., 2010). During his career, Crichton became intensely focused on mental illness, publishing a three-volume book entitled, *An Inquiry Into the Nature and Origin of Mental Derangement: Comprehending a Concise System of the Physiology and Pathology of the Human Mind and a History of the Passions and Their Effects*. In the second volume, Crichton noted that attention varied across people and within individuals at different times:

> The incapacity of attending with a necessary degree of constancy to any one object, almost always arises from an unnatural or morbid sensibility of the nerves, by which means this faculty is incessantly withdrawn from one impression to another. It may be either born with a person, or it may be the effect of accidental diseases. (as cited in Crichton, 2008, p. 203)

Crichton went on to say that when this inability to attend (focus) was not innate, then the cause could be related to nervous disorders:

> In this disease of attention, if it can with propriety be called so, every impression seems to agitate the person, and gives him or her an unnatural degree of mental restlessness. People walking up and down the room, a slight noise in the same, the moving a table, the shutting a door suddenly, a slight excess of heat or of cold, too much light, or too little light, all destroy constant attention in such patients, inasmuch as it is easily excited by

every impression. The barking of dogs, an ill-tuned organ, or the scolding of women, are sufficient to distract patients of this description to such a degree, as almost approaches to the nature of delirium. It gives them vertigo, and headache, and often excites such a degree of anger as borders on insanity. When people are affected in this manner, which they very frequently are, they have a particular name for the state of their nerves, which is expressive enough of their feelings. They say they have the fidgets. (as cited in Crichton, 2008, p. 203)

Despite this early mention of a possible medical tie to "abnormal attention," for many historians, true scientific investigation into what would come to be known as ADHD occurred in 1902, when British pediatrician Sir George Fredric Still identified a "defect of moral control" in some children in a series of lectures known as the Goulstonian Lectures (Barkley, 2006; Conners, 2000). This defect was a result of a lack of "control of action in conformity with the idea of the good of all" (Still, 1902, p. 1008), but without a "general impairment of intellect" (p. 1077). Still (1902) went on to note that this defect of moral control was displayed in a series of symptoms:

> (1) passionateness; (2) spitefulness—cruelty; (3) jealousy; (4) lawlessness; (5) dishonesty; (6) wanton mischievousness—destructiveness; (7) shamelessness—immodesty; (8) sexual immorality; and (9) viciousness. *The keynote of these qualities is self-gratification*, the immediate gratification of self without regard either to the good of others or to the larger and more remote good of self. (p. 1009, emphasis added)

Barkley (2006) noted that the reference to the need for immediate gratification is congruent with problems related to delayed gratification often associated with children with ADHD. Additionally, the "passionateness" Still (1902) identified as the first symptom of this defect in moral control was related to "a state of intense drivenness and impulsivity regarding some immediate goal" (Conners, 2000, p. 176). These lectures set the stage for the modern-day understanding of identification of children with ADHD with symptomologies related to impulsivity out of a need for instant gratification without regard for the consequences. Interestingly, Still noted that the ratio of boys to girls identified with this disorder was three to one (Barkley, 2006; Conners, 2000; Lange et al., 2010), a ratio that is similar to the current generally accepted rate of identification of four to one (Bauermeister et al., 2007; Biederman et al., 2005; Cuffe et al., 2005).

The connection to hyperactivity was first observed in 1932 by two German physicians, Franz Kramer and Hans Pollnow, when they reported "on hyperkinetic disease in infancy" (Conners, 2000). Similar to current symptomologies related to hyperactivity, Kramer and Pollnow (1932) described children as having marked motor restlessness, causing an inability to "stay still for a second, run up and down the room, climb about preferring high furniture, and are displeased when deterred from acting out their motor impulses" (as cited in Conners, 2000, p. 247). They noted that many of the impulsive actions carried out by the children that they observed appeared to be without specific purpose, but rather were "possibly due to a distinct distractibility by new and intensive stiumuli" (as cited in Conners, 2000, p. 247). Kramer and Pullnow also noted that many of the children afflicted with hyperkinetic disease had difficulty maintaining attention to tasks for more than a few minutes unless it was of interest to them, in which case they could maintain attention for extended periods of time, sometimes for hours (Conners, 2000).

It was not until the release of the DSM-II that Hyperkinetic Impulse Disorder was officially recognized in the United States (APA, 1968). The name was later changed to Attention Deficit Disorder in 1980. The scientific rational for this change was largely due to the belief that the presence of hyperactivity was not necessarily a common symptom, but rather a subtype, of the disorder (Gentry & Fugate, 2018; Holland & Higuera, n.d.). The publication of the DSM-III once again changed the designation of the disorder to "Attention Deficit Disorder with or without hyperactivity" (APA, 1980). Finally, with the 1987 revision of the DSM-III, the disorder was officially identified as Attention Deficit/Hyperactivity Disorder, or ADHD (APA, 1987). With the 1997 reauthorization of the Individuals With Disabilities Education Act, ADHD was officially recognized as an "other health impaired" condition, making a student diagnosed with this condition eligible for special education services in public schools (United States Department of Education, 1999).

During this time, it became understood that ADHD was not just a childhood disorder that disappeared over time, "but rather a chronic, persistent disorder remaining into adulthood in many cases" (Lange et al., 2010, p. 252). Lange et al. cautioned that researchers had been unable to locate a unique genetic marker for ADHD in clinical samples. They went on to point out that the objective diagnoses in community samples of school-aged children with ADHD may not always be reliable due to discrepancies between parent and teacher ratings; thus, they suggested, "the issue of the clinical entity of ADHD remains therefore an open question that requires further investigation" (p. 254).

However, since this study, the National Human Genome Research Institute (NHGRI, n.d.) determined that there were strong genetic correlations in the occurrence of ADHD in families and undertook a study to determine if there was in fact a genetic link to ADHD. Based upon this work, medical, psychological, and educational professionals have begun to better understand the nature of ADHD. Specifically, NHGRI (n.d.) classified ADHD as "a neurological disorder that affects a person's ability to control their behavior and pay attention to tasks" (para. 1). NHGRI noted that children diagnosed with ADHD were more likely to have a close biological relative who had also been identified with the same condition, thereby rejecting the notion of a lack of a genetic link that had been cautioned by Lange et al. (2010).

Further, through brain imaging, Lange et al. (2010) identified differences in size and function in some parts of the brain of children with ADHD when compared to children without the disorder. They determined a possible link between these differences and the brain chemicals that are required in sustaining attention and regulating behaviors. More recently, Jin et al. (2019) conducted a study to advance understanding of the brain architecture of people with ADHD, specifically the role of Cell Adhesion Molecule 1, or CADM1 gene, a protein that facilitates cell adhesion in the prefrontal lobe. Their preliminary findings showed "evidence to implicate the roles of CADM1 in relation to prefrontal brain activities, inhibition function, and ADHD, indicating a potential 'gene-brain-behavior' relationship of the CADM1 gene" (p. 2).

Characteristics of ADHD

Some characteristics commonly associated with ADHD include problems sustaining attention, difficulty listening attentively, difficulty with task commitment and follow-through, lack of attention to detail, difficulty with organization and time management, fidgeting, and excessive talking (APA, 2013). A continuum based upon the severity of these characteristics exists from clinically diagnosed, to those who are undiagnosed or with characteristics related to ADHD. Both clinic-referred and community-based samples of students— those selected from behavioral ratings—are referred to as ADHD and are equivalent in characteristics, outcomes, underlying skill deficits, and responses to intervention (see Barbaresi et al., 2007; Epstein et al., 1991; Merrell & Tymms, 2001; Powers et al., 2008), making differences in degree more than in type among these groups. However, clinically diagnosed samples of children with ADHD are more likely to represent children with co-occurring learning deficiencies in academic areas commonly seen in classrooms, such as in reading and/or mathematics (e.g., reading recognition, math calculation), and may experience difficulties in developing higher order thinking skills in these areas (Zentall, 2006).

Creativity and ADHD

Researchers have long focused on the importance of creativity in education (e.g., Davis, 2004; Guilford, 1967; Lewis, 2009; Renzulli, 1994). Creativity has been documented as a predictor of future performance and success in the workplace (e.g., Tierney et al., 1999; Torrance, 1972, 1981) and a factor in healthy emotional development, interpersonal relationships (e.g., Russ, 1998), and career advancements in science, technology, engineering, art, and mathematics (Plucker et al., 2004; Sternberg, 1999). Although there have been many studies focused on creativity, researchers have failed to agree upon a definition (Davis, 2004; Plucker et al., 2004). For this reason, this section includes an examination of the personality, behavioral, cognitive, and performance characteristics that are associated with creativity and ADHD found in the extant literature.

Although children with ADHD experience a number of challenges within the school environment, they may also possess strengths that go unrecognized. For example, children with ADHD in school-based samples tell more creative stories with novel themes and plots (Zentall, 1988). Furthermore, researchers have reported an overlap in behavioral characteristics between those individuals with creativity—specifically divergent thinking and the ability to identify alternative or unusual uses for objects and/or ways to solve a problem—and those with ADHD (e.g., Baum & Olenchak, 2002; Fugate et al., 2013; Webb et al., 2005). For example, researchers have reported that creative students may have difficulty (a) maintaining attention due to an active imagination and frequently daydreaming, (b) completing tasks because of their varied interests, and (c) focusing attention on activities that are not captivating or personally interesting (e.g., Baum & Olenchak, 2002; Cramond, 1994a).

When making more systematic comparisons between creative and noncreative adolescents, the creative students had characteristics that were similar to ADHD. Using the Conners' Parent Rating Scales–Revised and Conners' Teacher Rating Scale–Revised (Conners, 1997), Healey and Rucklidge (2006) measured ADHD symptomology in 67 children, 10–12 years in age. Those children who received a score at or above the clinical level on either the parent or teacher rating scales and were identified as creative based upon Creativity Index scores on the Torrance Tests of Creative Thinking (TTCT; Torrance 1966/2006) were then interviewed using the behavioral section of the Schedule for Affective Disorders and Schizophrenia for School-aged Children—Present and Lifetime Version (Kaufman et al., 1996). Although none of the students in the creativity group met the full qualifications for a diagnosis of ADHD, Healey and Rucklidge (2006) found that they did possess characteristics related to ADHD, such as inattentiveness, reduced information processing speed, and slower reaction time to external stimuli.

Overall, the literature suggests greater potential for creativity and creative achievement in the ADHD population than in the neurotypical population (e.g., Abraham et al., 2006; Carson et al., 2003; Cramond, 1994a; Fugate et al., 2013; White & Shah, 2006). If these indicators reflect a more general trait (i.e., creativity) in students with ADHD, then perhaps alternative approaches to education focused on developing creativity could be implemented, thus reducing negative outcomes for this population. In fact, researchers have noted the importance of approaching education from a strength-based perspective rather than focusing on remediating weaknesses (e.g., Fugate et al., 2013; Nielsen, 2002; Nielsen & Higgins, 2005).

Associations Between Creativity and Personality/Behavioral Traits

Davis (2004) suggested that personality, cognitive abilities, and biographical traits work together to produce creativity. He conducted an analysis of the creativity literature from 1961 to 2003 with the goal of identifying recurrent personality traits of creative people. Although not all traits applied to all creative people, he identified 22 high-frequency traits: 16 "positive" (e.g., independent, risk-takers, high energy, curious, humorous, artistic, emotional) and six "negative" (e.g., impulsive, hyperactive, argumentative; see Table 3.1). This list of characteristics has been followed by reports of an overlap between those individuals with creativity and those with ADHD (e.g., Baum & Olenchak, 2002). Other researchers have suggested that this overlap could be attributed to the characteristics of giftedness and not to an association with ADHD (Webb et al., 2005). That is, students with giftedness may have more difficulty (a) maintaining attention due to an active imagination and a propensity to daydream, (b) completing tasks because of their varied interests, and (c) focusing attention on activities that are not captivating or personally interesting (e.g., Baum & Olenchak, 2002; Cramond, 1994a).

TABLE 3.1
Summary of Davis's (2004) Personality Traits of Creative People

Personality Trait	Definition
Awareness of creativity	A habit of creative productivity; creative consciousness.
Originality	Continuously looking for new ways of doing things.
Independent	The desire to stand out, challenge traditions, and make changes as needed.
Risk-taking	The ability of the creative individual to expose themselves to failure or criticism.
High energy	A sense of enthusiasm and spontaneity.
Curiosity	Having a wide variety of interests and a desire to know how things work.
Sense of humor	Often takes a playful approach to problem solving.
Capacity for fantasy	May believe in the mysterious (e.g., mental telepathy, spirits).
Attraction to complexity	Has a preference for ambiguity and novelty.
Artistic	Interests in music, dance, plays, and art are often present.
Open minded	Open to new ideas and a willingness to look at problems from different perspectives.
Thorough	A commitment to completing tasks; being organized and disciplined.
Needs time alone	Preference for working alone; needs time for reflection when problem solving.
Perceptive	Ability to see relationships.
Emotional	May experience emotional swings, heightened activity levels, and a strong sense of right and wrong.
Ethical	Sensitivity to the needs of others.
Egotistical	Selfish, often intolerant of others.
Impulsive	May impatiently act without any thought for consequences.
Argumentative	Questions rules and authority.
Childish	May behave in an immature manner.
Absent minded	Easily forgetful, may spend a great deal of time daydreaming.
Neurotic	May have difficulty controlling emotions.
Hyperactive	Often restless and overactive both physically and mentally.

Associations Between Creativity and Cognitive Indicators

Creative abilities have also been associated with cognitive traits of divergent thinking (e.g., fluency, flexibility, originality, elaboration) and with information-processing abilities (e.g., using existing knowledge as a basis for new ideas, questioning norms and assumptions, finding problems; Davis, 2004). These information-processing abilities could explain the association often presumed between creativity and highly intelligent individuals. However, some researchers have reported data supporting Threshold Theory, which has been defined by findings of a weaker association between creativity and intelligence when overall IQ is above 120 than when IQ is below 120 (Getzels & Jackson, 1962; Guilford & Christensen, 1973; MacKinnon, 1962). Also arguing against the relationship between creativity and giftedness is the failure to find differences in the size of the relationship between creativity and intelligence of students above or below the 120 IQ threshold (see Preckel et al., 2006). What may explain divergent findings is the failure of these studies to specify and assess the two components of intelligence: crystallized intelligence, which reflects accumulated knowledge, and fluid intelligence, which reflects the ability to flexibly reason, induce rules and patterns, problem solve, and manipulate new information (Fugate et al., 2013; Furnham et al., 2008; Preckel et al., 2006).

When fluid intelligence is isolated, there is evidence of an association between creativity and divergent thinking, which are interrelated and needed for problem solving (Batey et al., 2010; Furnham et al., 2008; Lewis, 2009; Preckel et al., 2006; Silva, 2008). However, there is also a mediating variable between fluid intelligence and the outcomes of creativity and problem solving. This mediator—working memory, or the ability to hold information in mind needed to carry out a specific task—has been found to have positive associations with fluid intelligence (e.g., Baddeley, 2003; Hornung et al., 2011).

Perhaps the ability to hold information in mind allows individuals to reorder elements in new and useful ways, seeing new possibilities and divergent outcomes. This is supported by small to moderate correlations reported between working memory tasks (e.g., backward digit span, spatial working memory) and reasoning tasks related to creativity (e.g., verbal and figural analogies) for neurotypical university undergraduate students and staff members (Süß et al., 2002). More specifically, in a review of working memory as it was related to both analytical and creative problem solving, Wiley and Jarosz (2012) concluded that working memory could have positive and negative influences. Although the ability to narrow and sustain attention to information can be useful during the performance of analytical tasks (e.g., performing sequences of steps in mathematical problem solving, multiple movement possibilities in a problem-solving task), this restricted range of attentional focus can disrupt performance when creative problem solving may be improved by attention to peripheral cues. In other words, the mediating effect of working memory on creativity depends on the type of task to be performed (Fugate et al., 2013).

Group Comparisons of Creative Performance

Typically, creative performance has been operationally defined by tasks assessing originality or the production of divergent strategies and solutions. Using this definition, individuals with ADHD appear to have skills related to generating unique solutions, at least under specific performance conditions and with some tasks (Fugate et al., 2013). For example, students and/or adults with ADHD and with equivalent intelligence to those without ADHD used more visual imagery and strategies during problem solving in response to stimulating videos and games (Lawrence et al., 2002; Shaw & Brown, 1999); contributed to higher percentages of correct problem solutions in cooperative groups compared to small groups without a student with ADHD (Kuester & Zentall, 2011; Zentall et al., 2011); and performed significantly better than non-ADHD peers when measured on their ability to generate original ideas (Abraham et al., 2006). However, when the practicality of idea generation was measured, it was the equivalent-IQ neurotypical individuals who scored higher and who also preferred clarifying and developing ideas more than the ADHD group (Abraham et al., 2006).

There are also some tasks and measures that have not produced statistical differences in creative performance. For example, although Abraham et al. (2006) found differences in originality of idea generation, they failed to find creative performance differences on several tasks: (a) fluency or uniqueness differences on an untimed production of alternative and unusual uses of common objects, such as a newspaper or a brick; (b) the ability to extend or loosen preexisting boundaries that required imagining and drawing two new species of animals that might live on a planet wholly unlike Earth (conceptual expansion, coded as deviations from representing bilateral systems, common appendages, and features); or (c) the ability to assemble objects (e.g., furniture) using a sequence of three-dimensional figures (creative imagery). Similarly, Healey and Rucklidge (2005) reported no differences between ideas generated by students with ADHD and those generated by students without ADHD when given a variety of tools and asked to develop as many ideas as possible as to how they could use these tools to connect a set of strings. In general, these tasks were untimed and required using or modifying a sequence of concrete visual structures. It is these types of multiple component tasks that may be more likely improved by working memory (see Wiley & Jarosz, 2012), which are different from problem-solving tasks that are performed better with fewer steps and when ignoring the immediate context and details.

Fugate et al. (2013) noted that more consistent positive effects have been reported in research investigating divergent thinking and creative achievement in adults with ADHD. There is evidence of greater real-world creative achievement (a self-reported measure of creative achievement) in college-age students with ADHD (who self-reported prior ADHD diagnosis and ratings of ADHD symptoms) than in neurotypical college peers (White & Shah, 2011). Also, using a self-report preference scale for problem identification, idea generation, solution development, and solution implementation, White and Shah reported a preference for idea generation in their ADHD group, while the neurotypical group preferred solution development—similar to Abraham et al.'s (2006) findings in adolescents.

In sum, there is evidence of creative performance for individuals with ADHD and average to above-average IQ related to the generation of unique solutions (e.g., alternative uses and unique ideas, themes/plots, and strategies), primarily during the performance of short duration tasks (Fugate et al., 2013). These effects were documented more often when performance was brief or timed and when there were few preexisting stimuli to hold in mind. Perhaps under these task conditions, the poor working memory documented for the ADHD population (e.g., Carson et al., 2003; Kofler et al., 2010; Rhodes et al., 2012) would not be expected to offset creative abilities.

Group Comparisons of Assessed Creativity

The task attributes of creativity could be operationalized using normative assessments of divergent thinking. Using the Torrance Tests of Creative Thinking (TTCT), Cramond (1994b) reported that 32% of 34 participants with ADHD (ages 6–15) scored at or above the 90th percentile and 50% scored above the 70th percentile on the Creativity Index. Similarly, Shaw and Brown (1991) identified two equivalent groups of high-IQ 11- to 12-year-old students with and without ADHD, and reported that the students with ADHD attained higher scores on the TTCT than the students without ADHD. However, Healey and Rucklidge (2005) also examined 10- to 12-year-old students with equivalent but average IQ and reported no differences between groups, with only 9% of the ADHD group scoring higher than the 90th percentile on the TTCT. Thus, the 2005 study reported no evidence of creativity in an average-IQ ADHD sample. However, when these researchers later compared creative and noncreative students, defined by Creativity Index scores above the 90th percentile on the TTCT, 40% of those creative students were at risk for ADHD, a rate that was 4 times higher than the 9% that would be expected within the general population (Healey & Rucklidge, 2006).

In Review

Although there is no generally accepted definition of creativity, in psychology, creative thinking has been defined as the process of incorporating seemingly irrelevant and unrelated information to solve problems (Runco, 2004). This suggests that a wide focus of attention, often described as distractibility and documented for individuals with ADHD, may be useful for creative thought and insight. Prior findings reporting higher creative thinking ability in ADHD groups than in neurotypical groups have (1) annotated an overlap of social behavioral characteristics between creativity and ADHD; (2) documented creative performance on divergent thinking tasks, such as telling more creative stories, using more nonverbal information and strategies during problem solving, generating more alternative and unusual uses of objects, and contributing to higher percentages of correct problem solutions in cooperative groups; and (3) been self-reported by adults with ADHD as attaining more creative achievements and as preferring generating ideas to clarifying ideas. The literature that failed to find differences in creativity between individuals with and without ADHD appears to have assessed untimed and extended task performance requiring synthesis of preexisting stimuli (Fugate et al., 2013).

Giftedness and ADHD

Arguments have been made for the possible misdiagnosis of ADHD in students who should have instead been identified as gifted (e.g., Baum & Olenchak, 2002; Webb et al., 2005); however, no empirical evidence exists regarding the frequency that this may occur. Foley-Nicpon et al. (2011) reviewed 17 empirical studies related specifically to giftedness and ADHD that were conducted over a 20-year span. Shaw and Brown (1991) conducted the earliest study cited. In this study, the researchers reported that elevated scores on behavioral rating scales "undoubtedly would influence test performance" (Foley-Nicpon et al., 2011, p. 9). Foley-Nicpon et al. noted that these researchers also associated stable characteristics, such as high figural creativity, with the combined presence of high intelligence and ADHD. The authors also looked at a qualitative study of three boys with ADHD conducted by Cramond (1994a), who found that the participants exhibited high levels of creativity when given an assessment of divergent thinking. Finally, Foley-Nicpon et al. examined Baum et al.'s (1998) qualitative case study finding that environmental influences could result in inattentive behaviors when taking standardized assessments, posing difficulties in recognizing high ability. Although this review identified only three empirical studies conducted in the 1990s, Foley-Nicpon et al. found that interest in this population subsequently increased. This is most likely due to the fact that ADHD has become the most common behavioral disorder identified in children (Neihart, 2003) with an estimated 6.4 million students identified (Visser et al., 2016).

Academic Characteristics and Challenges

Cognitive processing difficulties often found in students with ADHD can lead to IQ scores that are typically 5–10 points lower than similar-ability neurotypical peers (Castellanos, 2000; Hughes, 2011). Because these scores may not truly reflect students' potential, educators could fail to recognize giftedness in students with ADHD, especially those in school districts that rely on IQ scores for identification (Hughes, 2011; Moon, 2002; Silverman, 2002). Conversely, the presence of giftedness often delays the age at which ADHD is recognized, so that the higher the IQ, the later an ADHD diagnosis tends to occur (Moon, 2002). Other common characteristics affecting the academic performance of students who are gifted with ADHD are a lack of organizational skills, poor short-term and working memory abilities, the inability to maintain attention, impulsive tendencies, and poor metacognitive skills (Davis et al., 2017; Moon & Reis, 2004; Nielsen, 2002; Zentall et al., 2001).

Social-Emotional Challenges

In 1988, Baum and Owen conducted one of the first studies looking at the social-emotional challenges of gifted students with learning disabilities, including those with ADHD. They discovered that although these twice-exceptional students often had higher levels of creative potential, they had a tendency for disruptive behaviors and achieved at lower levels than their peers. Baum and Owen noted that these disruptive behaviors may have been an outward sign of the students' feelings of inadequacy and low self-esteem. Twice-exceptional students can display emotional intensity, experience extreme depression, have a sense of inferiority, lack self-confidence, and experience frustration that leads to a general lack of motivation (Baum et al., 2001; Hughes, 2011; Moon & Reis, 2004; Olenchak & Reis, 2002). These characteristics often lead to challenges for gifted students with ADHD when relating to same-age peers, as they may feel a sense of alienation because of their inability to control verbal and/or physical impulsivity (Moon et al., 2001; Renzulli & Reis, 2009). Table 3.2 shows some characteristics associated with giftedness, learning disabilities, and twice-exceptional students who are gifted with ADHD.

Girls, ADHD, and Giftedness

As demonstrated in this chapter, there has been extensive research examining the effects of ADHD, as well as on being gifted and diagnosed with ADHD. However, there exists an inequity of gifted/ADHD research between the sexes, with more attention focused on boys. It is important to understand that, although there may be some similarities in the ways that giftedness and ADHD manifest between the sexes, there are realities of being gifted and ADHD that are specific to girls and must be understood.

The Centers for Disease Control (2019) reported that a total of 13.2% of boys have ever been diagnosed with ADHD, compared with only 5.6% of girls. However, the limited number of studies focused on girls with ADHD has increased only slightly in recent years. Further, researchers have noted that girls face social pressures as they enter their secondary education years that are distinctly different from those faced by their male counterparts, and these pressures can be exacerbated by ADHD and by giftedness (e.g., Blachman & Hinshaw, 2002; Fugate, 2019; Fugate & Gentry, 2016; Greene et al., 2001).

The manifestation of ADHD characteristics in girls can result in lowered self-esteem, heightened emotional reactions, a lack of focus, and difficulty with peer and family relationships (Fugate, 2014; Fugate & Gentry, 2016). These effects may become particularly amplified as these girls enter adolescence and can place additional stress on both academic and personal performance (Owens et al., 2009), leading to increased incidences of underachievement (Reid & McGuire, 1995; Reis & McCoach, 2000). Grskovic and Zentall (2010) studied 262 girls with and without ADHD. They found that girls with ADHD were verbally impulsive, hyperactive, faster in conversation and schoolwork, easily bored, often at the center of trouble among peers, impatient, and more

TABLE 3.2

Comparison of Characteristics of Gifted,
ADHD, and Gifted With ADHD

Domain	Students Who Are Gifted	Students With ADHD	Students Who Are Gifted With ADHD
Academic	High level of concentration	Easily distracted during repetitive tasks; difficulty completing tasks independently	Difficulty shifting attention when focused on a high interest activity; difficulty completing tasks due to broad areas of interest
	Learns easily	Difficulty following directions and sustaining attention to routine tasks	Easily bored with routine tasks; underachievement
	Enjoys learning	Easily frustrated by academic tasks, especially mathematics facts	Easily frustrated by difficulties verbalizing academic responses
Social Emotional	Able to get along with others of similar IQ	Ease at initiating but difficulty maintaining friendships	Difficulty developing close relationships; loner
	Behaves maturely	Poor judgment when interacting with others and overly emotional	Emotionally intense
	Keen sense of humor	Spontaneous and can be fun or silly	Displays humor at inappropriate times
	Good organizational skills	Disorganized and careless	Disorganized and careless
	Self-confident	Low self-esteem and self-efficacy	Critical of self and others; poor self-image

Note. Data are from Baum & Olenchak, 2002; Cramond, 1994a; Davis et al., 2017; Moon et al., 2001; Nielsen, 2002; Renzulli & Reis, 2009; Zentall et al., 2001. From "Attention Deficit/ Hyperactivity Disorder in Gifted Students," by M. Gentry and C. M. Fugate, in *APA Handbook of Giftedness and Talent* (pp. 575–584), 2018, American Psychological Association. Copyright 2018 by American Psychological Association. Reprinted with permission.

easily prone to moodiness, anger, and stubbornness than their peers without ADHD. However, participants with ADHD in this study were also able to relate prosocial behaviors with high self-esteem. Specifically, these girls were able to discriminate between their own appropriate and inappropriate behaviors, understanding "that they were more likely to react with strong feelings than other groups of girls" (p. 181).

The socialization process becomes particularly challenging for girls with ADHD who have higher rates of peer rejection than their male counterparts and "often serve as 'negative social catalysts,' fueling conflictual social interactions among their peers" (Blachman & Hinshaw, 2002, p. 625). The exhibition of ADHD behaviors in girls has been found to be setting specific, with girls more likely to repress ADHD behaviors in the classroom environment where teacher disapproval is more likely. However, these behaviors become more prominent in social settings that "involve more complex rules and requirements, which may involve delayed and indirect consequences," the result of which is increased peer rejection (Grskovic & Zentall, 2010, p. 170). Mikami et al. (2004) found that, because of their social difficulties, girls with ADHD run the risk of being "doubly disliked" by both peers and adults. These girls have a heightened awareness of the social consequences of their behaviors, which can result in a poor perception of relationships with their teachers, lowered self-esteem, and increased rates of depression and anxiety (Rucklidge & Tannock, 2001).

Because girls with ADHD are at greater risk of social impairment, when rejected by their peers, they have an increased possibility of poor adolescent and adult adjustment that often leads to depressed and/or anxious behaviors (Greene et al., 2001; Mikami & Hinshaw, 2006). Researchers have identified links between peer rejection and academic underachievement and increased incidents of substance abuse within this population (e.g., Barkley et al., 2006). Further, if issues related to ADHD are left unaddressed, these girls find themselves at higher risk for low self-esteem (Becker et al., 2013) and teen pregnancy (Quinn, 2005). These problems are likely to carry into adulthood, where they have been found to experience higher divorce rates, financial problems, and difficulties with time management (Nadeau & Quinn, 2002; Rodin & Lithman, 2002; Rucklidge et al., 2007). Interestingly, Mikami and Hinshaw (2006) found that girls with ADHD who were more confident in their academic abilities demonstrated lowered incidences of these negative results and increased achievement over time.

Fugate (2014)[1] conducted the first study to look exclusively at gifted girls with ADHD during their secondary education years. The five girls in this col-

---

1 The remainder of this section on gifted girls with ADHD is adapted with permission from Fugate (2014).

lective case study reported several advantages and challenges to being gifted with ADHD. Patterns and themes were found in four major categories that provided insight into their lived experiences as they interacted throughout the school day with teachers and peers, their ability to make and maintain friendships, their relationships within their own families, and the coping mechanisms that they had developed over time to handle these pressures and to help them regain focus.

Analysis was conducted through the lens of symbolic interactionism, in order to examine how these girls viewed their own behaviors—known as the "I"—and how they perceived themselves to be viewed by others around them—the "me" (LeCompte et al., 1992). For these gifted girls with ADHD the "I" came through in the social-emotional and academic support acquired from family and close friends, as well as in recognizing how their own perseverance through the challenges they faced related to ADHD helped them achieve in school. The "me" was seen in their insecurities in their interactions with peers, perceptions of their parents' expectations, and the lack of understanding that some teachers had for the challenges that they faced.

Self-Concept

The gifted girls with ADHD in Fugate's (2014) study reported that they had insecurities about their ability to fit in with other same-age peers. They were acutely aware of the combined qualities of giftedness and ADHD that they possessed and felt that others might view them as "weird" (Grace, personal communication). They were uncomfortable asserting themselves when they were around others their age. Additionally, they worried that when they did start to get close to someone, they would eventually be rejected and "pushed aside" (Jenny, personal communication).

Faced with mounting pressures to fit in, these girls went out of their way to be someone who they thought others wanted or expected them to be. They felt as if they were constantly under scrutiny and being judged by others so they protected themselves by putting on a "public face" (Jenny, personal communication) in order to mask their true personality to shield them from the rejection that they were sure would eventually come. At times they feigned interest in things that were socially acceptable: "[Flappy Bird is] just what a lot of people are talking about; so if I talk about it, I fit in with them. I have something that helps me fit in" (Grace, personal communication). This ultimately led to feelings of low self-esteem because these girls were not appreciated for who they felt they truly were: "I just get tired of it because I just want them to like me for me" (Jenny, personal communication).

To cope with the social pressures of middle school, these girls turned to physical activities that helped them refocus, calm, and center themselves:

> If I seem bad or am hurt, I use that pain, and it's like what I'm running against. I push past it and keep running harder and longer. By the end of the run, I'm tired, but I got it out of my system. (Jenny, personal communication)

The girls also discussed the importance of having a creative outlet, supporting the findings of Fugate et al. (2013) that gifted students with ADHD had higher levels of creativity than their gifted peers without ADHD:

> When I need to calm down, I usually get into some sort of creative project. The last time I made a marionette out of a stuffed pig. I don't know, my mom says that I'm creative but mostly it just helps me calm down when I'm angry or upset. (Lily, personal communication)

Ultimately, the aspects of giftedness and ADHD that made them unique were the barriers that they felt kept them from building relationships with others: "I wouldn't say that I'm the average person because, well, I came in wearing a monkey hat. I think it's a little different for people. . . . My mom said it's creative, but I think most people think it's a little weird" (Grace, personal communication). These findings support past researchers who reported that girls with ADHD had difficulty developing friendships (e.g., Grskovic & Zentall, 2010; Mikami & Hinshaw, 2006; Owen et al., 2009) and gifted researchers, findings of increased social pressures as girls transition into middle school (e.g., Dai, 2002; Kerr et al., 2012; Rimm, 2002), leading to fears of social isolation (e.g., Reis, 2002; Reis & Callahan, 1989).

Regardless of how much they felt the need to fit in, these girls reported that they had little in common with other girls their own age, making it difficult for them to relate with peers in school. They saw their giftedness as one of the reasons for these differences. For some of these girls, this manifested in their lack of concern for what they saw as gender-specific interests common in other girls, such as boys, make-up, shopping, and social networks. For others it was their sense of social justice that they felt conflicted with girls their age who spent too much time "talking crap" about other people (Jenny, personal communication). Often, the only thing that they felt that they had in common with their peers was the mere fact that they were in the same school. However even then they felt that, unlike the other girls, they were "kind of interested in what they're teaching at school" (Lily, personal communication), implying that despite this one similarity, vast differences still existed. This contradicted Pepperell and Rubel (2009), who found that gifted girls transitioning into middle school were able to find common interests with their nongifted peers, thereby helping them fit into the social schema.

Added to their perceived dissimilarities resulting from their giftedness, were these girls' feelings that symptomologies of ADHD also differentiated them from other girls their age. They worried that they lacked appropriate social skills as a result of their impulsivity. Consistent with previous findings from researchers on ADHD (Zentall, 2006) and gifted-ADHD twice-exceptionality (Grskovic & Zentall, 2010; Zentall et al., 2001), these girls were concerned that their inability to control their words and actions set them apart: "I'm really hard to make mad, but when you get me mad, good luck. It's not pretty" (Jenny, personal communication). They found that their ADHD presented challenges, even with people that they were close to:

> There's one of my friends who, I mean it's not like she's a discourager to what I do, but I feel like she's not the most patient person in the world and she'll get annoyed with me sometimes—like forgetting things or even when we're playing board games, like directions if we're learning a new game. That's really hard. And just—people might get annoyed with that or just make snide comments, like I'm really slow with this, like why are you taking so long. (Teresa, personal communication)

These feelings resulted in a personal view that they were somehow flawed, while others were "perfect" and that they were left "off to the side in my own little world" (Grace, personal communication), a fact that was concerning given their self-reported tendencies toward depression.

Finally, specific to gifted girls with ADHD, there was a feeling of personal responsibility for others whom they saw as "outsiders" similar to themselves (Teresa, personal communication). Sometimes this sense of responsibility grew from regrets about past experiences that they carried with them and vowed to change:

> When I was in Scotland, there was this bully who was really mean to the kids in my grade. I saw that happening and I felt

really bad, but I didn't really do much and I've always sort of kicked myself for that and I wanted to fix that where I am now. I'm trying to fix that here and make sure that it doesn't happen again. (Grace, personal communication)

In the end, these girls had a need to feel as though they made "a difference" (Jenny, personal communication)—whether it was with someone whom they felt was somehow diminished in capacity, a group of people who they viewed as needing additional help or reinforcement, or members of their own family. This feeling of personal responsibility and the need to help others made these girls feel "strong" (Jenny, personal communication) and bolstered their self-esteem and self-worth.

Social Support

As discussed previously, dealing with the day-to-day social demands of school caused emotional challenges for these gifted girls with ADHD. Therefore, it was important that they had people to look to for support and encouragement. Supporting Reis's (1998) assertion of the importance of parental opinions, family was one of the primary groups of people who played an important role in their social development. The girls reported that they understood that their parents wanted them to have "nice friends" (Lily, personal communication) and to be able to interact with a wider variety of people who may have views different from their own:

> My mom does try to push me to do more things with my
> friends . . . she does want me to interact with more people . . .
> to see what's out there and know different personalities and
> interact with different things, to get into different situations
> and know how to react. My mom was the one with a lot of
> friends growing up and I think she wants that for me. (Grace,
> personal communication)

Additionally, these twice-exceptional girls depended on their parents to help them navigate the increasingly complicated social world that they found themselves in when they entered their secondary education years: "Socially, I'm able to talk with them a lot and work through my problems with them" (Teresa, personal communication).

Unlike the strong maternal influence reported in the literature for gifted girls (e.g., Callahan & Reis, 1996; Hébert et al., 2001; Reis, 1998), some of these girls reported that it was, in fact, their father with whom a special bond had formed: "My dad and I are closer than I am with my mom" (Lea, personal communication). Grace added, "My dad and I, every Saturday after my Irish class, we go to Culver's and have a yogurt, like a father-daughter date. So, if I've missed him during the week, we get time to catch up then" (personal communication).

However, the teenage years can also be particularly challenging for the parent/daughter relationship, and the challenges may be exacerbated when that daughter is also gifted and has ADHD. The verbal impulsivity that comes with having ADHD affects not only these girls' relationships with peers in school, but also their relationships with family: "I get mad sometimes. I don't get mad at my friends—that's really hard to make me mad—but my mom just ticks me off . . . she puts so many limitations on me and I don't like being limited; I feel trapped" (Jenny, personal communication). When these moments of frustration occurred, these girls turned to a small, close-knit circle of friends:

> I don't know, they always just, they can relate to me because I know there are a lot more families in a worse situation than me . . . I just go to my [best friend], and then we'll talk about the stuff that's bothering us, or the annoying things that other people talk about. She's that person I can go to and talk about pretty much everything. (Jenny, personal communication)

Unlike reports from researchers regarding the difficulties that girls with ADHD have in maintaining friendships (e.g., Grskovic & Zentall, 2010; Owen et al., 2009), assertions of the influence of like-IQ peers for gifted girls (e.g., Comallie-Caplan, 2008; Kerr et al., 2012), or claims that gifted girls feel they must choose between being smart or having friends (Silverman, 1995, 2005), these gifted girls with ADHD forged their own paths toward friendship. They sought out others who were like them behaviorally and built friendships based upon trust with a group of peers who withheld judgment, let them be who they were, and provided them with support and encouragement:

> I normally turn to my friends; they look to keep me going. If I'm sad they always find a way to make me happy . . . with them I can just sort of let myself be me. . . . Sometimes, like, I just—I don't know—I let myself behave how I want to behave. Not

how my brain wants me to, but how my heart feels. (Grace,
personal communication)

These close, personal connections were important, as these girls often felt
that they had to put on a different persona when they were around others
whom they perceived did not understand them: "I'm really enjoying my time
with my friends. We sort of have, it's a kind of unique group. We're not interested in any of the normal stuff, like parties or anything like that" (Teresa,
personal communication). Ultimately, it may be that the combination of gifted
and ADHD traits gave these girls the confidence to be themselves while building connections with a small group of like others.

Achievement and Motivation

The girls in this study reported several positive and negative effects on their
academic achievement and motivation as a result of being both gifted and having ADHD. Characteristics of giftedness—such as good memory, advanced
problem-solving ability, and attention to detail—were reported in the girls'
interview responses, but these gifted traits were mitigated by characteristics
related to their ADHD. These girls associated school with feelings of confusion, tension, and shame—more so than they did at home. They attempted to
compensate for their challenges through competition with others around them,
which would often become a source of social distress. However, distractibility
and failure to complete tasks such as homework were the two main academic
challenges these girls faced, findings that were consistent with the literature
on twice-exceptional students (e.g., Baum & Olenchak, 2002; McCoach et al.,
2001; Moon, 2002).

These girls had a difficult time maintaining focus and attention. Even the
slightest distraction, such as the presence of a fish tank close by in the classroom, could divert their attention: "I have a hard time paying attention if there
is something distracting . . . if someone's doing something wrong or chewing
gum loudly, that bothers me. It's the slightest things, and I have a hard time
paying attention" (Grace, personal communication).

Further, these girls became easily bored when faced with completing
homework that they saw as repetitive:

I cannot focus on my homework. I don't . . . it's not that I don't
like it, it's just that after a while I get bored and I don't want
to do anymore after a certain point. It's just the same material.

We've been doing it years before and I know it. . . . (Jenny, personal communication)

Suddenly, time doing homework became time not doing homework, a fact that they were cognizant of, but they could not bring themselves to do anything else, so they ended up spending time doing nothing at all: "I spend a lot of time doing homework or attempting to do homework. There's a lot of time spent not doing homework but not doing anything else either because I still have homework to do, if that makes sense" (Teresa, personal communication).

When homework was completed, the chances that it made it to the teacher were small, even when organizational systems were put into place. These girls were also keenly aware of the consequences related to their lack of focus on their achievement. "I forget my homework and when I don't have that, I don't really know that [material] as much" (Lea, personal communication). This, in turn, affected their motivation:

> [My teacher] gave out a lot of homework that I couldn't really finish, and if I did, I forgot to turn it in, so I got marked off a lot for that. Since I was GT, most of the kids got stuff faster than me, so I wouldn't really get the material. I wanted to cry. (Lily, personal communication)

Fortunately, for these girls this was, once again, where physical activity became an important compensatory strategy:

> I don't know what I would do without running because when I have energy, I feel like I'm gonna spaz out. I don't know. It tires me out, but then you get this runner's high, which is just an awesome feeling. And then I get home, I have enough energy I still can, like, function and do my homework. (Jenny, personal communication)

Seeing value in hard work, these girls also believed that ability alone was ineffective in the classroom. These girls were aware of the challenges that they faced as a result of their ADHD and were committed to overcoming them: "I just think that if I really work hard, I might make something of myself. When I want to be smart, I can. This is when I want to be. I think I'm really smart, but I actually have to work at it" (Jenny, personal communication). Their belief in their ability to persevere resulted in a growth mindset, seeing their abilities as malleable and connected to their effort: "I try my best and give my best effort even if I'm not very good at something" (Grace, personal communication). This is in contrast to findings that girls tend to have more fixed mindsets focused on ability (Dweck, 2006/2016; Good et al., 2012).

In addition to these external pressures, these girls faced many internalized symptoms as a result of their co-occurring conditions. Even at the middle school level, many of these girls were already looking beyond high school and considering their options for college: "We have this college book, the cover says '283 Good Colleges,' and I found William & Mary that I want go to, so I'm starting to get my grades up for that" (Grace, personal communication). Consistent with findings that perfectionist tendencies may be more prevalent in gifted girls than their nongifted peers, and because of the traits associated with their co-occurring ADHD, these twice-exceptional girls worried about their grades and become hypercritical of their own performance. A 94 in an English class and an 83 in an advanced math class were considered "only okay" with one girl who wished she had done better (Teresa, personal communication). Fortunately, these girls were also self-aware and able to reflect upon past failures and used them as positive motivation, traits that Speirs-Neumeister (2004) identified in self-oriented perfectionists:

> Sometimes I'm liable to give up, but I can't. I have to push myself to go forward. I have to care. You have to care to succeed. If you don't, you may succeed, but you won't get far. I've learned that there are times when I didn't care, and I got bad grades. That's going to show on my records for college. I have to get good grades to go to college. I have to keep pushing forward. (Lea, personal communication)

Although this drive and determination positively motivated some of these twice-exceptional girls, unreasonably high expectations resulted in low self-esteem for others, leaving their sense of self-image tied to the challenges of ADHD: "I mean I wish I could be a better person, able to get through things like tests quicker. I would like to have more time for other things and even read more and have a better memory" (Teresa, personal communication).

Academic Support

Twice-exceptional students face many obstacles in the classroom as a result of their learning and/or behavioral differences (Baum et al., 2001; Hughes, 2011; Moon & Reis, 2004; Olenchak & Reis, 2002) that require academic supports that address both their giftedness and their ADHD. All too often, these gifted girls with ADHD found themselves in classrooms settings where they felt alienated or misunderstood because teachers failed to fully realize the challenges that they faced on a daily basis. Grskovic and Zentall (2010) discussed the academic difficulties that girls with ADHD have, particularly in areas of math and science. Unfortunately for these gifted girls with ADHD, those could be some of their most unforgiving classes: "I kind of am slower at taking notes and I think that the teacher—because she's really good at science—she doesn't really know what it's like to not be good at science" (Lea, personal communication).

Additionally, these girls were often asked to perform tasks that highlighted their challenges, such as reading aloud in class: "I'll look over the words and I'll get really red in the face, and I want to crawl into a hole. I want to sound like I know what I'm talking about, but it's new material. I don't know; it just makes me nervous" (Jenny, personal communication). Consequently, if a teacher lost patience with these girls or failed to recognize their giftedness, learning preferences, or needs, motivation and achievement declined: "She makes me feel really bad about that when I don't get it. It makes me feel discouraged with myself. It just makes me not like the class as much" (Lea, personal communication).

Although incidents like these are likely unintentional, they highlight the need that exists for research-based professional development focused on differentiation and the needs of twice-exceptional learners in general, and gifted girls with ADHD in particular. The idea of differentiation to meet the needs of gifted learners in the classroom is not new. However, for these girls, differentiation was essential for their increased achievement, self-esteem, and self-efficacy. They required more hands-on and visual learning experiences that put discrete skills into a larger context that they could relate to and understand: "I learn by seeing, and I'm a hands-on learner. I don't learn by hearing and writing it down. I have to have something to relate it to" (Grace, personal communication). In addition to contextual, hands-on learning experiences, providing these girls with more opportunities to have choices in their learning honored their interests and increased their motivation:

> We're doing this book thing where we have to read a book that [our teacher] approves. They have to be award winning or notable. I asked [her] if Stephen King counts, and she said yes. I was like, "YES!" I just adore him, his books, his writing; he's a great author. (Lea, personal communication)

These findings support the literature on twice-exceptional learning differences suggesting that these students achieve when learning is presented from a strength-based perspective (Baum & Olenchak, 2002; McCoach et al., 2001; Neihart, 2000).

Just as important as differentiation are the relationships that educators develop with their students and the environment that they create in their classrooms and schools. First, when these girls felt that their learning differences were honored and supported, their motivation increased: "[My teacher] gets that I need more time on things or notes for things. If she's going through something on the board, she'll give [the notes] to me, but not in a really obnoxious, obvious manner, which I appreciate" (Teresa, personal communication). Consequently, when these girls felt that their teacher genuinely cared, they wanted to work harder for that teacher, and the byproduct was personal reflection on their own learning and understanding:

> She encourages us to do our best, to work hard. Especially since some of the problems don't take a short time to do, they take some time to think about them. It makes me think about how I'm doing and if I understand what I'm learning. . . . She encourages me to check over my stuff and make sure that I have it as good as I can make it. (Grace, personal communication)

Finally, these girls needed an environment, in their classrooms and in their schools, that met their unique needs and encouraged them to achieve:

> It's kind of a creative school. It's not all about math or science or reading or writing; it's about art, too. [Since moving to this school] my grades have gone up, so now I feel like I am smart, and I can do more. . . . I think more of the kids at this school have ADHD, too, and the teachers understand that. [My English teacher] is so supportive. We have creative stories sometimes, and she says that I write really well. (Lily, personal communication)

Unfortunately, these types of educational experiences were not always readily available to these girls. This is where the academic support received from their parents became so important. Parents have long been regarded as an important component in the success of gifted girls (Comallie-Caplan, 2008 Hébert et al., 2001; Kerr et al., 2012; Reis, 1998, 2002). These girls looked to their parents to be their advocates to ensure that they were provided every opportunity for success. They appreciated the lengths that their parents would go to make sure that they received the accommodations that they needed and that helped them better understand themselves as gifted learners with ADHD: "Academically, if they hadn't helped me to have gotten my accommodations that have been very helpful—like double time especially—I would have done much worse" (Teresa, personal communication). In addition to their advocacy, parents provided valuable motivational support: "My dad is really the one that encourages me academically. We do a weekly grade check and stuff like that" (Grace, personal communication).

Unfortunately, whether real or perceived, at times these twice-exceptional girls felt additional pressure as a result of what they saw as unreasonable expectations from their parents. When this happened, these girls became highly frustrated, wanting their parents to "lay off and let me take care of it myself" (Jenny, personal communication). This opened the door to the possibility for these girls to develop socially prescribed perfectionist tendencies (Speirs-Neumeister, 2004). Fortunately, they also seemed to understand that even though they may become easily frustrated by their parents' expectations, "I know she's doing it because she loves me" (Jenny, personal communication).

Meeting the Needs of ADHG Students

Although gifted students with ADHD may demonstrate varying degrees of difficulty in their academic and social worlds, there is evidence, dating as far back as the late 1980s, that students who are gifted, or demonstrate above-average intelligence, and have ADHD may have a greater potential for creativity and creative achievement (e.g., Fugate et al., 2013; Kuester & Zentall, 2011; Shaw & Brown, 1999; Zentall, 1988). Specifically, researchers have found that gifted students with ADHD scored higher on tests of creative thinking (Cramond 1994b; Fugate et al., 2013); told more creative stories with novel themes (Zentall, 1988); used more visual imagery and strategies during problem solving in response to high states of arousal, such as when watching and playing videos and games (Lawrence et al., 2002; Shaw & Brown, 1999); and contributed to higher percentages of correct problem solutions in cooperative groups (Kuester & Zentall, 2011) when compared with their same-age peers. Further, when comparing college students with and without ADHD, White and Shah (2006) found that the students with ADHD outperformed their neurotypical peers in measures of divergent thinking in the areas of fluency, flexibility, and originality. Additionally, these students were found to be more innovative in their thinking (White & Shah, 2016) and reported higher levels of creative achievement (White & Shah, 2011).

Based upon these findings, Fugate and Gentry (2016) have suggested that these students be viewed as Attention Divergent Hyperactive Gifted (ADHG). This label alters the focus from the challenges that these students face and instead highlights their potential for creativity, innovation, and motivation.

Educators must pay attention to and cultivate the creativity and innovation inherent in these ADHG students, rather than let these qualities remain dormant and underdeveloped. In order to accomplish this, schools must implement a systematic approach to the identification of these students combined with in-class supports and strategies that highlight the strengths that these students possess and leverages those strengths to address their challenges.

Identification

There are an estimated 385,000 twice-exceptional students in the United States, although this may be a conservative estimate due to the lack of systematic procedures for identifying these students (Assouline et al., 2015). One reason for this is due to a phenomenon known as the masking effect (McCoach et al., 2001; Pfeiffer, 2013). Children who are gifted and have a learning and/or behavioral disability display characteristics of both conditions with one often hiding the characteristics of the other, the frequent result being that the student presents as "average" with neither their strengths nor their challenges being adequately addressed (Baum et al., 2001; Zentall et al., 2001). This can have serious academic consequences for these students, particularly under the Response to Intervention model. Although these students may be working below their potential, their performance may not be below that of their grade-level peers; therefore, they are never identified with an intervention need. Baum and Olenchak (2002) found that assessments for identification in gifted programs rarely occurred once a diagnosis for ADHD or another disability had been made. It has also been reported that, in instances when students were identified as both gifted and ADHD, they were apt to have been retained more often, performed poorly on standardized tests, and experienced higher rates of mood and anxiety disorders when compared to their gifted, non-ADHD peers (Antshel, 2008).

To address these concerns, Nielsen (2002) encouraged schools to establish a multidisciplinary task force that would advocate for, and raise awareness of, the needs of twice-exceptional students. This task force should include gifted education, special education, and general education teachers, as well as any diagnosticians responsible for the testing and identification of students for special education services. The primary functions of this group would be to establish and oversee a process of identification and the development of a continuum of service options that meets the unique needs of these ADHG students and "[focuses] on developing the talent while compensating for the disability" (Renzulli & Reis, 2009, p. 187). To increase awareness, the task force should seek out professional development opportunities for all stakeholders— teachers, administrators, diagnosticians, paraprofessionals, and parents. These opportunities would focus on recognizing the characteristics associated with these students for identification, as well as best practices for differentiation to meet their needs.

Nielsen (2002) further recommended that identification begin with a thorough examination of the special education records to identify students who have an IQ score of 120 or higher. Records should also be considered for students with IQs starting at 110, due to the 5- to 10-point difference that can exist when compared to similar-ability peers (Castellanos, 2000; Hughes, 2011). Additionally, an examination of the records of identified gifted students should also be conducted for any indications of a special need that might require further evaluation for special education services. During this process of records examination, Nielsen (2002) stressed the importance of carefully exploring any discrepancies between the results of abilities tests and measures of academic performance, as well as any extreme score variation on individual abilities subtests. Because students with ADHD often have deficiencies in cognitive processes related to indicators such as coding and digit span, the discrepant subscores and full-scale scores may not accurately reflect the ability of the student. Finally, it is important that multiple data sources be used for identification. Because creative thinking has been found to be a strength in ADHG students (Fugate et al., 2013), the use of measures that evaluate divergent thinking, such as the Torrance Tests of Creative Thinking, may be important when developing identification plans for these students.

Classroom Strategies

Teachers should incorporate a variety of classroom strategies that recognize that ADHG students are gifted first, addressing and enhancing their strengths, and then use those strengths to address the challenges that they face. The challenge for teachers is to create classroom environments in which "creativity is emphasized as a pathway to learning as well as an outcome of learning" (Fugate et al., 2013, p. 242). This type of environment encourages students to ask questions and make connections beyond just finding correct answers. It is an environment in which teachers encourage their students' interests and passions, and provide students with timely, positive feedback on work that is challenging, with realistic goals and time frames established with and/or by the students (Drapeau, 2014).

Hayes (2016) suggested some specific strategies that can easily be incorporated in the classroom when working with ADHG students. For instance, these students should be allowed to test out of units of study in which they demonstrate mastery. Additionally, when they are working on larger projects or are involved in coursework that is new or more challenging, tasks should be divided into smaller, more manageable chunks. The ability to successfully complete these subtasks builds positive self-efficacy and can help students take on larger tasks in the future. Further, offering students choice in how they learn, and in the types of products that they produce to demonstrate understanding, gives them an opportunity to develop autonomy and take responsibility for their own learning. As previously discussed, researchers found that students with ADHD were able to maintain high states of arousal when involved in games and videos. Therefore, the utilization of technology for high-level research, online classes, and educational games and programs can increase student interest and attention (Fugate, 2018).

Finally, these students have a reverse hierarchy of learning that is focused on "the big picture," as opposed to the discrete skills emphasized in the learning objectives often associated with district and state standards (Fugate, 2018). For example, if reading from a science textbook is the primary source of learning for a student with attention and processing deficiencies related to ADHD, a deficiency is created in science (Hughes, 2011). Instead, these students need to be exposed to authentic learning experiences that emphasize applied content knowledge over the process of acquisition of knowledge. Project-based learning is one example of a learning experience that provides this type of authentic learning and may be especially appropriate for ADHG students (Fugate, 2018; Fugate et al., 2013). Implications for creative writing and problem solving within science, social studies, literature, and mathematics can yield a variety of interest-based student products, including cartoons, role-playing, blogs, videos, and newspaper articles. Learning can then be deepened and broadened through the revision of these products for different audiences (Fugate et al., 2013).

Hayes (2016) offered several suggestions for teachers to consider when planning for authentic learning experiences. First, when planning your lesson, it is important to keep in mind how you would like your ADHG students to be able to demonstrate understanding. This requires that teachers identify the specific cognitive skills (e.g., using algebra as a tool to solve everyday problems), affective skills (e.g., working with others/team building), and metacognitive skills (e.g., how to conduct research) that they want their students to develop. Once this has been accomplished, create a list of those areas of mastery that you want them to develop (e.g., cause-and-effect relationships). The list might include specific questions that they could answer, topics they might explore, and/or online resources to get them started. Next, determine the amount of time that it will take to complete the project-based learning experience, understanding that ADHG students often need extended time to fully develop their ideas. Providing them with opportunities to "walk away" for a period of time allows for reflection in order to further build upon their ideas when they return to the project (Fugate, 2018).

When you are ready to present students with a project-based learning experience, clearly explain that the objective is to demonstrate mastery of the content through the process of the project, not through the final product itself. This will allow students to develop products that demonstrate their learning based upon individualized areas of interests. The prospect of choosing their own learning product may be new to ADHG learners; therefore, Hayes (2016) suggested providing them with examples of possible projects to spark their creativity (e.g., design a living history museum, design and develop a community garden, develop a website). To further promote opportunities for choice and to enhance learning, provide students with occasions to engage with others, as "the beauty of teaching through individual projects is that children can work on their own, in a group, with a partner, or engage in a combination of solo and group endeavors" (Hayes, 2016, p. 5). Next, work with students to create a self-checklist that breaks the project into smaller parts with periodic check-in times to obtain teacher support as needed. This will help students learn to self-regulate and stay on task while building their self-efficacy. Finally, allow students time to present their work in class. As Hayes (2016) pointed out, this allows them to not only share their own learning, but also learn from their peers "in a multi-modality, high-interest way" (p. 5).

Conclusion

For decades, researchers have focused on the importance of creativity in education, and the connections between levels of divergent thinking skills related to creativity and students who are diagnosed with ADHD. In order to foster creativity in the classroom, education must be approached from a strength-based perspective, as opposed to one that is focused on remediating weaknesses. This is particularly beneficial for Attention Divergent Hyperactive Gifted students who educators must start to see not as having a deficiency or disorder, but as motivated individuals with strengths, perseverance, and resilience—innate qualities that make them so very special.

FROM THE EDITORS

Student Vignettes

Paul

Paul is 14 years old and lives with his grandfather. Paul's father is no longer living, and his mother Jane is a recovering alcoholic. She began drinking at 14, dropped out of school, and was pregnant at age 17. She was a heavy alcohol user and experienced frequent blackouts during her first two trimesters of pregnancy, but stayed healthy during the final months. Depressed and struggling to remain sober, Jane relinquished custody of Paul to John, her father, just before Paul's second birthday. Health issues prevent John from working, but he cares deeply for his grandson and does his best to provide a stable home environment.

Paul loves spending time with his grandfather. Late nights listening to stories are often followed by late mornings, so Paul frequently misses the bus to school. When this occurs, his grandfather allows him to stay home. Paul's grandfather knows how difficult it is for Paul to sit still in school and remembers that Jane's brothers had similar problems before dropping out years ago. As adults, Jane's brothers struggle with alcoholism and seem to drift from job to job.

Paul is easily distracted and often forgets his homework, backpack, or both. He wishes he could stay home instead of going to school, where he finds it hard to pay attention and remain in his seat. He would rather run through the fields near his home or draw pictures of the birds and animals he sees. Although he has energy to spare, he is able to focus and draw for hours. The detailed pictures he creates are exquisite.

FROM THE EDITORS, *continued*

Miss Jenkins, Paul's English teacher, is concerned about Paul's truancy but is actually relieved when he's not in class. She feels guilty about the situation but is unsure how to handle Paul. When he is not daydreaming, he disrupts the class with humor and captivating stories. Miss Jenkins is also confused by Paul's performance in her classroom. He has failed nearly all tests in her class, which seems odd, given his high verbal ability. When Paul and his classmates take the state assessments, his performance is above grade level in mathematics but significantly below in reading. Comparing his current scores with the past few years of data, Miss Jenkins sees little if any growth in reading.

Discussion Questions

1. In what ways does Paul appear to be twice-exceptional? What are his strengths and challenges?
2. What, if anything, should Miss Jenkins do to help Paul?
3. How is it possible for a student with high energy to sit for hours making detailed drawings?

Max

Max was identified as gifted when he was in kindergarten. He has an advanced vocabulary and a keen sense of humor. He is inquisitive and creative, and has a knack for telling imaginative stories. Unfortunately, by the end of his kindergarten year and throughout first grade, it became clear that something else was going on. He quickly fell behind his peers in reading and often found himself in the principal's office due to his inability to control his behavior in the classroom.

Now in second grade, Max has been identified with ADHD Combined Type and dyslexia. Unfortunately, his self-esteem has started to decrease due to his challenges with his academics and behaviors. He is starting to find that other students are distancing themselves from him because they do not want to get in trouble or are frustrated by his impulsive behaviors in the classroom and on the playground. Mr. Sims, Max's teacher, is also the gifted coordinator for the school. He has been working with Max since he was identified in kindergarten. He knows that Max

FROM THE EDITORS, *continued*

is incredibly bright and creative. He always looks forward to the stories that Max often tells him when he comes into the classroom most mornings. However, on this particular morning, Max has entered the room and is not talking. It is clear that there is something weighing on his mind. After he has had a chance to get settled in, Mr. Sims calls Max over to his desk and asks him if everything is okay. Max looks at him and says, "Mr. Sims, I am stupid." Shocked, Mr. Sims looks at Max and asks why he would say such a thing. Max replies that everyone else in the class can read but him. He further states that no one wants to play with him anymore and he does not think that he wants to come to school anymore.

Discussion Questions

1. How are Max's challenges with ADHD related to his challenges with dyslexia?
2. What recommendations would you have for Mr. Sims to address Max's social-emotional needs?
3. How might Mr. Sims leverage Max's strength areas to mitigate his academic challenges?

Samantha

Samantha is 13 years old and in the seventh grade. Her primary interest is reading science fiction novels, and she one day hopes to become a sci-fi movie make-up artist in Hollywood.

Although she has never been formally identified as gifted by her school, her parents are both university professors and have instilled a love of learning in both her and her younger brother. Samantha was referred for ADHD evaluation by her parents and a speech and hearing pathologist at the age of 6. Samantha was demonstrating difficulty with staying on task, completing multistep commands, staying in her seat, sustaining attention, and interacting appropriately with her peers in school. The Wechsler Preschool and Primary Scale of Intelligence–Third Edition (WPPSI-III) was administered, and Samantha was found to have a Full-Scale Intelligence Quotient (FSIQ) of 111. The neuropsychologist

FROM THE EDITORS, *continued*

noted that a significant 25-point discrepancy existed between Samantha's performance on the mathematics portion of the WPPSI-III and her FSIQ. Also noted was a 20-point discrepancy between her Verbal IQ (118) and her Performance IQ (98). Ultimately, Samantha was diagnosed with ADHD Combined Type and at significant risk for developing a learning disability in mathematics and, to a lesser degree, in reading comprehension. Samantha currently takes 27 mg of methylphenidate in the morning with an additional 15 mg in the afternoon to help regulate her ADHD.

Samantha's performance in school is uneven. Mr. Simonds, her science teacher, does not seem to understand her needs as they relate to her ADHD. To "keep her quiet and focused," he has assigned her to a seat separate from the other students in the classroom. The seat so happens to be near the fish tank, and Samantha often finds her attention drawn to the fish. Often when asked to respond to a question in class, she is unable to answer because of this distraction. Mr. Simonds will then chastise her and tell her she needs to focus and pay attention. Added to this is the fact that she often struggles with completing her science homework, and when she does, she often fails to turn it in because she has left it at home.

Alternately, Ms. Bell is Samantha's teacher for literature, a class that she loves. Ms. Bell often creates assignments and projects that allow the students to explore their own personal interests through a literary lens. Most recently, she has asked the class to do an in-depth study of an author of their choice. Samantha eagerly inquired if she could research Stephen King, as he is her favorite author, to which Ms. Bell responded, "Of course!" Since starting this multiweek, multistep assignment, which includes the creation of a life-size cardboard cutout of the author as well as a dramatic reading of a passage from a novel, Samantha has been focused and is looking forward to submitting her final paper.

Discussion Questions

1. What might explain the wide discrepancies that were found in Samantha's test results? Do you think that she should be considered for gifted identification? Why, or why not?

FROM THE EDITORS, *continued*

2. What are the potential effects on Samantha's social-emotional well-being as a result of her interactions with Mr. Simonds?
3. What factors do you feel contribute to the differences in Samantha's academic performance in Ms. Bell's classroom?

Resources

- *ADHD and Education: Foundations, Characteristics, Methods, and Collaboration*, by Sydney Zentall: This book provides research-based strategies for addressing the needs of children with ADHD in the classroom.
- *Bright Not Broken: Gifted Kids, ADHD, and Autism*, by Diane Kennedy, Rebecca Banks, and Temple Grandin: For teachers and parents, this book provides insight into the lives of these twice-exceptional children, the potential for misdiagnosis, and what families and educators can do to address the needs of gifted students with ADHD and autism.
- The Mind Matters Podcast series hosted by Emily Kircher-Morris: This dynamic podcast series by Morris Creative Services, provides in-depth discussions with leaders in the fields of gifted education, psychology, and others on topics related to twice exceptionality. Episodes are appropriate for a wide variety of audiences, including researchers, educators, parents, and, most importantly, the students themselves. https://www. mindmatterspodcast.com
- *Misdiagnosis and Dual Diagnoses of Gifted Children and Adults: ADHD, Bipolar, OCD, Asperger's, Depression, and Other Disorders*, by James Webb, Edward Amend, Nadia Webb, Jean Goerss, Paul Beljan, and F. Richard Olenchak: This book addresses the potential for misdiagnosis of specific learning and/or behavioral disorders in gifted students.
- *Twice-Exceptional Gifted Children: Understanding, Teaching, and Counseling Gifted Students*, by Beverly Trail: This book guides educators through the development of a collaborative team of educators to identify twice-exceptional students in their schools, their unique needs,

and the development of a comprehensive plan to meet those needs through enrichment, modification, and accommodation.

- Uniquely Gifted (http://www.uniquelygifted.org): This website provides a comprehensive list of resources, designed for families of gifted students with special needs. Informative articles provide parents with a more complete understanding of twice-exceptionality, while personal stories from families and twice-exceptional children give insight into the experiences of these students. Included are also links for online support groups, information on specific learning needs (e.g., ADHD, autism, dyslexia), and much more.

References

Abraham, A., Windmann, S., Siefen, R., Daum, I., & Güntükün, O. (2006). Creative thinking in adolescents with attention deficit hyperactivity disorder (ADHD). *Child Neuropsychology, 12*(2), 111–123. https://doi.org/10.1080/09297040500320691

American Psychiatric Association. (1968). *Diagnostic and statistical manual of mental disorders* (2nd ed.).

American Psychiatric Association. (1980). *Diagnostic and statistical manual of mental disorders* (3rd ed.).

American Psychiatric Association. (1987). *Diagnostic and statistical manual of mental disorders* (3rd ed., Rev.).

American Psychiatric Association. (2013). *Diagnostic and statistical manual of mental disorders* (5th ed.). https://doi.org/10.1176/appi.books.9780890425596

Antshel, K. M. (2008). Attention-deficit hyperactivity disorder in the context of a high intellectual quotient/giftedness. *Developmental Disabilities Research Reviews, 14*(4), 293–299. https://doi.org/10.1002/ddrr.34

Assouline, S. G., Colangelo, N., VanTassel-Baska, J., & Lupkowski-Shoplik, A. (Eds.). (2015). *A nation empowered: Evidence trumps the excuses holding back America's brightest students* (Vol. 2). The University of Iowa, The Connie Belin & Jacqueline N. Blank International Center for Gifted Education and Talent Development.

Baddeley, A. D. (2003). Working memory: Looking back and looking forward. *Nature Reviews Neuroscience, 4*(10), 829–839. https://doi.org/10.1038/nrn1201

Barbaresi, W. J., Katusic, S. K., Colligan, R. C., Weaver, A. L., & Jacobsen, S. J. (2007). Modifiers of long-term school outcomes for children with attention-deficit/hyperactivity disorder: Does treatment with stimulant medication make a difference? Results from a population-based study. *Journal of Developmental & Behavioral Pediatrics, 28*(4), 274–287. https://doi.org/10.1097/DBP.0b013e3180cabc28

Barkley, R. A. (2006). *Attention-deficit hyperactivity disorder: A handbook for diagnosis and treatment* (3rd ed.). Guilford Press.

Barkley, R. A., Fischer, M., Smallish, L., & Fletcher, K. (2006). Young adult outcome of hyperactive children: Adaptive functioning in major life activities. *Journal of the American Academy of Child and Adolescent Psychiatry, 45*(2), 192–202. https://doi.org/10.1097/01.chi.0000189134.97436.e2

Barron, K. E., Evans, S. W., Baranik, L. E., Serpell, Z. N., & Buvinger, E. (2006). Achievement goals of students with ADHD. *Learning Disability Quarterly, 29*(3), 137–158.

Batey, M., Furnham, A., & Safiullina, X. (2010). Intelligence, general knowledge, and personality as predictors of creativity. *Learning and Individual Differences, 20*(5), 532–535. https://doi.org/10.1016/j.lindif.2010.04.008

Bauermeister, J. J., Shrout, P.E., Chávez, L., Rubio-Stipec, M., Ramírez, R., Padilla, L., Anderson, A., García, P., & Canino, G. (2007). ADHD and gender: Are risks and sequela of ADHD the same for boys and girls? *Journal of Child Psychology and Psychiatry, 4*(8), 831–839. https://doi.org/10.1111/j.1469-7610.2007.01750.x

Baum, S., & Owen, S. V. (1988). High ability/learning disabled students: How are they different? *Gifted Child Quarterly, 32*(3), 321–326. https://doi.org/10.1177/001698628803200305

Baum, S. M., Cooper, C. R., & Neu, T. W. (2001). Dual differentiation: An approach for meeting the curricular needs of gifted students with learning disabilities. *Psychology in the Schools, 38*(5), 477–490.

Baum, S. M., & Olenchak, F. R. (2002). The alphabet children: GT, AHDH, and more. *Exceptionality, 10*(2), 77–91. https://doi.org/10.1207/S15327035EX1002_3

Baum, S. M., Olenchak, F. R., & Owen, S. V. (1998). Gifted students with attention deficits: Fact and/or fiction? Or, can we see the forest for the trees? *Gifted Child Quarterly, 42*(2), 96–104. https://doi.org/10.1177/001698629804200204

Becker, S. P., McBurnett, K., Hinshaw, S. P., & Pfiffner, L. J. (2013). Negative social preference in relation to internalizing symptoms among children with ADHD predominately inattentive type: Girls fare worse than boys.

Journal of Clinical Child & Adolescent Psychology, 42(6), 784–795. https://doi.org/10.1080/15374416.2013.828298

Biederman, J., Kwon, A., Aleardi, M., Chouinard, V.-A., Marino, T., Cole, H., Mick, E., & Faraone, S. V. (2005). Absence of gender effects on attention deficit hyperactivity disorder: Findings in nonreferred subjects. *The American Journal of Psychiatry, 162*(6), 1083–1089. https://doi.org/10.1176/appi.ajp.162.6.1083

Blachman, D. R., & Hinshaw, S. P. (2002). Patterns of friendship among girls with and without attention-deficit/hyperactivity disorder. *Journal of Abnormal Psychology, 30*, 625–640. https://doi.org/10.1023/A:1020815814973

Callahan, C. M., & Reis, S. M. (1996). Gifted girls, remarkable women. In K. D. Arnold, K. D. Noble, & R. F. Subotnik (Eds.), *Remarkable women: Perspectives on female talent development* (pp. 171–192). Hampton Press.

Carson, S. H., Peterson, J. B., & Higgins, D. M. (2003). Decreased latent inhibition is associated with increased creative achievement in high-functioning individuals. *Journal of Personality and Social Psychology, 85*(3), 499–506. https://doi.org/10.1037/0022-3514.85.3.499

Castellanos, X. (2000). *ADHD or gifted: Is it either/or?* [Paper presentation]. Annual meeting of the National Association for Gifted Children, Atlanta, GA, United States.

Centers for Disease Control. (2019, October 15). *Data and statistics about ADHD.* https://www.cdc.gov/ncbddd/adhd/data.html

Comallie-Caplan, L. (2008). *Gifted girls to gifted women* [Conference session]. 2008 New Mexico Summer Institute for the Gifted Education, Albuquerque, NM, United States.

Conners, C. K. (1997). *Conners' rating scales-revised: Technical manual.* Multi-Health Systems.

Conners, C. K. (2000). Attention-deficit/hyperactivity disorder: Historical development and overview. *Journal of Attention Disorders, 3*(4), 173–191. https://doi.org/10.1177/108705470000300401

Cramond, B. (1994a). Attention-deficit hyperactivity disorder and creativity: What is the connection? *Journal of Creative Behavior, 28*(3), 193–210. https://doi.org/10.1002/j.2162-6057.1994.tb01191.x

Cramond, B. (1994b, April). *The relationship between attention-deficit hyperactivity disorder and creativity* [Paper presentation]. 1994 American Educational Research Association Annual Meeting, New Orleans, LA, United States.

Crichton, A. (2008). An inquiry into the nature and origin of mental derangement. On attention and its diseases. *Journal of Attention Disorders, 12*(3), 200–206. https://doi.org/10.1177/1087054708315137

Cuffe S. P., Moore C. G., & McKeown R. E. (2005). Prevalence and correlates of ADHD symptoms in the national health interview survey. *Journal of Attention Disorders, 9*(2), 392–401. https://doi.org/10.1177/108 7054705280413

Dai, D. Y. (2002). Are gifted girls motivationally disadvantaged? Review reflection and redirection. *Journal for the Education of the Gifted, 25*(4), 315–358. https://doi.org/10.4219/jeg-2002-283

Davis, G. A. (2004). *Creativity is forever* (5th ed.). Kendall Hunt.

Davis, G. A., Rimm, S. B., & Siegle, D. (2017). *Education of the gifted and talented* (7th ed.). Pearson.

Drapeau, P. (2014). *Sparking student creativity: Practical ways to promote innovative thinking and problem solving.* ASCD

Dweck, C. S. (2016). *Mindset: The new psychology of success.* Ballantine Books. (Original work published 2006)

Epstein, M. A., Shaywitz, S. E., Shaywitz, B. A., & Woolston, J. L. (1991). The boundaries of attention deficit disorder. *Journal of Learning Disabilities, 24*(2), 78–85. https://doi.org/10.1177/002221949102400204

Foley-Nicpon, M., Allmon, A., Sieck, B., & Stinson, R. D. (2011). Empirical investigation of twice-exceptionality: Where have we been? Where are we going? *Gifted Child Quarterly, 55*(1), 3–17. https://doi.org/10.1177/00 16986210382575

Fugate, C. M. (2014). *Lifting the cloak of invisibility: A collective case study of girls with characteristics of giftedness and ADHD* [Unpublished doctoral dissertation]. Purdue University.

Fugate, C. M. (2018). Attention divergent hyperactive giftedness: Taking the deficiency and disorder out of the gifted/ADHD label. In S. B. Kaufman (Ed.), *Twice exceptional: Supporting and educating bright and creative students with learning difficulties* (pp. 191–200). Oxford University Press. https://doi.org/10.1093/oso/9780190645472.003.0012

Fugate, C. M. (2019). Increasing the visibility of gifted girls with ADHD: A collective case study. *TEMPO, 40*(1), 13–20.

Fugate, C. M., & Gentry, M. (2016). Understanding gifted girls with ADHD: Motivated and achieving. *High Ability Studies, 27*(1), 83–109. https://doi.org/10.1080/13598139.2015.1098522

Fugate, C. M., Zentall, S. S., & Gentry, M. (2013). Creativity and working memory in gifted students with and without characteristics of attention deficit hyperactive disorder: Lifting the mask. *Gifted Child Quarterly, 57*(4), 234–246. https://doi.org/10.1177/0016986213500069

Furnham, A., Batey, M., Anand, K., & Manfield, J. (2008). Personality, hypomania, intelligence, and creativity. *Personality and Individual Differences, 44*(5), 1060–1069. https://doi.org/10.1016/j.paid.2007.10.035

Gentry, M., & Fugate, C. M. (2018). Attention deficit/hyperactivity disorder in gifted students. In S. I. Pfeiffer, M. Foley-Nicpon, & E. Shaunessy-Dedrick (Eds.), *APA handbook of giftedness and talent* (pp. 575–584). American Psychological Association.

Getzels, J. W., & Jackson, P. W. (1962). *Creativity and intelligence: Explorations with gifted students.* Wiley.

Good, C., Ruttan, A., & Dweck, C. S. (2012). Why do women opt out? Sense of belonging and women's representation in mathematics. *Journal of Personality and Social Psychology, 102*(4), 700–717. https://doi.org/10.1037/a0026659

Greene, R. W., Biederman, J., Faraone, S. V., Monuteaux, M. C., Mick, E., DuPre, E. P., Fine, C. S, & Goring, J. C. (2001). Social impairment in girls with ADHD: Patterns, gender comparisons, and correlates. *Journal of the American Academy of Child and Adolescent Psychiatry, 40*(6), 704–710.

Grskovic, J. A., & Zentall, S. S. (2010). Understanding ADHD in girls: Identification and social characteristics. *International Journal of Special Education, 25*(1), 170–183.

Guilford, J. P. (1967). *The nature of human intelligence.* McGraw-Hill.

Guilford, J. P., & Christensen, P. R. (1973). The one-way relation between creative potential and IQ. *Journal of Creative Behavior, 7*(4), 247–252. https://doi.org/10.1002/j.2162-6057.1973.tb01096.x

Hayes, M. (2016, September). Teaching 2e children. *2e Newsletter*, 3–6.

Healey, D., & Rucklidge, J. J. (2005). An exploration into the creative abilities of children with ADHD. *Journal of Attention Disorders, 8*(3), 88–95. https://doi.org/10.1177/1087054705277198

Healey, D., & Rucklidge, J. J. (2006). An investigation into the relationship among ADHD symptomatology, creativity, and neuropsychological functioning in children. *Child Neuropsychology, 12*(6), 421–438. https://doi.org/10.1080/09297040600806086

Hébert, T. P., Long, L. A., & Speirs-Neumeister, K. L. (2001). Using biography to counsel gifted young women. *Journal of Secondary Education, 12*(2), 62–89. https://doi.org/10.4219/jsge-2000-645

Holland, K., & Higuera, V. (n.d.). *The history of ADHD: A timeline.* https://www.healthline.com/health/adhd/history#Overview1

Hornung, C., Brunner, M., Reuter, R. A. P., & Martin, R. (2011). Children's working memory: Its structure and relationship to fluid intelligence. *Intelligence, 39*(4), 210–221. https://doi.org/10.1016/j.intell.2011.03.002

Hughes, C. E. (2011). Twice-exceptional children: Twice the challenges, twice the joys. In J. A. Castellano & A. D. Fraizer (Eds.), *Special populations in gifted education: Understanding our most able students from diverse backgrounds* (pp. 153–173). Prufrock Press.

Jin, J., Liu, L., Chen, W., Gao, Q., Li, H., Wang, Y., & Qian, Q. (2019) The implicated roles of Cell Adhesion Molecule 1 (*CADM1*) gene and altered prefrontal neuronal activity in Attention-Deficit/Hyperactivity Disorder: A "gene-brain-behavior relationship"? *Frontiers in Genetics, 10,* 882. https://doi.org/10.3389/fgene.2019.00882

Kaufman, J., Birmaher, B., Brent,, D., Rao, U., & Ryan, N. (1996). *The schedule for affective disorders for school-aged children—Present and lifetime version (version 1.0).* University of Pittsburg School of Medicine, Department of Psychiatry.

Kerr, B., Vuyk, M. A., & Rea, C. (2012). Gendered practices in the education of gifted girls and gifted boys. *Psychology in the Schools, 49*(7), 647–655. https://doi.org/10.1002/pits.21627

Kofler, M. J., Rapport M. D., Bolden, J., Sarver, D. E., & Raiker, J. S. (2010, February). ADHD and working memory: The impact of central executive deficits and exceeding storage/rehearsal capacity on observed inattentive behavior. *Journal of Abnormal Child Psychology, 38,* 149–161. https://doi.org/10.1007/s10802-009-9357-6

Kuester, D. A., & Zentall, S. S. (2011). Social interaction rules in cooperative learning groups for students at-risk for ADHD. *Journal of Experimental Education, 80*(1), 69–95. https://doi.org/10.1080/00220973.2011.566589

Lange, K. W., Reichl, S., Lange, K. M., Tucha, L., & Tucha, O. (2010). The history of attention deficit hyperactivity disorder. *Attention Deficit Hyperactivity Disorders, 2*(4), 241–255. https://doi.org/10.1007/s12402-010-0045-8

Lawrence, V., Houghton, S., Tannock, R., Douglas, G., Durkin, K., & Whiting, K. (2002, October). ADHD outside the laboratory: Boy's executive function performance on tasks in videogame play and on a visit to the zoo. *Journal of Abnormal Child Psychology, 30,* 447–462. https://doi.org/10.1023/A:1019812829706

LeCompte, M. D., Millory, W. L., & Preissle, J. (Eds.). (1992). *The handbook of qualitative research in education.* Academic Press.

LeFever, G. B., Villers, M. S., Morrow, A. L., & Vaughn, E. S. (2002). Parental perceptions of adverse educational outcomes among children diagnosed and treated for ADHD: A call for improved school/provider collaboration. *Psychology in the Schools, 39*(1), 63–71. https://doi.org/10.1002/pits.10000

Lewis, T. (2009, August). Creativity in technology education: Providing children with glimpses of their inventive potential. *International Journal of*

Technology and Design Education, 19, 255–268. https://doi.org/10.1007/ s10798-008-9051-y

MacKinnon, D. W. (1962). The nature and nurture of creative talent. *American Psychologist, 17*(7), 484–495. https://doi.org/10.1037/h0046541

McCoach, D. B., Kehle, T. J., Bray, M. A., & Siegle, D. (2001). Best practices in the identification of gifted students with learning disabilities. *Psychology in the Schools, 38*(5), 403–411. https://doi.org/10.1002/pits.1029

Merrell, C., & Tymms, P. B. (2001). Inattention, hyperactivity and impulsiveness: Their impact on academic achievement and progress. *British Journal of Educational Psychology, 71*(1), 43–56. https://doi.org/10.1348/0007099 01158389

Mikami, A. Y., Chi, T. C., & Hinshaw, S. P. (2004, September). Behavior ratings and observations of externalizing symptoms in girls: The role of child popularity with adults. *Journal of Psychopathology and Behavioral Assessment, 26,* 151–163. https://doi.org/10.1023/B:JOBA.0000022107.47515.85

Mikami, A. Y., & Hinshaw, S. P. (2006, December). Resilient adolescent adjustment among girls: Buffers of childhood peer rejection and attention deficit/hyperactivity disorder. *Journal of Abnormal Psychology, 34,* 825–839. https://doi.org/10.1007/s10802-006-9062-7

Moon, S. M. (2002). Gifted children with attention-deficit/hyperactivity disorder. In M. Neihart, S. M. Reis, N. M. Robinson, & S. M. Moon (Eds.), *The social and emotional development of gifted children: What do we know?* (pp. 193–204). Prufrock Press.

Moon, S. M., & Reis, S. M. (2004). Acceleration and twice-exceptional students. In N. Colangelo, S. G. Assouline, & M. U. M. Gross (Eds.), *A nation deceived: How schools hold back America's brightest students* (Vol. 2, pp. 109–119). The University of Iowa, The Connie Belin & Jacqueline N. Blank International Center for Gifted Education and Talent Development.

Moon, S. M., Zentall, S. S., Grskovic, J. A., Hall, A. & Stormont, M. (2001). Emotional, social, and family characteristics of boys with AD/HD and giftedness: A comparative case study. *Journal for the Education of the Gifted, 24*(3), 207–247. https://doi.org/10.1177/016235320102400302

Nadeau, K. G., & Quinn, P. O. (Eds.). (2002). *Understanding women with AD/HD.* Advantage Books.

National Human Genome Research Institute. (n.d.). *About attention deficit hyperactivity disorder.* https://www.genome.gov/Genetic-Disorders/Attention-Deficit-Hyperactivity-Disorder

Neihart, M. (2000). Gifted children with Asperger's syndrome. *Gifted Child Quarterly, 44*(4) 222–230. https://doi.org/10.1177/001698620004400403

Neihart, M. (2003). *Gifted children with attention deficit hyperactivity disorder (ADHD)* (ED482344). ERIC. https://files.eric.ed.gov/fulltext/ED482344.pdf

Nielsen, M. E. (2002). Gifted students with learning disabilities: Recommendations for identification and programming. *Exceptionality, 10*(2), 93–111. https://doi.org/10.1207/S15327035EX1002_4

Nielsen, M. E., & Higgins, L. D. (2005). The eye of the storm: Services and programs for twice-exceptional learners. *Teaching Exceptional Children, 38*(1), 8–15. https://doi.org/10.1177/004005990503800102

Olenchak, R., & Reis, S. M. (2002). Gifted children with learning disabilities. In M. Neihart, S. M. Reis, N. M. Robinson, & S. M. Moon (Eds.), *The social and emotional development of gifted children: What do we know?* (pp. 177–192). Prufrock Press.

Owens, E. B, Hinshaw, S. P., Lee, S. S., & Lahey, B. B. (2009). Few girls with childhood attention-deficit/hyperactivity disorder show positive adjustment during adolescence. *Journal of Clinical Child & Adolescent Psychology, 38*(1), 132–143. https://doi.org/10.1080/15374410802575313

Pepperell, J. L., & Rubel, D. J. (2009). The experience of gifted girls transitioning from elementary school to sixth and seventh grade: A grounded theory. *The Qualitative Report, 14*(2), 341–360. https://nsuworks.nova.edu/tqr/vol14/iss2/8

Pfeiffer, S. I. (2013). *Serving the gifted: Evidence-based clinical and psychoeducational practice.* Routledge.

Plucker, J. A., Beghetto, R. A., & Dow, G. T. (2004). Why isn't creativity more important to educational psychologists? Potentials, pitfalls, and future directions in creativity research. *Educational Psychologist, 59*(2), 83–96. https://doi.org/10.1207/s15326985ep3902_1

Polanczyk, G., de Lima, M. S., Horta B. L., Biederman, J., & Rohde, L. A. (2007). The worldwide prevalence of ADHD: A systematic review and metaregression analysis. *The American Journal of Psychiatry, 20*(6), 386–392.

Powers, R. L., Marks, D. J., Miller, C. J., Newcorn, J. H., & Halperin, J. M. (2008). Stimulant treatment in children with attention-deficit/hyperactivity disorder moderates adolescent academic outcome. *Journal of Child and Adolescent Psychopharmacology, 18*(5), 449–459. https://doi.org/10.1089/cap.2008.021

Preckel, F., Holling, H., & Wiese, M. (2006). Relationships in intelligence and creativity in gifted and non-gifted students: An investigation of threshold theory. *Personality and Individual Differences, 40*(1), 159–170. https://doi.org/10.1016/j.paid.2005.06.022

Quinn, P. O. (2005). Treating adolescent girls and women with ADHD: Gender-specific issues. *Journal of Clinical Psychology, 61*(5), 579–587. https://doi.org/10.1002/jclp.20121

Reid, B. D., & McGuire, M. D. (1995). *Square pegs in round holes—these kids don't fit: High ability students with behavioral problems* (RBDM9512). University of Connecticut, The National Research Center on the Gifted and Talented.

Reis, S. M. (1998). *Work left undone: Choices and compromises of talented females.* Creative Learning Press.

Reis, S. M. (2002). Gifted females in elementary and secondary school. In M. Neihart, S. M. Reis, N. M. Robinson, & S. M. Moon (Eds), *The social and emotional development of gifted children: What do we know?* (pp. 125–135). Prufrock Press.

Reis, S. M., & Callahan, C. M. (1989). Gifted females: They've come a long way—or have they? *Journal for the Education of the Gifted, 12*(2), 99–117. https://doi.org/10.1177/016235328901200203

Reis, S. M., & McCoach, D. B. (2000). The underachievement of gifted students: What do we know and where do we go? *Gifted Child Quarterly, 44*(3), 152–170. https://doi.org/10.1177/001698620004400302

Renzulli, J. S. (1994). *Schools for talent development: A practical guide for total school improvement.* Prufrock Press.

Renzulli, J. S., & Reis, S. M. (with Thompson, A.). (2009). *Light up your child's mind.* Little, Brown.

Rhodes, S. M., Park, J., Seth, S., & Coghill, D. R. (2012). A comprehensive investigation of memory impairment in attention deficit hyperactivity disorder and oppositional defiant disorder. *Journal of Child Psychology and Psychiatry, 53*(2), 128–137. https://doi.org/10.1111/j.1469-7610.2011.02436.x

Rimm, S. (2002). Peer pressures and social acceptance of gifted students. In M. Neihart, S. M. Reis, N. M. Robinson, & S. M. Moon (Eds.), *The social and emotional development of gifted children: What do we know?* (pp. 13–18). Prufrock Press.

Rodin, G. C., & Lithman, J. R. (2002). Fibromyalgia in women with AD/HD. In K. G. Nadeau & P. O. Quinn (Eds.), *Understanding women with AD/HD* (pp. 190–226). Advantage Books.

Rucklidge, J. J., Brown, D. L., Crawford, S., & Kaplan, B. J. (2007). Attributional styles and psychosocial functioning of adults with ADHD: Practice issues and gender differences. *Journal of Attention Disorders, 10*(3), 288–298. https://doi.org/10.1177/1087054706289942

Rucklidge, J. J., & Tannock, R. (2001). Psychiatric, psychosocial and cognitive functioning of female adolescents with ADHD. *Journal of the American*

Academy of Child and Adolescent Psychiatry, 40(5), 530–540. https://doi.org/10.1097/00004583-200105000-00012

Runco, M. A. (2004). Creativity. *Annual Review of Psychology, 55*, 657-687. https://doi.org/10.1146/annurev.psych.55.090902.141502

Russ, S. W. (1998). Play, creativity, and adaptive functioning: Implications for play interventions. *Journal of Clinical Child Psychology, 27*(4), 469–480. https://doi.org/10.1207/s15374424jccp2704_11

Shaw, G., & Brown, G. (1999). Arousal, time estimation, and time use in attention-disordered children. *Developmental Neuropsychology, 16*(2), 227–242. https://doi.org/10.1207/S15326942DN1602_6

Shaw, G. A., & Brown, G. (1991). Laterality, implicit memory and attention disorder. *Educational Studies, 17*(1), 15–23. https://doi.org/10.1080/0305569910170102

Silva, P. J. (2008). Another look at creativity and intelligence: Exploring higher-order models and probable confounds. *Personality and Individual Differences, 44*(4), 1012–1021. https://doi.org/10.1016/j.paid.2007.10.027

Silverman, L. K. (1995). To be gifted or feminine: The forced choice of adolescence. *Journal of Secondary Gifted Education, 6*(2), 141–156.

Silverman, L. K. (2002). *Upside-down brilliance: The visual-spatial learner.* DeLeon.

Silverman, L. K. (2005, November). *Who cares if I'm smart, am I thin enough?* [Paper presentation]. European Council of International Schools, Hague, Netherlands.

Speirs Neumeister, K. L. (2004). Understanding the relationship between perfectionism and achievement motivation in gifted college students. *Gifted Child Quarterly, 48*(3), 219–231. https://doi.org/10.1177/001698620404800306

Sternberg, R. J. (Ed.). (1999). *Handbook of creativity.* Cambridge University Press.

Still, G. F. (1902). The Goulstonian Lectures on some abnormal psychical conditions in children. *The Lancet, 159*(4104), 1163–1168. https://doi.org/10.1016/S0140-6736(01)74901-X

Süß, H.-M., Oberauer, K., Wittman, W. W., Wilhelm, O., & Schulze, R. (2002). Working memory capacity explains reasoning ability—And a little bit more. *Intelligence, 30*(3), 261–288. https://doi.org/10.1016/S0160-2896(01)00100-3

Subotnik, R. F., Olszewski-Kubilius, P., & Worrell, F. C. (2011). Rethinking giftedness and gifted education: A proposed direction forward based on psychological science. *Psychological Science in the Public Interest, 12*(1), 3–54. https://doi.org/10.1177/1529100611418056

Thomas, R., Sanders, S., Doust, J. Beller, E., & Glasziou, P. (2015). Prevalence of attention-deficit/hyperactivity disorder: A systematic review and meta-analysis. *Pediatrics, 135*(4), 994–1001. https://doi.org/10.1542/peds.2014-3482

Tierney, P., Farmer, S. M., & Graen, G. B. (1999). An examination of leadership and employee creativity: The relevance of traits and relationships. *Personnel Psychology, 52*(3), 591–620. https://doi.org/10.1111/j.1744-6570.1999.tb00173.x

Torrance, E. P. (1972). Career patterns and peak creative achievements of creative high school students twelve years later. *Gifted Child Quarterly, 16*(2), 75–88. https://doi.org/10.1177/001698627201600201

Torrance, E. P. (1981). Predicting the creativity of elementary school children (1958–1980)—and the teacher who "made a difference." *Gifted Child Quarterly, 25*(2), 55–62. https://doi.org/10.1177/001698628102500203

Torrance, E. P. (2006). *TTCT–Torrance tests of creative thinking (Form A)*. Scholastic Testing Services. (Original work published 1966)

United States Department of Education. (1999, June 24). *Assistance to the states for the education of children with disabilities: Final rule.*

Visser, S. N., Danielson, M. L., Wolraich, M. L., Fox, M. H., Grosse, S. D., Valle, L. A., Holbrook, J. R., Claussen, A. H., & Peacock, G. (2016). Vital signs: National and state-specific patterns of attention deficit/hyperactivity disorder treatment among insured children ages 2–5 years—United States, 2008–2014. *Morbidity and Mortality Weekly Report, 65*, 443–450. https://doi.org/10.15585/mmwr.mm6517e1

Webb, J. T., Amend, E. R., Webb, N. E., Goerss, J., Beljan, P., & Olenchak, F. R. (2005). *Misdiagnosis and dual diagnoses of gifted children and adults: ADHD, bipolar, OCD, Asperger's, depression, and other disorders*. Great Potential Press.

White, H. A., & Shah, P. (2006). Uninhibited imaginations: Creativity in adults with attention-deficit/hyperactivity disorder. *Personality and Individual Differences, 40*(6), 1121–1131. https://doi.org/10.1016/j.paid.2005.11.007

White, H. A., & Shah, P. (2011). Creative style and achievement in adults with attention-deficit/hyperactivity disorder. *Personality and Individual Differences, 50*(5), 673–677. https://doi.org/10.1016/j.paid.2010.12.015

White, H. A., & Shah, P. (2016). Scope of semantic activation and innovative thinking in college students with ADHD. *Creativity Research Journal, 28*(3), 275–282. https://doi.org/10.1080/10400419.2016.1195655

Wiley, J., & Jarosz, A. F. (2012). Working memory capacity, attention focus, and problem solving. *Current Directions in Psychological Science, 21*(4), 258–262. https://doi.org/10.1177/0963721412447622

Zentall, S. S. (1988, December). Production deficiencies in elicited language but not in the spontaneous verbalizations of hyperactive children. *Journal of Abnormal Child Psychology, 16,* 657–673. https://doi.org/10.1007/BF00 913476

Zentall, S. S. (2006). *ADHD and education: Foundations, characteristics, methods, and collaboration.* Pearson.

Zentall, S. S., Kuester, D. A., & Craig, B. A. (2011). Social behavior in cooperative groups: Students at-risk for ADHD and their peers. *Journal of Educational Research, 104*(1), 28–41. https://doi.org/10.1080/00220670903567356

Zentall, S. S., Moon, S., Hall, A. M., & Grskovic, J. (2001). Learning and motivational characteristics of boys with giftedness and/or attention deficit/hyperactivity disorder. *Exceptional Children, 67*(4), 499–519. https://doi.org/10.1177/001440290106700405

CHAPTER 4

Reading Skills, Developmental Dyslexia, and Twice-Exceptionality

Walter Edward Dunson

Speech Versus Reading

Spoken language evolved in humans thousands of years before writing was invented. In fact, for most of human history, spoken language existed without written forms (Seidenberg, 2017). In speech, the listener is provided with many clues as to the meaning of the speaker's words. Intonation, pitch, cadence, and body language all assist in the comprehension of auditory signals. Further, according to the "innateness hypothesis," children are equipped with a blueprint of the principles and properties of the grammars of all spoken human language called *universal grammar* (Fromkin et al., 2014). Barring neurologically based developmental delays, children do not require explicit instruction to master the spoken language. Speech develops without conscious effort or formal instruction, and it is deployed without children's awareness of its underlying logic (Pinker, 1994). Speech is acquired effortlessly through exposure, and its acquisition can only be seriously disrupted by extreme neglect or insult (Wolf et al., 2012). Universal grammar aids children in the task of constructing the spoken language. Structure dependency of the native language and coordinate structure constraint are inherent. Universal grammar automatically assembles the phonemes into words for the speaker and listener (Fromkin et al., 2014). In the first 3 years of life, children gain near-mastery of their native language (Chomsky, 1957; Pinker, 1994; Wolf et al., 2012). Additionally, through stages in oral communication, speakers learn from the surrounding linguistic environment the proper cadence, pitch, and intonation associated with the successful display of language ability, as well as language-specific grammar rules. That is why people from Brooklyn, NY, sound like they are from Brooklyn, and people from Boston, MA, sound like they are from Boston. All that is necessary to master spoken language is for humans to be exposed to it (Shaywitz, 1996). Children are wired for sound (Chomsky, 1957; Pinker, 1994; Wolf et al., 2012). This presents speech as a natural process (Fromkin et al., 2014; Shaywitz, 1996).

Although reading and speech share a linguistic foundation (Seidenberg, 2017), and reading is embedded in both the language system and writing system (Perfetti & Dunlap, 2008), reading involves quite a different process from speech for several reasons. First, unlike speech, the acquisition of written language skills is not innate. Reading skills are derived from intentional instruction and involve the comprehension of written codes and mapping them with speech sounds and morphology (Nakamura et al., 2012; Siegel, 2006). Although many believe that humans have been using oral language, from grunts to clear articulations, for hundreds of thousands of years, humans have only been writing for about 3,200 years. Humans began with pictograms and logograms; however, the first alphabet, the Phoenician alphabet, was introduced in approximately 1200 BC. The Phoenician alphabet was adapted from the early West Semitic alphabet (Kaltner & McKenzie, 2002) and is ultimately derived from Egyptian hieroglyphs (Howard, 2012). It became one of the most widely used writing systems, spread by Phoenician merchants across the Mediterranean world, where it was adopted and modified by many other cultural languages, including Aramaic, Greek, Latin, Cyrillic, and Hebrew. The time period from 1200 BC to now represents an incredibly small slice of human history. Further, during most of this time, writing only involved a small minority of humans—the priesthood, the elite, and scribes in pre-Ptolemaic Egypt (Zinn, 2013), and the Catholic Church during the Middle and Dark Ages (Bäuml, 1980). Even within relatively recent American and European society, reading was reserved for the upper class. Mass reading did not begin in the United States until the first public school was established in Dorchester, MA, in 1639 (Cremin, 1970).

According to the human timeline, written language is a relatively recent human construct (Wolf et al., 2012). Writing systems have undergone many variations in the course of human history, and each system places different demands on the brain (Bolger et al., 2005; Howard, 2012; Kaltner & McKenzie, 2002; Wolf et al., 2012). In the evolution of all writing systems, humans have designated symbols to represent the sounds of spoken language using conventional, visible marks (Balmuth, 2009; Katz & Frost, 1992; Seidenberg, 2017). The purpose of writing systems is to encode directly in correspondence to spoken words, not meaning (Bolger et al., 2005; Katz & Frost, 1992; Perfetti & Dunlap, 2008; Pugh & Verhoeven, 2018). This is Perfetti and Dunlap's (2008) most basic universal, the language constraint on writing systems. In the utilization of a writing system, spoken language is encrypted, and people access spoken language through their vision through the process of decryption (Dehaene, 2011; Seidenberg, 2017). This act requires connecting the symbols used in the written language with the corresponding sounds that they represent in the spoken language (Borleffs et al., 2019; Chall, 1983; Sprenger-Charolles & Siegel, 2013; Verhoeven & Perfetti, 2017) in all three of the world's major writing systems: alphabetic, syllabic, and logographic (Perfetti & Dunlap, 2008). Developing this knowledge is the most basic requirement of reading acquisition (Costenaro & Pesce, 2012; Wolf et al., 2012), and it is called sound-symbol correspondence (Borleffs et al., 2019; Chall, 1983; Sprenger-Charolles & Siegel, 2013; Verhoeven & Perfetti, 2017). Like deciphering the meanings of pictograms and logograms, it is not a naturally occurring process. A great deal of effort and repetition is required (Wolf, 2013; Wolf et al., 2012), as it is the designing feature of a writing system (Perfetti & Dunlap, 2008). Sound-symbol correspondence must be systematically and explicitly taught in a logical progression from the simple to complex (Pinker, 1994; Uhry, 2013) and drilled sufficiently until the association of sound to symbol and symbol to sound is automatic (Wolf, 2013). Different written languages have different phonics systems. Although some languages may use the same letters, they may assign different sounds to them (Balmuth, 2009; Dunson, 2013). Reading, therefore, must be viewed as a cultural invention. It does not occur naturally (Seidenberg, 2017; Wolf, 2013; Wolf et al., 2012).

Additionally, the code for written language is more complex because most visual and auditory cues must be inferred based upon two-dimensional symbolic representations called punctuation (Balmuth, 2009; Fromkin et al., 2014). Although universal grammar was specified for spoken language, written language is of a different process, and children must be explicitly taught the rules for written language. Further, students should be taught not only the phonemes and graphemes associated with the language, but also a phonics study that includes the myriad spelling rules governing usage and application (Balmuth, 2009; Dunson, 2013; Gillingham & Stillman, 1997; Pyles &

Algeo, 1993). For example, the choice between using "ai" and "ay," among other options, for graphically representing the / ā / phoneme within a spoken word depends upon the location of the long vowel phoneme within the word. If the long vowel phoneme / ā / appears in the middle of a one-syllable word, use "ai" (e.g., *rain, chain, pail*). If, however, the long vowel phoneme / ā / appears at the end of a one-syllable word, use "ay" (e.g., *day, pay, stay*; Dunson, 2013; Gillingham & Stillman, 1997).

The two key components of reading, which do not manifest themselves in speech, are word identification and concept imagery (Dunson, 2013; Fromkin et al., 2014). Word identification involves recognizing that words are a systematic string of individual letters or graphemes. Each individual sequential combination represents a different word. Students must string together individual sounds that are mapped to the letters or letter groups in order to produce these words (Borleffs et al., 2019; Chall, 1983; Sprenger-Charolles & Siegel, 2013; Verhoeven & Perfetti, 2017), all while taking into consideration vowel activity, vowel teams, consonants, consonant blends, consonant digraphs, syllable types, syllable division, and morphology (Dunson, 2013). This is the essence of decoding. Students who have weak word identification skills (word attack) will stumble and stammer as they clumsily attempt to read the printed language, producing errors in identification and pronunciation along the way. This deficit restrains students' ability to pull meaning from print, as the other half of the reading puzzle, concept imagery, involves comprehension of the meanings behind the sequential combinations of letters (Ostovar-Namaghi et al., 2015; Perfetti & Dunlap, 2008).

Concept imagery is the ability to form an image in the "mind's eye" based solely upon sensory input, whether visual, auditory, or tactile-kinesthetic. It represents the ability to take the next logical step toward comprehension. This process allows students to visualize the item or process represented by the printed words, and it relies solely upon the accurate identification and pronunciation of the sequential strings of graphemes and phonemes presented. Without word identification skills, students will not understand what was read.

The Neuronal Aspects of Reading

As a result of the limited evolutionary time period since humans began encrypting their spoken language with symbols, the human genome does not contain instructions for reading-specific brain circuits. Human brains are constructed to speak and hear language. They are not meant to read (Chomsky,

1957; Fromkin et al., 2014; Pinker, 1994; Shaywitz, 1996; Wolf et al., 2012). There has not been enough time for reading-specific circuits to naturally develop. So, humans must create these circuits by recycling existing brain systems that are influenced by the oral and written language environment (Dehaene, 2009; Moats, 2000; Wolf et al., 2012).

During reading acquisition, people transform some of the visual structures of their brains into a highly specialized interface between vision and language (Dehaene, 2011). Identified in the left hemisphere (the language hemisphere for the majority of humans) was a network in the brain showing common activation when reading a sentence and when listening to one (Dehaene, 2004, 2009; DeMille et al., 2018; Dennis et al., 2009; Galaburda et al., 2006; Mascheretti et al., 2017; Meng et al., 2005; Powers et al., 2013, 2016; Richlan, 2014; Scerri et al., 2017). This network included the left inferior frontal gyrus, precentral gyrus, left fusiform gyrus, inferior temporal gyrus, middle temporal gyrus, and bilateral superior temporal gyri (Bolger et al., 2005; Paulesu et al., 2000; Richlan, 2014). Dehaene (2011) recommended that the entire length of the superior temporal sulcus and the temporal-parietal junction be added to this list of activations. He further specified that these regions were not unique to the reading process, but rather were spoken language areas accessed through vision. These spoken language areas are already fully activated in the left hemisphere in babies who listen to their native language (Dehaene, 2011). All that remains is to acquire the visual interface to fully access the written language, and this involves recycling existing brain systems (Dehaene, 2011; Wolf, 2013).

Dehaene (2011) viewed the human brain as a collection of evolved devices inherited from evolutionary development. These devices naturally addressed problems, such as navigating space and remembering locations, representing time, acquiring a sense of number for concrete sets, recognizing objects and faces, and representing sounds, particularly the speech sounds typical of our species. These can be considered evolutionary survival skills. People take advantage of these evolutionary devices through education by recycling them for use—a process called neuronal recycling. This process represents the capacity of the human brain to form new circuits for cultural inventions from circuits developed through evolution (Dehaene, 2004; Wolf, 2013).

As children acquire reading skills, their brains must learn to identify and process a new form of visual input (written words; Cohen et al., 2002; Dehaene, 2009) and connect it to the spoken language network. To accomplish this, learners recycle the evolutionary device for recognizing objects and faces: their visual shape analysis system (Nakamura et al., 2012).

Reading involves recognizing strings of ordered letter identities. These ordered identities are known as visual word form (Cohen et al., 2002). Functional magnetic resonance imaging (fMRI) studies have demonstrated that a location on the left fusiform gyrus is activated by reading real words and pseudowords (Bouhali et al., 2014; Centanni et al., 2019; Cohen et al., 2002; Dehaene, 2011; Dehaene, 2004; Kronbichler et al., 2004; Mano et al., 2012; Nakamura et al., 2012; Pinel et al., 2014; Slotnick, 2013). This visual analysis system has been termed the "visual word form area" (VWFA). fMRI is a form of magnetic resonance imaging that is utilized concurrently as the study participant is performing a task. It uses the blood-oxygen-level dependent (BOLD) contrast and measures brain activity by detecting changes associated with blood flow. This technique relies on the fact that cerebral blood flow and neuronal activation are coupled. When an area of the brain is in use, blood flow to that region also increases, and neuroscientists can document the activity. It is how scientists know about the left hemisphere activation during reading tasks.

The lateral occipito-temporal VWFA is responsible for the perceptual analysis of written words and is part of the posterior left hemisphere network upon which reading relies (Nakamura et al., 2012). It responds strictly to visual stimuli, and it responds to all sorts of strings of letters (Centanni et al., 2019; Dehaene, 2011; Pinel et al., 2014; Richlan et al., 2010; Schuster et al., 2015). The VWFA is always found in the same location in the left lateral occipito-temporal sulcus, within a few millimeters, regardless of the individual or culture (Bolger et al., 2005; Cohen et al., 2002; Dehaene, 2011; Dehaene et al., 2002; Nakamura et al., 2012). It serves as a foundational component in the reading process, as lesions in this area of the brain cause acquired alexia, an inability to read in formally literate readers (Beeson & Insalaco, 1998; Cohen et al., 2002; Dehaene, 2011). With evidence-based literacy instruction, the VWFA will respond based upon a specific script and will activate more to a known script (Dehaene, 2011; Schuster et al., 2015; Wolf, 2013), regardless of cultural properties (e.g., capitalization or handwriting vs. print; Dehaene, 2011) or spatial location (Cohen et al., 2002). During reading acquisition, this area becomes more strongly activated. In strong readers, this area is highly developed and activated. In the brains of dyslexics and other struggling readers, this area is underdeveloped (Dehaene, 2011; Sprenger-Charolles & Siegel, 2013).

It is hypothesized that the posterior location of the VFWA aids in visuospatial analysis and is probably determined by its proximity and connections to cortical areas for spoken language. What is left to do is to connect the VFWA to the spoken language network. Connectivity is everything, but it has to be learned (Wolf, 2013).

Letters, letter patterns, and morphemes must be connected to their corresponding sounds and blended into words; morphemes and words must be automatically connected to their meanings and associations, as well as to their grammatical uses. A great deal of effort and repetition is required (Wolf, 2013; Wolf et al., 2012), as it is the designing feature of a writing system (Perfetti & Dunlap, 2008). Sound-symbol correspondence must be systematically and explicitly taught in a logical progression from the simple to complex (Pinker, 1994; Uhry, 2013) and drilled sufficiently until the association of sound to symbol and symbol to sound is automatic. The portion of the newly created reading circuitry, from visual recognition to semantic activation, needs to occur in "less than one-half second" (Wolf, 2013, p. 4).

The Planum Temporale

There is a second region that bears mentioning—the higher order cortical region involved in language processing (Caylak, 2009). It is called the planum temporale, and it is located on the superior temporal lobe. It forms the heart of Wernicke's area, and for most people, is larger in the left hemisphere. In most people a noticeable symmetry is seen. The left hemisphere is larger in close to 70% of the population, while the right hemisphere is larger in 11%. Harvard neurologist Norman Geschwind discovered an asymmetry in the temporale plane, determining that the ratio of left to right planum temporale is related to increased language performance (Caylak, 2009; Gayán Guardiola, 2001). Postmortem studies and, more recently, magnetic resonance imaging (MRI) revealed a symmetrical sized planum temporale in dyslexic readers (Gayán Guardiola, 2001). MRI is medical imaging that is based upon the principles of nuclear magnetic resonance. The main strength of the MRI is that it offers the best soft tissue (grey matter and white matter) contrast of all imaging modalities (Elnakib et al., 2014). The planum temporale is associated with the acquisition of phonemic awareness, phonological processing, verbal short-term memory, and grapheme-phoneme correspondences (also known as phonics). Activation in this area to spoken language doubles with literacy in good readers compared to struggling nonreaders. Likewise, dyslexics activate less than people without dyslexia because, in dyslexics, the connections between the VWFA and the planum temporale are not fully developed. As evidence-based reading instruction is pursued, new connections are progressively established between the VWFA and the planum temporale (Dehaene, 2009, 2011; Sprenger-Charolles & Siegel, 2013).

Phonemic Awareness

Phonemic awareness, a part of phonological awareness, is a strictly oral activity that is based upon auditory discrimination. Although phonological awareness is the knowledge and understanding that spoken words and syllables are made up of sequences of speech sounds called phonemes, phonemic awareness represents the ability to hear, identify the sequence and number, and manipulate sounds located within each spoken stream (Blachman, 1991; Caylak, 2010; Costenaro & Pesce, 2012; Fowler, 1991; Yopp, 1992). Because of its impact on early and struggling readers, phonemic awareness is the most researched aspect of the reading acquisition process (Sprenger-Charolles & Siegel, 2013). There have been hundreds of studies of the effects of phonemic awareness instruction on reading and spelling (Wolf et al., 2012; Uhry, 2013). Children who have difficulty with the relationship between the different sounds (phonological processing) will experience difficulty creating the associations between the sounds and letter patterns (Hairston et al., 2005). As a result, blending sounds to make words will be problematic (Wolf et al., 2012).

Phonemic awareness is vital because students must have the ability to identify and visually image the number, order, and identity of sounds and letters within words (Landerl et al., 2019). Reading Roman-based languages involves accurately mapping a sequence of phonemes, from left to right, onto a spatial sequence of graphemes, from first to last (Siegel, 2006; Uhry, 2013). Beyond learning the orthography of a native alphabetic writing system, children encounter an additional problem (Sprenger-Charolles et al., 2006; Ziegler & Goswami, 2005). Prior to mastery of the mapping skill, learners must first understand the spoken language at the phonemic level in order to develop the skills to accurately map the graphemes with the corresponding phonemes (Balmuth, 2009; Pugh & Verhoeven, 2018; Seidenberg, 2017; Siegel, 2006). Students must be able to isolate phonemes in a speech stream because phonemes are coarticulated. In words with three sounds, for example, the initial sound flows to the medial and then the final sound (Uhry, 2013). The vowel sound is difficult to isolate for students who are first learning to read because sounds are articulated so closely in the tract of articulation (Sprenger-Charolles & Siegel, 2013). Take, for example, *bag*, *beg*, *big*, *bog*, and *bug*. These sounds typically proved to be problematic in their identification for struggling readers. This difficulty has been demonstrated through many studies, including a collaborative study conducted by the Neuhaus Education Center, the University of Houston, and Haskins Laboratories, which stated that the least skilled readers have significantly more difficulty with stressed short vowel sounds than with stressed long vowel sounds (Post et al., 1999). Perhaps, it is because we have been singing our long vowel sounds since the very first time that we sang our ABCs.

Phonemic awareness abilities underlie accurate word attack, word recognition, reading fluency, and spelling (Costenaro & Pesce, 2012). Children who have phonemic awareness skills are likely to have an easier time learning to read and spell than children who have few or none of these skills. Weakness in these functions causes individuals to add, omit, substitute, and reverse sounds and letters within words while reading and spelling.

The five key skills that serve as the foundation of phonemic awareness are:

- **Phoneme replication:** The ability to repeat a sound that they hear.
- **Blending:** The ability to join a string of phonemes together to create a word.
- **Segmenting:** The ability to break a word into its individual phonemes.
- **Substitution/deletion:** The ability to replace a phoneme with a new phoneme, creating a new word.
- **Rhyming:** The ability to find words with the same rhyme

Phonemes are the smallest parts of sound in a spoken word. For example, the word *at* has two sounds or phonemes, / ă / / t /. The word *dog* has three phonemes, / d / / ŏ / / g /. Although the word *box* has three letters, it has four phonemes, / b / / ŏ / / k / / s /. As evidenced by the word *box*, phonemes are separate entities from the symbols that are called letters of the alphabet, or graphemes. A grapheme is the smallest part of written language that represents a phoneme in the spelling of a word. A grapheme may be just one letter, such as "t" or "d" or several letters, such as "aw" or "eigh." Graphemes represent the phonemes in written language.

Phonics

Phonics is the study of the predictable relationship between the phonemes or sounds in language and the graphemes or letters that are used to represent these sounds. Phonics is a morphological activity based upon sound-symbol correspondence, knowing which letters or group of letters create which sounds and when. The purpose of phonics instruction is to teach children the sound-symbol relationships and how to use those relationships to read words. To achieve this, phonics instruction must be explicit and systematic. It is explicit in that sound-symbol relationships are directly taught. Students are told, for example, that the letter "s" stands for the / s / sound; however, when the letter "s" sits between two vowels or follows a voiced sound at the end of a word, the letter "s" says / z /. Phonics instruction is systematic in that it follows a scope and sequence that allows children to form and read words early on. The skills taught are constantly reviewed and applied to real reading.

Further, there is a difference between traditional phonics instruction and multisensory phonics instruction. Multisensory phonics instruction revolves around the scientifically based concept that humans acquire and master spoken and written language through three distinct neurological pathways: visual processing (seeing), auditory processing (hearing), and tactile-kinesthetic processing (feeling; Dunson, 2013). In the last pathway, tactile refers to small muscle movements (handwriting, manipulation of the vocal tract and speech organs), and the kinesthetic refers to large muscle movements (movement of the arms/legs). The trifecta of dyslexia—deficits in phonological awareness, verbal short-term memory, and lexical memory—inhibits the effectiveness of traditional, unisensory, phonics instruction (Shams & Seitz, 2008). The multisensory aspect aids in phonological awareness, verbal short-term memory, and lexical memory and retention as auditory and visual information are integrated. Multisensory protocols are more effective for learning because people's experience in the world involves constant multisensory input in terms of human processing of sensory information (Calvert et al., 2004; Shimogo & Shams, 2001). Therefore, multisensory perceptual learning better resembles natural activities (Shams & Seitz, 2008). Further, early detection of said deficits is crucial, as intervention is more effective when it is applied earlier rather than later (Powers et al., 2013).

Reading Difficulties and Dyslexia

According to the fifth edition of the *Diagnostic Statistical Manual of Mental Disorders* (DSM-5; American Psychiatric Association, 2013), there are three main learning disorders that may be diagnosed in the during childhood: reading, writing, and math. Speech skills may also be affected (Powers et al., 2013). It is estimated that 80% of children with learning disorders have reading problems, making reading disability the most common form of learning disability. Reading disabilities have probably existed since the first humans (Gayán Guardiola, 2001). Long before writing systems were invented, people most likely struggled with the interpretation of the meanings behind man-made visual symbols (pictographs) that were based upon spoken language. Most citizens of Pre-Ptolemaic Egypt, the origins of the writing system upon which the West Semitic (Kaltner & McKenzie, 2002) and Phoenician alphabets (Howard, 2012) were based, were illiterate.

Dyslexia is a common disorder that hinders the development of reading skills, and it is characterized by deficits in phonological awareness, accurate and fluent word and pseudoword reading, rapid naming, spelling abilities, verbal working memory, and reading comprehension (Diamanti et al., 2018; Lyon et al., 2003; Seidenberg, 2017; Siegel, 2006). The construct of verbal short-term memory (verbal working memory) refers to the mechanism by which sensory information for speech is stored for a short time and processed in the service of other mental operations (Döhla & Heim, 2016; Döhla et al., 2018; Mann & Liberman, 1984; Nittrouer et al., 2016). Verbal short-term memory is a dual-component system in which verbal information is stored in a durable phonological code, recovered via the phonological loop, and information may be held for a short period of time. When combined in a phonological loop, the active rehearsal process and the phonological loop, together, allow individuals to retain information for a longer period of time (Döhla & Heim, 2016; Döhla et al., 2018).

Further research concluded that children who were identified as dyslexic will likely continue to have reading difficulties through adulthood (Bruck, 1990; Diamanti et al., 2018; Galaburda et al., 2006; Raskind et al., 2012; Shaywitz et al., 1999; Siegel, 2006). Some researchers refer to dyslexia as a visual processing disorder that is neurological in nature; varied definitions are used throughout medical, educational, and governmental institutions, although few mention phonological processing as the primary cognitive deficit (Kearns et al., 2019; Seidenberg, 2017). Current cognitive neuroscientific research indicates that dyslexia is based upon underlying core deficits in phonological processing, resulting in weak phonemic awareness and phonological decoding (Caylak, 2010; Costenaro & Pesce, 2012; Galaburda et al., 2006; Raskind et al., 2012; Shaywitz et al., 1999; Wise & Snyder, 2003). Because humans access spoken language through their vision, the process of reading is the decryption of the written symbols into the sounds that they represent (Dehaene, 2011; Seidenberg, 2017). This act requires connecting the symbols used in the written language with the corresponding sounds that they represent in the spoken language (Sprenger-Charolles & Siegel, 2013).

Word identification is one of the key components of reading, and it involves recognizing that words are a systematic string of individual letters. Each individual sequential combination represents a different word. Students must be able to string together the sounds that are mapped on the letters or letter groups in order to produce these words, all while taking into consideration vowel activity, vowel teams, consonants, consonant blends, consonant digraphs, syllable types, syllable division, and morphology (Dunson, 2013). Dyslexics, in general, are affected, as they suffer from a faulty processing of speech sounds (Dehaene, 2009; Temple, 2002). The phonological deficit underlying dyslexia manifests in:

- poor phonological awareness—the knowledge and understanding that spoken words and syllables are made up of sequences of speech sounds called phonemes that must be identified and manipulated (Blachman, 1991; Caylak, 2010; Costenaro & Pesce, 2012; Fowler, 1991; Yopp, 1992);
- poor verbal short-term memory—the ability to retain a string of sounds or letters (Caylak, 2010; Diamanti et al. 2018; Galaburda et al., 2006; Mann & Liberman, 1984; Raskind et al., 2013); and
- slow lexical memory—the ability to remember the graphemes and words of our language (Diamanti et al., 2018; Galaburda et al., 2006; Raskind et al., 2013; Richlan, 2014).

Processes beyond those involving the sounds of speech are implicated. Multiple studies have shown that working memory (Raskind et al., 2012) and executive functions (Berninger et al., 2006; Lyon & Krasnegor, 1996; Raskind et al., 2013) in working memory are impaired with dyslexia. In the educational setting, students with learning disabilities are impeded compared to their neurotypical peers, resulting in nocuous psychological, social, and socioeconomic results (Powers et al., 2016). Gender-related information is somewhat mixed. In terms of reading disability (dyslexia) and spelling ability (dysgraphia), many studies have found an excess of males, with male to female ratios ranging from one to five and three to one (Raskind et al., 2013). Dyslexia is defined by the International Dyslexia Association (2002) as:

> a specific learning disability that is neurobiological in origin. It is characterized by difficulties with accurate and/or fluent word recognition and by poor spelling and decoding abilities. These difficulties typically result from a deficit in the phonological component of language that is often unexpected in relation to other cognitive abilities and the provision of effective classroom instruction. Secondary consequences may include problems in reading comprehension and reduced reading experience that can impede growth of vocabulary and background knowledge.

Dyslexics struggle with language acquisition skills despite having been exposed to scientific-based reading teaching methodologies. Some estimates suggest that 5% to 17% of children in the United States have dyslexia (Dehaene, 2009; Ramus et al., 2003; Sexton et al., 2011), while others suggest that approximately 20% have dyslexia (Shaywitz, 2020, pp. 6–7). Dehaene (2009) felt that, based upon this model, this percentage is rather high and may be based upon the threshold to define the impairment and the setting of an arbitrary criterion for what is "normal." Siegel (2006) provided foundation for Dehaene's concern when she wrote, "The distinction between dyslexia and normal reading is arbitrary; where the cutoff point is drawn varies from study to study" (p. 581). She further explained that this definition of dyslexia is based upon the test given, as reading is measured on a continuum and there is no cutoff score on a reading test that will clearly divide individuals into dyslexic and neurotypical groups.

Simply because a student has language-based difficulty in reading does not mean that they have dyslexia (Seidenberg, 2017; Uhry, 2013). Some children have vocabulary deficits without a biological connect, but simply because of inadequate early childhood experience with rich language (Moats, 2000; Wolf, 2013). Studies have shown that young children from professional and middle-class homes hear dramatically more words, and dramatically more different words, than do children from families in poverty (Hart & Risley, 1995; Wolf et al., 2012). Others may have experienced misdiagnosed auditory deficits or poor educational environments (Dehaene, 2009). Finally, the English orthography system is quite deep and contains components from eight different cultural influences: Latinate, Greek, Anglo-Saxon, French, Spanish, Native American, Kemetic, and Scandinavian (Balmuth, 2009; Dunson, 2013; Pyles & Algeo, 1993). This situation requires explicit and systematic phonics instruction to master sound-symbol correspondence of such a complex orthography that involves a vast number of stored memory representations (Costenaro & Pesce, 2012; Dunson, 2013; Richlan, 2014). To suggest a diagnosis of dyslexia, all of these possible causes of a reading deficit must be examined and discarded (Dehaene, 2009).

Genetic Cause of Dyslexia

Reading disability has a genetic component and is inherited (Caylak, 2010; Döhla & Heim, 2016; Powers et al., 2013; Raskind et al., 2012). Researchers have known for quite some time that there was a genetic link between dyslexics and their families (Compston, 2016; Gayán Guardiola, 2001; Hallgren, 1950; Meng et al., 2005; Orton, 1928; Powers et al., 2013, 2016; Valentine, 2019).

Since the late 1970s, studies have shown that up to 50% of children of dyslexic parents are affected (Finucci et al., 1976; Meng et al., 2005). Further, 50% of siblings of dyslexics and 50% of parents of dyslexic children are affected as well. Heritability estimates range from 44% to 75% (Caylak, 2010, Raskind et al., 2012).

As there is no universally accepted definition of dyslexia, there is, in keeping, no universally accepted cause (Conner, 2017). Cognitive neuroscience, however, has added a new tool to get to the genetic roots of the disorder. The new tool is the "imaging-genetic" approach, which integrates neuroimaging data, genetic data, and cognitive data (Gayán Guardiola, 2001; Mascheretti et al., 2017). Using this new interdisciplinary approach, researchers have identified several chromosomal sites as candidates for dyslexia susceptibility (DeMille et al., 2018; Dennis et al., 2009; Galaburda et al., 2006; Mascheretti et al., 2017; Meng et al., 2005; Powers et al., 2013; Raskind et al., 2013).

Through studies on genetic association and chromosomal translocation, at least nine developmental dyslexia risk loci, named DYX1-DYX9, have been identified on eight different chromosomes: 1p36-p34, 2p16-15, 3p12-q13, 6p22.3, 6q13-16.2, 11p15.5, 15q21.3, 18p11.2, and Xq27.3 (Mascheretti et al., 2017). Several genes across these DXY loci have been implicated as the source of reading disability: DYX1C1, C2ORF3, MRPL19, FAM176A, NRSN1, KIAA0319L, FMR1, KIAA0319, DCDC2, and ROBO1 (DeMille et al., 2018; Dennis et al., 2009; Galaburda et al., 2006; Mascheretti et al., 2017; Meng et al., 2005; Powers et al., 2013; Powers et al., 2016; Raskind et al., 2013; Scerri et al., 2017). The one discovered to have received the most attention is the DCDC2 gene, the gene proposed to be the primary candidate gene for reading disability (DeMille et al., 2018; Mascheretti et al., 2017; Meng et al., 2005; Powers et al., 2013).

In November of 2005, Dr. Jeffrey Gruen, an associate professor at Yale School of Medicine, and his research team discovered that reading ability is influenced by a gene called DCDC2. This gene is located on chromosome 6 (Converse, 2001). The team studied 153 families with dyslexic children and identified an altered stretch of DNA within the DCDC2 gene of the study group that correlated to a severe reading disability. Recently discovered, within the past 6 years or so, is a region of the DCDC2 gene that has a binding protein called BV677278 (Powers et al., 2013), and this protein is believed to act as a modifier of the expression of the DCDC2 gene. It is termed as a regulatory element associated with dyslexia 1 or 'READ1' (DeMille et al., 2018; Powers et al., 2013, 2016).

Development dyslexia-susceptibility genes affect neuronal migration, the process by which the neurons of the fetus migrate during pregnancy (Dehaene,

2009; Mascheretti et al., 2017). During their migration, they are formed by cell division as they travel to their final position on the appropriate level of the cerebral cortex (Dehaene, 2009). While performing autopsies on the brains of dyslexics, Galaburda et al. (1985) discovered that neuronal migration had not occurred properly. They found numerous ectopias, neuron clusters, indicating that the neurons had not been placed correctly during the migration process. The incorrectly placed neurons clustered around the planum temporale (Dehaene, 2009; Vanderauwera et al., 2018) and the visual word form area (Cohen et al., 2002; Dehaene, 2009).

The History of Dyslexia Research

Finding mutual agreement as to the definition and causes of dyslexia has proven to be difficult and contentious (Siegel, 2006). The first theories of dyslexia began in Europe and focused on defects or damage to the human brain. The study of reading disability began with the findings of early researchers into aphasia. Although research into aphasia and alexia began in 1676 by German-Austrian surgeon Johann Schmidt (Benton, 2000; Gayán Guardiola, 2001), the term *dyslexia* was originally coined by German ophthalmologist Rudolf Berlin in 1887 (Wagner, 1973). Berlin concluded that dyslexia was due to a brain lesion, and his research was based upon the research of his mentor, German physician Adolph Kussmaul (Kirby, 2018).

In 1877, Kussmaul had identified the deficits in reading ability in his aphasic adult patients that were later described by Berlin, utilizing the term first used by Schmidt, "Wortblindheit" or "word-blindness" (Benton, 2000; Compston, 2016). As he was unable to identify any weakness in the vision of the adults who suffered from a reading disability, Kussmaul concluded that the problem lay within the human brain itself. Initially, early researchers of reading disability assumed that it was based upon a general mental defect, and children who exhibited reading difficulty were described as partial imbeciles (feeble minded; Orton, 1928).

In 1892, while French physician and anatomist Paul Broca identified parts of the brain that housed language functions, French neurologist Joseph Dejerine identified lesions in the parietal and occipital lobes that caused reading difficulty, concluding that dyslexia was a neurological disorder caused by cerebral trauma. His findings fell in line with Berlin and Kussmaul, who believed that brain damage was the root of reading disability (acquired dyslexia; Gayán Guardiola, 2001).

Eventually, in 1896, cases began to be published of children of normal intelligence who suffered from a reading disability. British physician W. Pringle Morgan noted in a case study that a young boy with whom he worked had a defective or absent visual memory for words, which is equivalent to saying that he was what Kussmaul had termed "word blind" (Orton, 1928). This position was reinforced by Scottish optic surgeon James Hinshelwood in 1917 (Compston, 2016; Gayán Guardiola, 2001; Kirby, 2018). He compared those who exhibited congenital word blindness with acquired word blindness (blindness that may result from regional brain destruction).

Hinshelwood was one of the earlier dyslexia researchers who postulated that there existed a congenital defect of development of the brain area for registration of visual memories of words, "congenital word blindness" (Orton, 1928). Hinshelwood, through a series of articles in medical books that were clinical in nature, is considered the foremost researcher who turned dyslexia into a medical issue of great importance (Gayán Guardiola, 2001).

British psychologist Lucy Fildes, through a series of experiments in 1921 involving readers and nonreaders, disputed that students who struggled with reading were partial imbeciles. She concluded that there was no connection between reading disability and intelligence (Compston, 2016; Fildes, 1921; Gayán Guardiola, 2001; Valentine, 2019). Further, she determined that this difficulty was not confined to words. Students in her experiments who struggled with reading also had difficulty with shapes and numbers; however, like her predecessors, Fildes determined that there was damage in the region of the human brain responsible for visual processing, and she added that there may also be damage in the region of the brain responsible for auditory processing (Valentine, 2019).

Neuropsychiatrist and pathologist Samuel Orton was the first American to research the phenomenon, attributing reading difficulty to the visual processing system, and termed it "congenital word blindness." In 1925, Orton, as the director of the Green County Mental Clinic in Iowa, initially tested the 125 students referred to the clinic. Only one clearly fit Hinshelwood's measure for congenital word blindness; others were determined to be intellectually challenged. Through a series of tests, Orton (1928) observed that, as vision is based in the occipital lobe, visual function was the key.

Orton continued his research into language disabilities between 1925 and his death in 1948, studying approximately 3,000 children and adults. He first noted correlations between reading disability and left-handedness (Compston, 2016; Gayán Guardiola, 2001; Kirby, 2018; Orton, 1928). Later, he observed a large number of reading and writing errors that were based upon the inversions of letters within words. Noting this, Orton became the first to argue that dyslexia was not based upon damage to the brain, shaking the research community. He, instead, argued that there must be a syndrome that is unrelated to brain damage. He termed it *strephosymbolia* or "twisted signs" (Compston, 2016; Orton, 1928; Valentine, 2019), and he believed that reading difficulties ran in families.

Even though Orton's conclusions regarding "cerebral dominance" have been dispelled by research (Kirby, 2018), he completely changed how dyslexia was addressed, removing it from the realm of physicians to the public arena. He revolutionized modern thought concerning learning disabilities, determining that language-based disorders were biological and not environmental in origin. He brought together neuroscientific information and principles of remediation, having extensively studied children with the kind of language processing difficulties now commonly associated with dyslexia, and formulated a set of teaching principles and practices for such children. He strongly believed that such disorders would respond to specific training if properly diagnosed and if the proper training methods to meet the needs of each particular case were instituted. Working with Anna Gillingham, a gifted educator, psychologist, and school administrator, the two devised methods of teaching these students based on the principles formulated by Orton. The method is called the Orton-Gillingham approach, and Gillingham compiled and published the instructional materials. *The Gillingham Manual*, which Gillingham wrote with Bessie Stillman (1997), still serves as the leading instruction manual of the Orton-Gillingham approach.

Orton's legacy has been championed by the International Dyslexia Association (formerly the Orton Society and later, the Orton Dyslexia Society, founded upon his death in 1948) and its allied group of psychologists, researchers, and of late, cognitive neuroscientists, who keep dyslexia research moving forward.

As the Orton Society was in its infancy, research into reading disabilities was waning in Europe; however, strides were still being made through the 1950s and 1960s. In Scandinavia, Bertil Hallgren published, "Specific Dyslexia (Congenital Word-Blindness); a Clinical and Genetic Study" in 1950, which detailed, after several studies, that dyslexia was inherited (Gayán Guardiola, 2001; Hallgren, 1950).

In the following years, psychologists began to analyze dyslexic abilities and disabilities. Psychiatric consequences of dyslexia were also investigated. Soon, a new aspect of dyslexia study began—neuroanatomy. This was when, as previously discussed, in the late 1960s, Harvard neurologist Norman Geschwind discovered an asymmetry in the temporale plane, determining that the ratio of left to right planum temporale is related to increased language performance (Caylak, 2009; Gayán Guardiola, 2001). Postmortem studies, and more recently MRI, revealed a symmetrical sized planum temporale in dyslexic readers (Galaburda et al., 1985; Gayán Guardiola, 2011). This research led to the eventual development of the phonological deficit hypothesis at the end of the 1970s and the beginning of the 1980s.

In the past 20 years or so, certain tools have provided a clearer picture of brain phonological processing and the acquisition of language: magnetic resonance imaging (MRI), functional magnetic resonance imaging (fMRI), and positron emission testing (PET) scans. Currently, the "imaging-genetic" approach has allowed researchers to identify several chromosomal sites as candidates for dyslexia susceptibility (DeMille et al., 2018; Dennis et al., 2009; Galaburda et al., 2006; Mascheretti et al., 2017; Meng et al., 2005; Powers et al., 2013; Raskind et al., 2013; Scerri et al., 2017).

The Dyslexic Brain and Reading

The brain of the English reader (Roman alphabet) is visibly different in terms of activation of the key left hemisphere network than that of a reader of Chinese or Japanese Kanji or Japanese kana (Liu et al., 2013; Paulesu et al., 2001; Richlan, 2014; Welty et al., 2014; Wolf et al., 2012). Further, the dyslexic brain functions differently than the nondyslexic brain in reading tasks. There are two prevailing theories as to the origins: the phonological deficit hypothesis and the double-deficit hypothesis. Paulesu et al. (2000) used positron emission tomography (PET), an imaging test that uses a radioactive tracer to reveal how tissues and organs are functioning, to compare the brains of skilled adult readers. Identified in the left hemisphere was a network in the brain showing common activation of all participants that included the left inferior frontal gyrus, precentral gyrus, left fusiform gyrus, inferior temporal gyrus, middle temporal gyrus, and bilateral superior temporal gyri (Bolger et al., 2005; Paulesu et al., 2000; Richlan, 2014) These are the areas responsible for phonological processing.

This study was followed up by Paulesu et al. in 2001. In the second study, the group again investigated the activations of the left hemisphere's language areas. This time, the focus was on the left-lateralized brain activations and their relationships to dyslexia. Using the same activation tasks of the previous study, PET scans were obtained of dyslexic and nondyslexic students from the United Kingdom, France, and Italy (Paulesu et al., 2001). The European countries have languages that share common origins, and all, like English, use the Roman alphabet (Bolger et al., 2005). The researchers identified a large cluster in the left hemisphere composed of the bilateral superior temporal gyri (corresponding to phonological processing), middle temporal gyrus (corresponding to semantic processing), and inferior temporal gyrus (corresponding to orthographic processing). This cluster had higher levels of activation in neurotypical readers than with dyslexic readers (Temple, 2002). These results were unilateral, regardless of the orthography. Under activation of this left hemisphere, this cluster occurred in readers of the orthographies of Italian, French, and English (Dehaene, 2009; Paulesu et al., 2001; Richlan, 2014). Considering that all dyslexic participants were selected based upon phonological deficits, the results were interpreted as evidence for a universal neurocognitive basis for dyslexia in cultures with an alphabetic writing system (Richlan, 2014).

When an fMRI study using adults was used to compare the activations based upon an alphabetic writing system with the activations based upon Chinese, a logographic writing system, the clusters in the left hemisphere showed increased activation of the English adults but not in the Chinese adults (Richlan, 2014). It was concluded that the left hemisphere phonological network reorganized differently in readers of alphabetic writing systems versus readers of logographic writing systems (Liu et al., 2013; Paulesu et al., 2001; Richlan, 2014). This has been challenged. Hu et al. (2010) found that there was a writing system-specific difference in activation between English and Chinese nonimpaired readers, with Chinese readers having a higher level of activation in the left inferior frontal sulcus. Chinese and English dyslexic readers shared a common pattern of underactivation compared to nonimpaired readers (Hu et al., 2010; Richlan, 2014). Because the phonological deficit underlying dyslexia manifests in poor phonological awareness, poor verbal short-term memory, and slow lexical memory (Blachman, 1991; Caylak, 2010; Costenaro & Pesce, 2012; Diamanti et al., 2018; Fowler, 1991; Galaburda et al., 2006; Mann & Liberman, 1984; Richlan, 2014; Yopp, 1992), researchers agreed that the cross-linguistic underactivation of the left hemisphere in the Chinese and English impaired readers is because dyslexics, across orthographies, have difficulty computing and remembering how phonology is linked to written symbols, reinforcing the phonological deficit hypothesis (Brady & Shankweiler, 1991; Ramus et al., 2003).

The double-deficit hypothesis of developmental dyslexia differs from the phonological deficit hypothesis in that naming speed is added to the equation. Rapid automatized naming works alongside phonological awareness in young readers to determine reading ability. Students with deficits in both abilities are most affected (Landerl et al., 2019; Norton & Wolf, 2012; Pugh & Verhoeven, 2018; Vukovic & Siegel, 2006). Rapid automatized naming (RAN) is the ability to name a series of high-frequency numbers, letters, colors, or objects presented in random order within a specific time period (Vukovic & Siegel, 2006).

The time period obtained is compared to time periods that are normed. The double-deficit hypothesis advanced the existence of three subtypes of reading disorder: (1) the phonological deficit subtype, in which the phonological deficit occurs with average naming speed; (2) the naming speed-deficit subtype, in which a naming speed deficit occurs with average phonological skills; and (3) the double-deficit hypothesis, in which naming speed and phonological deficits are both present (Caylak, 2010; Landerl et al., 2019; Norton & Wolf, 2012; Pugh & Verhoeven, 2018; Vukovic & Siegel, 2006; Wolf & Bowers, 1999). On RAN tests, a standard score that is one standard deviation below the mean is used to indicate a naming speed deficit (Vukovic & Siegel, 2006). Concern remains within the double-deficit hypothesis community because, like dyslexia diagnoses, the determination is task specific and, therefore, somewhat arbitrary, although some RAN studies have demonstrated that naming speed is a predictor of reading skill in several alphabetic languages (Landerl et al., 2019).

Orthography and Dyslexia

Although dyslexia is recognized as a global phenomenon, there is some discord about the universality of the syndrome because research studies have shown that the frequency of the diagnosis differs across languages (Landerl et al., 1997; Paulesu et al., 2001), marking dyslexia with culture-specific manifestations. Specifically, the frequency of occurrence seems to be related to the shallowness of the language's orthography. Incidences of dyslexia in Italy, which has a shallow orthography, are half of what they are in the United States (Paulesu et al., 2001) due to the depth of the English orthography. Orthographic depth refers to the reliability of print-to-speech correspondences (Richlan, 2014; Schmalz et al., 2015; Widjaja & Winskel, 2004). In different written languages, the rate of grapheme-phoneme correspondence may vary.

Each language has its prerequisite number of sounds (Fromkin et al., 2014). In English, for example, there are 44 (see Figure 4.2). There are five short vowel sounds, five long vowel sounds, six r-controlled vowel sounds, four advanced vowel sounds, 18 "basic" consonant sounds, and six "advanced" consonant sounds (Dunson, 2013; Gillingham & Stillman, 1997). These 44 sounds can be represented by 1,120 graphemes (Georgiou et al., 2012).

In addition to the phonological aspect of spoken language required for decoding, there are eight different languages that contribute to the production of these 44 sounds (Balmuth, 2009; Dunson, 2013; Pyles & Algeo, 1993):

1. Latinate = 55%
2. Anglo-Saxon = 25%

FIGURE 4.2
Vowel and Consonant Sounds

Short Vowel Sounds	Long Vowel Sounds	R-Controlled Vowel Sounds
/ă/ as in *hat*	/ā/ as in *skate*	/χr/ as in *herd*
/ě/ as in *bed*	/ē/ as in *Pete*	/ar/ as in *car*
/ĭ/ as in *fish*	/ī/ as in *kite*	/or/ as in *born*
/ŏ/ as in *stop*	/ō/ as in *note*	/ear/ as in *fear*
/ŭ/ as in *cup*	/ū/ as in *flute*	/air/ as in *hair*
		/oor/ as in *floor*

Basic Consonant Sounds		
/b/ as in *big*	/k/ as in *king*	/s/ as in *silly*
/d/ as in *dog*	/l/ as in *lips*	/t/ as in *test*
/f/ as in *fish*	/m/ as in *man*	/v/ as in *van*
/g/ as in *go*	/n/ as in *no*	/w/ as in *win*
/h/ as in *hat*	/p/ as in *pan*	/y/ as in *yellow*
/j/ as in *jelly*	/r/ as in *rabbit*	/z/ as in *zipper*

Advanced Vowel Sounds	Advanced Consonant Sounds
/oo/ as in *book*	/sh/ as in *shut*
/ow/ as in *cow*	/ch/ as in *chin*
/oy/ as in *boy*	/zh/ as in *measure*
/aw/ as in *saw*	/ng/ as in *thing*
	/th/ as in *thimble*
	/th/ as in *this*

3. Greek = 11%
4. Spanish = < 3%
5. Kemetic = < 3 %
6. French = 3%
7. Native American = < 3%
8. Scandinavian = < 3%

English is as a polyglot mix with an opaque or deep orthographic system. Most letters of the English alphabet are symbols for a single-speech sound. However, there are exceptions (Balmuth, 2009; Dunson, 2013; Gillingham & Stillman, 1997; Pyles & Algeo, 1993). The letter "c" can make the / k / sound as in *king* or the / s / as in *silly*. The letter "g" can make the / g / sound as in *go* or the / j / as in *jelly*. The letter "s" can make the / s / as in *silly* or the / z / in *nose*. The letter "x" represents two phonemes, the / k / and / s / sounds. The sounds are pronounced in sequence. The / k / sound is immediately followed by the / s / sound as in the word *box*. When the letter "x" begins a word, it makes the / z / sound as in *xylophone*. When a word begins with an "e" and the letter "x" immediately follows it and the "x" is followed by a vowel, the "x" says / gz / as in the words *exit* or *exam*. "qu" also represents two sounds, the / k / sound immediately followed by the / w / sound. It is important to note that the letter "q" is never found in the English language without being immediately followed by the letter "u" (e.g., *queen, quiet, quick, quack*, etc.). Lastly, in words adopted from the French code, "qu" says / k / as in *mosquito* or *liquor* (Dunson, 2013; Gillingham & Stillman, 1997).

Consider "ch." In Spanish, a shallow or transparent orthography system, the "ch" says /ch//ĕ/. Every time that you see it, it will say, /ch//ĕ/. In fact, the regularity of grapheme-to-phoneme correspondence in the Spanish language is 94% (Sprenger-Charolles & Siegel, 2013). By and large, the Spanish language is WYSIWYG (i.e., what you see is what you get).

In contrast, due to the deep orthography system of English, the regularity of grapheme-to-phoneme correspondence is only 48% (Sprenger-Charolles & Siegel, 2013). As a result, incidences of dyslexia are higher in the English language than other alphabetic writing systems, as myriad grapheme-phoneme correspondences have to be retrieved from stored memories (Richlan, 2014) held in verbal short-term memory and then mapped based upon phonological principles (Diamanti et al., 2018; Galaburda et al., 2006; Mann & Liberman, 1984; Seidenberg, 2017; Yopp, 1992). This represents the "trifecta" of the primary deficits found with dyslexia. The likelihood of choosing the wrong pronunciation in English is far greater than in shallow orthographies. Look at "ch" again, but this time, through the lens of English orthography. Without specific language training, in this case, morphology, students of English will not know if it says / ch / from the Anglo-Saxon influence, / k / from the Greek influence, or / sh / from the French influence. Without proper instruction, students must either guess or memorize. To demonstrate the importance of this information, what is the first question that successful students ask when they are presented a word in a spelling bee? Yes, word origin.

Because the English language is a polyglot with multiple cultural influences, there are multiple spellings for many of the sounds and multiple sounds for many of the written symbols (e.g., two sounds of "c," two sounds of "g," three sounds of "y," three sounds of "ea," two sounds of "-tion," etc.). There are also multiple spellings that produce the same sounds, yet they are not interchangeable (e.g., "au" and "aw" both say / aw /, "ie" and "ei" both say / ē /, "oi" and "oy" both say / ō / / ē /, "ou" and "ow" both say / ŏ / / oo /, "g" and "j" both say / j /, etc.). Figure 4.3 includes some additional examples.

Orthographic depth has been identified as one of the most important environmental factors influencing learning to read (Richlan, 2014; Seymour et al., 2003), and it may be viewed as a continuum. At one end of the continuum is a very deep or opaque orthography, like English, with its grapheme-phoneme correspondence rate of vowels of 48% (Sprenger-Charolles & Siegel, 2013). At the other end of the continuum is a shallow or transparent orthography, such as:

- Finnish (Aro & Wimmer, 2003; Bolger et al., 2005);
- German (Ellis et al., 2004; Wimmer & Hummer, 1990);
- Greek (Diamanti et al., 2018; Ellis et al., 2004; Goswami et al., 1997);
- Italian (Bolger et al., 2005; Ellis et al., 2004; Thorstad, 1991);
- Spanish (Ellis et al., 2004; Goswami et al., 1998; Sprenger-Charolles & Siegel, 2013);
- Turkish (Ellis et al., 2004; Öney & Durgunoglu, 1997); or
- Welsh (Ellis & Hooper, 2001; Ellis et al., 2004).

Learning to read these written languages is easier than learning to read an orthographically opaque language, such as French, Danish, or English (Aro & Wimmer, 2003; Borleffs et al., 2017; Goswami et al., 1997; Landerl et al., 1997; Marinelli et al., 2018; Navas et al., 2014; Perfetti & Dunlap, 2008; Seymour et al., 2003). English has 44 unique sounds compared to French, which has 34. However, the number of unique sounds is not the issue here. The grapheme-phoneme correspondence rate is. The German language has 45 phonemes, one more than English, but the letters in German more consistently produce the same sounds when they are found in different words. German has a shallow orthography. The grapheme-phoneme correspondence rate of a deep orthography means that the WYSIWYG factor is low, and decoding becomes problematic without specific phonics training due to the lack of phonological transparency (Aro & Wimmer, 2003; Costenaro & Pesce, 2012; Dunson, 2013; Schmalz et al., 2015).

The orthographic depth hypothesis (Katz & Frost, 1992) theorized that shallow orthographies should be easier to read in the word-recognition pro-

FIGURE 4.3
Sample Graphemes

The long "a" (/ ā /) sound	"a,"	"a-e"	"ai"	"ay"	"ea"	"ei"	"eigh"	"ey"	"et"
The long "e" (/ ē /) sound	"e"	"e-e"	"ee"	"ea"	"ei"	"ey"	"i"	"ie"	"y"
The long "i" (/ ī /) sound	"i"	"i-e"	"igh"	"y"	"ie"	"y-e"			
The long "o" (/ ō /) sound	"o"	"o-e"	"oa"	"ow"	"oe"				
The long "u" (/ ū /) sound	"u"	"u-e"	"ue"	"ew"	"eu"	"ui"	"oo"	"ou"	

cess that was involved in the language's phonology. Richlan (2014) supported this and stated, "in shallow orthographies, phonology can be derived relatively easily and directly from print" (p. 1). Here, what you see is what you get. Additionally, the majority of languages with a shallow orthography are taught using highly structured phonics methods that explicitly and systematically teach sound-symbol correspondence (Costenaro & Pesce, 2012). This is a concept that is still in its infancy in the United States, despite the National Reading Panel's 2000 report (Dunson, 2013).

Highly structured phonics methods that explicitly and systematically teach sound-symbol correspondence are crucial for a deep orthography such as that of English. In deep orthographies, where there are multiple spellings for each sound and multiple sounds for many of the written symbols, grapheme-phoneme correspondences have to be retrieved from stored memories (Richlan, 2014). This makes learning to read difficult to master (Aro & Wimmer, 2003; Diamanti et al., 2018; Pugh & Verhoeven, 2018). In 2003, Seymour et al. demonstrated that this was true. They compared the abilities of first-grade children to read familiar words and simple nonwords in English and 12 other European orthographies. The results showed that children from most European countries were accurate and fluent in reading before the end of the first school year, with word reading accuracies exceeding 90% in all except the deeper orthographies of Portuguese, French, Danish, and, particularly, English. Because all aspects of reading are linked to the characteristics of the orthography (Bolger et al., 2005; Richlan, 2014; Schmalz et al., 2015), research on reading acquisition has consistently shown that the achievement of reading accuracy is a slower process for children learning to read in a deep orthography (Frith et al., 1998). Richlan (2014) concluded that orthographic depth "has a direct effect on how easy or difficult it is for children to translate a new letter string into a phonological code by which phonological word forms can be accessed" (p. 1).

Decoding a deep orthography such as that of English is a monumental task due the amount of grapheme-phoneme correspondences that must be stored in memory to accurately map lexical sequences with the appropriate sounds. The reservoir of stored memories for representations, as discussed by Richlan (2014), must be vast and highly organized to produce the mapping of sounds that is required for fluent and accurate decoding of such a confluence of cultural contributions. For students who are learning the English language, this process is further complicated by dyslexia.

Coexistence of Dyslexia With Other Learning Difficulties

The most common learning disabilities involve language (Powers et al., 2013). As the trifecta of dyslexia involves poor phonological awareness, poor verbal short-term memory, and slow lexical memory (Blachman, 1991; Caylak, 2010; Costenaro & Pesce, 2012; Diamanti et al., 2018; Fowler, 1991; Galaburda et al., 2006; Mann & Liberman, 1984; Richlan, 2014; Yopp, 1992), the coexistence of other language-dependent disorders may occur. Among them are specific language impairment (SLI), dysgraphia, and Attention Deficit/Hyperactivity Disorder (ADHD).

Specific Language Impairment

Specific language impairment (SLI) has been referred to using other terms, including developmental dysphasia, language impairment, language learning disability, developmental language disorder, delayed speech, and deviant language (Ullman & Pierpont, 2005). SLI is characterized by difficulty with language that is not caused by known neurological, sensory, intellectual, or emotional deficit (Ervin, 2001). It is common for children with SLI to learn to talk late, as the development of vocabulary, grammar, and discourse skills can be affected (Ervin, 2001; Raskind et al., 2012). As dyslexia is an impairment in processing written language, specific language impairment is an impairment in processing and expressing spoken language, and children with specific language impairment are at increased risk for developing a reading disability (Powers et al., 2012) and slow processing speed (Raskind et al., 2013). Reading and speech share a linguistic foundation (Döhla & Heim, 2016; Seidenberg, 2017), and research has recently identified an altered stretch in the KIAA0319 gene on Chromosome 6 (Paracchini et al., 2008). Along with the DCDC2 gene on chromosome 6, the KIAA0319 gene has now been implicated not only as a source of reading disability (DeMille et al., 2018; Dennis et al., 2009; Galaburda et al., 2006; Mascheretti et al., 2017; Meng et al., 2005; Paracchini et al., 2008; Powers et al., 2013, 2016), but also as a source of specific language impairment (Döhla & Heim, 2016; Döhla et al., 2018). Correspondingly, children with specific language impairment have difficulty with short-term verbal memory, a trait common in dyslexia (Bishop & Adams, 1990; DeMille et al., 2018; Dennis et al., 2009; Galaburda et al., 2006; Mascheretti et al., 2017; Meng et al., 2005; Powers et al., 2013, 2016).

Dysgraphia

Dysgraphia is a disorder characterized by difficulties in the acquisition of writing and spelling skills, and the prevalence is 7%–15% among school-aged children (Döhla & Heim, 2016; Döhla et al., 2018). Dysgraphia is closely related to dyslexia, and at one time, dysgraphia was originally included in the definition of dyslexia. Additionally, the dyslexia trifecta of poor phonological processing, poor verbal short-term memory, and slow lexical memory has connections with dysgraphia.

In terms of phonological processing, sound-symbol correspondence is key. Specifically, grapheme-to-phoneme correspondence is important to reading, but phoneme-to-grapheme correspondence is necessary for writing. Students must be able to string together the individual sounds that are mapped on the letters or letter groups in order to produce these words, all while taking into consideration vowel activity, vowel teams, consonants, consonant blends, consonant digraphs, syllable types, syllable division, and morphology (Dunson, 2013). This is the essence of decoding. Encoding requires the same knowledge, only in reverse. Phonological processing is a key aspect of both reading and writing.

Dyslexics score poorly on phonological assessments due to poor auditory discrimination and sequencing, as the tasks require verbal short-term memory. Writing, in keeping, requires auditory discrimination and verbal working memory to hold information so that a child can accurately map the phoneme to the appropriate grapheme. Poor phonological processing and poor verbal short-term memory, combined with slow lexical retrieval of phonological code stored in long-term memory, make writing problematic (Caylak, 2010; Landerl et al., 2019; Norton & Wolf, 2012; Pugh & Verhoeven, 2018; Vukovic & Siegel, 2006). Reading requires grapheme-to-phoneme correspondence, a challenge for readers with dyslexia that is made more difficult with a deep orthography (Aro & Wimmer, 2003; Borleffs et al., 2019; Goswami et al., 1998; Landerl et al., 1997; Marinelli et al., 2018; Navas et al., 2014; Seymour et al., 2003). Writing requires phoneme-to-grapheme correspondence, a greater challenge for students with dyslexia, as the phonological code for the English language that is stored in memory must be vast due to the depth of the orthography (Döhla & Heim, 2016; Döhla et al., 2018; Richlan, 2014). Coexistence with dysgraphia is more likely than not for dyslexia. Interestingly, the prevalence for dyslexia and the prevalence for dysgraphia both range between 7%–15% (Dehaene, 2009; Döhla & Heim, 2016; Temple, 2002)

Attention Deficit/Hyperactivity Disorder

ADHD is the disorder with the highest rate of coexistence with dyslexia (Carroll et al., 2005; Sexton et al., 2011). ADHD is a pattern of behavior characterized by deficits in executive functioning (Gray & Climie, 2016), inattention, hyperactivity, and impulsivity (American Psychiatric Association, 2013; Sexton et al., 2011). ADHD is composed of three behavioral subtypes: predominantly inattentive type, predominantly hyperactive-impulsive type, and combined type (Raskind et al., 2012). Worldwide prevalence of ADHD was 5.3%, with slightly higher estimates in North America (Sexton et al., 2011), and it is primarily observed in males compared to females.

Studies investigating the efficacy of interventions to improve the reading ability of children with both ADHD and specific learning disorder with impaired reading (SLD-R) are few in number (Gray & Climie, 2016). "Specific learning disorder" has become the umbrella term for mathematics, reading, and written expression disorders in the updated DSM-5. The DSM-IV classified these as separate diagnoses. Now, these disorders are housed under one diagnosis with added specifiers (e.g., specific learning disorder with impaired reading; Medina, 2018).

Research studies that have focused on reading interventions for children who have both ADHD and specific learning disorder with impaired reading (dyslexia) have predominantly included the use of medication treatments with stimulants and nonstimulants, although there is a plethora of empirical studies on the two individually (Gray & Climie, 2016). Based upon the few studies undertaken of both disorders together, some researchers have suggested that attention had a direct impact on the development of reading and writing skills (Döhla & Heim, 2016). They hypothesized that the distortion in the development of orthographic and phonological development was an indirect consequence of the deficits in spatial attention. As orthographic and phonological skills are key components of the writing process, writing skills would be adversely affected.

There are four primary manifestations of ADHD. Three are well known: inattention, hyperactivity, and impulsivity. Lack of focus and attention frequently results in poor academic performance and outcomes (Gray & Climie, 2016). Although some believe that distortion in the development of orthographic and phonological development was an indirect consequence of the deficits in spatial attention, executive functioning exhibits a trait that has been demonstrated, through extensive research (Raskind et al., 2012), to impact the development and utilization of phonological and orthographical development: working memory. A deficit in verbal short-term working memory has been shown to compromise the grapheme-to-phoneme correspondence required for reading (Caylak, 2010; Diamanti et al., 2017; Galaburda et al., 2006; Mann & Liberman, 1985) and the phoneme-to-grapheme correspondence required for writing (Diamanti et al., 2018; Galaburda et al., 2006; Richlan, 2014; Snowling, 2001). Poor verbal short-term memory combined with slow lexical retrieval of phonological code stored in long-term memory makes encoding and decoding difficult and labor intensive (Caylak, 2010; Landerl et al., 2019; Norton & Wolf, 2012; Pugh & Verhoeven, 2018; Vukovic & Siegel, 2006; Wolf & Bowers, 1999).

Twice-Exceptional Students With Dyslexia

Federal attention began to be directed toward students who are both gifted and have a disability in 2004 with the reauthorization of the Individuals With Disabilities Education Act (IDEA; Josephson et al., 2018). The concept is known as twice-exceptionality, or 2e. Twice-exceptional students are those who are intellectually gifted but also have difficulties, such as dyslexia, dysgraphia, ADHD, dyspraxia, or other sensory disorders (Reis et al., 2014).

Research on 2e has increased in the past 30 years, but like learning disabilities in general, many schools fail to understand the concept and, as a result, fail to meet the needs of these students. This lack of understanding of learning disabilities, like in the case of dyslexia, may lead to the misidentification of 2e students as underachievers and required interventions not being provided (Josephson et al., 2018).

The concept of students who are intellectually gifted while displaying a physical, hearing, or visual deficit is not new. Helen Keller and Stephen Hawking are prime examples (Lovett & Lewandowski, 2006). What is new is that scholars are now embracing the aforementioned learning disabilities of dyslexia—and its frequent coexisting differences, dysgraphia and ADHD—as they relate to aptitude/achievement discrepancies and processing deficits (Brody & Mills, 1997; Lovett & Lewandowski, 2006). Accepted today is the belief that the presence of a specific learning difficulty does not mean that a child is any less intellectually gifted. Dyslexia, dysgraphia, ADHD, and specific language impairment can coexist with intellectual potential in the same way as can physical, hearing, or visual deficits (Lovett & Sparks, 2011; Reis et al., 2014). Because these students are gifted, it is important that a strength-based approach to education is required (Baum et al., 2017). The biggest difficulty is often in persuading schools and local authorities to implement necessary support (Blustain, 2019).

Strategies and Interventions

1. Twice-exceptional students must be seen as gifted first. Therefore, enhanced remediation, or additional context, is required to meet their need for advanced content. Enhanced remediation augments the level of depth and complexity that goes beyond simply addressing the challenges of struggling readers.

2. Students should work with a highly qualified reading specialist who is trained in a methodology that has been scientifically proven to be effective for struggling readers to help with the remediation process. The approach used should follow a systematic and sequential path toward mastery of sound-symbol relationships in an effort to promote greater phonological awareness.

3. Language concepts should be taught using multisensory techniques in order to strengthen visual and auditory memory for language.

4. Reading instruction must be delivered with intensity and optimally, in very small groups or one to one. Research indicates that the reading

instruction is most effective when it is taught comprehensively and explicitly.

5. Students should receive this specialized reading instruction 5 days a week, at a minimum. Remediation and instruction should be of sufficient duration. One of the most common errors in teaching a student with reading challenges to read is to withdraw, prematurely, the instruction that seems to be working.

6. Students should be placed in an academic environment where class sizes and auditory/visual distractions are limited. This will allow them to receive the individualized attention that they require without sensory overload. Additionally, the school environment should be one where learning preferences are actively discussed and properly accommodated within the context of the academic curriculum.

7. Students should develop and use cursive writing skills in their written work. Consistent and legible cursive writing is a key kinesthetic element, and it is necessary for reinforcing reading and spelling concepts and communicating knowledge. Cursive writing teaches the words of the English language as cohesive strings or units.

8. Students with language-based reading disorders benefit from a multisensory, structured, sequential, cumulative, cognitive, flexible, emotionally sound, and diagnostic-prescriptive approach to reading instruction. The approach should be a phonics-based system that teaches the basics of word formation before whole meanings. As sound-symbol correspondence is not a naturally occurring process, it must be systematically and explicitly taught in a logical progression from the simple to complex. This approach places students in position to master the 85% of the English code that is phonetic. Further, and most importantly, it allows them to make intelligent choices towards mastering the remaining 15% of the English code that must be analyzed in order to be applied properly.

9. Students should engage in activities specifically designed to increased automatic recognition of letter patterns and reading rate while reinforcing phonics skills and sight word recognition.

10. Students should engage in activities specifically designed to develop the sensory-cognitive brain functions necessary for language and literacy development.

Resources

- Orton-Gillingham-based instructional materials and *The Gillingham Manual: Remedial Training for Students With Specific Disability in Reading, Spelling, and Penmanship*
- Recipe for Reading (https://eps.schoolspecialty.com/products/literacy/reading-intervention/recipe-for-reading/about-the-program)
- Wilson Reading System (https://www.wilsonlanguage.com/programs/wilson-reading-system)
- The Lindamood Phoneme Sequencing Program for Reading, Spelling, and Speech (https://ganderpublishing.com/content/lips-overview.asp)
- Visualizing and Verbalizing Program of Concept Imagery for Comprehension and Thinking (http://ganderpublishing.com/content/visualizing-and-verbalizing-overview.asp)
- Great Leaps for Reading (https://greatleaps.com)
- Six-Way Paragraphs (https://www.mheducation.com/prek-12/product/six-way-paragraphs-introductory-walter-pauk/9780844221243.html)

FROM THE EDITORS

Student Vignette

Leah

At 11, Leah is arguably one of the most well-liked girls in the sixth grade. Friends describe her as smart, cute, and fun. They envy her ability to get along with everyone; popular kids, smart kids, jocks, and nerds all like Leah. She skis competitively, has a great voice, and knows the lyrics to "all" of the songs. Although classroom work is not easy for Leah, she loves attending school. She likes the interaction with her classmates and enjoys several of her classes. She finds science interesting, especially class demonstrations and experiments. She actively participates in social studies and language arts class discussions but finds keeping up with the reading to be an ongoing challenge. Choir is her favorite, and math has become increasingly difficult for her.

FROM THE EDITORS, *continued*

Teachers enjoy Leah in class, describing her as a "respectful and conscientious student." Comments shared by teachers during conferences and on report cards indicate Leah's assignments are thorough and on time. Although group work, experiential learning, and projects are particular strengths for Leah, classroom and achievement test scores are typically in the average to low-average range. This is somewhat surprising given her third-grade Cognitive Abilities Test (CogAT) score of 132 and past participation in the elementary gifted program.

When Leah admits during her sixth-grade conference that homework can, at times, seem overwhelming, her teachers are surprised. They assume her contributions to class discussions reflect a wide range of knowledge and above-average reading ability. They are not aware that Leah reads very slowly, often rereading passages many times for basic comprehension. Leah realizes she spends far more time on her homework than her peers and is beginning to wonder if something is wrong. She is exhausted and discouraged by late nights of study. Once confident, she now questions her own capability and if she will be allowed to take the enriched and accelerated courses that interest her.

At the request of Leah's family, a special needs assessment is conducted to determine if Leah has all compensatory components required for reading. During a preliminary interview with Leah, the assessment team notes that she is highly verbal, is articulate, and uses advanced vocabulary appropriately. She presents herself as an intelligent and pleasant young lady who is clearly frustrated by issues with homework. When the team reviews Leah's records and discovers a descending pattern of achievement, they determine further investigation is needed. They begin with reading assessments. They note the discrepancy and Leah's difficulties with spelling and sequencing, which make problem solving and note-taking difficult. Further, Leah's difficulties with sequencing, working memory, and reading also impact her ability to complete numerical operations and story problems in math.

When the team shares their assessment findings with Leah's parents, they note many of her weaknesses are consistent with those found in students with dyslexia. They recommend consultation with a dyslexia specialist. Leah's parents are surprised but relieved to know that their daughter has received a thorough assessment and that a diagnosis may lead to a solution.

FROM THE EDITORS, *continued*

Discussion Questions

1. What is Leah's greatest school challenge? As she moves through the school system, are the challenges she faces likely to increase or decrease? Why, or why not?
2. In what ways can classroom teachers modify the curriculum to address the needs of twice-exceptional students with reading difficulties? Should the grading rubric be modified as well? Why, or why not?
3. What type of assessment is likely to provide the most accurate picture of Leah's strengths and relative weaknesses? Why? What conversation, if any, would you have with Leah prior to assessment?
4. Should twice-exceptional students be allowed to take accelerated classes? Why, or why not?
5. How would professional development training help classroom teachers identify a twice-exceptional student?

References

American Psychiatric Association. (2013). *Diagnostic and statistical manual of mental disorders* (5th ed.). https://doi.org/10.1176/appi.books.9780890425596

Aro, M., & Wimmer, H. (2003). Learning to read: English in comparison to six more regular orthographies. *Applied Psycholinguistics, 24*(4), 621–635. https://doi.org/10.1017/S0142716403000316

Balmuth, M. (2009). *The roots of phonics: A historical introduction* (Rev. ed.). Brookes.

Baum S. M., Schader, R. M., & Owen, S. V. (2017). *To be gifted and learning disabled: Strength-based strategies for helping twice-exceptional students with LD, ADHD, ASD, and more* (3rd ed.). Prufrock Press.

Bäuml, F. H. (1980). Varieties and consequences of medieval literacy and illiteracy. *Speculum, 55*(2), 237–265. https://doi.org/10.2307/2847287

Beeson, P. M., & Insalaco, D. (1998). Acquired alexia: Lessons from successful treatment. *Journal of the International Neuropsychology Society, 4*(6), 621–635. https://doi.org/10.1017/S1355617798466116

Benton, A. (2000). *Exploring the history of neuropsychology: Selected papers.* Oxford University Press.

Berninger, V. W., Nielsen, K. H., Abbott, R. D., Wijsman, E., & Raskind, W. (2008). Writing problems in developmental dyslexia: Under-recognized and under-treated. *Journal of School Psychology, 46*(1), 1–21.

Bishop, D. V., & Adams, C. (1990). A prospective study of the relationship between specific language impairment, phonological disorders and reading retardation. *Child Psychology and Psychiatry and Allied Disciplines, 31*(7), 1027–1050. https://doi.org/10.1111/j.1469-7610.1990.tb00844.x

Blachman, B. A. (1991). Phonological awareness: Implications form prereading and early reading instruction. In S. A. Brady & D. P. Shankweiler (Eds.), *Phonological processes in literacy: A tribute to Isabelle Y. Liberman* (pp. 29–36). Erlbaum.

Blustain, R. (2019). *Twice exceptional, doubly disadvantaged? How schools struggle to serve gifted students with disabilities.* The Hechinger Report. https://hechingerreport.org/twice-exceptional-doubly-disadvantaged-how-schools-struggle-to-serve-gifted-students-with-disabilities

Bolger, D. J., Perfetti, C. A., & Schneider, W. (2005). Cross-cultural effect on the brain revisited: Universal structures plus writing system variation. *Human Brain Mapping, 25*(1), 92–104. https://doi.org/10.1002/hbm.20124

Borleffs, E., Maassen, B. A. M., Lyytinen, H., & Zwarts, F. (2019). Cracking the code: The impact of orthographic transparency and morphological-syllabic complexity on reading and developmental dyslexia. *Frontiers in Psychology, 9,* 2534. https://doi.org/10.3389/fpsyg.2018.02534

Bouhali, F., Thiebaut de Schotten, M., Pinel, P., Poupon, C., Mangin, J. F., Dehaene, S., & Cohen, L. (2014). Anatomical connections of the visual word form area. *Journal of Neuroscience, 34*(46), 15402–15414. https://doi.org/10.1523/JNEUROSCI.4918-13.2014

Brady, S. A., & Shankweiler, D. P. (Eds.). (1991). *Phonological processes in literacy: A tribute to Isabelle Y. Liberman.* Erlbaum.

Brody, L. E., & Mills, C. J. (1997). Gifted children with learning disabilities: A review of the issues. *Journal of Learning Disabilities, 30*(3), 282–296. https://doi.org/10.1177/002221949703000304

Bruck, M. (1990). Word-recognition skills of adults with childhood diagnoses of dyslexia. *Developmental Psychology, 26*(3), 439–454. https://doi.org/10.1037/0012-1649.26.3.439

Calvert, G., Spence, C., & Stein, B. E. (2004). *The handbook of multisensory processes*. MIT Press.

Carroll, J. M., Maughan, B., Goodman, R., & Meltzer, H. (2005). Literacy difficulties and psychiatric disorders: evidence for comorbidity. *The Journal of Child Psychology and Psychiatry, 46*(5), 524–532. https://doi.org/10.111 1/j.1469-7610.2004.00366.x

Caylak, E. (2009). Neurobiological approaches on brains of children with dyslexia: Review. *Academic Radiology, 16*(8), 1003–1024. https://doi.org/10. 1016/j.acra.2009.02.012

Caylak, E. (2010). The studies about phonological deficit theory in children with developmental dyslexia: Review. *American Journal of Neuroscience, 1*(1), 1–12.

Centanni, T., Norton, E., Ozernov-Palchik, O., Park, A., Beach, S., Halverson, K., Gaab, N., Gabrieli, J. (2019). Disrupted left fusiform response to print in beginning kindergartners is associated with subsequent reading. *Neuroimage: Clinical, 22*, 101715. https://doi.org/10.1016/j.nicl.2019.101 715

Chall, J. S. (1983). *Stages of reading development*. McGraw-Hill.

Chomsky, N. (1957). *Syntactic structures*. Mouton.

Cohen, L., Lehéricy, S., Chochon, F., Lemer, C., Rivaud, S., & Dehaene, S. (2002). Language-specific tuning of visual cortex? Functional properties of the visual word form area. *Brain, 125*, 1054–1069.

Compston, D. A. (2016). A psychological inquiry into the nature of the condition known as congenital word-blindness. By Lucy G. Fildes. *Brain* 1921; 44: 286–307. With a neurological appraisal of familial congenital word-blindness. By Arthur L. Drew. From Department of Neurology, University of Michigan, Ann Arbor, Michigan, USA. *Brain* 1956; 79: 440–60. *Brain, 139*(10), 2804–2808. https://doi.org/10.1093/brain/aww210

Conner, L. (2017). Understanding dyslexia: Competing theories, expanding definitions and ongoing controversy. *The STeP Journal: Student Teacher Perspectives, 4*(2), 11–18.

Converse, P. J. (2001). *Doublecortin domain-containing protein 2; DCDC2*. https://www.omim.org/entry/605755

Costenaro, V., & Pesce, A. (2012). Dyslexia and the phonological deficit hypothesis: Developing phonological awareness in young English language learners. *EL.LE, 1*(3). http://doi.org/10.14277/2280-6792/38p

Cremin, L. A. (1970). *American education: the colonial experience, 1607–1783*. Harper and Row.

Dehaene, S. (2004). Evolution of human cortical circuits from reading to arithmetic: the "neuronal recycling" hypothesis. In S. Dehaene, J.- R. Duhamel,

M. D. Hauser, & G. Rizzolatti (Eds.), *From monkey brain to human brain: A Fyssen Foundation Symposium*. MIT Press.

Dehaene, S. (2009). *Reading in the brain: The new science of how we read*. Penguin Books.

Dehaene, S. (2011). The massive impact of literacy on the brain and its consequences for education. In A. M. Battro, S. Dehane, & W. J. Singer (Eds.), *Human neuroplasticity and education: The proceedings of the Working Group 27–28 October 2010* (pp. 19–32, 237–238). Pontifical Academiae Scientiarvm, Vatican City.

Dehaene, S., Le Clec'H, G., Poline, J.-B., Le Bihan, D., & Laurent, C. (2002). The visual word form area: A prelexical representation of visual words in the fusiform gyrus. *Neuroreport, 13*(3), 321–325.

DeMille, M. M. C., Tang, K., Mehta, C. M., Geissler, C., Malins, J. G., Powers, N. R., Bowen, B. M., Adams, A. K., Truong, D. T., Frijters, J. C., & Gruen, J. R. (2018). Worldwide distribution of the DCDC2 READ1 regulatory element and its relationship with phoneme variation across languages. *Proceedings of the National Academy of Sciences of the United States, 115*(19), 4951–4956. https://doi.org/10.1073/pnas.1710472115

Dennis, M. Y., Paracchini, S., Scerri, T. S., Prokunina-Olsson, L., Knight, J. C., Wade-Martins, R., Coggill, P., Beck, S., Green, E. D., & Monaco, A. P. (2009). A common variant associated with dyslexia reduces expression of the KIAA0319 gene. *PLOS Genetics, 5*(3), e1000436. https://doi.org/10.1371/journal.pgen.1000436

Diamanti, V., Goulandris, N., Campbell, R., & Protopapas, A. (2018). Dyslexia profiles across orthographies differing in transparency: An evaluation of theoretical predictions contrasting English and Greek. *Scientific Studies of Reading, 22*(1), 55–69. https://doi.org/10.1080/10888438.2017.1338291

Döhla, D., & Heim, S. (2016). Developmental dyslexia and dysgraphia: What can we learn from the one about the other? *Frontiers in Psychology, 6*, 2045. https://doi.org/10.3389/fpsyg.2015.02045

Döhla, D., Willmes, K., & Heim, S. (2018). Cognitive profiles of developmental dysgraphia. *Frontiers in Psychology, 9*, 2006. https://doi.org/10.3389/fpsyg.2018.02006

Dunson, W. E. (2013). *School success for kids with dyslexia and other reading difficulties*. Prufrock Press.

Elnakib, A., Soliman, A., Nitzken, M., Casanova, M. F., Gimel'farb, G., & El-Baz, A. (2014). Magnetic resonance imaging findings for dyslexia: a survey. *Journal of Biomedical Nanotechnology, 10*(10), 1–28. https://doi.org/10.1166/jbn.2014.1895

Ellis, N. C., & Hooper, A. M. (2001). It is easier to learn to read in Welsh than in English: Effects of orthographic transparency demonstrated using frequency-matched cross-linguistic reading tests. *Applied Psycholinguistics, 22*, 571–599.

Ellis, N. C., Natsume, M., Stavropoulou, K., Hoxhallari, L., Van Daal, V. H. P., Polyzoe, N., Tsipa, M.-L., & Petalas, M. (2004). The effects of orthographic depth on learning to read alphabetic, syllabic, and logographic scripts. *Reading Research Quarterly, 39*(4), 438–468. https://doi.org/10.1598/RRQ.39.4.5

Ervin, M. (2001). SLI: What we know and why it matters. *The ASHA Leader, 6*(12), 4–31. https://doi.org/10.1044/leader.FTR1.06122001.4

Fildes, L. G. (1921). A psychological inquiry into the nature of the condition known as congenital word-blindness. *Brain: A Journal of Neurology, 44*(3), 286–307. https://doi.org/10.1093/brain/44.3.286

Finucci, J. M., Guthrie, J. T., Childs, A. L., Abbey, H., & Childs, B. (1976). The genetics of specific reading disability. *Annals of Human Genetics, 40*(1), 1–23. https://doi.org/10.1111/j.1469-1809.1976.tb00161.x

Fowler, A. E. (1991). How early phonological development might set the stage for phonemic awareness. In S. A. Brady & D. P. Shankweiler (Eds.), *Phonological processes in literacy: A tribute to Isabelle Y. Liberman* (pp. 97–117). Erlbaum.

Frith, U., Wimmer, H., & Landerl, K. (1998) Differences in phonological recoding in German and English-speaking children. *Scientific Studies of Reading, 2*(1), 31–54. https://doi.org/10.1207/s1532799xssr0201_2

Fromkin, V., Rodman, R., & Hyams, N. (2014). *An introduction to language* (10th ed.). Cengage Learning.

Galaburda, A. M., LoTurco, J., Ramus, F., & Fitch, R. H., & Rosen, G. D. (2006). From genes to behavior in developmental dyslexia. *Nature Neuroscience, 9*, 1213–1217. https://doi.org/10.1038/nn1772

Galaburda, A. M., Sherman, G. F., Rosen, G. D., Aboitiz, F., & Geschwind, N. (1985). Developmental dyslexia: Four consecutive patients with cortical anomalies. *Annals of Neurology, 18*(2), 222–233. https://doi.org/10.1002/ana.410180210

Gayán Guardiola, J. (2001). The evolution of research on dyslexia. *Anuario Psicologia, 32*(1), 3–30.

Georgiou, G. K., Torppa, M., Manolitsis, G., Lyytinen, H., & Parrila, R. (2012). Longitudinal predictors of reading and spelling across languages varying in orthographic consistency. *Reading and Writing: An Interdisciplinary Journal, 25*(2), 321–346. https://doi.org/10.1007/s11145-010-9271-x

Gillingham, A., & Stillman, B. W. (1997). *The Gillingham manual: Remedial training for students with specific disability in reading, spelling, and penmanship* (8th ed.). Educators Publishing Service.

Goswami, U., Gombert, J. E., & de Barrera, L. F. (1998). Children's orthographic representations and linguistic transparency: Nonsense word reading in English, French, and Spanish. *Applied Psycholinguistics, 19*(1), 19–52. https://doi.org/10.1017/S0142716400010560

Goswami, U., Porpodas, C., & Wheelwright, S. (1997) Children's orthographic representations in English and Greek. *European Journal of Psychology of Education, 12,* 273. https://doi.org/10.1007/BF03172876

Gray, C., & Climie, E. A. (2016). Children with attention-deficit/hyperactivity disorder and reading disability: A review of the efficacy of medication treatments. *Frontiers in Psychology, 7,* 988. https://doi.org/10.3389/fpsyg.2016.00988

Hairston, W. D., Burdette, J. H., Flowers, D. L., Wood, F. B., & Wallace, M. T. (2005). Altered temporal profile of visual–auditory multisensory interactions in dyslexia. *Experimental Brain Research, 166,* 474–480. https://doi.org/10.1007/s00221-005-2387-6

Hallgren, B. (1950). *Specific dyslexia ("congenital word-blindness"): A clinical and genetic study.* Munksgaards Forlag.

Hart, B., & Risley, T. R. (1995). *Meaningful differences in the everyday experience of young American children.* Brookes.

Howard, M. C. (2012). *Transnationalism in ancient and medieval societies: The role of cross-border trade and travel.* McFarland.

Hu, W., Lee, H. L., Zhang, Q., Liu, T., Geng, L. B., Seghier, M. L., Shakeshaft, C., Twomey, T., Green, D. W., Yang, Y. M., & Price. C. J. (2010). Developmental dyslexia in Chinese and English populations: Dissociating the effect of dyslexia from language differences. *Brain, 133*(6), 1694–1706. https://doi.org/10.1093/brain/awq106

International Dyslexia Association. (2002). *Definition of dyslexia.* https://dyslexiaida.org/definition-of-dyslexia

Josephson, J., Wolfgang, C., & Mehrenberg, R. (2018). Strategies for supporting students who are twice-exceptional. *The Journal of Special Education Apprenticeship, 7*(2). https://files.eric.ed.gov/fulltext/EJ1185416.pdf

Kaltner, J., & McKenzie, S. (2002). *Beyond Babel: A handbook for biblical Hebrew and related languages.* Brill Academic.

Katz, L., & Frost, R. (1992). The reading process is different for different orthographies: The orthographic depth hypothesis. *Advances in Psychology, 94,* 67–84. https://doi.org/10.1016/S0166-4115(08)62789-2

Kearns, D. M., Hancock, R., Hoeft, F., Pugh, K. R., & Frost, S. J. (2019). The neurobiology of dyslexia. *Teaching Exceptional Children, 51*(3), 175–188. https://doi.org/10.1177/0040059918820051

Kirby, P. (2018, March). A brief history of dyslexia. *The Psychologist, 31,* 56–59.

Kronbichler, M., Hutzler, F., Wimmer, H., Mair, A., Staffen, W., & Ladurner, G. (2004). The visual word form area and the frequency with which words are encountered: Evidence for a parametric fMRI study. *NeuroImage, 21*(3), 946–953. https://doi.org/10.1016/j.neuroimage.2003.10.021

Landerl, K., Freudenthaler, H. H., Heene, M., De Jong, P. F., Desrochers, A., Manolitsis, G., Parrila, R., & Georgiou, G. K. (2019). Phonological aware-ness and rapid automatized naming as longitudinal predictors of read-ing in five alphabetic orthographies with varying degrees of consistency. *Scientific Studies of Reading, 23*(3), 220–234. https://doi.org/10.1080/108 88438.2018.1510936

Landerl, K., Wimmer, H., & Frith, U. (1997). The impact of orthographic consistency on dyslexia: A German-English comparison. *Cognition, 63*(3), 315–334. https://doi.org/10.1016/S0010-0277(97)00005-X

Liu, L., Tao, R., Wang, W., You, W., Peng, D., & Booth, J. R. (2013, October). Chinese dyslexics show neural differences in morphological processing. *Developmental Cognitive Neuroscience, 6,* 40–50. https://doi.org/10.1016/j.dcn.2013.06.004

Lovett, B. J., & Lewandowski, L. J. (2006). Gifted students with learning dis-abilities: Who are they? *Journal of Learning Disabilities, 39*(6), 515–527. https://doi.org/10.1177/00222194060390060401

Lovett, B. J., & Sparks, R. L. (2011). The identification and performance of gifted students with learning disability diagnoses: A quantitative synthesis. *Journal of Learning Disabilities, 46*(4), 304–316.

Lyon, G. R., & Krasnegor, N. A. (1996). *Attention, memory, and executive func-tion.* Brookes.

Lyon, G. R., Shaywitz, S. E., & Shaywitz, B. A. (2003). A definition of dyslexia. *Annals of Dyslexia, 53*(1), 1–14. https://www.jstor.org/stable/23764731

Mann, V. A., & Liberman, I. Y. (1984). Phonological awareness and verbal short-term memory. *Journal of Learning Disabilities, 17*(10), 592–599. https://doi.org/10.1177/002221948401701005

Mano, Q. R., Humphries, C., Desai, R. H., Seidenberg, M., Osmon, D. C., Stengel, B. C., & Binder, J. (2012). The role of left occipitotemporal cortex in reading: reconciling stimulus, task, and lexicality effects. *Cerebral Cortex, 23*(4), 988–1001.

Marinelli, C., Putzolu, A., Salvatore, M., Iaia, M., & Angelelli, P. (2018). Developmental phonological dyslexia and dysgraphia in a regular orthography: A case study. *Journal of InterDisciplinary Research Applied to Medicine*, 2(1), 67–82.

Mascheretti, S., De Luca, A., Trezzi, V., Peruzzo, D., Nordio, A., Marino, C., & Arrigoni, F. (2017). Neurogenetics of developmental dyslexia: From genes to behavior through brain neuroimaging and cognitive and sensorial mechanisms. *Translational Psychiatry, 7*, e987. https://doi.org/10.1038/tp.2016.240

Medina, J. (2018). *Specific learning disorder*. Psych Central. https://psychcentral.com/disorders/specific-learning-disorder

Meng, H., Smith, S. D., Hager, K., Held, M., Liu, J., Olson, R. K., Pennington, B. F., DeFries, J. C., Gelernter, J., O'Reilly-Pol, T., Somlo, S., Skudlarski, P., Shaywitz, S. E., Shaywitz, B. A., Marchione, K., Wang, Y., Paramasivam, M., LoTurco, J. J., Page, G. P., & Gruen, J. R. (2005). DCDC2 is associated with reading disability and modulates neuronal development in the brain. *Proceedings of the National Academy of Sciences of the United States of America, 102*(47), 17053–17058. https://doi.org/10.1073/pnas.0508591102

Moats, L. (2000). *Speech to print: Language essentials for teachers*. Brookes.

Monzalvo, K., Fluss, J., Billard, C., Dehaene, S., & Dehaene-Lambertz, G. (2012). Cortical networks for vision and language in dyslexic and normal children of variable socio-economic status. *Neuroimage, 61*(1), 258–274. https://doi.org/10.1016/j.neuroimage.2012.02.035

Nakamura, K., Jui-Wen, K., Pegado, F., Cohen, L., Tzeng, O., & Dehaene, S. (2012). Universal brain systems for recognizing word shapes and handwriting gestures during reading. *Proceedings of the National Academy of Sciences of the United States of America, 109*(50), 20762–20767. https://doi.org/10.1073/pnas.1217749109

National Reading Panel. (2000). *Teaching children to read. An evidence-based assessment of the scientific research literature on reading and its implications for reading instruction*. U. S. Department of Health and Human Services. https://www.nichd.nih.gov/publications/pubs/nrp/smallbook

Navas, A. L. G. P., Ferraz, É. C., & Borges, J. P. A. (2014). Phonological processing deficits as a universal model for dyslexia: Evidence from different orthographies. *CoDAS, 26*(6), 509–519. http://dx.doi.org/10.1590/2317-1782/20142014135

Nittrouer, S., Lowenstein, J. H., Wucinich, T., & Moberly, A. C. (2016). Verbal working memory in older adults: The roles of phonological capacities and processing speed. *Journal of Speech, Language, and Hearing Research, 59*(6), 1520–1532. https://doi.org/10.1044/2016_JSLHR-H-15-0404

Norton, E. S., & Wolf, M. (2012). Rapid automatized naming (RAN) and reading fluency: Implications for understanding and treatment of reading disabilities on brain activity of listeners: An fMRI Study. *Annual Review of Psychology, 63*, 427–452.

Öney, B., & Durgunoğlu, A. Y. (1997). Beginning to read in Turkish: A phonologically transparent orthography. *Applied Psycholinguistics, 18*(1), 1–15. https://doi.org/10.1017/S014271640000984X

Orton, S. T. (1928). Specific reading disability—strephosymbolia. *Journal of the American Medical Association, 90*(14), 1095–1099.

Ostovar-Namaghi, S. A., Hosseini, S. M., & Norouzi, S. (2015). Reading fluency techniques from the bottom up: A grounded theory. *International Journal of Applied Linguistics and English Literature, 4*(5), 2200–3592. http://dx.doi.org/10.7575/aiac.ijalel.v.4n.5p.29

Paracchini, S., Steer, C. D., Buckingham, L. L., Morris, A. P., Ring, S., Scerri, T., Stein, J., Pembrey, M. E., Ragoussis, J., Golding, J., Monaco, A. P. (2008). Association of the KIAA0319 dyslexia susceptibility gene with reading skills in the general population. *American Journal of Psychiatry, 165*(12), 1576–1584. https://doi.org/10.1176/appi.ajp.2008.07121872

Paulesu, E., McCrory, E., Fazio, F., Menoncello, L., Brunswick, N., Cappa, S. F., Cotelli, M., Cossu, G., Corte, F., Lorusso, M., Pesenti, S., Gallagher, A., Perani, D., Price, C., Frith, C. D., & Frith, U. (2000). A cultural effect on brain function. *Nature Neuroscience, 3*, 91–96. https://doi.org/10.1038/71163

Paulesu, E., Démonet, J.-F., Fazio, F., McCrory, E., Chanoine, V., Brunswick, N., Cappa, S. F., Cossu, G., Habib, M., Frith, C., & Frith, U. (2001). Dyslexia: cultural diversity and biological unity. *Science, 291*(5511), 2165–2167.

Perfetti, C. A., & Dunlap, S. (2008). Learning to read: General principles and writing system variations. In K. Koda & A. M. Zehler (Eds.), *Learning to read across languages: Cross-linguistic relationships in first- and second-language development* (pp. 13–35). Routledge.

Pinel, P., Lalanne, C., Bourgeron, T., Fauchereau, F., Poupon, C., Artiges, E., Le Bihan, D., Dehaene-Lambertz, G., & Dehaene, S. (2014). Genetic and environmental influences on the visual word form and fusiform face areas. *Cerebral Cortex, 25*(9), 2478–2493. https://doi.org/10.1093/cercor/bhu048

Pinker, S. (1994). *The language instinct*. Pelican Books.

Post, Y. V., Swank, P. R., Hiscock, M., & Fowler, A. E. (1999). Identification of vowel speech sounds by skilled and less skilled readers and the relation with vowel spelling. *Annals of Dyslexia, 49*, 161–194.

Powers, N. R., Eicher, J. D., Butter, F., Kong, Y., Miller, L. L., Ring, S. M., Mann, M., & Gruen, J. R. (2013). Alleles of a polymorphic ETV6 binding site in DCDC2 confer risk of reading and language impairment. *American*

Journal of Human Genetics, 93(1), 19–28. https://doi.org/10.1016/j.ajhg.
2013.05.008

Powers, N. R., Eicher, J. D., Miller, L. L., Kong, Y., Smith, S. D., Pennington, B. F., Willcutt, E. G., Olson, R. K., Susan M Ring, S. M., & Gruen, J. R. (2016). The regulatory element READ1 epistatically influences reading and language, with both deleterious and protective alleles. *Journal of Medical Genetics, 53,* 163–171.

Pugh, K., & Verhoeven, L. (2018). Introduction to this special issue: Dyslexia across languages and writing systems. *Scientific Studies of Reading, 22*(1), 1–6. https://doi.org/10.1080/10888438.2017.1390668

Pyles, T., & Algeo, J. (1993). *The origins and development of the English language.* Thomson Learning.

Ramus, F., Rosen, S., Dakin, S. C., Day, B. L., Castellote, J. M., White, S., & Frith, U. (2003). Theories of developmental dyslexia: insights from a multiple case study of dyslexic adults. *Brain, 126*(4), 841–865. https://doi.org/10.1093/brain/awg076

Raskind, W. H., Peter, B., Richards, T., Eckert, M. M., & Berninger, V. W. (2012). The genetics of reading disabilities: From phenotypes to candidate genes. *Frontiers in Psychology, 3,* 601. https://doi.org/10.3389/fpsyg.2012.00601

Reis, S. M., Baum, S. M., & Burke, E. (2014). An operational definition of twice exceptional learners: Implications and applications. *Gifted Child Quarterly, 58*(3), 217–230. https://doi.org/10.1177/0016986214534976

Richlan, F. (2014). Functional neuroanatomy of developmental dyslexia: the role of orthographic depth. *Frontiers in Human Neuroscience, 8,* 347. https://doi.org/10.3389/fnhum.2014.00347

Richlan, F., Sturm, D., Schurz, M., Kronbichler, M., Ladurner, G., & Wimmer, H. (2010). A common left occipito-temporal dysfunction in developmental dyslexia and acquired letter-by-letter reading? *PLOS ONE 5*(8), e12073. https://doi.org/10.1371/journal.pone.0012073

Scerri, T. S., MacPherson, E., Martinelli, A., Wa, W. C., Monaco, A. P., Stein, J., Zheng, M., Sun-Han Ho, C., McBride, C., Snowling, M., Hulme, C., Hayiou-Thomas, M. E., Waye, M. M. Y., Talcott, J. B., & Paracchini, S. (2017). The *DCDC2 deletion is not a risk factor for dyslexia. Translational Psychiatry, 7,* e1182. https://doi.org/10.1038/tp.2017.151

Schmalz, X., Marinus, E., Coltheart, M., & Castles, A. (2015). Getting to the bottom of orthographic depth. *Psychonomic Bulletin and Review, 22,* 1614–1629. https://doi.org/10.3758/s13423-015-0835-2

Schuster, S., Hawelka, S., Richlan, F., Ludersdorfer, P., & Hutzler, F. (2015). Eyes on words: A fixation-related fMRI study of the left occipito-temporal cortex during self-paced silent reading of words and pseudowords. *Scientific Reports, 5,* 12686. https://doi.org/10.1038/srep12686

Seidenberg, M. (2017). *Language at the speed of sight: How we read, why so many can't, and what can be done about it.* Basic Books.

Sexton, C. C., Gelhorn, H. L., Bell, J. A., & Classi, P. M. (2011). The co-occurrence of reading disorder and ADHD. *Journal of Learning Disabilities, 45*(6), 538–564.

Seymour, P. H. K., Aro, M., & Erskine, J. M. (2003). Foundation literacy acquisition in European orthographies. *British Journal of Psychology, 94*(2), 143–174. https://doi.org/10.1348/000712603321661859

Shams, L., & Seitz, A. R. (2008). Benefits in multisensory learning. *Trends in Cognitive Neuroscience, 12*(11), 411–417.

Shaywitz, S. (2020). *Overcoming dyslexia* (2nd ed.). Knopf.

Shaywitz, S. E. (1996, November). *Dyslexia.* Scientific American. https://www.scientificamerican.com/article/dyslexia

Shaywitz, S. E., Fletcher, J. M., Holahan, J. M., Shneider, A. E., Marchione, K. E., Stuebing, K. K., Francis, D. J., Pugh, K. R., & Shaywitz, B. A. (1999). Persistence of dyslexia: The Connecticut longitudinal study at adolescence. *Pediatrics, 104*(6), 1351–1359. https://doi.org/10.1542/peds.104.6.1351

Shimogo, S., & Shams, L. (2001). Sensory modalities are not separate modalities: Plasticity and interactions. *Current Opinion in Neurobiology, 11*(4), 505–509. https://doi.org/10.1016/S0959-4388(00)00241-5

Siegel, L. S. (2006). Perspectives on dyslexia. *Paediatrics & Child Health, 11*(9), 581–587. https://doi.org/10.1093/pch/11.9.581

Slotnick, S. (2013). *Controversies in cognitive neuroscience.* Palgrave Macmillan.

Snowling, M. J. (2001). From language to reading and dyslexia. *Dyslexia, 7*(1), 37–46. https://doi.org/10.1002/dys.185

Sprenger-Charolles, L., Colé, P., & Serniclaes, W. (2006). *Reading acquisition and developmental dyslexia.* CRC Press.

Sprenger-Charolles, L., & Siegel, L. (2013, Winter). Reading acquisition and dyslexia in languages varying in orthographic depth. *Perspectives on Literacy and Language*, 23–31.

Temple, E. (2002). Brain mechanisms in normal and dyslexic readers. *Current Opinion in Neurobiology, 12*(2), 178–183. https://doi.org/10.1016/S0959-4388(02)00303-3

Thorstad, G. (1991). The effect of orthography on the acquisition of literacy skills. *British Journal of Psychology, 82*(4), 527–537. https://doi.org/10.1111/j.2044-8295.1991.tb02418.x

Uhry, J. (2013, Winter). The role of phonemic awareness in learning to read and spell successfully. *Perspectives on Language and Literacy*, 11–16.

Ullman, M. T., & Pierpont, E. I. (2005). Specific language impairment is not specific to language: The procedural deficit hypothesis. *Cortex, 41*(3), 399–433.

Valentine, E. (2019). A lady of unusual ability and force of character. *The Psychologist, 32,* 76–78.

Vanderauwera, J., Altarelli, I., Vandermosten, M., DeVos, A., Wouters, J., & Ghesquière, P. (2018). Atypical structural asymmetry of the planum temporale is related to family history of dyslexia. *Cerebral Cortex, 28*(1), 63–72. https://doi.org/10.1093/cercor/bhw348

Verhoeven, L. T. W., & Perfetti, C. (2017). *Learning to read across languages and writing systems.* Cambridge University Press.

Vukovic, R. K., & Siegel, L. S. (2006). The double deficit hypothesis: A comprehensive analysis of the evidence. *Journal of Learning Disabilities, 39*(1), 25–47. https://doi.org/10.1177/00222194060390010401

Wagner, R. (1973). Rudolf Berlin: Originator of the term dyslexia. *Bulletin of the Orton Society, 23,* 57–63. https://www.jstor.org/stable/23769538

Welty, Y. T., Menn, L., & Oishi, N. (2014). Developmental reading disorders in Japan—Prevalence, profiles, and possible mechanisms. *Topics in Language Disorders, 34*(2), 121–132.

Widjaja, V., & Winskel, H. (2004). Phonological awareness and word reading in a transparent orthography: Preliminary findings on Indonesian. In S. Cassidy, F. Cox, R. Mannell, & S. Palethorpe (Eds.), *Proceedings of the 10th Australian international conference on speech science and technology: Macquarie University, Sydney, 8–10 December, 2004* (pp. 370–375). Australian Speech Science and Technology Association.

Wimmer, H., & Hummer, P. (1990). How German-speaking first graders read and spell: Doubts on the importance of the logographic stage. *Applied Psycholinguistics, 11*(4), 349–368. https://doi.org/10.1017/S014271640000 09620

Wise, B., & Snyder L. (2003, August 27–28) *Clinical judgments in identifying and teaching children with language-based reading difficulties* [Paper presentation]. Learning Disabilities Summit: Building a Foundation for the Future, Washington, DC, United States.

Wolf, M. (2013, Fall). *A Literate Nation white paper: How the reading brain resolves the reading wars.* Literate Nation.

Wolf, M., & Bowers, P. G. (1999). The double-deficit hypothesis for the developmental dyslexias. *Journal of Educational Psychology, 91*(3), 415–438. https://doi.org/10.1037/0022-0663.91.3.415

Wolf, M., Ullman-Shade, C., & Gottwald, S. (2012). The emerging, evolving reading brain in digital culture. *Journal of Cognitive Education and Psychology, 11*(3). https://doi.org/10.1891/1945-8959.11.3.230

Yopp, H. K. (1992). Developing phonemic awareness in young children. *The Reading Teacher, 45*(9), 696–703. https://www.jstor.org/stable/20200960

Ziegler, J. C., & Goswami, U. (2005). Reading acquisition, developmental dyslexia, and skilled reading across languages: A psycholinguistic grain size theory. *Psychological Bulletin, 131*(1), 3–29. https://doi.org/10.1037/0033-2909.131.1.3

Zinn, K. (2013). Literacy, pharaonic Egypt. In R. S. Bagnall, K. Brodersen, C. B. Champion, A. Erskine, & S. R. Hueber (Eds.), *The encyclopedia of ancient history*. Wiley-Blackwell. https://doi.org/10.1002/9781444338386.wbeah15244

CHAPTER 5

Gifted Learners and Dyslexia

Designing Interventions Without Labels

Eleonoor van Gerven[1]

This chapter focuses on gifted learners with characteristics of dyslexia. The scientific definition of dyslexia, the causes of dyslexia, or the diagnostics of dyslexia are not disputed, nor is the identification process of giftedness combined with dyslexia. Instead, this chapter explores what may affect the education of gifted learners with severe reading and/or spelling difficulties, and opportunities to optimize the education of this group of twice-exceptional learners. In order to do this, this chapter first stresses the unicity of the educational profile of gifted students with dyslexia.

In this context, educational needs are defined. Second, working definitions for giftedness, dyslexia, and twice-exceptionality are explained. Third, why gifted students with dyslexia may be hard to identify is explored by focusing on two key concepts: severe and persevering problems. Fourth, this chapter explores how a systemic intervention matrix enables teachers to set up a custom educational design for their gifted students with dyslexia, addressing strengths and talents, and weaknesses.

---

1 This chapter could not have been written without the help and support of Annemieke Weterings, MEP.

165

There are no two gifted learners with dyslexia who have identical strengths and weaknesses (Maddocks, 2020; van Gerven, 2018); each student is unique (Foley-Nicpon et al., 2011; Reis et al., 2014). Differences in students' profiles are determined by (1) their strengths and weaknesses in their intelligence profile, (2) their strengths and weaknesses defined by dyslexia, (3) the interplay of being gifted and dyslexic, and (4) the interplay between their educational needs and the responses of their ecological systems (Foley-Nicpon & Kim, 2018; van Gerven, 2018). As a result of their individual profiles, there is no single intervention that is a meaningful response for all gifted students with dyslexia. Consequently, every strategy that is described in this chapter has its own nuances in a teacher's practice. They all require adjustments in order to become the best match for students' educational needs and an understanding that one-size-fits-all curriculum does not work, nor does it make it easier for teachers. Having a twice-exceptional learner in your classroom means that you have to switch from "pret à portée to haute couture," and that is what this chapter is about.

Crossing the T's and Dotting the I's

Defining Educational Needs

The notion of educational needs is the reference point for the design of meaningful educational responses for gifted learners with characteristics of dyslexia. Educational needs exceed academic needs (Pameijer & Van Beukering, 2007). Educational needs represent the spectrum of all pedagogical and didactical needs students have (van Gerven, 2015). All students have different educational needs (Florian & Black-Hawkins, 2011). If meaningful responses to these needs are withheld, the student's development can be negatively affected (Pameijer & Van Beukering, 2007; van Meersbergen & de Vries, 2017). Seeing, understanding, and responding to educational needs form the underpinning of solid education for all learners, including gifted and twice-exceptional learners (van Gerven, 2018). Using the notion of educational needs in this context means there is no need for a label. Thus, intervention strategies presented in this chapter do not require that a student is identified as both gifted and dyslexic. The intervention strategies are entirely based on identifying strengths and weaknesses in a student's profile and finding the optimal responses to those needs (Baum et al., 2017; Trail, 2011).

Interventions described in this chapter are underpinned by the change- and solution-focused approach (Cauffman & van Dijk, 2009; Coleman & Johnsen, 2011; de Shazer et al., 2012; Pameijer & Van Beukering, 2007; van Gerven, 2015; van Meersbergen & de Vries, 2017). This approach is useful for classroom teachers, as it aims to optimize students' learning processes using general teaching competencies to design interventions (see also Chapter 2, this volume). In this approach, students' learning processes determine how teachers can fine-tune the interplay between students and their ecological system (i.e., teacher, physical learning environment, curriculum, peers, family; van Meersbergen & de Vries, 2017; van Meersbergen & Jeninga, 2012; van Swet, 2009).

Defining Giftedness

The operational definition of *giftedness* used this chapter is based on Gagné's (2010) Differentiation Model for Giftedness and Talent, which uses a threshold of 1.3 standard deviations above the norm, including learners with an IQ > 120. This chapter will not differentiate between gifted, highly gifted, or profoundly gifted. This choice is made because most gifted students will be educated in the general classroom, and consequently, they all may require a differentiated response to needs that are not addressed by general teaching strategies (van Gerven & Hoogenberg, 2011).

Defining Dyslexia

This chapter will not differentiate between *dyslexia* and *dysgraphia*. From an educational perspective, both can be seen as two sides of the same coin: the process of decoding needed for reading and the coding needed to process and produce written information (Verhoeven et al., 2014). The working definition of dyslexia used in this chapter focuses on the three core problems (de Bruin-de Boer, 2009; Elliot & Grigorenko, 2014; Kroesbergen, 2017; Verhoeven et al., 2014) and how they may interfere with the learning process: (1) severe and persevering problems with reading and spelling at word-identification level, (2) severe and persevering problems with fast and accurate reading of different types of texts in all academic subjects (decoding), and (3) severe and persevering problems with fast and accurate spelling while writing in all academic subjects (coding).

Defining Twice-Exceptionality

What does the phrase "intellectually gifted learners hindered by characteristics of dyslexia" mean? Intellectually gifted learners with dyslexia have, on one hand, high IQ, and on the other hand, they are hindered by severe and persevering reading and/or spelling problems (Kroesbergen, 2017; van Viersen et al., 2014; see also Chapter 4, this volume). Problems with decoding and coding written information both cause complex situations in the education of gifted learners (Baum et al., 2017; de Bruin-de Boer, 2009; Trail, 2011). Assouline et al. (2010) suggested that twice-exceptional learners struggle in the academic domain that is directly affected by their disability, but that they do not have the same intense struggle in domains not affected by the disability. Research by Maddocks (2018) seems to confirm this and emphasizes the unicity of the individual student's profile. Maddocks found that twice-exceptional students exhibited contrasting achievement patterns. The patterns matched differentiated diagnoses of intellectual giftedness combined with learning disabilities, such as having problems with reading and/or spelling (dyslexia) or being intellectually gifted and having mathematical problems (dyscalculia; see Chapter 6, this volume). So although intellectually gifted learners exhibiting characteristics of dyslexia may struggle with all tasks that include reading and/or spelling, that does not necessarily mean that they will also struggle in domains or tasks that do not require reading and/or spelling. They may even excel in these domains, depending on their individual profile of strengths and challenges.

Keep in mind that the effects of dyslexia are not limited to reading and/or spelling problems in language arts. In the early years, these students are often not as severely hindered by their inabilities. At this stage, only a limited amount of tasks require reading and writing, and the required level of automation and processing speed has not increased to an extent when being intellectually gifted no longer offers adequate compensation skills (de Bruin-de Boer, 2009). In the higher grades, those subjects in which information processing and producing are applied require more focus on written information, presenting a challenge for students who are gifted and have dyslexia.

Where Do Educators Go Wrong Interpreting Students' Results?

In a traditional classroom, the curriculum and the teacher's instructional strategies are often based on the notion of a bell curve (Borland, 2005). That implies that the way teachers traditionally differentiate is based on what they may expect regarding educational needs in a three-tiered structure: below average, average, and above average (van Gerven, 2017a). The more students deviate from this standard, the more likely it is that their educational needs are not fully met (Borland, 2005; Oliver, 1996). Based on this traditional approach to teaching and Gagné's (2010) threshold for giftedness, one can assume that intellectually gifted learners are able to meet the achievement standards at the level of the "above-average student" without having to make a real effort (Heacox & Cash, 2019). However, the achievement standards for grade levels have a so-called didactical ceiling. As a result, well-balanced and good-performing intellectually gifted learners will be able to achieve at the highest level, and it may go unnoticed that they are able to learn at a far higher level than what is provided (van Gerven, 2017b). As long as students achieve within the bandwidth of teacher expectations, it is unlikely that teachers will be alarmed that their achievements do not match their potential (Kieboom & Venderickx, 2017; Missett, 2018). If a teacher is not aware of a student being intellectually gifted, average achievements for reading and/or spelling and an average tempo displayed during their coursework are often interpreted as a sign of average ability (de Bruin-de Boer, 2009; Weterings, 2017).

If a teacher is aware of a student being intellectually gifted, average achievements, including those for reading and/or spelling, are often interpreted as a sign of a lack of interest for these specific academic subjects or underachievement (Weterings, 2017). Maddocks (2020) showed that twice-exceptional learners have a significantly lower processing speed and perform particularly poorly on tasks requiring fluency compared to gifted learners without learning challenges. That means in daily education, twice-exceptional students need more time for their coursework than other gifted learners. Again, teachers may interpret this relatively slow pace as a signal of demotivation or even laziness, not realizing that a student is hindered by severe reading and/or spelling problems or dyslexia. The misinterpretation of these signs has to do with the mental framework educators use to interpret academic achievements. Daring to doubt their interpretations of observed behavior is, in this context, an admirable quality for teachers. It enables them to reflect on action (What am I about to do?

What have I done?) and in action (Is what I am doing meaningful and relevant for the student in question?). As a result of misinterpreted behavior and achievements, these gifted learners are denied access to education that calls on their individual strengths (Baum et al., 2017; Foley-Nicpon et al., 2011; Misset, 2018). This results in the normativity of the notion of "severe problems."

Interpreting "Severe Problems"

The notion of "severe problems" references situations in which students are unable to perform at their intellectual potential. In the context of a learning disability, the word *severe* refers to a situation in which a student is compared with students with similar intellectual abilities and falls within 4% of students who earn the lowest grades for reading and/or spelling (de Bruin-de Boer, 2009; Kroesbergen, 2017; Lovett, 2013). Students who are gifted and have dyslexia may be hindered and unable to perform at a level commensurate to their intellectual ability. These challenges may lead to underachievement and increased drop-out rates.

Comparing potential twice-exceptional students with nongifted students with similar educational histories and working at an identical didactical and instructional level may lead to findings that twice-exceptional students achieve at an average level or a slightly above-average level (de Bruin-de Boer, 2009; Foley-Nicpon & Kim, 2018; Kroesbergen, 2017; Lovett, 2013). Consequently, such comparisons may not identify a student as a struggling reader and/or speller. If the student's struggle goes unnoticed, it becomes clear that the notion of having "severe problems" has a different meaning. Related to other gifted learners, this student has severe problems. Related to the average learner, the teacher may define the problems as minimal. If the teacher does not know that the student in question is intellectually gifted, it is not likely this comparison will lead to the student being identified as gifted and dyslexic (McCallum et al., 2013; van Viersen et al., 2014). Unfortunately, in daily practice, the comparison with nongifted classmates is often made. Teachers use the achievements of their class as a reference to what is considered to be "normal." Only when the teacher is aware of the student's intellectual giftedness will these relatively low results raise concerns that something is going on. "Severe" gets the weight that it should have in the context of being intellectually gifted.

Although teachers are not diagnosticians, they are qualified to assess a student's strengths and weaknesses, and relate this information to characteristics of giftedness and/or dyslexia (McCallum et al., 2013; van Gerven, 2017c). This systematic exploration of strengths and weaknesses precedes a referral for further diagnostics. Sometimes teachers doubt if one of their students is an underachiever or a potential twice-exceptional student. At that time, it is relevant to compare this student's developmental process and achievements for reading and/or spelling to the process and achievements of other intellectually gifted learners in the same age group and exposed to a similar curriculum. An observed intrapersonal discrepancy cannot be conclusive. This concept denies the existence of the heterogeneity of the individual student's profile with individual strengths and weaknesses (Maddocks, 2018; Sternberg et al., 2011).

Persevering Problems

In the context of a learning disability, the notion of persevering becomes relevant. The difference between a problem with reading and/or spelling or being dyslexic is defined by the answer to the question of whether the student's achievement gaps can be remediated (Kroesbergen, 2017; Verhoeven et al., 2014; Weterings, 2017; see also Chapter 4, this volume). In other words, teachers have to exclude the possibility that the process of learning how to read and/or spell in the past was not negatively affected by flaws in the didactical strategies used during the learning process (Weterings, 2017). The use of incorrectly applied instructional strategies and curricular insufficiencies result in what are called *misdidactics* (van Gerven & Weterings-Helmons, 2014–2020; van Groenestijn et al., 2011). The notion of misdidactics does not imply that the teacher does not know how to teach in general. Rather, it refers to a situation in which an individual student's educational needs are not sufficiently met. As a result of this mismatch, the student has developed gaps in knowledge and skills that may be problematic but can be fixed. This process of excluding the possibility of misdidactics should either "fix" the problem or prove the perseverance of the problem.

During this process, interventions for stimulating, compensating, and remediating (R) reading and/or spelling skills are needed. If during this process the problems with reading and/or spelling are solved and the student's achievements increase, it is likely that they were caused by misdidactics. In the case of a learning disability, although the student's performance and achievements may increase, the core problem still exists, and it is unlikely that this student will reach the achievement levels of a gifted student not challenged by dyslexia. As a result, learning new content at a higher level can be as difficult as it was in the previous stage. A disability means that the problem is resistant to remediation (de Bruin-de Boer, 2009; Verhoeven et al., 2014). Dyslexia does not disappear as a result of a good education, but it becomes more manageable.

Having a high IQ can help to develop compensation strategies to make it even more manageable (van Viersen et al., 2014). The more effective the compensation strategies, the more likely it is that learning at a higher level can become a positive experience.

Losing the Need for a Label

This section shifts from a focus on teaching students who are gifted and dyslexic to findings strategies to personalize the education of students so that it matches their individual strengths, talents, and weaknesses. The strategy presented is, therefore, not dependent on labels but dependent on the need for the diversification of teaching.

According to Biesta (2018), core issues in education are qualification, socialization, and subjectification. Qualification refers to (academic) development of students, enabling them to become qualified adults, capable of participating as responsible members of our society. Socialization refers to the developmental process of becoming this responsible person in interaction with significant others. Subjectification refers to the process of students knowing who they are as human beings, accepting their personal qualities, and using these qualities, not only for their own well-being, but also for the benefit of society. Once educators accept these premises and make them the core objectives of education, there is no need for a label when responding to a student's educational needs. Addressing the educational needs of twice-exceptional students is transferred to addressing the educational needs of all students.

Translating these principles to education means that a change- and solution-focused approach can underpin the teacher's professional behavior (van Gerven, 2015). This approach involves five questions: (1) What is to be learned? (2) How can set objectives be acquired? (3) What has to be organized to optimize the learning process? (4) What could be the best place to provide these meaningful responses? (5) How can we assess results of the learning process in a way that we do justice to the educational process and the student's achievements (Chandra Handa, 2009; Roberts & Inman, 2015; van Gerven, 2014; Winstanley, 2010)?

The Systemic Intervention Protocol (SIP) is a tool that is designed to optimize complex educational dilemmas as they can occur to teach (potentially) gifted learners with severe and persevering reading and/or spelling problems (van Gerven, 2014, 2019). The SIP is constructed as a matrix and helps teachers understand what they could change in instructional strategies or the curriculum for a single student in order to enhance success (van Gerven, 2014, 2019). The SIP helps teachers explore their educational strategies for single cases. Each column in the matrix focusses on how a different (f)actor in the ecological system interplays with the educational process. Students' ecological systems consist of five components in a direct interplay with student development: the teacher, a student's family, peers, the curriculum, and the physical learning environment (van Gerven, 2015; van Meersbergen & Jeninga, 2012). As interplay suggests mutuality between two or more components, not only do these components influence the student, but also the student influences these components. The basic assumption is that teachers have a mandate to influence four (f)actors: (1) the individual student, (2) the curriculum, (3) the learning environment, and (4) the teacher's strategies.

Table 5.1 is an abridged matrix that can be easily extended by asking more questions per constructed cell. Teachers can easily design their own additional questions. One can easily add a fifth column (parents) or even a sixth column (school as an organization). Each row in the matrix aims for a different aspect to be explored from that specific ecological perspective. This exploration can vary from thinking strategies and the use of (or call on) executive skills to the ability for cooperative or collaborative learning.

Teachers using the SIP for the first time should restrict themselves to this abridged version of the matrix. It helps to narrow down the interventions and keeps them simple and small. Interventions needed to successfully teach these students follow logically from the use of the matrix. The following instruction can be used to fill in the SIP.

The first column focuses on the student in the current situation and is directly related to the educational objectives the teacher has set. Without exception, always use the question in the first cell of Column 1 as a starting point. The question in Cell 2 asks teachers to concretely describe what they already know about the student's knowledge and skills in relation to the set objective. Continuing to Cell 3, describe the student's strength regarding the different levels of thinking skills—based on Bloom's revised taxonomy (Anderson & Krathwohl, 2001) or Marzano and Kendall's (2007) taxonomy. Do not expand to an overall description of the student's functioning in every cell, but stay focused on the description related directly to the set objective. In doing so, the teacher constructs a systematic inventory of the student's knowledge and skills related to the set objective and easily attends to the student's educational needs.

Column 2 helps teachers explore which assignments or projects provide the optimal match for this student. Similar to Column 1, questions include: (1) What assignments do you think match the set objectives? (2) What knowledge and skills are required at the start of the assignment? (3) How does the

TABLE 5.1

Example Systemic Intervention Protocol Matrix

	Student	Assignments and Materials	Physical Learning Environment	Teacher
Objectives (of/in)	What is the next educational objective for this student, and why is this objective relevant?	Which assignments and/or materials are a match with the objective(s) stipulated?	What is the best learning environment for these objectives?	What do I have to do to align the objective, assignment/material, and environment?
Content and student efficacy	What is the student's current knowledge and skill level related to the assignment?	What content knowledge and skills are required for the student to be successful?	What content-based resources do I have available to support students' work?	What do I need to do to support student efficacy? What responses are needed to match current knowledge and skills with required knowledge and skills? What environmental supports are available to the student?
Thinking skills	Which of Bloom's or Marzano and Kendall's cognitive thinking skills are strengths for this student?	What thinking skills are developed by doing this assignment? How does this assignment utilize these thinking skills?	Which resources are available to support the student during the learning process?	How do I modify the learning environment in a way that learning is optimized to develop these thinking skills?
Product	What kind of product would align with the student's capacities and preferences?	What alternative curricular materials are available to replace the product if it does not meet the student's needs?	Within reason, what products can be made in this learning environment?	What interventions are necessary to align the objective, assignment, product, and learning environment? How can I make learning visible and relate the results to the objectives?

TABLE 5.1, *continued*

	Student	Assignments and Materials	Physical Learning Environment	Teacher
Regulation skills	To what extent is this student ready for self-regulated learning? What do you know about the student's executive skills?	What level of self-regulation is required of the student while working on the assignment? How does the assignment utilize the student's regulation skills?	How does the learning environment influence the student's use of regulation skills? What level of self-regulation skills are required in this environment?	How can I support this student's self-regulation in relation to the objective, task requirements, and environmental conditions?
Cooperative and collaborative	To what extent is this student able to learn in a situation where cooperation or collaboration is required?	To what extent is cooperative/collaborative learning a condition for successfully working on this assignment?	To what extent is cooperative/collaborative learning possible in the learning environment? What requirements for cooperative and collaborative learning are met in the learning environment?	How do I adjust the learning environment in order to achieve the required level of cooperation/collaboration?
Emotions	What are the student's emotional responses when they are learning? How does the student deal with limited success or even a lack of success?	What are the emotional responses I might expect when the student is working on this assignment?	What resources are available to increase the possibility of a positive learning experience?	What can I do in order to help the student with their emotional responses during the learning process?

Note. From *Knapzak Praktijkgidsen: Uitdagend onderwijs* (pp. 82–83), by E. van Gerven, 2014, Leuker.nu. Copyright 2014 by E. van Gerven. Reprinted with permission of the author.

assignment utilize specific thinking skills? (4) What level of self-regulation is required?

When comparing the results between Columns 1 and 2, it is normal to conclude that there is a gap between the student's starting level and the level of knowledge and skills required for the task. If not, the task may not be in the zone of proximal development (Vygotsky, 1978). This gap can be bridged with interventions explored in Columns 3 and 4. In Column 3, teachers consider how the learning environment can contribute to a successful learning process. For example, what resources regarding knowledge and skills are available for the student once they are working on the assignment? How can the student ask for help? How is the learning environment prepared for the required level of self-regulation? To what extent is the physical learning environment a match for what is required? Is collaboration with other students possible?

Learning in the zone of proximal development means that the student is about to take on an assignment that forces them to stretch toward the next developmental level within the safety of an effective support system that is available, if needed (Vygotsky, 1978). Having completed the assignment and having met the objectives means that the student has acquired new knowledge and skills. Based upon items explored in Columns 1–3, the teacher describes their role in supporting students as they master the objective.

Working with students having educational needs that require teachers to diversify their pedagogical and didactical strategies is not about doing more or intervening more. It is about doing something slightly different or doing the same thing at a slightly different time. Sometimes it is not about what the teacher does while the student is working on the assignment, but about what the teacher has done prior to the lesson to enhance independent learning. All of these things will sound familiar. Teachers are used to providing this support for all students in their classroom (van Meersbergen & de Vries, 2017). Work based on the SIP shows teachers that detailed preparation can be very effective for all learners, especially when they are dealing with complex learners or with situations in which education is not as successful as initially thought. The SIP is not about ready-to-use interventions, but about using common sense for intervention design. It is not about work based on general assumptions about a certain group of learners, but shows teachers how to create custom-made interventions. These interventions may be applicable for a wider group, and the discussion of whether the student is a gifted learner with dyslexia is irrelevant.

FROM THE EDITORS

Student Vignette

Akita

During his early elementary years, Akita knew there was something "different" about him. Although he made decent grades, he felt like he had to work harder than his friends who always made it look so easy. When the teacher would ask him to read aloud, he would hesitate, knowing that what would come out of his mouth would elicit giggles from his classmates, letting him know that what he had "read" was not what was on the page. Still, he loved learning and looked forward to going to school each day.

Unfortunately, this changed when he began the fourth grade. It was soon clear to Akita that his teacher was frustrated with him and his inability to read at the level expected of the typical student his age. This frustration grew as the year progressed, and at one point, his teacher told him that she was concerned that he would not even be qualified to work as a fast food cashier if he did not learn to read. Akita's love for school began to decline, but his love of learning did not.

The next year brought new promise. Akita's fifth-grade teacher recognized his challenges, but also recognized something more. She took the time to get to know him and began assessing his reading abilities. She assured him that he was extremely bright and just struggled with reading, and together they would find out why. Working with the special education teacher, Akita was assessed, it was determined that he was dyslexic, and he began to receive services to address these needs. Additionally, his teacher provided him with opportunities for enrichment in those areas that he excelled in, and Akita's love for school began to bloom again.

After graduating from high school, Akita went into the military and then, ultimately, entered college to earn his degree in education. His professors quickly realized that he was someone to watch, that he was someone whom they knew would go on to do great things in education. Once Akita graduated and entered the classroom, he vowed to be the type of educator that his fifth-grade teacher had been to him. He began to work with students who had been identified with dyslexia and who felt that they had been deemed as a lost cause by other teachers. As a

FROM THE EDITORS, *continued*

result of his dedication to these students, their academic achievement has grown—something that has been recognized by the administration in his school. His school is now asking Akita if he would allow other teachers to observe in his classroom and consider providing professional development to those teachers about the work that he is doing.

Discussion Questions

1. Thinking about Akita's experience, what are the social-emotional ramifications for students with dyslexia as they navigate the school environment? How are these effects amplified or mitigated by the co-occurring presence of giftedness?
2. Would Akita have benefited from an earlier intervention? Why?
3. How could Akita's fourth-grade teacher have better served his educational needs? What additional supports would you recommend for her?
4. Why was Akita's fifth-grade teacher able to help him?
5. What personality traits allowed Akita to succeed?
6. What is Akita's most critical role as an educator?

References

Anderson, L., & Krathwohl, D. R. (Eds.). (2001). *A taxonomy for learning, teaching, and assessing: A revision of Bloom's taxonomy of educational objectives* (Complete ed.). Longman.

Assouline, S. G., Whiteman, C., & Foley-Nicpon, M. (2010). Cognitive and psychosocial characteristics of gifted students with written language disability. *Gifted Child Quarterly, 55*(2), 102–115. https://doi.org/10.1177/0016986209355974

Baum, S. M., Schader, R. M., & Owen, S. V. (2017). *To be gifted and learning disabled: Strength-based strategies for helping twice-exceptional students with LD, ADHD, ASD, and more* (3rd ed.). Prufrock Press.

Biesta, G. (2018). Persoonsvorming in het onderwijs: over vorming-van-personen en vorming-tot-persoon-willen zijn. In G. Geerdink & F. de Beer (Eds.), *Kennisbasis Lerarenopleiders: Katern 6: Vorming in de lerarenopleidingen* (pp. 21–34). Velon.

Borland, J. H. (2005). Gifted education without gifted children: The case for no conceptions of giftedness. In R. J. Sternberg & J. E. Davidson (Eds.), *Conceptions of Giftedness* (2nd ed., pp. 1–19). Cambridge University Press.

Cauffman, L., & van Dijk, D. J. (2009). *Handboek oplossingsgericht werken in het onderwijs*. Coutinho.

Chandra Handa, M. (2009). Learner-centred differentiation model: A new framework. *Australasian Journal of Gifted Education, 18*(2), 55–66.

Coleman, M. R., & Johnsen, S. K. (2011). *RtI for gifted students*. Prufrock Press.

de Bruin-de Boer, A. (2009). Hoogbegaafdheid en dyslexie. In E. van Gerven (Ed.), *Handboek hoogbegaafdheid* (pp. 212–230). Koninklijke van Gorcum.

de Shazer, S., Dolan, Y., Korman, H., Trepper, T., McCollum, E., & Berg, I. K. (2012). *More than miracles: The state of the art of solution-focused brief therapy*. Routledge.

Elliot, J. G., & Grigorenko, E. L. (2014). *The dyslexia debate*. Cambridge University Press.

Florian, L., & Black-Hawkins, K. (2011). Exploring inclusive pedagogy. *British Educational Research Journal, 37*(5), 813–828. https://doi.org/10.1080/01411926.2010.501096

Foley-Nicpon, M., Allmon, A., Sieck, B., & Stinson, R. D. (2011). Empirical investigation of twice-exceptionality: Where have we been and where are we going? *Gifted Child Quarterly, 55*(1), 3–17. https://doi.org/10.1177/0016986210382575

Foley-Nicpon, M., & Kim, J. Y. C. (2018). Identifying and providing evidence-based services for twice-exceptional students. In S. I. Pfeiffer (Ed.), *Handbook of giftedness in children: Psychoeducational theory, research, and best practices* (2nd ed., pp. 349–362). Springer.

Gagné, F. (2010). *Building gifts into talents: Brief overview of the DMGT 2.0*. Université du Québec à Montréal.

Heacox, D., & Cash, R. M. (2019). *Differentiation for gifted learners: Going beyond the basics* (Rev. ed.). Free Spirit.

Kieboom, T., & Venderickx, K. (2017). *Meer dan intelligent alleen*. Lannoo.

Kroesbergen, E. (2017). Begaafde leerlingen met dyslexie. In E. van Gerven (Ed.), *De gids. Over begaafdheid in het basisonderwijs* (pp. 243–252). Nieuwolda.

Lovett, B. J. (2013). The science and politics of gifted students with learning disabilities: A social inequality perspective. *Roeper Review, 35*(2), 136–143. https://doi.org/10.1080/02783193.2013.766965

Maddocks, D. L. S. (2018). The identification of students who are gifted and have a learning disability: A comparison of different diagnostic criteria. *Gifted Child Quarterly, 62*(2), 175–192. https://doi.org/10.1177/0016986 217752096

Maddocks, D. L. S. (2020). Cognitive and achievement characteristics of students from a national sample identified as potentially twice-exceptional (gifted with a learning disability). *Gifted Child Quarterly, 64*(1), 3–18. https://doi.org/10.1177/0016986219886668

Marzano, R. J., & Kendall, J. S. (2007). *The new taxonomy of educational objectives* (2nd ed.). Corwin.

McCallum, R. S., Bell, S. M., Coles, J. T., Miller, K. C., Hopkins, M. B., & Hilton-Prillhart, A. (2013). A model for screening twice-exceptional students (gifted with learning disabilities) within a response to intervention paradigm. *Gifted Child Quarterly, 57*(4), 209–222. https://doi.org/10.1177/ 0016986213500070

Missett, T. C. (2018). Twice-exceptional students: gifted students with disabilities impacting learning. In C. M. Callahan & H. L. Hertzberg-Davis (Eds.), *Fundamentals of gifted education: Considering multiple perspectives* (2nd ed., pp. 361–371). Routledge.

Oliver, M. (1996). *Understanding disability: From theory to practice.* St Martin's Press. https://doi.org/10.1007/978-1-349-24269-6

Pameijer, N., & Van Beukering, T. (2007). *Handelingsgericht werken: een handreiking voor de intern begeleider.* Acco.

Reis, S. M., Baum, S. M., & Burke, E. (2014). An operational definition of twice-exceptional learners: implications and applications. *Gifted Child Quarterly, 58*(3), 217–230. https://doi.org/10.1177/0016986214534976

Roberts, J. L., & Inman, T. F. (2015). *Strategies for differentiating instruction. Best practices for the classroom* (3rd ed.). Prufrock Press.

Sternberg, R. J., Jarvin, L., & Grigorenko, E. L. (2011). *Explorations in giftedness.* Cambridge University Press.

Trail, B. A. (2011). *Twice-exceptional gifted children. Understanding, teaching, and counselling gifted students.* Prufrock Press.

van Gerven, E. (2014). *Knapzak Praktijkgidsen: Uitdagend Onderwijs.* Leuker. nu.

van Gerven, E. (2015). *De cirkel van zorg voor de intern begeleider.* Leuker.nu.

van Gerven, E. (2017a). Begaafde leerlingen met ADHD. In E. van Gerven (Ed.), *De Gids: Over begaafdheid in het basisonderwijs* (2nd ed., pp. 279–296). Leuker.nu.

van Gerven, E. (2017b). Begaafde leerlingen met een autismespectrum stoornis. In E. Van Gerven (Ed.), *De Gids: Over begaafdheid in het basisonderwijs* (2nd ed., pp. 199–224). Leuker.nu.

van Gerven, E. (2017c). Inclusie en onderwijs aan begaafde leerlingen: twee geloven op één kussen? In E. Van Gerven (Ed.), *De Gids: Over begaafdheid in het basisonderwijs* (2nd ed., pp. 19–36). Leuker.nu.

van Gerven, E. (2018). *Addressing the needs of twice-exceptional students in the classroom.* Slim! Educatief. https://www.slimeducatief.nl/artikelen/download/29

van Gerven, E. (2019). *Ecologisch begeleiden van begaafde leerlingen (BBM mei 2019).* https://www.lbbo.nl/materialenbank/ecologisch-begeleiden-van-begaafde-leerlingen-bbm-mei-2019

van Gerven, E., & Hoogenberg, I. (2011). *Begaafd begeleiden: de competentiematrix voor de Specialist Begaafdheid.* Koninklijke van Gorcum.

van Gerven, E., & Weterings-Helmons, A. (2014–2020). *Specialist Dubbel-Bijzondere Leerlingen.* https://www.slimeducatief.nl/cursus/specialist-dubbel-bijzonder

van Groenestijn, M., Borghouts, C., & Janssen, C. (2011). *Protocol ernstige rekenwiskunde-problemen en dyscalculie.* Koninklijke van Gorcum.

van Meersbergen, E., & de Vries, P. (2017). *Handelingsgericht werken in passend onderwijs.* Utrecht.

van Meersbergen, E., & Jeninga, J. (2012). De ecologie van de leerling: Een systeemgericht model voor het onderwijs. *Tijdschrift voor Orthopedagogiek, 51*(4), 175–185.

van Swet, J. (2009). Diagnostiek vanuit een oplossingsgericht perspectief. In E. van Gerven (Ed.), *Handboek hoogbegaafdheid* (pp. 38–57). Van Gorcum.

van Viersen, S., Kroesbergen, E. H., Slot, E. M., & de Bree, E. H. (2014). High reading skills mask dyslexia in gifted children. *Journal of Learning Disabilities, 49*(2), 1–11. https://doi.org/10.1177/0022219414538517

Verhoeven, L., de Jong, P., & Wijnen, F. (2014). *Dyslexie 2.0.* Maklu.

Vygotsky, L. (1978). *Mind in society. The development of higher psychological processes.* Harvard University Press.

Weterings, A. (2017). Begaafde leerlingen met ernstige reken- en wiskundeproblemen en dyscalculie. In E. van Gerven (Ed.), *De Gids: Over begaafdheid in het basisonderwijs* (2nd ed., pp. 255–278). Leuker.nu.

Winstanley, C. (2010). *The ingredients of challenge.* Trentham Books.

CHAPTER 6

Giftedness and Math Difficulty

Nancy Fike Knop and Stephen H. Chou

Long before humans understood how or why it worked, humans learned math and taught each other. Just as human brains are wired to understand language, they are wired to understand quantity (e.g., number, distance, brightness, loudness, time). Given the initial wiring for both language and math and the plasticity that allows them to change with experience, human brains are primed to learn and use corresponding symbol systems and sophisticated concepts. Once upon a time, people taught each other one-to-one, passing down knowledge from parent to child, from master to apprentice, by direct instruction and experience. But eventually, as people began to believe it would be good for everyone to develop literacy and numeracy, they began to teach each other in groups, then in classrooms. The idea that everyone would be able to read and write, that everyone would be able to calculate, is relatively recent. Scientists are gathering ever more sophisticated data about brains and behavior to understand how and why people learn. Educators can apply that understanding to better teach students in the 21st century.

In the second half of the 20th century, enough cognitive science and neuroscience accumulated to shed light on the reading wars between phonics and

183

whole language. It is now understood that even though some will learn to read no matter how they are taught, up to 20% may never learn without direct, explicit instruction in how the sounds in words are related to the symbols that represent the sounds—in other words, without phonological awareness (see Melby-Lervåg et al., 2012). Without this base, literacy will not develop for everyone. Similar understandings, although still in an experimental phase, are now developing for mathematics. Cognitive scientists and neuroscientists are accumulating bodies of evidence that are leading to new ways of thinking about how to develop students' numeracy. Whereas the understanding, insight, evaluation, and interventions for literacy are more robust, the same cannot be said about numeracy.

Children are understood as gifted when their ability is significantly above the norm for their age (National Association for Gifted Children [NAGC], n.d.-b). Another definition from the Columbus Group (Institute for the Study of Advanced Development [ISAD], n.d.) that also includes intensity, sensitivity, and overexcitabilities as primary characteristics of the highly gifted states:

> Giftedness is asynchronous development in which advanced cognitive abilities and heightened intensity combine to create inner experiences and awareness that are qualitatively different from the norm. This asynchrony increases with higher intellectual capacity. The uniqueness of the gifted renders them particularly vulnerable and requires modifications in parenting, teaching and counseling in order for them to develop optimally.

All children may have different rates of mastery in different academic subjects; gifted children may experience challenges in mathematics as well, performing significantly below their potential. These children may be what is termed twice-exceptional, which, "also referred to as '2e,' is used to describe gifted children who have the characteristics of gifted students with the potential for high achievement and give evidence of one or more disabilities as defined by federal or state eligibility criteria" (NAGC, n.d.-a).

What can educators do to recognize the strengths and overcome the challenges some gifted children face so that they can reach math mastery? In addition to studying brain changes with typical math learning, there is also a great deal of recent research in the area of math disability and developmental dyscalculia (e.g., Bartelet et al., 2014; Berch et al., 2016; Butterworth, 2018; Castaldi et al., 2018; Fuchs et al., 2016; Geary, 2011; Kersey et al., 2019; L. Peters & De Smedt, 2018; Wu et al., 2017).

Gifted mathematicians may be recognized in early childhood, but others who have gifts for mathematical thought may never be noticed. The reasons why some have unrecognized gifts may have to do with math education in general—related to issues that affect all children, not just those who are gifted. When is the problem for gifted children due to cultural mindsets about math, about math anxiety that may affect them more than others, or about math teaching that does not see their strengths or meet their challenges?

This chapter looks closely at twice-exceptional students who struggle in math. What are the reasons for their lack of ability and achievement in math? Genetics, brain lesions, and current research all provide evidence for a neurological deficit—dyscalculia—a core deficit in the approximate number system that allows subitizing (instant recognition of small quantities), estimation, and comparison of quantities (e.g., Butterworth, 2018; Cantlon et al., 2006; Castaldi et al., 2018; Vanbinst et al., 2016). But other factors that may impact math for gifted children include environmental factors and math anxiety. Dyscalculia exists in gifted children, but math difficulty is a much broader issue. Have educational methods left twice-exceptional students without the foundations they need to build math knowledge? Has math anxiety stifled their ability to think and caused them to avoid subjects that involve math? Increasingly, educators have the tools to recognize, diagnose, and remediate the difficulties that gifted children have in math.

Why Learn Math?

Why is math so important? Arguments have been raging for more than a century about how to formulate and address this question (Geary, 2011; National Council of Supervisors of Mathematics & National Council of Teachers of Mathematics, 2018; Schoenfeld, 2004). Is math important for the competitive success of a country on the international stage or for military dominance? Is learning mathematics important because math knowledge is linked to access to career paths and social mobility? Mathematics is part of world knowledge and culture that everyone should have a chance to learn. Indeed, math has historically been much more translatable across multilingual societies than language. Because confident numeracy is linked to better health (E. Peters et al., 2019), numeracy is as essential as literacy and may even have a greater impact on individual lives (Parsons & Bynner, 2005). People face issues of population growth, climate impacts, economics, migration, and citizenship, and every day, people live with calendars, schedules, directions, music, cooking, shopping, grades, taxes, etc.—all with solutions globally and personally dependent on numeracy. The future depends on the leadership and achievement of young people and adults who understand, use, and interpret mathematics, from addition and subtraction to statistics and calculus. Some truly gifted children and adults struggle with math, perhaps in greater proportions than others. The world needs their gifts.

What Happens When People Learn?

Marian Diamond and colleagues published the first scientific evidence of brain anatomy changes with learning (brain plasticity) at the University of California, Berkeley in 1964. In 1997, French neuroscientist Stanislaus Dehaene published the first edition of his prominent book, *The Number Sense*. This book reviewed the extensive evidence that he, his colleagues, and others collected from brain lesions and early brain imaging to describe brain areas uniquely designated for math. With the development of increasingly sophisticated brain imaging methods, the understanding of how brains develop through childhood and adolescence began to accumulate (Gogtay et al., 2004). Cognitive scientists have studied the behavior of math learning, including David Geary at the University of Missouri, Lynn Fuchs at Vanderbilt University in Tennessee, and Brian Butterworth in England. Scientists at the University of Chicago have examined the embodiment and environment of learning in the importance of gesture (Goldin-Meadow 2003, Hynes-Berry et al., 2019) and the impact of anxiety (Beilock & Willingham, 2014). The work of neuroscientists and cognitive scientists is being integrated: Recent work by Jessica Cantlon and colleagues (e.g., Kersey et al., 2019) and at Stanford by neuroscientist Vinod Menod and colleagues (e.g., Jolles, Supekar, et al., 2016; Jolles, Wasserman, et al., 2016; Wu et al., 2017) has shown how children's and adults' brains differ in math processing and how specific math teaching and learning change brain pathways. The connections between education and learning and the neurobiology of the brain for math are ever increasing.

Some math education programs fit well with the emerging science, but some do not. Change is needed, but change is not easy. How can the work of neuroscientists and cognitive scientists be integrated into educational practice? More collaboration is needed with teachers and curriculum developers.

People Are Born to Do Math

People are born to do math. Babies and preschool children know exactly the quantity of one to three or four things, can compare quantities, and understand some math concepts (Barth et al., 2005). Humans are not the only ones: Elephants, bees, birds, fish, lemurs, macaques, and others have number sense, too. The brain system in humans naturally recognizes magnitude in things that are continuous, like loudness and brightness, and things that are discrete, like countable quantities. This system—widely referred to as the approximate number system (ANS)—is about more than numbers. It is understood as the core brain system that involves the nonsymbolic ability to approximate number representations, and it is involved in building symbolic mathematic understanding (e.g., Bonny & Lourenco, 2013; Feifer & Clark, 2016). It is based upon subitizing (the ability to instantly recognize how many are in a small set), estimating, and comparing.

The ANS is analogous to the brain system that allows infants to hear and learn their native language. In learning language, infants and children build on an inborn ability to develop phonological awareness; in learning math, infants and children use the inborn ANS. Built upon the foundation of the ANS, children then learn to focus in on specific quantities, count with one-to-one correspondence, and recognize ordinality (the sequence) and cardinality (the total number counted). To begin reading, children continue to build on phonological awareness to match sounds (phonemes) to symbols (graphemes). To begin math, children continue to build on the ANS to build symbolic number processing (Vanbinst et al., 2016). In fact, Wang et al. (2017) showed that approximate number sense is related to math giftedness in teens enrolled in the Center for Talented Youth program at Johns Hopkins Although these systems for developed word and number knowledge are analogous, the processes are different and are located in different areas of the brain. For language, they are primarily located in the temporal lobe, specializing on the left side, and for mathematics, they are largely located in the parietal lobes on both sides, although other areas are also identified. Research continues: The cerebellum is still less understood, even though 80% of the brain's neurons are in the cerebellum (Herculano-Houzel, 2019). Because math involves spatial-temporal understanding, the cerebellum may play more than one important role in mathematics (Moore et al., 2017; Vandervert, 2017). Indeed, many areas of the brain are utilized to do math (Kubas et al., 2015).

Once learning begins, and as learning develops, brains change. Importantly, in the last few decades, it has become possible to use functional magnetic resonance imaging (fMRI) with young children, allowing investigation of the development of math understanding (Kersey et al., 2019). A goal for reading is to build automatic knowledge of enough words to begin building reading fluency. For math, the goal is to build automatic knowledge of enough number facts and procedures to be able to compute fluently. Over the last half-century, awareness has grown about the need to build word knowledge through the process of learning the sounds in words and then using this to build word knowledge, leading to sight recognition of a large vocabulary. There is less awareness, however, of the necessary steps for building knowledge of mathematics. In both literacy and numeracy learning, the early stages of learning require effort and brain power. During the development of automatic retrieval of number facts and basic math procedures, there is considerable domain-general (widely used brain areas) work. The hippocampus and surrounding areas dedicated to moving information into long-term memory are particularly active during this domain-general stage, much more so than before or after that stage (Qin et al., 2014). It takes brain power to learn number facts. Once these are learned, the brain can utilize automaticity (and less brain power) to solve mathematical problems, moving toward domain-specific learning (the development of one set of skills independent from the development of other types of skills). (See Figure 6.1.)

One of the continuing debates in math curriculum development is whether or not it is necessary to memorize math facts and procedures. For all students, there is a striking barrier to progress in math when rational numbers—fractions, decimals, and percentages—are introduced. Without automatic retrieval of math facts and procedures, it is even more difficult. The core system that was adapted to learn counting and math facts does not so easily adapt for numbers that do not share the characteristics of counting (Jacobs Danan & Gelman, 2017). At this stage, if automatic retrieval of number facts is not available, there is not enough working memory to recreate them at the same time as new number systems are learned. These increasing demands, without automatic retrieval, greatly burden the brain. Even if there is enough working memory, it takes too long, even with above-average processing speed. What worked until now is not sufficient any longer in school settings. Even gifted brains become overloaded. And it gets worse every year. But if automatic retrieval is established, there is a shift in brain activity. Math does not take so much work. Brain circuits that support math thinking emerge, and math thinking is more efficient (Battista et al., 2018). Price et al. (2013) showed that brain activity responsible for fluent retrieval of math facts was correlated with success on the PSAT Math in high school.

FIGURE 6.1

Representation of Similar But Separate Development in Math and Language

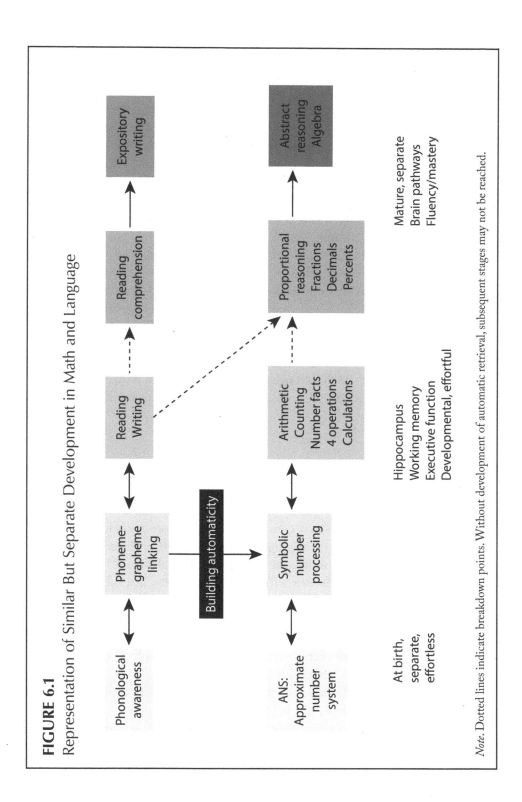

Note. Dotted lines indicate breakdown points. Without development of automatic retrieval, subsequent stages may not be reached.

There are at least two factors in the math wars at play, with collateral damage. First, gaining automaticity has been downplayed, even denounced as "rote memorization" or "drill and kill," pretty awful-sounding approaches. And, of course, calculators are available. Second, many textbooks, in a current wave of emphasis on making math meaningful in the real world, have included more and more "story problems." These problems may be full of interesting details, but the details may have nothing to do with the actual math needed to solve them—more detractions than additional context to help make math real. Although the goal is admirable, word problem teaching methods may not serve students well. Increasingly, students are asked to imagine and write about real-world situations to match math problems, or to explain their own mathematical solutions in writing. The difficulty with this approach is that words and numbers are processed differently, and although the words may make math more realistic, translating between words and numbers makes math more difficult (Wu et al., 2017). Talking about these situations is one thing, but using written words is another. Math recorded in problem solutions uses a language of its own—the language of math—with its own structure and grammar. Once a mathematical solution is shown, following mathematical structure and grammar, it is complete. It should not need to be translated into written words to be completely understandable. We can encourage math understanding in its own language.

The Barriers to Numeracy

Although mathematics may come naturally and more easily for some, difficulties in mathematics exist. The range of math difficulty reported in the literature is from a dyscalculia/math learning disability prevalence of 3%–7%, which is commonly cited (e.g., Butterworth et al., 2011; Geary, 2011; Haberstroh & Schulte-Korne, 2019; Kaufmann & von Aster, 2012), to the much higher prevalence of functional disability due to math anxiety (Ashcroft & Moore, 2009). No matter the actual percentage, there is general agreement about the impact of low math achievement on individuals and societies; it affects career choices, social mobility, and even health.

The barriers to numeracy are generally described in both education and psychology. The Individuals With Disabilities Education Act (IDEA, 1990) defined a specific learning disability as "a disorder in one or more of the basic psychological processes involved in understanding or in using language, spoken or written, that may manifest itself in the imperfect ability to listen, think, speak, read, write, spell, or to do mathematical calculations." The American Psychiatric Association (APA, 2013) defined "Specific Learning Disorder with Impairment in Mathematics" as mathematical achievements that are:

> substantially and quantifiable below those expected for the individual's chronological age, and cause significant inter-ference with academic or occupational performance, or with activities of daily living, as confirmed by individually adminis-tered standardized achievement measures and comprehensive clinical assessment . . . but may not fully manifest until the demands for those affected academic skills exceed the individ-ual's limited capacities. (p. 67)

In math, these struggles manifest with difficulties mastering number sense, number facts, or calculation, or difficulties with mathematical reasoning. In addition, with regard to giftedness and learning difficulties, APA (2013) stated:

> Specific learning disabilities may also occur in individuals identified as intellectually "gifted." These individuals may be able to sustain apparently adequate academic functioning by using compensatory strategies, extraordinarily high effort, or support, until the learning demands or assessment procedures (e.g., timed tests) poses barriers to their demonstrating their learning or accomplishing required tasks. (p. 69)

This suggests significantly discrepant performance in comparison to measured intellectual potential.

Although difficulties in math can be described within education and psy-chology, performance in mathematical achievement that is below expected for chronological age and intellectual potential may derive from many root causes. These barriers may include, but are not limited to:

- brain activity specifically related to math (domain-specific: nonsym-bolic magnitude and number sense)—dyscalculia;
- general kinds of brain processing (domain-general: intelligence, work-ing memory, processing speed);
- environmental factors that affect math development (parents, culture, schooling);
- math anxiety that leads to the avoidance of math, hindering math devel-opment; or
- interactions between all of these barriers.

What Is Dyscalculia?

Dyscalculia was first defined in 1974 by Ladislav Košč as:

> a structural disorder of mathematical abilities which has its
> origin in a genetic or congenital disorder of those parts of the
> brain that are the direct anatomico-physiological substrate of
> the maturation of the mathematical abilities adequate to age,
> without a simultaneous disorder of general mental functions.
> (p. 47)

Shalev (2004) described dyscalculia as a "specific learning disability affect-ing the normal acquisition of arithmetic skills in spite of normal intelligence, emotional stability, scholastic opportunity, and motivation" (p. 766). Rosselli et al. (2006) described dyscalculia as:

> specific math-related deficits, including difficulty learning
> and retrieving math-related deficits, difficulty executing math
> calculation procedures when engaged in problem solving, or
> lack of basic number sense and concept development skills to
> utilize a particular strategy when problem solving. (as cited in
> Feifer & Clark, 2016, p. 2)

Szucs et al. (2013) also shared "a popular view is that DD [developmental dyscalculia] is the consequence of the deficit of a core amodal magnitude rep-resentation often called the 'number sense'" (p. 34). There are also several sub-types of dyscalculia noted in the literature. Table 6.1 summarizes the subtypes.

No matter the various definitions and subtypes, a review of literature about dyscalculia asserts that it is a brain-based disorder (DeFina & Moser 2011, 2013; Košč, 1981; Macaruso & Sokol, 1998; Szucs & Goswami 2013; von Aster, 1994). Notably, APA (2013) also mentioned dyscalculia in a notation as an "alternative term use to refer to a pattern of difficulties characterized by problems processing numerical information, learning arithmetic facts, and performing accurate or fluent calculations" (p. 67).

Dyscalculia seems to be biologically based, with a core deficit that is likely within the ANS and its number sense/magnitude sense (e.g., Butterworth, 2018; Cantlon et al., 2006; Castaldi et al., 2018; Vanbinst et al., 2016). This domain-specific deficit or subsequent domain-general and environmental fac-tors may prevent development of the link between number and the symbols for numbers, and then, as a result, processes for calculations using number

TABLE 6.1
Dyscalculia Subtypes

Reference	Dyscalculia Subtype	Characteristics
Košč (1974)	Verbal	Disturbed ability with mathematical terms and relations. Difficulty with math language.
	Practognostic	Disturbance of mathematical manipulation with real or pictured objects.
	Lexical	Disability in reading mathematical symbols.
	Graphical	Disability in writing mathematical symbols; analogous to lexical dyscalculia.
	Ideognostical	Disability in understanding mathematical ideas and relations and in mental calculation.
	Operational Development	Disability in carrying out mathematical operations.
Raja and Kumar (2012)	Sequential	Difficulty counting numbers in sequence. Difficulty calculating time, checking schedules, tracking direction, and taking measurement.
Feifer and Clark (2016)	Procedural	One or more deficits in the ability to count, order, or sequence numbers and/or sequence mathematical procedures when problem solving.
	Verbal	Difficulty with rapid number identification skills and deficits retrieving or recalling stored mathematical facts or overlearned information.
	Semantic	Deficit in deciphering magnitude representations among numbers in visual-spatial or conceptual components.

symbols. Fortunately, just as with developmental dyslexia, it is possible to train brain pathways that compensate for the deficit. Unfortunately, however, by the time this problem is detected, many environmental factors have compounded the problem, making it complex enough to require individual diagnosis and remediation. Although methods are now being developed to detect lack of symbolic number sense in preschoolers (Hawes et al., 2019), it is often unidentified until second or third grade. But for gifted children, basic math difficulty may be surreptitious and not identified until middle school.

Gaps in Knowledge Acquisition

Mathematics is relentlessly cumulative. Robust mathematical foundations are vital in learning math. Gaps in the foundations of mathematical knowledge can occur from a variety of reasons. These reasons include, but are not limited to, the following:

- Unexpected life events (e.g., major moves/immigration, greatly impactful illnesses, or divorce) may affect students' academic engagement. Other-focused attentions may detract from academic learning. Missing a step in the step-wise mathematical learning process can affect later acquisition of knowledge.
- Teaching that did not connect. Mode and speed of education through curricula and pacing can also interfere.
- Learning in a second language can cause gaps in acquisition for mathematics.
- Inadequate educational opportunity due to socioeconomic constraints causes foundational gaps.
- Math anxiety passed on from teachers and parents can compound other issues, especially when new methods do not match students' past experience with math calculation.

Understanding if an interruption or disturbance in the acquisition of math knowledge or if a neurobiological influence is rendering mathematical difficulty is vital in accurate assessment and intervention (Ottmar, 2017; Secher Schmidt, 2016; Siemann & Petermann, 2018).

Math Anxiety

Math anxiety is a well-documented, extensively studied, specific condition that affects far too many—young and old, students, parents, and teachers (Chang et al., 2017; Eden et al., 2013; Luttenberger et al., 2018; Ramirez et al., 2018). All of the factors previously discussed can lead to math anxiety. It is distinct from general anxiety, although math anxiety does have some overlap with test anxiety. Estimates of how common it is are varied, but it seems likely that math anxiety affects one fourth of 4-year college students and one third of 15-year-old students internationally (e.g., Foley et al., 2017). Math anxiety is important to address.

Math anxiety is not the result of lower cognitive ability; in fact, higher math achievers from all over the world experience more math anxiety and suffer greater performance impacts (Foley et al., 2017). Math anxiety interacts with motivation and self-efficacy, further affecting the opportunity to develop mathematical ability. It is a downward spiral.

Scientists studying math anxiety agree that it dramatically reduces working memory capacity (Beilock & Willingham 2014; Skagerlund et al., 2019). Because working memories, including visual-spatial working memory and verbal working memory (for word problems), are key cognitive abilities associated with math achievement, the effect of math anxiety is dramatic, especially for those whose working memories are naturally strong. Math anxiety will impact more advanced problem solving, so the impact increases with age and mathematics level. But math anxiety also impacts the number processing used for basic arithmetic (Skagerlund et al., 2019). Because math anxiety leads to avoidance of courses or career choices that involve mathematics, it severely impacts not only individual lives, but also whole societies.

Stealth Dyscalculia

Why does any gifted person struggle in math? Unfortunately, there is currently little to no information about the hybridized state of giftedness and dyscalculia, another fascinating twice-exceptionality, or other mathematics difficulties/disorders. Even so, anecdotal information exists.

Eide and Eide (2015) coined the phrase *stealth dyslexia* to describe children with:

> characteristic dyslexic difficulties with word processing and written output [who have] findings on neurological and neuropsychological testing consistent with the auditory, visual, language, and motor processing deficits characteristic of dyslexia, and reading skills that appear to fall within the normal or even superior range for children their age, at least on silent reading comprehension. (p. 1)

Although not yet employed within the literature, we propose that stealth dyscalculia may be a viable parallel to describe those twice-exceptional individuals who are both gifted and dyscalculic. Some gifted students may have easily recognizable math disability/dyscalculia. Stealth dyscalculia will be identified when characteristic dyscalculic difficulties are identified through neuropsychological testing even if mathematical skills appear to fall within the average or even superior range for their age, especially when additional time or other accommodation is provided. These children often go undetected until much later in their educational careers, as their brightness/giftedness offers compensatory mechanisms concealing their dyscalculic processing such that both the brightness/giftedness and the dyscalculia may be masked.

These 2e students may not develop automatic retrieval of number facts and basic procedures in the early grades. Instead, these gifted students may display an ability to keep figuring them out every time by utilizing greater verbal reasoning, stronger working memory, or better fluid intelligence to circumvent typically developing or required mathematics processing for problem solving. By the time the problem size becomes too big even for their compensatory mechanisms, these students have bypassed significant math foundation building. This is not helped by modern curricula that deemphasize storing number facts and basic procedures in long-term memory and emphasize written language. Because these students did not need this math knowledge in the early grades, they did not store it. Nobody insisted on it or discovered that they needed extra help doing it; therefore, these students' struggles went further unnoticed. For students with basic deficits, math development requires explicit instruction and practice they did not experience. Is it any wonder that gifted students suffer higher rates of math anxiety?

For gifted students in our clinical practice, math disability is becoming evident later, and they are working much harder to solve problems without good retrieval of facts and procedures. They may use their fingers to count and calculate. They may ask for directions. They may have difficulties with time and money. They focus upon verbal interactions to understand math. They need calculators. As with any discrepant ability, the difficulty is unexpected and difficult to acknowledge. These students often need remedial help in middle school in order to reach their potential in mathematics. They must gain automatic retrieval of number facts, and they deserve a chance to step back to see (again) the conceptual basis for certain number facts. These students need the math language and the pencil-and-paper procedures. It is well worth learning facts and basic procedures well enough that they can be automatically recalled and applied, and it is essential for moving beyond the four operations (addition, subtraction, multiplication, and division) into proportional reasoning, algebra, geometry, trigonometry, statistics, and calculus. Gifted students may resist repetition; however, sufficient repetition is vital for math facts and procedural fluency. The foundation must be solid and in place to build into the mathematical areas that require logical, abstract, and creative reasoning—and, the more multisensory and contextual, the better.

Differential Diagnoses/ Co-Occurring Conditions: Diagnosing Math Difficulty

School assessments, standardized year-end tests, teacher comments and interviews, and parent and student interviews all give valuable evidence about math difficulty. Additional evaluations inclusive of educational to neuropsychological assessments may also be provided to ascertain if a mathematics disorder/disability is present. Ad hoc skills assessments provide insight. The Numeracy Screener developed at Western University in Ontario, Canada, is a 2- to 4-minute downloadable test that assesses symbolic and nonsymbolic number understanding in children in Pre-K–grade 3 (Nosworthy et al., 2013). The Feifer Assessment in Math (Feifer & Clark, 2016) provides norm-referenced standardized measures of aspects of dyscalculia. It includes a shorter screening test and can be used beginning in Pre-K. Many other measures are also available, from published norm-referenced standardized tests, to screening tests devised by individual curricula, teachers, and educational resource specialists. Evaluations that determine intellectual potential and mathematics achievement levels, as well as other sensory processing and neurological areas (attention/executive functioning, memory, etc.), are oftentimes provided to identify if a math difficulty is diagnosable and where the math difficulties are rooted.

Math difficulties, whether qualitatively observed or statistically demonstrated, may derive from a variety of root causes. Consequently, when exploring and evaluating math difficulties, proper identification is vital in determining relevant and appropriate interventions and accommodations.

Differential Diagnosis

Difficulties in mathematics may derive from external factors, such as unexpected life events, traumatic affectations (Jacobson, n.d.), inadequate or incompatible math instruction, language factors, socioeconomic opportunities, and math anxiety. Appropriate and detailed examination of an individual's educational, cultural/immigration/language, socioeconomic, and family histories is important to distinguish these factors from dyscalculia. General physical and mental health are important.

Difficulties in mathematics may derive from endogenous biological factors, such as intellectual disability (intellectual developmental disorder), Attention Deficit/Hyperactivity Disorder (ADHD), difficulties with working memory and processing speed, and dyslexic processing. Appropriate background information gained from clinical interviews; gathering information from other collateral contacts, including a student's family and school; and apposite psychological and neuropsychological evaluation are vital in establishing these diagnoses.

Attention Deficit/Hyperactivity Disorder

According to APA (2013), ADHD is a:

> neurodevelopmental disorder defined by impairing levels of inattention, disorganization, and/or hyperactivity-impulsivity. Inattention and disorganization entail inability to stay on task, seeming not to listen, and losing materials, at levels that are inconsistent with age or developmental level. Hyperactivity-impulsivity entails overactivity, fidgeting, inability to stay seated, intruding into other people's activities, and inability to wait—symptoms that are excessive for age or developmental level. (p. 31)

Attention is important for math learning (Geary, 2013). Therefore, difficulties with focus and hyperactivity/impulsivity may impair an individual's ability to attend to and engage in mathematics, potentially resulting in holes in learning. This is not a mathematics disorder; rather, mathematics difficulties are secondary to ADHD as sustained attention is needed for memory of mathematics and reasoning of multistep math problems.

Working Memory and Processing Speed

Neurodevelopmental disorders that distress working memory and processing speed, as cognitive efficiency is directly correlated to mathematics mastery, may also contribute to problems in math. Working memory is required to recognize, retrieve, and manipulate information mentally and to concertize material learned into long-term memory for automaticity. Both verbal memory and visual-spatial working memory are necessary for problem solving as needed concepts are identified, necessary math facts are retrieved, procedural steps are followed, and successful completion is recognized. Working memory is related to brain structure, and its function changes between childhood and adulthood (Bathelt et al., 2018).

If processing speed is impaired, mathematic processing will also be impaired. Although math fluency is often used as an indicator of math ability, it is actually an ability statistically separable from untimed math performance (Petrill et al., 2012). Given sufficient time, students may be able to demonstrate otherwise unrecognized strength in mathematics. But school math almost always requires fluency in the absence of special accommodations.

Dyslexic Processing

Dyslexic processing may be dysphonetic (i.e., an inability to hear the separate sounds that make up words), dyseidetic (i.e., an impairment in the ability to recognize words visually), or a combination of the two. Dyseidetic dyslexia may affect math as well as reading because both involve symbolic mastery (Cheng et al., 2018; Lander et al., 2009). But given the extent to which written words have become part of the math curricula, dyslexic processing in any form will impair math performance. Differential diagnoses of dyslexia from dyscalculia may be gained through appropriate assessment of educational history with evidence that early learning of mathematics remained intact (i.e., numeracy was within normal limits and expectations for the individual), and neuropsychological evaluation that mathematical conceptual knowledge remains relatively commensurate to intellectual potential even though math calculations and math facts fluency may be compromised.

Visual and Auditory Perception

Visual perception is important for success in school math (Cheng et al., 2018). A routine eye examination outside a clinic may conclude that a child has 20:20 vision. This only means that each eye, acting independently, could focus at a distance of 20 feet. This may not be enough for any kind of successful school performance, which involves focusing both eyes together at the same time and place at book, writing, and manipulation distance; tracking successfully across a line of words or an equation or down a column of numbers; and refocusing on the next line or next necessary information. Visual perception is the precursor to visual-spatial working memory and is essential for mathematical thinking. Binocular focusing and tracking issues can be diagnosed and remediated by developmental optometrists. Similarly, auditory processing affects the ability to perform well in academic settings and should also be evaluated. When math is taught through verbal means, it may be important to assess for auditory processing, which involves the ability to receive, organize, and process this auditory mathematical information.

Dysgraphia

Dysgraphia affects the ability to successfully communicate mathematical thinking. Dysgraphia can affect math through difficult-to-read calculations; inconsistent spacing between numbers and symbols; omitting numbers, letters, and words in writing math answers; or difficulty copying numbers from the board, avoiding tasks involving drawing or writing (Cherry, 2016). Unlike tools available for difficulty communicating in words, there are no easy-to-use math typing or dictation programs available to school children for communicating in numbers.

Accommodations can help. Rarely is enough space provided for clearly seeing or thoroughly and clearly solving math problems. Leaving clear spacing between problems helps. Providing ample space for solutions or requiring that work be shown on separate pages helps. Faintly lined grid paper (1/4 inch or larger) may help. Giving instructions in more than one format—in writing as well as by voice, in backup online format—can help reading, attention and auditory processing issues. Allowing for sufficient/extra time can help with processing speed. These problems must be recognized to be accommodated and/or remediated.

Co-Occurring Conditions

Specific learning disorder in mathematics may commonly co-occur with neurodevelopmental, processing, or other mental disorders (e.g., anxiety disorders, depressive and bipolar disorders). These:

> comorbidities do not necessarily exclude the diagnosis specific learning disorder but may make testing and differential diagnosis more difficult, because each of the co-occurring disorders independently interferes with the execution of activities of daily living, including learning. Thus, clinical judgment is required to attribute such impairment to learning difficulties. If there is an indication that another diagnosis could account

for the difficulties learning keystone academic skills . . . specific learning disorder should not be diagnosed. (APA, 2013, p. 74)

Recommendations

As neuroscience and cognitive science reveal more and more about inborn math abilities and how math abilities (may or may not) develop, educators can learn a great deal about how math teaching could bring numeracy to everyone. We strongly recommend revised approaches that would help gifted children avoid hitting walls in upper elementary and middle school. These would allow educators to act on the belief that numeracy is as important as literacy.

Important Considerations

1. Gifted learners typically learn new skills at an accelerated pace when compared with other learners.
2. Gifted learners generally do not need the number of repetitions that other students require.
3. Gifted learners will achieve at greater levels if instruction builds conceptual understanding along with the development of automatic recall.
4. Acknowledging a disability or asking for help may be difficult for a student who typically excels in other areas.

Developmental science has shown that successful math learning involves different brain pathways than the pathways used for successful reading. Math pathways starting out in the ANS share common brain areas with reading (the hippocampus and nearby areas) during storage of basic math facts and procedures in long-term memory (Qin et al., 2014), but become more independent of language pathways as mastery is achieved (Amalric & Dehaene, 2018; see Figure 6.1).

The development of automatic recall of basic math facts depends upon curriculum and upon methods of teaching and individual learning. As it stands now, when that development takes place is highly variable, and that is unfortunate, because mastery is based on automaticity. All students should leave third grade able to retrieve number facts and basic procedures so that they are ready to build the new brain pathways needed for fractions, decimals, and percentages in fifth and sixth grade; progression in grade 8 or 9 to algebra; and preparation for high school geometry, calculus, and statistics before they graduate. The underpinning for success in this progression is fluent retrieval of number facts (Price et al., 2013).

Recent math curricula have increased emphasis on story problems, in an effort to make math relevant to real life. But recent research at Vanderbilt University, an important center for understanding math learning, suggests that this may not be the best approach (Fuchs et al., 2016). Fuchs et al.'s research suggests that training in solving word problems did not improve calculation, and training in calculation did not improve solving word problems. Although similar processes are called upon, the brain processes are different. In fact, too much emphasis on word problems in the early elementary grades will interfere with developing skill in calculation. Learning to solve word problems is an important goal for numeracy, but the conceptual and skill development for this understanding is separate and intensive in its own right, requiring development over the long term (David Berg, Making Math Real Institute, personal communications, July 15, 2019; January 26, 2020).

Teachers must use words to teach math, but in early grades these words can be spoken rather than written, demonstrated with multisensory approaches, and recorded in the mathematical language of symbols (e.g., numbers, operation signs, equal signs). Learning number facts (and basic arithmetic procedures) so that they are available for immediate retrieval requires storage in long-term memory (Geary et al., 2012), but this need not be painful. Repeated practice is essential, but multisensory methods, games, and problem solving in math language (number and operation symbols) allow sufficient practice without pain. This important work can be interesting, fun, and rewarding. It must not be dismissed as "rote memorization" or "drill and kill."

Both words and time affect math learning (see Table 6.2). Processing speed develops with age and brain maturation. When this development occurs is variable, and in addition, gifted children often have asynchronous development that can include delayed development of and relatively lower processing speed. All children should have a chance to learn and perform at a speed consistent with their own current development. Better test, quiz, and homework design can allow sufficient time for thoughtful responses that measure understanding more than processing speed.

Multisensory teaching and learning involves hearing, seeing, touching, and movement. A variety of math manipulatives are necessary. It involves hands and gestures (Hynes-Berry et al., 2019). In Asian countries, abacus training that leads to mental calculation improves both calculation skills and conceptual

TABLE 6.2

For Effective Math Teaching, Address These Issues

Words	Time
■ Recognize that math and language have separate brain pathways. ■ Use math symbols, fewer written words. ■ Emphasize fact automaticity before story problems requiring them. ■ Omit requirements for word writing until math language is well developed. ■ Teach word problem solving as a separate development.	■ Recognize that speed does not equal math knowledge. ■ Acknowledge brain development and allow time for it. ■ Reduce time pressure. ■ Value thoughtfulness as much as speediness. ■ Support variability in processing speed. ■ Consider the cognitive load.

knowledge (Li et al., 2016). Weng et al. (2017) reported brain changes with abacus-based mental calculation (AMC) training that may improve visual-spatial information processing. Cho and So (2018) showed that children ages 6–8 given this training first master calculation with specific hand gestures and a physical abacus, then move to mental calculation using the same gestures, and ultimately gain mastery through visual-spatial processing even without hand gestures. Math teaching and learning involves pencil-and-paper work. It requires questioning and analyzing student understanding and prescribing incremental next steps accordingly (Berg, n.d.). Games allow engaged practice. But projects and games should be focused on the work necessary to achieve automaticity in early elementary grades rather than providing a diversion from this essential brain development.

As already discussed, twice-exceptional children with mathematical difficulties may not have solid retrieval of number facts because they could always "figure it out" using compensating strategies in the time allowed. But eventually, problems to be solved place too much demand on even the best working memories. Stored number facts, fewer words, and less time pressure will help all children, including gifted children, reach full numeracy.

Just as with dyslexia, dyscalculia can be remediated. New brain pathways can be established with professional help. Several recent studies show significant brain changes in key math brain pathways with specific one-to-one tutoring for time periods as short as 8 weeks. These brain changes were associated with improved performance (Jolles, Supekar, et al., 2016; Jolles, Wasserman, et al., 2016; Supekar et al., 2015).

Math anxiety is a key factor that must be addressed in the remediation of any math difficulty. Poor math performance certainly can lead to math anxiety, but math anxiety may cause poor math performance, particularly among students whose good working memory is compromised (Ramirez et al., 2018).

Math-anxious parents and teachers add to environmental factors that can cause math anxiety. A program initiated at the University of Chicago gave families iPads and access to a program, Bedtime Math, designed to encourage comfortable math interactions with children through stories and thinking about math questions together. The children's math achievement improved significantly across the school year compared to a control group that had access to a reading program, and this was especially true for children with parents who had math anxiety (Berkowitz et al., 2015). Positive math experiences and attitudes toward math from birth are an important step in the right direction (Chen et al., 2018).

Remediation of foundation gaps can reduce math anxiety. Supekar et al. (2015) found significant reduction in math anxiety after only 8 weeks of one-to-one tutoring with math-anxious third graders. In this study, tutoring three times a week focused on number concepts and skills, including speeded practice based on an approach developed by Fuchs et al. (2013). Before and after measures resulted in reduced math anxiety, improved math performance, and remediated aberrant brain responses across brain regions, including the amygdala and, prefrontal and parietal cortices.

Interpretation of math difficulty may be an important source of math anxiety, one that can be remediated. Students who have difficulty may conclude that they have poor ability, and this interpretation can lead to anxiety. This can lead to even more difficulty, as well as to avoidance of future math (and the opportunities math provides). These students can be coached to reinterpret their difficulty, to reframe math as an acceptable challenge, rather than an impossible barrier. For students motivated to do well and who take on the challenge, a little math anxiety led to optimal performance. These students could see and meet the challenge by reframing their interpretation. Students can benefit from understanding that peak performance is achieved under situations of moderate stress (Ramirez et al., 2018). Another effective strategy involved journaling about math concerns, which served to reduce anxiety and/or give insight into reasons for it sufficient to set it aside (Park et al., 2014).

There is some gender involvement with math anxiety. Although it is possible that differences in spatial processing may be involved, it is much more likely that gender differences are due to stereotypic thinking and cultural misappropriations of academics that are gender-specific. This, too, can be remediated with internal narratives and good coaching. Devine et al. (2013) found similar math ability in boys and girls.

There is no single published curriculum that meets the needs of 2e students with math difficulty. Making Math Real (http://www.makingmathreal.org) is a multisensory structured methodology, but it is not a curriculum. It is a learning institute for teachers and parents to enable them to reach the full diversity of learning styles, including in students who have learning disabilities, are gifted, or are twice-exceptional. It is consistent with cognitive science and neurobiology. Ultimately, it is the teaching that matters. A successful teacher or tutor will use structured, multisensory methods to develop and follow a prescriptive program based on an accurate diagnosis of the difficulty.

Conclusion

Being identified as gifted does not guarantee success in math. There are a variety of reasons why math can be difficult, including dyscalculia, foundational gaps in math education, life events, math anxiety, or math avoidance and lost opportunity. Evidence from neuroscience and cognitive science shows numeracy is not only stepwise, but also developmental (Fuchs et al., 2010). Math processing uses brain pathways and brain areas that are separate from those for reading, and there is a critical period of intense activity in brain areas dedicated to long-term storage and automatic retrieval of foundational knowledge: number facts/basic procedures for math. Math has its own language, grammar, and syntax. Consequently, math educators benefit most from teachings that focus upon this language of math without overemphasis upon math fluency (speed). When conceptual and calculation difficulties are present due to difficulties with the Approximate Number System, this is understood as dyscalculia, which then requires a prescriptive multisensory approach.

For those who are twice-exceptional (2e) with giftedness and math difficulties from dyscalculia, we propose the descriptive term *stealth dyscalculia* to describe math-based difficulty that may remain undetected due to strong compensation mechanisms with verbal, fluid reasoning and working memory strengths.

Math difficulties can be overcome with targeted accommodations and prescriptive remediation, and new brain pathways can be established. In addition, math anxiety may interact with other math difficulties and can impact gifted/high-achieving math students disproportionately. Building confidence also matters. For the sake of twice-exceptional children, dyscalculia and math difficulty must be recognized, researched, and remediated.

FROM THE EDITORS

Student Vignettes

Alexa

Alexa is curious about the world around her and has wide-ranging interests. At 3, she was able to amuse herself for hours looking at books or at rocks under a magnifying glass. Her love of learning continues, and as a fourth grader, she enjoys her science, social studies, language arts, and art classes. Despite her interests, she struggles in math and dislikes music class.

Alexa's parents believe she is very bright and are puzzled by her struggles in math. Despite their efforts to help, she seems unable to grasp math basic concepts. Homework has become a daily battle, and Alexa is clearly frustrated by her poor performance on math assignments and tests. After Alexa's parents discuss their concerns with her teacher, she is recommended for a special needs assessment. A thorough assessment reveals Alexa has talent in several domains, as well as dyscalculia, a mathematical disability in which a person has unusual difficulty solving arithmetic problems and grasping math concepts.

With an IQ score of 141 and dyscalculia, Alexa is a twice-exceptional student, meaning that she has dual exceptionalities. She is gifted and has a learning disability. Although her gifts coupled with her interests and motivation could make her a candidate for accelerative instruction, a whole grade of acceleration would be inappropriate given her dyscalculia. Alexa might, however, benefit from subject (content-based) acceleration in science and language arts.

Discussion Questions

1. How can Alexa's dyscalculia be addressed?
2. In what ways can Alexa's parents and teachers support her talents and interests?
3. Is it possible to accelerate instruction in some content areas but not others?
4. In what ways can and should schools support students who are twice-exceptional?

FROM THE EDITORS, *continued*

Sarah

A car accident left Sarah, 28, with a severe concussion and broken arm 6 months ago. Although her arm healed quickly, daily headaches and fatigue remain an ongoing battle. Despite these challenges Sarah is anxious to return to work at the law firm where she was employed before the accident. Before she is allowed to do so, her employer requires her to pass a full battery of tests to prove that she is both physically and cognitively able to work.

After passing the physical assessment, Sarah made an appointment to take the cognitive test. She remembered taking the Critical Cognitive Aptitude Test (CCAT) during the interview process for her job as a paralegal. Even though it reminded her of the Cognitive Abilities Test (CogAT) she had taken in grade school, she passed the CCAT. She has suffered from test anxiety after taking the CogAT and learning that she had not qualified for the gifted program. Discovering she would have to requalify for her job terrified her.

Following the completion of the online test, she met with the psychologist to review her results in each of three categories: verbal reasoning, logic and math, and spatial reasoning. The psychologist assured Sarah that her cognitive functioning placed her well above average. Sarah had scored 85 in the spatial reasoning portion of the test measuring her ability to visualize, make spatial judgements, and problem solve. Her verbal ability score, measuring reasoning, comprehension of words, constructive thinking, and attention to detail was 82. Sarah's math and logic score was considerably lower at 45. When she heard the results, Sarah sighed—math had never been her strong suit, and simple computations were still a challenge—so much so that she often joked that she would be lost without the calculator on her phone.

After clearing Sarah to return to work, the psychologist asked about her school experience. Given the discrepancy between her scores, he wondered about her performance in math classes. Sarah told him how she had struggled with basic algebra, multiplication, and division. Number sequences were hard, and word problems a complete disaster. Sarah confessed that had her math skills been better, she would have applied to law school.

FROM THE EDITORS, *continued*

Discussion Questions

1. What characteristics of a twice-exceptional learner does Sarah exhibit?
2. Is it important for Sarah to understand her test scores?
3. In what ways might Sarah's school and career experience been different had she understand her exceptionality?
4. At 28, is it possible for Sarah to benefit from further assessment and intervention?

Resources

- 2eNews: https://www.2enews.com
- Bedtime Math: http://bedtimemath.org
- Dyscalculia.org: https://www.dyscalculia.org
- Making Math Real Institute: http://www.makingmathreal.org
- National Association for Gifted Children: https://www.nagc.org
- ST Math: https://www.stmath.com (see Wendt et al., 2018)
- Understood.org: https://www.understood.org

References

Amalric, M., & Dehaene, S. (2018). Cortical circuits for mathematical knowledge: Evidence for a major subdivision within the brain's semantic networks. *Philosophical Transactions of the Royal Society B, 373*(1740). https://doi.org/10.1098/rstb.2016.0515

American Psychiatric Association. (2013). *Diagnostic and statistical manual of mental disorders* (5th ed.). https://doi.org/10.1176/appi.books.9780890425596

Ashcroft, M. H., & Moore, A. M. (2009). Mathematics anxiety and the affective drop in performance. *Journal of Psychoeducational Assessment, 27*(3), 197–205. https://doi.org/10.1177/0734282908330580

Bartelet, D., Ansari, D., Vaessen, A., & Blomert, L. (2014). Cognitive subtypes of mathematics learning difficulties in primary education. *Research in Developmental Disabilities, 35*(3), 657–670. https://doi.org/10.1016/j.ridd.2013.12.010

Barth, H., La Mont, K., Lipton, J., & Spelke, E. S. (2005). Abstract number and arithmetic in preschool children. *PNAS, 102*(39), 14116–14121. https://doi.org/10.1073/pnas.0505512102

Bathelt, J., Gathercole S. E., Johnson, A., & Astle, D. E. (2018). Differences in brain morphology and working memory across childhood. *Developmental Science, 21*(3), e12579. https://doi.org/10.1111/desc.12579

Battista, C., Evans, T. M., Ngoon, T. J., Chen, T., Chen, L., Kochalka, J., & Menon, V. (2018). Mechanisms of interactive specialization and emergence of functional brain circuits supporting cognitive development in children. *npj Science of Learning, 3*(1). https://doi.org/10.1038/s41539-017-0017-2

Beilock, S. L., & Willingham, D. (2014). Math anxiety: Can teachers help students reduce it? Ask the cognitive scientist. *American Educator, 38*(2), 28–32.

Berch, D. B., Geary, D. C., & Koepke, K. M. (Eds.). (2016). *Development of mathematical cognition: Neural substrates and genetic influences.* Academic Press.

Berg, D. (n.d.). *Learn how to close the gap in achievement and reach the full diversity of learners.* Making Math Real. http://www.makingmathreal.org/about

Berkowitz, T., Schaeffer, M. W., Maloney, E. A., Peterson, L., Gregor, C., Levine, S. C., & Beilock, S. L. (2015). Math at home adds up to achievement in school. *Science, 350*(6257), 196–198. https://doi.org/10.1126/science.aac7427

Bonny, J. W., & Lourenco, S. F. (2013). The approximate number system and its relation to early math achievement: Evidence from the preschool years. *Journal of Experimental Child Psychology 114*(3), 375–388. https://doi.org/10.1016/j.jecp.2012.09.015

Butterworth, B. (2018). The implications for education of an innate numerosity-processing mechanism. *Philosophical Transactions of the Royal Society B, 373*(1740). https://doi.org/10.1098/rstb.2017.0118

Butterworth, B., Varma, S., & Laurillard, D. (2011). Dyscalculia: from brain to education. *Science, 332*(6033), 1049–1053. https://doi.org/10.1126/science.1201536

Cantlon, J. F., Brannon, E. M., Carter, E. J., & Pelphrey, K. A. (2006). Functional imaging of numerical processing in adults and 4-yr-old children. *PLoS Biology, 4*(5), e125. https://doi.org/10.1371/journal.pbio.0040125

Castaldi, E., Mirassou, A., Dehaene, S., Piazza, M., & Eger, E. (2018). Asymmetrical interference between number and item size perception provides evidence for a domain specific impairment in dyscalculia. *PLOS ONE, 13*(12), e0209256. https://doi.org/10.1371/journal.pone.0209256

Chang, H., Sprute, L., Maloney, E. A., Beilock, S. L., & Berman, M. G. (2017). Simple arithmetic: Not so simple for highly math anxious individuals. *Social Cognitive and Affective Neuroscience, 12*(12), 1940–1949. https://doi.org/10.1093/scan/nsx121

Chen, L. Bae, S. R., Battista, C., Qin, S., Chen, T., Evans, T. M., & Menon, V. (2018). Positive attitude toward math supports early academic success: behavioral evidence and neurocognitive mechanisms. *Psychological Science, 29*(3), 390–402. https://doi.org/10.1177/0956797617735528

Cheng, D., Xiao, Q., Qian, C., Cui, J., & Zhou, X. (2018). Dyslexia and dyscalculia are characterized by common visual perception deficits. *Developmental Neuropsychology, 43*(6), 497–507. https://doi.org/10.1080/87565641.2018.1481068

Cherry, J. (2016, April 4). https://study.com/academy/lesson/dysgraphia-math-difficulties-accommodations.html

Cho, P. S., & So, W. C. (2018, August). A feel for numbers: The changing role of gesture in manipulating the mental representation of an abacus among children at different skill levels. *Frontiers in Psychology, 9*, 1267. https://doi.org/10.3389/fpsyg.2018.01267

DeFina, P. A., & Moser, R. S. (2011). An overview of neuroscience contributions to the understanding of dyscalculia in children. In A. S. Andrew (Ed.), *Handbook of pediatric neuropsychology* (pp. 683–687). Springer.

DeFina, P. A., & Moser, R. S. (2013). Psychopathology of mathematics disorder and dyscalculia. In A. S. Davis (Ed.), *Psychopathology of childhood and adolescence: A neuropsychological approach* (pp. 133–139). Springer.

Dehaene, S. (1997). *The number sense: How the mind creates mathematics*. Oxford University Press.

Devine, A., Soltész, F., Nobes, A., Gosami, U., & Szűcs, D. (2013, October). Gender differences in developmental dyscalculia depend on diagnostic criteria. *Learning and Instruction, 27*, 31–39. https://doi.org/10.1016/j.learninstruc.2013.02.004

Diamond, M. C., Krech, D., & Rosenzweig, M. R. (1964). The effects of an enriched environment on the histology of the rat cerebral cortex. *Journal of Comparative Neurology, 123*(1), 111–120. https://doi.org/10.1002/cne. 901230110

Eden, C., Heine, A., & Jacobs, A. M. (2013). Mathematics anxiety and its development in the course of formal schooling—a review. *Psychology, 4*(6B), 27–35. https://dx.doi.org/10.4236/psych.2013.46A2005

Eide, B., & Eide, F. (2015). *Stealth dyslexia: How some dyslexic students escape detection*. Understood. https://www.understood.org/en/community-events/blogs/the-inside-track/2015/03/04/stealth-dyslexia-how-some-dyslexic-students-escape-detection

Feifer, S. G., & Clark, H. K. (2016). *Feifer Assessment of Mathematics: Professional manual.* PAR.

Foley, A. E., Herts, J. B., Borgonovi, F., Guerriero, S., Levine, S. C., & Beilock, S. L. (2017). The math anxiety-performance link: A global phenomenon. *Current Directions in Psychological Science, 26*(1), 52–58. https://doi.org/10.1177/0963721416672463

Fuchs, L. S., Geary, D. C., Compton, D. L., Fuchs, D., Hamlett, C. L., & Bryant, J. D. (2010). The contributions of numerosity and domain-general abilities to school readiness. *Child Development, 81*(5), 1520–1533. https://doi.org/10.1111/j.1467-8624.2010.01489.x

Fuchs, L. S., Geary, D. C., Compton, D. L., Fuchs, D., Schatschneider, C., Hamlett, C. L., DeSelms, J., Seethaler, P. M., Wilson, J., Craddock, C. F., Bryant, J. D., Luther, K., & Changas, P. (2013). Effects of first-grade number knowledge tutoring with contrasting forms of practice. *Journal of Educational Psychology, 105*(1), 58–77. https://doi.org/10.1037/a0030127

Fuchs, L. S., Geary, D. C., Fuchs, D., Compton, D. L., & Hamlett, C. L. (2016). Pathways to third-grade calculation versus word-reading competence: Are they more alike or different? *Child Development, 87*(2), 558–567. https://doi.org/10.1111/cdev.12474

Geary, D. C. (2011). Consequences, characteristics, and causes of mathematical learning disabilities and persistent low achievement in mathematics. *Journal of Developmental and Behavioral Pediatrics, 32*(3), 250–263. https://doi.org/10.1097/DBP.0b013e318209edef

Geary, D. C. (2013). Early foundations for mathematics learning and their relations to learning *disabilities. Current Directions in Psychological Science, 22*(1), 23–27. https://doi.org/10.1177/0963721412469398

Geary, D. C., Hoard, M. K., & Bailey, D. H. (2012). Fact retrieval deficits in low achieving children and children with mathematical learning disability. *Journal of Learning Disabilities, 45*(4), 291–307. https://doi.org/10.1177/0022219410392046

Gogtay, N., Giedd, J. N., Lusk, L., Hayashi, K. M., Greenstein, D., Vaituzis, A. C., Nugent, T. F., III, Herman, D. H., Clausen, L. S., Toga, A. W., Rapoport, J. L., & Thompson, P. M. (2004). Dynamic mapping of human cortical development during childhood through early adulthood. *PNAS, 101*(21), 8174–8179. https://doi.org/10.1073/pnas.0402680101

Goldin-Meadow, S. (2003). *Hearing gesture: How our hands help us think*. Harvard University Press.

Haberstroh, S., & Schulte-Korne, G. (2019). Clinical practice guideline: The diagnosis and treatment of dyscalculia. *Deutsches Arzteblatt International, 116*, 107–114.

Hawes, Z., Nosworthy, N., Archibald, L., & Ansari, D. (2019, February). Kindergarten children's symbolic number comparison skills relate to 1st grade mathematics achievement: Evidence from a two-minute paper-and-pencil test. *Learning and Instruction, 59*, 21–33. https://doi.org/10.1016/j.learninstruc.2018.09.004

Herculano-Houzel, S. (2019, November 26). *Your big brain makes you human— count your neurons when you count your blessings.* The Conversation. https://theconversation.com/your-big-brain-makes-you-human-count-your-neurons-when-you-count-your-blessings-127398

Hynes-Berry, M., McCray, J. S., & Goldin-Meadow, S. (2019). The role of gesture in teaching and learning math. In J. S. McCray, J.-Q. Chen, & J. Eisenband Sorkin, *Growing mathematical minds: Conversations between developmental psychologists and early childhood teachers* (pp. 83–108). Routledge.

Individuals With Disabilities Education Act, 20 U.S.C. §1401 *et seq.* (1990). https://sites.ed.gov/idea/statuteregulations

Institute for the Study of Advanced Development. (n.d.). *The Columbus Group*. https://www.gifteddevelopment.com/isad/columbus-group

Jacobs Danan, J. A., & Gelman, R. (2017). The problems with percentages. *Philosophical Transactions of the Royal Society B, 373*(1740). https://dx.doi.org/10.1098/rstb.2016.0519

Jacobson, R. (n.d.). *How to spot dyscalculia*. Child Mind Institute. https://childmind.org/article/how-to-spot-dyscalculia

Jolles, D., Supekar, K., Richardson, J., Tenison, C., Ashkenazi, S., Rosenberg-Lee, M., Fuchs, L., & Menon, V. (2016, October). Reconfiguration of parietal circuits with cognitive tutoring in elementary school children. *Cortex, 83*, 231–245. https://doi.org/10.1016/j.cortex.2016.08.004

Jolles, D., Wassermann, D., Chokhani, R., Richardson, J., Tenison, C., Bammer, R., Fuchs, L., Supekar, K., & Menon, V. (2016, April). Plasticity of left perisylvian white-matter tracts is associated with individual differences in math learning. *Brain Structure & Function, 221,* 1337–1351. https://doi.org/10.1007/s00429-014-0975-6

Kaufmann, L., & von Aster, M. (2012). The diagnosis and management of dyscalculia. *Deutsches Ärzteblatt International, 109*(45), 767–778. https://doi.org/10.3238/arztebl.2012.0767

Kersey, A. J., Wakim, K.-M., Li, R., & Cantlon, J. F. (2019, October). Developing, mature, and unique functions of the child's brain in reading and mathematics. *Developmental Cognitive Neuroscience, 39,* 100684. https://doi.org/10.1016/j.dcn.2019.100684

Košč, L. (1974). Developmental dyscalculia. *Journal of Learning Disabilities, 7*(3), 164–177. https://doi.org/10.1177/002221947400700309

Košč, L. (1981). Neuropsychological implications of diagnosis and treatment of mathematical learning disabilities. *Topics in Learning and Learning Disabilities, 1*(3), 19–30.

Kubas, H. A., & Hale, J. B. (2015, March 17). *LDs in Mathematics: Evidence-based interventions, strategies, and resources.* LD@school. https://www.ldatschool.ca/evidence-based-interventions-for-math

Lander, K., Fussenegger, B., Moll, K., & Willburger, E. (2009). Dyslexia and dyscalculia: Two learning disorders with different cognitive profiles. *Journal of Experimental Child Psychology, 103*(3), 309–324. https://doi.org/10.1016/j.jecp.2009.03.006

Li, Y., Chen, F., & Huang, W. (2016). Neural plasticity following abacus training in humans: a review and future directions. *Neural Plasticity,* 1213723. http://dx.doi.org/10.1155/2016/1213723

Luttenberger, S., Wimmer, S., & Paechter, M. (2018, August). Spotlight on math anxiety. *Psychology Research and Behavior Management, 11,* 311–332. https://doi.org/10.2147/PRBM.S141421

Macaruso, P., & Sokol, S. M. (1998). Cognitive neuropsychology and developmental dyscalculia. In C. Donlan (Ed.), *The development of mathematical skills* (pp. 201–225). Taylor & Francis.

Melby-Lervåg, M., Lyster, S.-A. H., & Hulme, C. (2012). Phonological skills and their role in learning to read: A meta-analytic review. *Psychological Bulletin, 138*(2), 322–352. https://doi.org/10.1037/a0026744

Moore, D. M., D'Mello, A. M., McGrath, L. M., & Stoodley, C. J. (2017, April). The developmental relationship between specific cognitive domains and grey matter in the cerebellum. *Developmental Cognitive Neuroscience, 24,* 1–11. https://doi.org/10.1016/j.dcn.2016.12.001

National Association for Gifted Children. (n.d.-a). *Twice-exceptional students.* https://www.nagc.org/resources-publications/resources-parents/twice-exceptional-students

National Association for Gifted Children. (n.d.-b). *What is giftedness?* https://www.nagc.org/resources-publications/resources/what-giftedness

National Council of Supervisors of Mathematics & National Council of Teachers of Mathematics. (2018). *Building STEM Education on a sound mathematical foundation: A joint position statement on STEM from the National Council of Supervisors of Mathematics and the National Council of Teachers of Mathematics.* https://www.nctm.org/Standards-and-Positions/Position-Statements/Building-STEM-Education-on-a-Sound-Mathematical-Foundation

Nosworthy, N., Bugden, S., Archibald, L., & Evans, B. (2013). A two-minute paper-and-pencil test of symbolic and nonsymbolic numerical magnitude processing explains variability in primary school children's arithmetic competence. *PLOS ONE, 8*(7), e67918. https://doi.org/10.1371/journal.pone.0067918

Ottmar, E. R. (2017). Book review of "Development of mathematical cognition: Neural substrates and genetic influences" (2016) edited by D. B. Berch, D. C. Geary, & K. M. Koepke. *Journal of Numerical Cognition, 3*(3), 716–722. https://doi.org/10.5964/jnc.v3i3.143

Park, D., Ramirez, G., & Beilock, S. L. (2014). The role of expressive writing in math anxiety. *Journal of Experimental Psychology: Applied, 20*(2), 103–111. https://doi.org/10.1037/xap0000013

Parsons, S., & Bynner, J. (2005). *Does numeracy matter more?* National Research and Development Centre for Adult Literacy and Numeracy. http://www.nrdc.org.uk/?p=19

Peters, E., Tompkins, M. K., Knoli, M. A. Z., Ardoin, S. P., Shoots-Reinhard, B., & Simon Meara, A. (2019). Despite high objective numeracy, lower numeric confidence related to worse financial and medical outcomes. *PNAS, 116*(3), 19386–19391. https://doi.org/10.1073/pnas.1903126116

Peters, L., & De Smedt, B. (2018, April). Arithmetic in the developing brain: A review of brain imaging studies. *Developmental Cognitive Neuroscience, 30*, 265–279. https://doi.org/10.1016/j.dcn.2017.05.002

Petrill, S., Logan, J., Hart, S., Vincent, P., Thompson, L., Kovas, Y., & Plomin, R. (2012). Math fluency is etiologically distinct from untimed math performance, decoding fluency, and untimed reading performance: Evidence from a twin study. *Journal of Learning Disabilities, 45*(4), 371–381. https://doi.org/10.1177/0022219411407926

Price, G. R., Mazzocco, M. M. M., & Ansari, D. (2013). Why mental arithmetic counts: Brain activation during single digit arithmetic predicts high school math scores. *Journal of Neuroscience, 33*(1), 156–163. https://doi.org/10.1523/JNEUROSCI.2936-12.2013

Qin, S., Cho, S., Chen, T., Rosenberg-Lee, M., Geary, D. C., & Menon, V. (2014). Hippocampal-neocortical functional reorganization underlies children's cognitive development. *Nature Neuroscience, 17*(9) 1263–1269. https://doi.org/10.1038/nn.3788

Raja, W. R, & Kumar, S. P. (2012). Findings of studies on dyscalculia—A synthesis. *Journal on Educational Psychology, 5*(3), 41–51.

Ramirez, G., Shaw, S. T., & Maloney, E. A. (2018). Math anxiety: Past research, promising interventions, and a new interpretation framework. *Educational Psychologist, 53*(3), 145–164. https://doi.org/10.1080/00461520.2018.144 7384

Schoenfeld, A. H. (2004). The math wars. *Educational Policy, 18*(1), 253–286. https://doi.org/10.1177/0895904803260042

Secher Schmidt, M. C. (2016). Dyscalculia ≠ math difficulties. An analysis of conflicting positions at a time that calls for inclusive practices. *European Journal of Special Needs Education, 31*(3), 407–421. https://doi.org/10.1080 /08856257.2016.1163016

Shalev, R. S. (2004). Developmental dyscalculia. *Journal of Child Neurology, 19*(10), 765–771. https://doi.org/10.1177/08830738040190100601

Siemann, J., & Petermann, F. (2018, April). Innate or acquired?–Disentangling number sense and early number competencies. *Frontiers in Psychology, 19.* https://doi.org/10.3389/fpsyg.2018.00571

Skagerlund, K., Ostergren, R., Vastfjall, D., & Traff, U. (2019). How does mathematics anxiety impair mathematical abilities? Investigating the link between math anxiety, working memory, and number processing. *PLOS ONE, 14*(1), e0211283. https://doi.org/10.1371/journal.pone.0211283

Supekar, K., Iuculano, T., Chen, L., Menon, V. (2015). Remediation of childhood math anxiety and associated neural circuits through cognitive tutoring. *Journal of Neuroscience, 35*(36), 12574–12583. https://doi.org/10.1523/JNEUROSCI.0786-15.2015

Szucs, D., Devine, A., Soltesz, F., Nobes, A., & Gabriel, F. (2013). Developmental dyscalculia is related to visuo-spatial memory and inhibition impairment. *Cortex, 49*(10), 2674–2688. https://doi.org/10.1016/j.cortex.2013.06.007

Szucs, D., & Goswami, U. (2013). Dyscalculia: Fresh perspectives. *Trends in Neuroscience and Education, 2*(2), 33–37. https://doi.org/10.1016/j.tine.20 13.06.004

Vanbinst, K., Ansari, D., Ghesquière, P., & De Smedt, B. (2016). Symbolic numerical magnitude processing is as important to arithmetic as phonological awareness is to reading. *PLOS ONE, 11*(3), e0151045. https://doi. org/10.1371/journal.pone.0151045

Vandervert, L. (2017). The origin of mathematics and number sense in the cerebellum: With implications for finger counting and dyscalculia. *Cerebellum & Ataxias, 4,* 12. https://doi.org/10.1186/s40673-017-0070-x

von Aster, M. (1994). Developmental dyscalculia in children: Review of the literature and clinical validation. *Acta Paedopsychiatrica: International Journal of Child & Adolescent Psychiatry, 56*(3), 169–178.

Wang, J. J., Halberda, J., & Feigenson, L. (2017, May). Approximate number sense correlates with math performance in gifted adolescents. *Acta Psychologica, 176,* 78–84. https://doi.org/10.1016/j.actpsy.2017.03.014

Wendt, S., Rice, J., & Nakamoto, J. (2018*). A cross-state evaluation of MIND Research Institute's ST Math program and math performance.* WestEd. https://www.wested.org/resources/st-math-evaluation

Weng, J., Xie, Y., Wang, C., & Chen, F. (2017, August 18). The effects of long-term abacus training on topological properties of brain functional networks. *Scientific Reports, 7,* 8862. https://doi.org/10.1038/s41598-017-08955-2

Wu, S. S., Chen, L., Battista, C., Smith Watts, A. K., Willcutt, E. G., & Menon, V. (2017, September). Distinct influences of affective and cognitive factors on children's non-verbal and verbal mathematical abilities. *Cognition, 166,* 118–129. https://doi.org/10.1016/j.cognition.2017.05.016

CHAPTER 7

Giftedness and Autism Spectrum Disorders

Claire E. Hughes

The ABC television series *The Good Doctor* highlights the challenges that a highly skilled surgeon with autism faces as he tries to work, make friends, and navigate the various requirements of being an independent adult. The series is unusual because the doctor's diagnoses are clearly stated and the challenges of inclusion into mainstream are not minimized, but what is perhaps most unusual is that the concept of being gifted with autism is mainstream enough to make for "good television" (Shore, 2019). Although many movies deal with the tension between ability and significant disability (Hughes, 2019), rarely does popular media explicitly explore in depth what it means to be gifted and diagnosed with autism.

Evolving Definitions and Concepts of Autism Spectrum Disorders

In 1943, the first mention of "autism" was published in English by Leo Kanner, a psychiatrist at Johns Hopkins University, who used "early infantile autism" to describe children with severe language deficiencies who exhibited social difficulties and repetitive behaviors or obsessions. Around the same time, in 1944, Hans Asperger wrote in German about "Autistic psychopathy in children." However, the children in his study often spoke fluently, but in the manner of adults, rather than children (Pearce, 2005). Asperger's work received little attention and was not translated into English until 1981; for 40 years, the concept of "autism" was thought to be exhibited primarily by children with significant developmental delays and limited intelligence. In 1979, Wing and Gould determined that autism is not a categorical diagnosis, but a dimensional one, in which the question is not whether or not a child has autism but in what ways the child demonstrates autism. In 1994, "Asperger's Disorder" was added into the fourth edition of the *Diagnostic and Statistical Manual of Mental Disorders* (DSM-IV; Autism Society, n.d.), an essential medical resource for diagnoses of mental and psychological issues, as a separate but related condition to autism. In 2013, the fifth edition of the DSM was introduced, and it subsumed multiple types of autistic-like conditions, such as Asperger's and Pervasive Developmental Disorder-Not Otherwise Specified (PDD-NOS) and Childhood Disintegrative Disorder into code 299.00 under the category "autism spectrum disorders," often abbreviated as ASD. Although the term "Asperger's" has been subsumed under autism spectrum disorders, there are many who still use the term to distinguish students with autism who have grammatical language, but challenges using it in social situations, from students with autism with significant language impairments and more intense needs (Autism Society, n.d.).

This role of language is a complex issue in autism and is highly connected to social use. The DSM uses two criteria for autism (American Psychiatric Association [APA], 2013): (1) persistent deficits in social communication and social interaction, and (2) restricted, repetitive patterns of behavior, interests or activities. The first criterion of ASD defines communication deficits that must appear across multiple contexts, meaning that they cannot occur in only one place or around one person. Examples of communication deficits can include challenges with back-and-forth conversation, failure to initiate or respond to communication, and/or a reduced sharing of interests or emotions. Examples also include issues with nonverbal communication, such as a lack of gestures, facial expressions, and/or eye contact. Lastly, the communication aspect of ASD must also be found in the problematic use of language, such as adjusting behavior and language in different social contexts and sharing imaginative play.

The second criterion of ASD involving behavior states that two of four possible aspects of "restriction or repetitive" must be present, either at the current time, or in the past. These restrictions include:

1. repetitive movements and use of objects or speech, such as lining up toys, repeated phrases, or physical movements;
2. insistence on sameness, rituals, or routines, such as the need to eat the same food every day, scripts for greetings, and distress when the routines are not followed;
3. highly restricted or fixated interests that are abnormal in intensity or focus; and
4. hypo- or hyperreactions to sensory input or interest in sensory input from the environment, such as lack of awareness of pain or fascination with lights or movement.

The DSM-5 clarified that ASD is not a "positive/negative" diagnosis, but that it varies according to levels of severity. The severity of the autism is defined as the ability to function in an environment. Levels of support needed range from Level 1, which is a mild level of support, to Level 3 which is "substantial support" (APA, 2013). Support systems in a school might range from a 1:1 paraprofessional, to provision of the day's schedule on the board. Although types of support are highly situational, the emphasis is on the fit between the individual and the demands of the environment. This flexible model of support emphasizes the social model of disability, in which the presence and severity of a disability is not diagnosed by a doctor, but is determined by those within the environment based on the social and behavioral demands and the individual's need of assistance to meet those demands (Shakespeare & Watson, 2001).

As the definition of autism has changed, so too has its rate of prevalence. As of September 2019, the Centers for Disease Control (CDC, 2020) has estimated that one in 59 children in the United States was found to be identified with autism, with 4 times as many boys as girls. This means that one in approximately 37 boys will be identified with autism, while one in 148 girls will. In the 1980s, about one in 2,000 children was diagnosed with autism, and since 2000, the prevalence of autism has increased from .067% of the population to 1.68% of the population, moving it from a low-incidence category of special education to a moderate-incidence category (CDC, 2020). And autism is clearly not an issue found solely in the United States. Although the reported rates of diagnosed autism fluctuate from country to country (almost 0% in Oman and 2.64% in South Korea), the typical range is 1%–2% across the world, using modern instruments (CDC, 2019b). Although researchers have yet to determine causes for this increase in prevalence rates, educators need to understand the characteristics related to autism and interventions that can support these students as they move through their educational years.

Social Model and Neurodiversity

Perhaps one of the most significant impacts in the field of autism in recent years has been the "neurodiversity" movement. Neurodiversity is a concept originating in the 1990s from Judy Singer (1999) that connects human cognition to "biodiversity," in which an ecosystem is stronger the more diverse it is. Silberman (2015) stated that:

> the notion that conditions like autism, dyslexia, and attention-deficit/hyperactivity disorder (ADHD) should be regarded as naturally occurring cognitive variations with distinctive strengths that have contributed to the evolution of technology and culture rather than mere checklists of deficits and dysfunctions. (p. 6)

From this concept has come the rise of a social model of autism, rather than a medical one.

The social model of disability defines disability as emerging from the social environment around an individual and focuses on issues related to barriers, attitudes, and exclusion, as opposed to the medical model, which seeks to identify what is wrong with an individual and then provide treatment (Shakespeare & Watson, 2001). A study that examined college students' beliefs about their autism found that those who perceived their autism as "difference" were significantly more likely to be focused on career development with higher self-perceptions than those who perceived autism as a "deficit" (Griffin & Pollack, 2009). Many of those who perceived autism as "difference" reported being active in neurodiversity support groups and online supports.

Such a shift in emphasis has had tremendous impact on both individuals and the language of disability. As one researcher said:

> We prefer the term ASC (Autism Spectrum Condition) rather than ASD (Autism Spectrum Disorder) because it is less stig-

matizing. Also, ASC is more consistent with the fact that these individuals have not only disabilities requiring a medical diagnosis, but also areas of cognitive strength. (Dudas et al., 2017, p. 1)

Renowned British autism researcher Simon Baron-Cohen (2010) noted that without the term *disorder*, implying that something is out of order or is wrong, American insurance companies would not pay doctors for treatment. Although his statement implies a cultural criticism, it also indicates an American value on treatment and cure, rather than a management or facilitation of behaviors.

This divide in the field of autism is exemplified by two of the major organizations. For more than 20 years, the advocacy group Autism Speaks has been responsible for raising the profile of autism and has been very successful at raising money for research purposes. However, one of the organization's founding tenets was to "cure" autism (Luterman, 2020). In contrast, the Autistic Self Advocacy Network (n.d.) has as its motto, "Nothing about us without us," and is a strong proponent of autism as a neurological variation. Both groups are focused on policy development and research but have very different belief structures.

One of the areas in which the neurodiversity model has made a significant impact is in the language of disability. Since the 1990s, special education has emphasized the use of "person-first" language, in which it is understood that people with disabilities are people first and then have a disability (Kirk et al., 2015). Thus, they are people with disabilities, such as a child with dyslexia and a student with an emotional disorder. However, in his impactful essay, Sinclair (1999) stated that:

Saying "a person with autism" suggests that autism is something bad—so bad that it isn't even consistent with being a person. Nobody objects to using adjectives to refer to characteristics of a person that are considered positive or neutral. We talk about left-handed people, not "people with left-handedness". . . . It is only when someone has decided that the characteristic being referred to is negative that suddenly people want to separate it from the person. I know that autism is not a terrible thing and that it does not make me any less of a person. (p. 3)

There are two other fields of exceptionality that do not consistently use person-first language. According to the Disability Language Style Guide (National Center on Disability and Journalism, 2020), the Deaf community has historically rejected person-first language as an implied rejection of its culture. People in the Deaf community often distinguish between "Deaf" as a culture with a capital D, "deaf" as an audiological condition, and the person-first phrase "hard of hearing" for those who do not identify as part of the Deaf community. In addition, the field of gifted education primarily uses the term *gifted child*, as evidenced by the National Association for Gifted Children.

This chapter will use both terms, *with autism* and *autistic*, determined by the flow of the sentence. Whenever possible, however, the word *autistic* will be used out of respect for the neurodiversity movement and its relationship to the twice-exceptional (2e) movement.

Causes of Autism

Although autism as a diagnosis has only been around for 80 years, it has clearly been present in society for quite some time. Kanner (1943) said that "I never discovered autism . . . it was there before" (as cited in Donvan & Zucker, 2016, p. 16). In the 1800s, doctors created a category called "idiot" to describe those with lower intelligence, but it often included people with different social and communication skills. In a history of autism, Donvan and Zucker (2016) described how Dr. Samuel Gridley Howe, husband of Julia Ward Howe of "Battle Hymn of the Republic" fame, sought to determine the difference between those who could be educated and those who could not. He hoped that his efforts to describe different groups of people would help guide educational decisions, but he noted that "Science . . . has not yet thrown her certain light upon its remote, or even its proximate causes" (as cited in Donvan & Zucker, 2016, p. 34). The search for a cause continues today.

Myths and Misconceptions

Perhaps nowhere in the annals of medicine has a medical hoax had such an impact on the perception of a disability. The most common myth about autism is that it is caused by immunizations—a myth established by an unethical doctor who faked the results of his study and tried to market his own immunization formula (Davidson, 2017). Autism is not caused by immunizations.

This has been stated and proven over and over again by government agencies (CDC, 2015; National Institute of Neurological Disorders and Stroke, 2019); large-scale studies in the United States (Jain et al., 2015), United Kingdom (Kaye et al., 2001), and Denmark (Hviid et al., 2019); numerous individual studies (American Academy of Pediatrics, 2018); and metanalyses (Taylor et al., 2014). The information that dispels this myth is based on scientific evidence that includes an inability to replicate the original flawed and unethically determined "results," the removal of potentially offending mercury from immunizations that did not decrease the rate of autism, and a similar rate of autism found among unimmunized groups.

However, in the myth that autism is caused by immunizations, it should be noted that there is not only a factual issue, but also serious ethical and public health issues. Children who are not immunized run the risk of dying from preventable diseases. This would indicate that families would prefer the risk of death to the risk of autism (Picciuto, 2017). In addition to the ethical issue of choosing death over autism, there is a significant public health issue. Although the possibility of dying from autism is zero, the possibilities of dying and suffering from measles, mumps, and polio—all easily prevented with an immunization—are small but possible; 5%–10% of patients die when infected with diphtheria alone. The World Health Organization (2019) estimated that 140,000 children died from measles in 2018, primarily due to outbreaks by people in industrialized countries unwilling to get an immunization who spread the disease to children in underdeveloped countries unable to get immunizations. The United States had its highest rates of measles outbreaks in 25 years, while Albania, the Czech Republic, Greece, and the United Kingdom all had measles return to their countries after eliminating it. "Measles anywhere is a threat to children everywhere," stated Henrietta Fore, UNICEF's executive director (World Health Organization, 2019, p. 19).

However, immunizations are not the only myth about the cause of autism. Another myth that has been disproven is that poor parenting causes autism (National Institute of Neurological Disorders and Stroke, 2019). In his original studies, Kanner (1943) noted that mothers and children had "cold" relationships, while Bettleheim (1967) hypothesized that "refrigerator mothers" were the cause of the child's difficulties. What both researchers failed to take into consideration is that autism characteristics will impact the dynamic between parents and children (Crowell et al., 2019). Having a child with autism can add stress to a parent, but just as with typical children, parenting practices can impact the development of their children. Although poor parenting practices can exacerbate the effects of autism, there is no evidence that parenting practices can either cause or cure autism (Waltz, 2015).

Related Factors

Although it is known what does not cause autism, there is no one clear point of consensus about what does cause autism. Autism appears to exist as a result of a combination of genetic and environmental factors (Autism Speaks, n.d.).

Genetic and Biologic Factors. There is considerable evidence that autism runs in families (Autism Speaks, n.d.). Heritability of autism may even be as close as 90% (Freitag, 2007). However, there is no one clearly established genetic "pattern," and up to 100 genes on different chromosomes may have mutations that play a role in autism (National Institute of Child Health and Human Development, 2017). The mutations appear to affect both what symptoms of autism are presented and how severely these symptoms are demonstrated.

In addition to genes directly affecting autism, autism may emerge from differences in other biological systems impacted by genetic issues, including:

1. how the brain is connected and communicates from one area to another through differences in white matter and fiber tracts (Shen & Piven, 2017),
2. brain volume in which children with autism tend to have larger brain mass than other children (Hazlett et al., 2017), and
3. "leaky gut," or increased gut permeability in which studies have found that gastrointestinal issues range from 23%–70% of children with autism (Cao et al., 2013).

Studies have shown that children born prematurely have a much higher rate of autism at 7%–9% than infants born full term at .5%–2% (Agrawal et al., 2018), and children with autism often exhibit characteristics of children born prematurely in their gut biomes, abnormal cardiac activity, low vagal nerve activity, and cerebellar abnormalities (Sajdel-Sulkowska et al., 2018).

In addition to other biological issues, there is a distinct overlap between children with autism and children with epilepsy. Approximately 20% of children with epilepsy have autism, and approximately 20% of children with autism have epilepsy, with estimates ranging from 8% of children with average to high intelligence to as high as 30% among autistic children with diminished intelligence and more severe autism (Besag, 2017). Whether autism causes epilepsy, whether epilepsy causes autism, or what the relationship truly is between autism and epilepsy remains unclear, but there is a distinct overlap.

Interaction With Environmental Factors. There do not appear to be any specific known environmental causes of autism (National Institute of Neurological Disorders and Stroke, 2019), although scientific research is ongoing.

However, there are a number of correlations of factors, which appear to impact growth of the developing brain (Autism Speaks, n.d.; Baron-Cohen et al., 2019; Tordjman et al., 2014). These include:

- advanced age of mother or advanced age of father;
- exposure to certain chemicals, such as mercury or lead;
- exposure to viral infections;
- elevated exposures to hormones;
- exposure to pollution; and
- parental immigration and significant changes in environments during gestation.

Although there is no clear-cut explanation of environmental factors that cause autism, there does appear to be a relationship between the exposure of an environmental or triggering agent in the environment and a genetic susceptibility (Tordjman et al., 2014). That would explain why some individuals who are exposed to various toxins in the environment would have autism and others would not. Although there are some things that do not cause autism, such as vaccines and poor parenting, there are no known medical or environmental factors that do.

Interventions for ASD

Although no singular list of effective practices exists, there are several databases of well-researched practices; most significant are the National Standards Project from the National Autism Center (2015) and the National Clearinghouse on Autism Evidence and Practice (Wong et al., 2014). Each group conducted rigorous research, analyses, and meta-analyses of research studies, and 27 different activities were determined to be evidence-based effective interventions. Some of these strategies are applicable to classroom teachers, while others are designed to be conducted in more therapeutic situations.

The lists of effective practices can be classified into three different areas of emphasis (Hughes & Henderson, 2017), including (1) applied behavior analysis-based interventions, (2) social/communication interventions, and (3) cognitive and physical supports.

ABA-Based Interventions

Applied behavior analysis (ABA) is a system of rewards and consequences designed to increase positive behaviors and decrease negative behaviors (Wong et al., 2014). There are many elements of this practice that can be helpful when working with children with autism, including (National Autism Center, 2015; Wong et al., 2014):

- Modeling and video modeling, in which the adult demonstrates the desired behavior for the child to imitate, either in person or through a recording. Such activities might include using social greetings, practicing the distance to stand in a social setting, or looking at the bridge of the nose to approximate looking someone in the eye.
- Functional behavioral assessment (FBA), in which the purpose or function of the inappropriate behavior is sought and a replacement behavior is taught to the child to accomplish the same purpose. An example would be determining that a meltdown might be due to being hungry. Providing a communication board that would allow the child to ask for food would reduce the tantrum and support the positive behavior of using communication.
- Antecedent-based intervention, in which the events or circumstances that precede an interfering behavior are determined and changed. Examples might include the use of a written schedule on the child's desk to providing warning of changes in schedule before the child is surprised by a change in routine or the removal of certain noises or flickering lights.

Communication/Social Interaction Strategies

Many of the evidence-based practices are focused on improving the social and communication aspects of autism. Nonverbal communication and expressive and receptive language are targeted as a means of improving communication efforts to peers and adults. Numerous strategies have been found, including (National Autism Center, 2015; Wong et al., 2014):

- Language training provides modeling and reinforcement for children with ASD to imitate and then initiate specific verbalizations.
- The Picture Exchange Communication System (PECS) provides children with a series of picture cards to express their communication needs. This is often used by replacing words with pictures in the classroom for children to refer to and to communicate through.

- Scripting is an activity in which an autistic child engages in a set script for a particular situation. Some of these include what to say when speaking to an adult or how to respond when asked a question.
- Social narratives or Social Stories (Gray, 1992) are short vignettes of a situation that include specific information about what is going to happen and responses that the child can provide, such has how to clean their teeth or how to ask for help.
- Peer training and structured play groups train peers on how to initiate and respond to communication efforts by an autistic child, including how to get their attention, how to provide help, and how to include them in play activities.

Cognitive-Based and Physical Approaches

There are numerous interventions that take a less-targeted approach and work with the "whole child" of the autistic child. These approaches are focused on improving the child's response to either a communication issue or an issue related to their repetitive behaviors (National Autism Center, 2015; Wong et al., 2014) and include the following:

- Exercise has been found to reduce negative responses to some situations; running around the track can reduce inattentiveness and "meltdowns" due to task demands.
- Cognitive behavioral intervention teaches the child about their own learning process, allowing them to exert control and adjust their own responses through an examination of their own emotional response.
- Similarly, self-management teaches a child to monitor their own behavior and to reward themselves for behaving appropriately, such as with self-determined breaks and self-evaluations.
- Visual supports and visual schedules are environmental supports that aid in supporting a student. Examples in a classroom might be the use of a small rug to define an individual work area, calendars, maps, and other organizational systems.

There are others in the two sets of evidence-based practices from the National Standards Project from the National Autism Center (2015) and the National Clearinghouse on Autism Evidence and Practice (Wong et al., 2014) that include both commercial and individual therapeutic practices, but these are perhaps the most common.

Many of these suggested interventions are relatively easy to implement. GT Independence (K, 2016) recommended Pokémon Go groups, which are a form of structured play groups, as a way for autistic people to meet and engage with others. Exercise is a low-cost, high-impact intervention that reduces anxiety and allows the individual opportunity for self-regulation. Other strategies, such as the "stress thermometer" (see Figure 7.1) or a "5-point scale" (Buron, 2004), where the student selects a color or a number to indicate a state of arousal or anxiety, are forms of cognitive behavioral intervention/language training. There are numerous products and programs available that meet the descriptions of these evidence-based strategies.

What is particularly interesting is what is *not* on the list. Not on the list are many popular interventions, such as sensory rooms, animal therapy, or the gluten-free casein-free (GFCF) diet. Although these may have potential, they do not yet have enough data to make them evidence-based. Although some interventions have had significant results, such as transcranial magnetic stimulation or cannabinoids, these appear to help with other issues and not the core issues associated with autism (Autism Science Foundation, n.d.).

ASD and Twice-Exceptionality

Although the definition of ASD is specifically not tied to intellectual functioning and asks practitioners to specify if the autism is "with or without accompanying intellectual impairment" (Reynolds & Kamphaus, 2013, p. 2), there does appear to be a relationship. Amongst children identified with autism, approximately 70% were found to also have significantly low IQ test scores with intellectual delays and disorders (Clarke et al., 2016). However, although there is a strong overlap with decreased intellectual functioning, the identification process does define intellectual development as a separate construct from autism and provides the possibility of both being gifted and having autism.

In contrast to the findings of autism highly associated with low IQ scores, there is an overrepresentation of children with high IQs among the students with Level 1 support needs, leading to what researcher Crespi (2016) called a "high intelligence imbalance" (p. 20) as a factor of autism. Not only are high IQ scores overrepresented among autistic children who have less severe needs, but also ASD is overrepresented among the gifted population, particularly prodigies. Ruthsatz and Urbach (2012) found in a study of eight prodigies in music, art, and math, that although they did not all score high on IQ tests,

FIGURE 7.1
Stress Thermometer

5	VERY upset
4	Upset
3	Moderately upset
2	A little distressed
1	Mostly calm

they did all score exceedingly high in working memory and had a relatively high autism-spectrum quotient (AQ)—a commonly-used normed assessment of autistic traits (Baron-Cohen et al., 2001).

This relationship between giftedness and autism has led to some possible confusion between the two. A. Singer (2017) noted that with the amalgamation of Asperger's syndrome into the definition of autism, the full spectrum has become lost in popular media, and distinctions between those with significant needs and those with more socially-acceptable forms of autism have begun to blur lines of communication about what is needed to help children. Webb et al. (2016) suggested that although many experts trained in a medical identification model will identify children with autism, they may actually be identifying characteristics of giftedness. Prior to the inclusion of Asperger's syndrome into the ASD definition, Amend et al. (2008) developed the Gifted/Asperger's Disorder Checklist (GADC) to help teachers and parents distinguish demonstrations of giftedness from the challenges of Asperger's syndrome. Used as a screening instrument, characteristics of children with Asperger's syndrome and gifted children are contrasted side-by-side, and a parent or practitioner places a checkmark in the appropriate column. For example, a parent might distinguish between "Extensive, advanced vocabulary" to determine giftedness and "Advanced use of words with lack of comprehension for all language used" to determine if the child has Asperger's syndrome. What might be considered a symptom of a disability through one lens might be considered a symptom of strength through another.

Characteristics of GTASD

Although it is possible to be gifted and autistic, there is a distinct difference in how certain behaviors are perceived by different practitioners and in different contexts. Gifted educators are trained to view student characteristics through a strength-based perspective, while special educators often view the same characteristics through a deficit perspective. Strength-based approaches are rooted in positive psychology and seek to identify the source of the imbalance between the individual and the environment. The approaches are designed to help individuals see themselves as valuable and participatory in changing their own experiences through an examination of what they can do (Stoerkel, 2019). In contrast, special education labels are often defined through the deficit model of identifying what individuals cannot do (Harry & Klingner, 2007). Table 7.1 outlines how some of the characteristics related to autism (CDC, 2019a) might be viewed differently through these different lenses; the same behavior may have different interpretations.

As noted by APA (2013), the severity of autism is determined by the demands of the environment and the resultant needs for supports. Whether the issue is a problem or a strength is often determined by the environment and the demands that are placed upon an individual. The difference between a child who "perseverates" and one who "perseveres" is determined by what else the child is being asked to do. If the child is working on a difficult math problem during their free time, the quality of perseverance is valued. However, if the class needs to start a science lab and a child will not stop working on a math problem, that could be perceived as perseveration.

The areas of language and imagination are perhaps where the most clearly distinct differences emerge between a perspective that perceives strengths and one that perceives deficits. Crespi et al. (2016) found that although intelligence can be quite high in autistic children, there were significant differences between children with autism and those without in the area of imagination. In addition, children with autism might have a high level of language, but not be able to switch their use of language in different contexts.

However, although there are some aspects of autism that are very similar to aspects of giftedness, there are a number of possible aspects of autism that can create challenges in numerous situations (CDC, 2019a). Although not every child with autism will exhibit these characteristics, many of these more common problematic autistic behaviors can include:
- Social issues:
  - Avoids or resists physical contact.
  - Cannot be comforted by others during distress.

TABLE 7.1

Paradoxical Characteristics of GTASD

Symptoms From a Deficit Perspective	Symptoms From a Strength-Based Perspective
Social Skills	
▪ Prefers to play alone. ▪ Does not share interests with others. ▪ Only interacts to achieve a desired goal.	▪ Often prefers the company of adults; often prefers to play by themselves. ▪ Often has unusual or "adult" interests. ▪ Intense focus on topics of interest.
Communication	
▪ Repeats words or phrases. ▪ Low verbal scores/inappropriate use of language.	▪ Persists in asking questions. ▪ Significant strengths in nonverbal measures.
Interests and Behaviors	
▪ Lines up toys or other objects. ▪ Likes parts of objects. ▪ Is very organized. ▪ Has to follow certain routines. ▪ Gets upset by minor changes. ▪ Obsessive interests.	▪ Enjoys patterns. ▪ Notices small details. ▪ Can create systems of organization. ▪ Questions existing rules and structures. ▪ Emotionally intense. ▪ Areas of passion.
Other	
▪ Unusual sleeping habits. ▪ Hyperactivity. ▪ Temper tantrums. ▪ Unusual mood or emotional reactions. ▪ Unusual reactions to the way things sound, smell, taste, look, or feel.	▪ Does not sleep much. ▪ Often highly active and intense in physical movements. ▪ Can be intense emotionally. ▪ Can have intense reactions to sensory stimuli.

Note. Symptoms are adapted from CDC, 2019a.

- o   Has trouble understanding others' feelings or talking about their own feelings.

- ■   Communication issues:
  - o   Delayed speech and language skills.
  - o   Reverses or confuses pronouns.
  - o   Does not point or respond to pointing.
  - o   Does not pretend in play.
  - o   Does not understand jokes, sarcasm, or teasing.

- ■   Unusual interests and behaviors:
  - o   Has to follow certain routines.
  - o   Flaps hands, rocks body, or spins self in circles.

- ■   Other behaviors:
  - o   Difficulty with eye contact.
  - o   Causes self-injury.
  - o   Struggles with eating disorders or eating restrictions.

Many of these issues can create challenges in the social and emotional climate of a classroom. Many teachers may feel the need to resort to punishment for behaviors that are characteristic of the child's condition, rather than teaching more appropriate behaviors and adapting reward systems to the capabilities of the child (Buckman, n.d.). Great care needs to be taken to ensure that children with autism are not bullied, because they are often the target of bullying more than typical children (Autism Speaks, 2018). It is important to build a classroom climate that understands behaviors of an autistic person and focuses on strengths, while teaching and supporting for growth.

Strategies and Interventions for GTASD

When working with GTASD students, educators must recognize that there is a dual goal: (1) to develop the ability of the child, while (2) mediating the difficulties created by the disability (Hughes, 2017). See Figure 7.2.

Strategies to develop a child's abilities are typically drawn from gifted education. They include adapting content/concept/process/product aspects (VanTassel-Baska, 2016), and linking these adaptations to the child interests, readiness level, and learning profile (Tomlinson, 2014). These models of differentiation for gifted learners involve adapting the standards of the regular

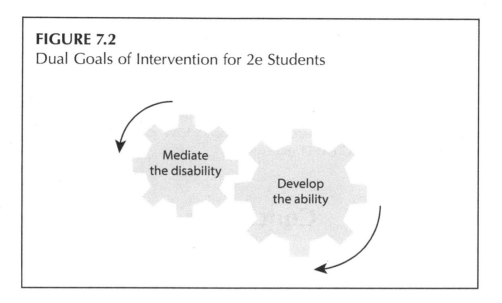

FIGURE 7.2
Dual Goals of Intervention for 2e Students

Mediate the disability

Develop the ability

classroom and extending the content through enriched and accelerated opportunities, as well as connecting the content to larger organizing concepts. The ability is developed through curriculum and content. Providing multiple ways to present the content for learning and multiple means to demonstrate learning is directly related to tenets of Universal Design for Learning (UDL), in which individual variations of learning are accommodated in the classroom (Novak, 2016). The intervention goal of gifted education is to identify and develop student strengths, often thereby inspiring future educational opportunities and career paths (Renzulli & Reis, 2014).

In contrast, strategies to mediate the impact of autism are focused on "increasing developmentally appropriate skills . . . [and] decreasing behaviors that interfere with life functioning" (National Autism Center, 2015, p. 37, 39). The interventions for children with autism are designed to increase developmental skills, including academic, communication, interpersonal, and self-regulation skills. Although these are general life skills, they are areas in which children with autism typically struggle. Although it is important to increase some skills, the National Autism Center strives to decrease those skills that impede social connections and intrapersonal skills, including:

- general mental health issues that may or may not be associated with autism;
- problem behaviors that can harm the child, others, or property;
- maladaptive, nonfunctional patterns of speech or thoughts, such as compulsive behaviors or restricted interests; and

■ sensory or emotional regulation where an individual can modify their level of arousal to function effectively in the environment.

Educators must help twice-exceptional students simultaneously identify and develop their talents while mediating the impacts of autism. Because the environment is so important in determining the intensity of the autism as well as the ability, the school, classroom, and teacher have to be prepared to meet the intricate needs of GTASD students.

Conclusion

Many of the characteristics of autism need to be seen through a gifted lens. This means that although "perseveration" is a bad thing, "perseverance" is a good thing. "Obsession" is a bad thing, but "area of passion" is often a characteristic of giftedness. Although many of the characteristics of autism cannot be "flipped" to be strengths, a strength-based approach can build from the characteristics and adapt the environment to fit the needs of the individual so that the strengths can be demonstrated. Dual differentiation is a process through which the needs of the child can be mediated so that the development of talents can occur. The goal of intervention cannot be to "cure" the child or even to "make them normal," but to help them deal with some of the disabling conditions that interfere with the development of their abilities.

All children deserve an education that provides a supportive environment to make mistakes, feedback about how to correct mistakes, and opportunities to learn about topics and areas of interest so that individuals can grow into better versions of themselves—all within a community of learners, teachers, and administrators who understand them and care about them. Gifted autistic children deserve an education that allows them to be fully themselves. Just as Shaun, the autistic doctor in *The Good Doctor* saves lives, teachers need to be providing an education that values the lives, experiences, and abilities of gifted children with autism.

FROM THE EDITORS

Student Vignettes

Estrella

Estrella is in first grade. She is really excited to be in school because her family only came to the United States 2 years ago and she really wants to learn like an American. She is also a little afraid because sometimes she does not know how to talk to the other kids. She is either too shy to say something or impulsively says too much, too loudly. She does not know why she does either one. She also thinks some people talk too loudly or want to touch her. She really does not like either of those.

Sometimes Estrella wants to tell her schoolmates what she knows about cells and what they do in the body. But she tried that before when she was learning about origami. No one wanted to hear about all she had learned. They would say, "Not again. We're tired of hearing you talk and talk and talk about that. Let's go play." So she decided to go play something by herself. She does not really like to play the games that the other students like, but she has learned that going out and running or swinging can help her calm down and not worry so much about how she does not really fit with the others in her class. She will just keep learning about the things she is curious to know.

Estrella's teacher has learned some things about Estrella. She sees how the other students cannot relate to the way Estrella thinks. She sees how bright Estrella is about things that interest her. She thinks it is interesting that Estrella can talk about all sorts of content and has a million ideas, but she does not relate to the other students and her physical skills are a little behind those of her age-mates. There are times when Estrella just cannot control her feelings or her mouth. Her teacher is going to have to learn more about Estrella so that she can help her grow academically and socially.

Discussion Questions

1. Which traits of ASD does Estrella exhibit? Which traits of giftedness?
2. Do these traits indicate that Estrella is twice-exceptional? Why, or why not?

FROM THE EDITORS, *continued*

3. In what ways could Estrella's teacher help Estrella build some self-management skills? Should she teach her these "soft skills"?
4. How might the teacher link Estrella's interests to help her with social development?
5. In what ways may the teacher adjust Estrella's classroom environment to facilitate her learning?

Raphael

Miss Warner is puzzled by a new student in her sixth-grade classroom. Raphael is tall for his age, quiet, and rarely makes eye contact. Miss Warner assumes he is shy and still adjusting to his new school. She quickly discovers that Raphael is a good student with talents and a special interest in math. His overall performance places him at the top of the class.

Despite his apparent abilities, Raphael does not participate in class discussions. Hoping to engage him, Miss Warner calls on him frequently. She is surprised that Raphael is slow to answer and seemingly at loss for words. Whether he is shy or not, she is also concerned about reports of Raphael's rude behavior in the hallway and lunch line. Because he walks with his head down, he often bumps into other students. When he does, he says nothing and continues walking. He does not respond when challenged by his classmates or reprimanded by school staff.

Hoping to keep a closer eye on him, Miss Warner moves Raphael's seat to the front of the classroom. It is only then that she notices how little interaction Raphael has with his classmates and the subtle way he rocks when reading.

Discussion Questions

1. What, if any, characteristics of giftedness or twice-exceptionality does Raphael exhibit?
2. What, if anything, should Miss Warner do?
3. What, if any, services or systems of support would help Raphael?
4. Could or should Raphael's schedule be modified in any way?

Resources

There are numerous resources for GTASD children, particularly online. For educators, it is worthwhile to look at public and private schools that serve twice-exceptional students and to look at online resources to support GTASD students in the classroom.

Schools

There are numerous schools designed for twice-exceptional students opening up regularly. Although not explicitly for GTASD students, these schools work with parents and prepare teachers to work with them:

- Montgomery County Public School's Twice Exceptional Students and Services: https://www.montgomeryschoolsmd.org/curriculum/enriched/gtld
- Bridges Academy: https://www.bridges.edu
- Arete Academy: https://www.areteacademymn.org

Facebook Groups

- Parents of Twice-Exceptional Children (2e)
- Raising Poppies

Research Centers

- Frank Porter Graham Center at the University of North Carolina with the TEACCH program: https://teacch.com/research
- Vanderbilt University Kennedy Treatment and Research Institute for Autism Spectrum Disorders (TRIAD): https://vkc.mc.vanderbilt.edu/vkc/triad/services
- National Autism Center in Randolph, MA: https://www.nationalautismcenter.org

Documentaries

- *2e* and *2e2* are two movies that have been made about being twice-exceptional and teaching twice-exceptional students.

Graduate Programs

- The Bridges Graduate School of Cognitive Diversity in Education: https://graduateschool.bridges.edu
- Johns Hopkins University's Master of Science in Education–Gifted Education: https://education.jhu.edu/academics/gifted

References

Agrawal, S., Rao, S. C., Bulsara, M. K., & Patole, S. K. (2018). Prevalence of autism spectrum disorders in preterm infants: A meta-analysis. *Pediatrics, 142*(3), e20180134. https://doi.org/10.1542/peds.2018-0134

Amend, E. R., Beaver-Gavin, K., Schuler, P., & Beights, R. (2008). *Giftedness/ Asperger's Disorder Checklist (GADC) pre-referral checklist.* Amend Psychological Services.

American Academy of Pediatrics. (2018). *Vaccine safety: Examine the evidence.* https://www.healthychildren.org/English/safety-prevention/immuniza tions/Pages/Vaccine-Studies-Examine-the-Evidence.aspx

American Psychiatric Association. (2013). *Diagnostic and statistical manual of mental disorders* (5th ed.). https://doi.org/10.1176/appi.books.978089042 5596

Autism Science Foundation. (n.d.). *Beware of non-evidence-based treatments.* https://autismsciencefoundation.org/what-is-autism/beware-of-non-evidence-based-treatments

Autism Society. (n.d.). *Asperger's syndrome.* https://www.autism-society.org/ what-is/aspergers-syndrome

Autism Speaks. (n.d.). *What causes autism?* https://www.autismspeaks.org/ what-causes-autism

Autism Speaks. (2018). *Top ten facts parents, educators and students need to know about bullying.* https://www.autismspeaks.org/tool-kit-excerpt/top-ten-facts-parents-educators-and-students-need-know-about-bullying

Autistic Self Advocacy Network. (n.d.). https://autisticadvocacy.org

Baron-Cohen, S. (2010). *Autism: Difference or disorder?* https://www.theneuro typical.com/autism_difference_or_disorder.html

Baron-Cohen, S., Tsompanidis, A., Auyeung, B., Norgaard-Pedersen, B., Hougaard, D. M., Abdallah, M., Cohen, A., & Pohl, A., (2019, July). Foetal oestrogens and autism. *Molecular Psychiatry.* https://doi.org/10.1038/s41 380-019-0454-9

Baron-Cohen, S., Wheelwright, S., Skinner, R., Martin, J., & Clubley, E. (2001, February). The autism-spectrum quotient (AQ): Evidence from Asperger syndrome/high-functioning autism, males and females, scientists and mathematicians. *Journal of Autism and Developmental Disorders, 31,* 5–17. https://doi.org/10.1023/A:1005653411471

Besag, F. M. C. (2017). Epilepsy in patients with autism: Links, risks and treatment challenges. *Neuropsychiatric Disease and Treatment, 2018*(14), 1–10. https://doi.org/10.2147/NDT.S120509

Bettleheim, B. (1967). *The empty fortress: Infantile autism and the birth of the self.* Free Press.

Buckman, S. (n.d.). *Consequences and autism in the classroom.* Autism Support Network. http://www.autismsupportnetwork.com/news/consequences-and-autism-classroom-330491134

Buron, K. D. (2004). *The incredible 5-point scale: Assisting students with autism spectrum disorders in understanding social interactions and controlling their emotional responses.* Autism Asperger Publishing Company.

Cao, X., Lin, P., Jiang, P., & Li, C. (2013). Characteristics of the gastrointestinal microbiome in children with autism spectrum disorder: A systematic review. *Shanghai Arch Psychiatry, 25,* 342–352.

Centers for Disease Control. (2015). *Vaccines do not cause autism.* https://www.cdc.gov/vaccinesafety/concerns/autism.html

Centers for Disease Control. (2019a). *Signs and symptoms of autism spectrum disorders.* https://www.cdc.gov/ncbddd/autism/signs.html

Centers for Disease Control. (2019b). *Summary of autism spectrum disorder (ASD) prevalence studies.* https://www.cdc.gov/ncbddd/autism/documents/ASDPrevalenceDataTable2016-508.pdf

Centers for Disease Control. (2020). *Autism data visualization tool.* https://www.cdc.gov/ncbddd/autism/data/index.html

Clarke, T.-K., Lupton, M. K., Fernandez-Pujals, A. M., Starr, J., Davies, G., Cox, S., Pattie, A., Liewald, D. C., Hall, L. S., Macintyre, D. J., Smith, B. H., Hocking, L. J., Padmanabhan, S., Thomson, P. A., Hayward, C., Hansell, N. K., Montgomery, G. W., Medland, S. E., Martin, N. G., Wright, M. J., Porteous, D. J., Dreary, I. J., & McIntosh, A. M. (2016). Common polygenic risk for autism spectrum disorder (ASD) is associated with cognitive ability in the general population. *Molecular Psychiatry, 21*(3), 419–425. https://doi.org/10.1038/mp.2015.12

Crespi, B., Leach, E., Dinsdale, N., Mokkonen, M., & Hurd, P. (2016, May). Imagination in human social cognition, autism, and psychotic-affective conditions. *Cognition, 150,* 181–199. https://doi.org/10.1016/j.cognition.2016.02.001

Crespi, B. J. (2016, June). Autism as a disorder of high intelligence. *Frontiers in Neuroscience, 10*(300). https://doi.org/10.3389/fnins.2016.00300

Crowell, J. A., Keluskar, J., & Gorecki, A. (2019, April). Parenting behavior and the development of children with autism spectrum disorder. *Comprehensive Psychiatry, 90*, 21–29. https://doi.org/10.1016/j.comppsych.2018.11.007

Davidson, M. (2017). Vaccination as a cause of autism- myths and controversies. *Dialogues in Clinical Neuroscience, 19*(4), 403–407.

Donvan, J., & Zucker, C. (2016, January). *The early history of autism in America.* Smithsonian Magazine. https://www.smithsonianmag.com/science-natu re/early-history-autism-america-180957684

Dudas, R. B., Lovejoy, C., Cassidy, S., Allison, C., Smith, P., & Baron-Cohen, S. (2017). The overlap between autism spectrum conditions and borderline personality disorder. *PLOS ONE, 12*(9), e018447. https://doi.org/10.1371/journal.pone.0184447

Freitag, C. M. (2007, January). The genetics of autistic disorders and its clinical relevance: A review of the literature. *Molecular Psychiatry, 12*, 2–22. https://doi.org/10.1038/sj.mp.4001896

Gray, C. (1992). *How to write social stories.* Jenison Public Schools.

Griffin, E., & Pollack, D. (2009). Student experiences of neurodiversity in higher education: Insights from the BRAINHE Project. *Dyslexia, 15*(1), 23–41. https://doi.org/10.1002/dys.383

Harry, B., & Klingner, J. (2007). Discarding the deficit model. *Educational Leadership, 64*(5), 16–21.

Hazlett, H. C., Gu, H., Munsell, B. C., Kim, S. H., Styner, M., Wolff, J. J., Ellison, J. T., Swanson, M. R., Zhu, H., Botteron, K. N., Collins, D. L., Constantino, J. N., Dager, S. R., Estes, A. M., Evans, A. C., Fonov, V. S., Gerig, G., Kostopolous, P., McKinstry, R. C., Pandey, J., Paterson, S., Pruett, J. R., Schultz, J. T., Shaw, D. W., Zwaigenbaum, L., & Piven, J. (2017, February). Early brain development in infants at high risk for autism spectrum disorder. *Nature, 542*, 348–351.

Hughes, C. E. (2017). Focusing on strengths: Twice-exceptional students. In W. W. Murawski & K. Lynn Scott (Eds.), *What really works with exceptional learners* (pp. 302–318). Corwin.

Hughes, C. E. (2019, November). *Disability as blessing, burden or battle* [Conference session]. Annual Teacher Education Division, Council for Exceptional Children, New Orleans, LA, United States.

Hughes, C. E., & Henderson, L. M. (2017). Addressing the autism spectrum disorder "epidemic" in special education. In W. W. Murawski & K. Lynn Scott (Eds.), *What really works with exceptional learners* (pp. 225–243). Corwin.

Hviid, A., Hansen, J. V., Frisch, M., & Melbye, M. (2019). Measles, mumps, rubella vaccine and autism: A nationwide cohort study. *Annals of Internal Medicine, 170*(8), 513–520. https://doi.org/10.7326/M18-2101

Jain, A., Marshall, J., Buikema, A., Bancroft, T., Kelly, J. P., & Newschaffer, C. J. (2015). Autism occurrence by MMR vaccine status among US children with older siblings with and without autism. *JAMA, 313*(15), 1534–1540. https://doi.org/10.1001/jama.2015.3077

K., A. (2016). *Pokémon Go: Life-changing benefits for those with autism.* GT Independence. https://www.gtindependence.com/pokemon-go-life-changing-benefits-for-those-with-autism

Kanner, L. (1943). Autistic disturbances of affective contact. *Nervous Child, 2,* 217–250.

Kaye, J. A., del Melero-Montes, M., & Jick, H. (2001). Mumps, measles, and rubella vaccine and the incidence of autism recorded by general practitioners: A time trend analysis. *British Medical Journal, 322*(7288), 720. https://dx.doi.org/10.1136/bmj.322.7284.460

Kirk, S., Gallagher, J., & Coleman, M. R. (2015). *Educating exceptional children* (14th ed.). Cengage Learning.

Luterman, S. (2020, February 14). *The biggest autism advocacy group is still failing too many autistic people.* The Washington Post. https://www.washingtonpost.com/outlook/2020/02/14/biggest-autism-advocacy-group-is-still-failing-too-many-autistic-people

National Autism Center. (2015). *National standards project, phase 2.* https://www.nationalautismcenter.org/national-standards-project/phase-2

National Center on Disability and Journalism. (2020). *Disability language style guide.* https://ncdj.org/style-guide

National Institute of Child Health and Human Development. (2017). *What causes autism?* https://www.nichd.nih.gov/health/topics/autism/conditioninfo/causes

National Institute of Neurological Disorders and Stroke. (2019). *Autism spectrum disorder fact sheet.* https://www.ninds.nih.gov/Disorders/Patient-Caregiver-Education/Fact-Sheets/Autism-Spectrum-Disorder-Fact-Sheet

Novak, K. (2016). *UDL now!: A teacher's guide to applying universal design for learning in today's classrooms.* CAST.

Pearce, J. M. S. (2005). Kanner's infantile autism and Asperger's syndrome. *Journal of Neurology, Neurosurgery and Psychiatry, 76,* 205. http://doi.org/10.1136/jnnp.2004.042820

Picciuto, E. (2017, April 14). *Enough is enough: Twisted anti-vaxxer parents choose fatal diseases over autism.* The Daily Beast. https://www.thedailybeast.com/twisted-anti-vaxxer-parents-choose-fatal-diseases-over-autism

Renzulli, J. S., & Reis, S. M. (2014). *The Schoolwide Enrichment Model: A how-to guide for talent development* (3rd ed.). Prufrock Press.

Reynolds, C. R., & Kamphaus, R. W. (2013). *Behavior assessment system for children* (3rd ed.). Pearson.

Ruthsatz, J., & Urbach, J. B. (2012). Child prodigy: A novel cognitive profile places elevated general intelligence, exceptional working memory and attention to detail at the root of prodigiousness. *Intelligence, 40*(5), 419–426. https://doi.org/10.1016/j.intell.2012.06.002

Sajdel-Sulkowska, E. M., Makowska-Zubrycka, M., Czarzasta, K., Kasarello, K., Aggarwal, V., Mialy, M., Szczepanska-Sadowska, E., & Cudnoch-Jedrzejewska, A. (2018). Common genetic variants link the abnormalities in the gut-brain axis in prematurity and autism. *The Cerebellum, 18*(2), 255–265. https://doi.org/10.1007/s12311-018-0970-1

Shakespeare, T., & Watson, N. (2001), The social model of disability: An outdated ideology? In S. N. Barnartt & B. M. Altman (Eds.), *Exploring theories and expanding methodologies: Where we are and where we need to go* (Vol. 2, pp. 9–28). Emerald Group.

Shen, M. D., & Piven, J. (2017). Brain and behavior development in autism from birth through infancy. *Dialogues in Clinical Neuroscience, 19*(4), 325–333.

Shore, D. (October, 2019). *Interview with David Shore, producer of "The Good Doctor."* Vision & Leadership 2e Symposium, Bridges 2e Center for Research and Professional Development, North Hollywood, CA, United States.

Silberman, S. (2015). *Neurotribes: The legacy of autism and the future of neurodiversity.* Penguin Books.

Sinclair, J. (1999). *Why I dislike person-first language.* Autism Mythbusters. https://autismmythbusters.com/general-public/autistic-vs-people-with-autism/jim-sinclair-why-i-dislike-person-first-language

Singer, A. (2017). *Portrayals of autism on television don't showcase full spectrum.* Spectrum News. https://www.spectrumnews.org/opinion/viewpoint/portrayals-autism-television-dont-showcase-full-spectrum

Singer, J. (1999). Why can't you be normal for once in your life? From a "problem with no name" to the emergence of a new category of difference. In M. Corker & S. French (Eds.), *Disability discourse* (pp. 59–67). Open Universty Press.

Stoerkel, E. (2019). *What is a strength-based approach?* https://positivepsychol ogy.com/strengths-based-interventions

Taylor, L. E., Swerdferger, A. L., & Eslick, G. D. (2014). Vaccines are not associated with autism: An evidence-based meta-analysis of case control and cohort studies. *Vaccine, 32*(29), 3623–3629. https://doi.org/10.1016/j. vaccine.2014.04.085

Tomlinson, C. A. (2014). *The differentiated classroom: Responding to the needs of all learners* (3rd. ed). ASCD.

Tordjman, S., Somogyi, E., Coulon, N., Kermarrec, S., Cohen, D., Bronsard, G., Connot, O., Weisman-Arcache, C., Botbol, M., Lauth, B., Ginchat, B., Roubertoux, P., Barburoth, M., Kovess, V., Geoggra, M.-M., & Xavier, J. (2014, August). Gene x environment interactions in autism spectrum disorders: Role of epigenetic mechanisms. *Frontiers in Psychiatry, 5.* https:// doi.org/10.3389/fpsyt.2014.00053

VanTassel-Baska, J. (2016). Introduction to the Integrated Curriculum Model. In J. VanTassel-Baska & C. A. Little (Eds.), *Content-based curriculum for high-ability learners* (3rd ed., pp. 15–33). Prufrock Press.

Waltz, M. M. (2015). Mothers and autism: The evolution of a discourse of blame. *AMA Journal of Ethics, 17*(4), 353–358. https://doi.org/10.1001/ journalofethics.2015.17.4.mhst1-1504

Webb, J. T., Amend, E. R., Webb, N. E., Goerss, J., Beljan, P., & Olenchak, F. R. (2016). *Misdiagnosis and dual diagnosis of gifted children: ADHD, bipolar, OCD, Asperger's, depression, and other disorders.* Great Potential Press.

Wing, L., & Gould, J. (1979, March). Severe impairments of social interaction and associated abnormalities in children: Epidemiology and classification. *Journal of Autism and Developmental Disorders, 9,* 11–29.

Wong, C., Odom, S. L., Hume, K. Cox, A. W., Fettig, A., Kucharczyk, S., Brock, M.E., Plavnick, J. B., Fleury, V. P., & Schultz, T. R. (2014). *Evidence-based practices for children, youth, and young adults with Autism Spectrum Disorder.* University of North Carolina, Frank Porter Graham Child Development Institute, Autism Evidence-Based Practice Review Group. https://cidd. unc.edu/Registry/Research/Docs/31.pdf

World Health Organization. (2019, December 5). *More than 140,000 die from measles as cases surge worldwide.* https://www.who.int/news-room/detail/05- 12-2019-more-than-140-000-die-from-measles-as-cases-surge-worldwide

CHAPTER 8

Anxiety and Gifted Children

Teresa Argo Boatman and Anne E. Boatman

Anxiety is a normal human emotion that has origins as a useful survival response to dangers in the world. Anxiety and fear act as signals of danger, threat, or motivational conflict, and trigger appropriate adaptive responses. There is a distinction between anxiety and fear: Anxiety is a response to an unknown threat or internal conflict, and fear is focused on known external danger. Anxiety and fear are adaptive and defensive reactions to escape the source of danger or motivational conflict. These reactions include active responses to escape the threat, which have been labeled as fight or flight, and passive responses, labeled freeze, when the threat appears inescapable (Harvard Health Publishing, 2018b).

The biological response consistent with fear and anxiety has been traced back to primate ancestors and can be found throughout the animal kingdom. The fight-flight-freeze response is generated in the amygdala of the brain, where the threat or danger is processed and sends a distress signal to the hypothalamus. The hypothalamus is the command center that communicates with the autonomic nervous system. It acts as the regulator of involuntary systems like breathing, heart rate, and dilation/constriction of blood vessels. Within the autonomic nervous system, the sympathetic nervous system is the activator, or gas pedal, and the parasympathetic system is the deactivator, or brake. When there is a perceived or actual threat, the hypothalamus sends chemicals that start the gas pedal of the sympathetic adrenomedullary system (SAM), which results in specific physical responses. Blood pressure, heart rate, and breathing increase; skin may become pale or flushed; pupils dilate to allow for better vision; muscles tense and become ready for action; and nonvital systems of digestion and fighting infection are put on hold. This reaction can happen before an individual is aware of a threat, such as jumping backward when a car swerves toward them. The system is designed to bypass the cognitive brain and move immediately to increase chances of survival in dangerous situations (Godoy et al., 2018).

After an acute stress response occurs and the perceived threat remains, the hypothalamus can engage the HPA axis (hypothalamus, pituitary, and adrenal glands), which acts to keep the body in stress response, essentially holding down the gas pedal. The parasympathetic system must engage at some point to dampen the stress response and return the brain and body systems to normal, putting on the brakes. It can take up to 60 minutes for the body to return to a resting state, and those with an anxiety disorder can sometimes be slower in their return to a more relaxed state. Individual differences in genetic predisposition and early adverse experiences, as well as coping or affective styles, appear to be critical predisposing factors for anxiety-related disorders (Godoy et al., 2018; Harvard Health Publishing, 2018b; Steimer, 2002).

History of the Diagnosis of Anxiety

The physical reactions of anxiety have been present since prehistoric times; however, anxiety as a medical diagnosis is a more recent category. Crocq (2017) discussed references to medical disorders, which have commonalities with anxiety in the writings of Hippocrates, ancient Latin philosophical writings, and throughout ancient Indo-European writings. Then, for centuries, the identification of anxiety as a separate set of symptoms disappeared into other categories of illness, such as melancholia, a combination of depression and anxiety. In 1869, George Miller Beard, one of the first successful American authors in psychiatry, used the term *neurasthenia* to describe a cluster of symptoms similar to anxiety. Contemporaries of Beard, such as Freud and Kraepelin, began integrating terms such as *neuroses* and *anxious distress* into their diagnosing of patients.

Modern psychiatric medical diagnosis became standardized through the *Diagnostic and Statistical Manual* (DSM), first published in 1952 by the American Psychiatric Association (APA). The DSM is a tool that is broadly used by psychologists, physicians, and other medical professions to diagnose a wide range of psychiatric conditions. The manual lists etiologies, symptoms, and severity of disorders. In the first DSM, anxiety-type disorders were categorized as psychoneurotic disorders, and in the DSM-II, they were called neuroses. With the publication of the DSM-III in 1980, the category of Anxiety Disorders was first presented with three distinct categories: phobic disorders, anxiety states (which were divided into generalized anxiety disorder, panic disorder, and obsessive compulsive disorder), and post-traumatic stress disorder. Small changes were made between the 1980 publication and the 2013 publication of the DSM-5, but anxiety as a category was consistently utilized in the medical classification terminology (Crocq, 2017).

Current Classifications of Anxiety as a Diagnosis

The DSM-5 (APA, 2013) is the most current comprehensive classification system of mental health disorders. Increasing knowledge of brain circuitry, underlying stress, panic, and obsessions/compulsions, as well as the commonalities of neurobiology, genetic, and psychological features, led to the identification of three main groupings. Anxiety disorders, which include disorders connected with stress, panic, and phobias, are classified as generalized anxiety disorder, panic disorder, specific phobia, social anxiety disorder, and separation anxiety disorder. Obsessive-compulsive disorder, which had previously been grouped under anxiety disorder, moved to be grouped with other disorders consistent with repetitive thoughts or compulsive behaviors. Finally, trauma and stress-related disorders become the overall category for disorders consistent with exposure to severe trauma and/or acute stress, such as post-traumatic stress disorder, acute stress disorder, and reactive attachment disorder.

Generalized Anxiety Disorder

Generalized anxiety disorder (GAD) is characterized by having worry that occurs on more days than not for a period of 6 months or more. This worry is hard to control and leads to a wide variety of physiological symptoms, including fatigue, fidgetiness, sleep disturbance, and muscle tension. In order for GAD to be diagnosed, there must be subjective distress about the feelings of worry (APA, 2013). GAD in a school setting includes children being tense or worried and having physical symptoms, such as stomachaches, nail biting, and nervous tics. Youth may be anxious about doing poorly on tests, health, family or peers, or the world. These worries may interfere with developmental processes, classroom performance, and relationships with others.

Panic Disorder

Panic disorder is classified through the presence of recurrent unexpected panic attacks (APA, 2013). Panic attacks are the sudden onset of fear accompanied by symptoms, which include sweating, trembling or shaking, feelings of choking, accelerated heart rate, and sensations of shortness of breath. Diagnosis of panic disorder requires there to be a period of at least a month following a panic attack that is marked by intense worry or change in behavior to avoid future panic attacks (APA, 2013). Panic symptoms can last from 15–30 minutes, and students who experience panic in school may have difficulty remaining in the classroom environment. Panic can occur with or without a specific anxiety-related situation, which may make it hard for students to identify triggers if they are not always consistently present. During a panic attack, students will not be able to concentrate on work and can be shaken and disoriented for a period of time afterward.

Social Anxiety Disorder

Social anxiety disorder (SAD) is defined as the "marked fear about one or more social situations in which the individual is exposed to possible scrutiny by others" (APA, 2013, p. 202). The social situation must provoke fear or anxiety in the child beyond the actual threat of the situation. The child must also exhibit avoidance behaviors around the situation. Students who have social anxiety disorder may tend to avoid situations in which they have to engage with unfamiliar people. They may avoid asking questions of teachers, classroom discussions, raising their hand in class, and interactions with peers in the lunchroom, classroom, or afterschool activities. Social anxiety can lead to a panic attack accompanying the avoidant behaviors.

Specific Phobia

Specific phobia is "fear or anxiety around a specific object or situation" (APA, 2013, p. 197). This fear must be persistent, lasting at least 6 months, and it must provoke immediate anxiety that must be out of the range appropriate to the level of danger from the situation. A phobia commonly seen in school is test anxiety, which is an anxiety response that interferes with a child's ability to concentrate and access learned material during a testing situation. Additionally, school phobia, or fear of attending school, can lead to school refusal. Other phobias may interfere with learning, such as a phobia of bees, which results in a child being unable to engage with school experiences during recess or field trips outside.

Separation Anxiety Disorder

Separation anxiety disorder is "excessive fear or anxiety concerning separation from those to whom the individual is attached" (APA, 2013, pp. 190–191). It includes significant distress when experiencing or anticipating separation and might include worry about harm coming to the attachment person or self if not with the attachment person, fear of being alone, and reluctance to go places without the attachment person. Separation anxiety is a common precursor to school refusal and also may interfere with a child's ability to enter a classroom experience. This is more commonly seen in younger children than children over the age of 12.

Obsessive-Compulsive Disorder

Obsessive-compulsive disorder (OCD) is identified by recurrent and persistent thoughts, impulses or images and repetitive behaviors (e.g., hand-washing, ordering, checking) or mental acts (e.g., praying, counting, repeating words) the person feels driven to perform (APA, 2013). Large amounts of time can be lost within a child's school day responding to both obsessions and compulsions. Children who have OCD may fear contamination, feeling a compulsion to wash their hands or use hand sanitizer repeatedly throughout the day. Compulsions can also include preoccupation with specific movements, such as tapping or touching in specific orders or times. Children can spend time engaging in writing and erasing until letters are performed perfectly or within a balanced number of strokes.

Webb et al. (2016) provided a guideline of distinguishing between OCD-type thinking and behaviors and the involvement of gifted children in fixations on topics of interests and pursuits of goals, which generally starts in early childhood for most gifted children. Exploring the motivation of highly focused behaviors assists in avoiding a misdiagnosis. In gifted children, high areas of interests are usually connected to understanding and exploring the world versus the fear and anxiety, which pushes the OCD thoughts and rituals. A meta-analysis of 98 studies, which included IQ data among individuals with OCD and a nonpsychiatric comparison group, found a small effect size for lower IQ among the OCD group (Abramovitch et al., 2018). This is the opposite of a common conception that there is more OCD among brighter individuals. Given that current research does not support that gifted children are at higher risk of an OCD diagnosis, it will not be explored in more detail in this chapter. Perfectionism, which has some behaviors consistent with OCD obsessive thinking, has been researched in its relationship to giftedness and will be explored in more detail later in the chapter.

Post-Traumatic Stress Disorder and Acute Stress Response

Post-traumatic stress disorder and acute stress response are both categorized by the responses of individuals after exposure to a trauma event, such as threatened death, serious injury, or sexual violence. Symptoms include distressing memories or dreams of the event, trauma reenactment, psychological distress and physiological reactions to the trauma, avoidance or the distressing memories, and alterations in moods or cognitions after the trauma event or increased reactivity associated with the trauma event. Students with trauma and stress-related disorders can have wide-ranging reactions, ranging from intense reactivity and behavioral outbursts, to being overly quiet and not engaging in the classroom. The current sensitivity to trauma-based responses in schools has led to the development of a wide variety of research and interventions for childhood trauma, the exploration of which is beyond the scope of this chapter. Further information can be found through resources such as the National Child Trauma Stress Network and https://traumasensitiveschools.org.

Research on Anxiety

Anxiety affects one in 20 children and adolescents in the United States at any given time (National Institute of Mental Health, 2017). There was a 56% increase in diagnosed anxiety disorders from 2003 to 2012, from 5.4% of children diagnosed with anxiety or depression in 2003 to 8.4% in 2011–2012 (Bitsko et al., 2018). The National Institute of Mental Health (NIMH, 2017) identified the lifetime prevalence rate of any anxiety disorder for adolescent females at 38% and adolescent males at 26.1%. The state of Minnesota collects an annual survey of students to monitor risk and protective factors. Table 8.1 shows the responses of fifth graders in 2013, 2016, and 2019, who responded "agree" or "strongly agree" with the statement "I worry a lot" (Minnesota Department of Education, 2019).

Questions about worry and anxiety given to Minnesota high school students have changed depending upon the year of data collection. In 2013, approximately 23% of ninth- and 11th-grade males and 41% of ninth- and 11th-grade females reported that over the past 12 months they had significant problems with "feeling very anxious, nervous, tense, scared, panicked or like something bad was going to happen" (Minnesota Department of Education, 2019). Questions in 2019 asked students to respond whether "in the past two weeks they had not been able to stop or control worrying." Among males, 12.4% of ninth graders and 14.5% of 11th graders responded more than half or nearly all days. Among females, 29.8% of ninth graders and 32.3% of 11th graders responded more than half or nearly all days.

Minnesota data appear to be consistent with national data, in that a significant percentage of students perceived that worry is a common experience for them, impacting up to one third of students at any given time (Minnesota Department of Education, 2019). These data did not include students who had been diagnosed or treated for an anxiety disorder. One estimate by the Centers for Disease Control and Prevention in 2016 indicated that 7% of children ages 3–17 had a current diagnosis of anxiety, and less than 60% of children and adolescents who met the criteria for an anxiety disorder received treatment (Ghandhour et al., 2019).

In a meta-analytic review of studies, Bandelow and Michaelis (2015) found lifetime prevalence rates for anxiety in adults to be as high as 33.7%. Broken down by specific diagnosis, they found the lifetime prevalence of GAD to be as high as 6.2%, panic disorder to be as high as 5.2%, SAD to be as high as 13%, and specific phobia as high as 13.8%. The lifetime prevalence for these

TABLE 8.1

Percentage of Minnesota Students Responding "I Agree" or "I Strongly Agree" With the Statement "I Worry a Lot"

Year	Fifth-Grade Males	Fifth-Grade Females
2013	27.6	38.0
2016	29.6	38.9
2019	29.5	42.0

Note. Data are from Minnesota Department of Education, 2019.

disorders in adolescents is lower, ranging from 3.1% (panic disorder) to 10.1% (specific phobia).

The impact of anxiety on child and adolescent outcomes was examined by a qualitative synthesis of 19 robust studies on youth and anxiety (de Lijster et al., 2018). The researchers examined the extent of problems in social and academic functioning and found consistent results showing decreased social competence in the areas of social performance, assertiveness, friendliness, and judging self to be performing worse in social situations. Anxious children have more difficulty with friendships, romantic relationships, school relationships, and higher levels of loneliness. They are also less socially accepted, and some studies show higher levels of victimization, like bullying. Academically, there were not consistent data indicating impairment in academic outcomes due to anxiety. Higher levels of school refusal were consistent among studies, as was evidence that anxious children were entering college with less frequency than non-anxious peers (de Lijster et al., 2018).

Definition of Giftedness and Characteristics of Gifted Children

The Columbus Group (1991) provided a definition of giftedness, which incorporates three major components of the gifted child's experience: asynchronous development, advanced cognitive abilities, and heightened intensity. The extension beyond intellectual and cognitive attributes to include developmental characteristics of the gifted experience makes it useful in examining the twice-exceptional nature of giftedness and anxiety:

> Giftedness is *asynchronous development* in which *advanced cognitive abilities* and *heightened intensity* combine to create inner

experiences and awareness that are qualitatively different from the norm. This asynchrony increases with higher intellectual capacity. The uniqueness of the gifted renders them particularly vulnerable and requires modifications in parenting, teaching and counseling in order for them to develop optimally. (emphasis added)

Asynchrony is the uneven development in the cognitive, emotional, and physical characteristics of the gifted child (Silverman, 1997). Gifted children are identified by advanced cognitive capability (2 or more years advanced depending upon level of giftedness), which does not always correlate with advanced emotional control or social functioning (Eren et al., 2018). An "in sync" child proceeds along development tasks in the areas of cognitive, emotional, and physical development at a generally similar rate of advancement predicted by age. For example, a typically developing 7-year-old child of average intelligence has the emotional control and physical capabilities expected of a 7-year-old. An asynchronous 7-year-old gifted child may have the verbal skills of a 10-year-old, interests consistent with a 15-year-old in specific areas, and the emotional control of a 7-year-old or younger child. The experience of interacting with this 7-year-old may be a deep discussion on the impact of global warming on the Earth at a great depth of knowledge, followed by loss of emotional control when bedtime is enforced. This gap between cognitive understanding and emotional readiness for content can also lead to internal distress for the gifted child, such as wanting to solve the problem of global warming and having the limitation of resources available to a 7-year-old.

Asynchrony can also be apparent between areas of cognitive skill. A child can score well above peers in math and spatial abilities, but have average verbal abilities on an out-of-level test, such as on the Scholastic Aptitude Test (SAT) taken at age 13 (Benbow & Minor, 1990), or score higher on verbal areas and average on performance (visual spatial and reasoning) of the Wechsler Intelligence Scale for Children when taken for identification for gifted services (Rowe et al., 2014). Asynchrony also occurs within a content area when a child is highly verbally capable but struggles with literary basics like handwriting grammar and punctuation or is highly capable in high-level mathematical reasoning but struggles with computation skills (Akin, 2005).

Advanced cognitive abilities of gifted children can be traced to specific differences in the brains of gifted children. Sousa (2009) provided a summary of the brain structures and characteristics that may be related to above-average intelligence. Gifted children may have a greater rate of change in the development of the cortex, where sophisticated information processing occurs, starting thinner, becoming thicker later, and pruning (or thinning again) at a later time than children of average intelligence, providing a higher degree of neural plasticity (Shaw et al., 2006). Intelligence also may be related to more organized white matter, the part of the brain that contains myelinated nerve fibers, in individuals with higher intelligence. More organized white matter leads to higher speed, and larger cortical areas lead to higher processing power. The faster speed and processing power may maintain individual differences within gifted children, which leads to differing ways and speeds in approaching problem solving. Gifted individuals have also been shown to solve problems faster and at earlier stages than other students, to have more efficient memories, and to make the transition from novel or new learning to routine in less time and with fewer exposures than the average brain (Sousa, 2009). Gifted math learners have demonstrated more brain activation in a number of regions when working on challenging problems than nongifted learners (Desco et al., 2011). These researchers correlated this with higher levels of visuospatial processing and logical reasoning in problem solving. As the understanding of the brain continues to become more specific and identified, it is possible that greater understanding of the underlying biology will lead to greater understanding of advanced cognitive abilities within the gifted child.

The heightened intensity or overexcitability (OE) of the gifted child has been explored through the work of Dabrowski (1964) and Daniels and Piechowski (2009). OEs or intensity (the original Polish word most accurately translates as *superstimulatability*) is the heightened experience of response and intake of information of an individual. Dabrowski identified five forms of intensity, which include psychomotor, sensual, emotional, imaginational, and intellectual:

1. Psychomotor intensity is a heightened excitability of the neuromuscular system. This is a capacity for being active and energetic, an enjoyment and need of physical movement, and a surplus of energy. Highly psychomotor intense children are movers in the classroom, frequently up and out of their seats. They blurt out answers without first being called and may have a strong need for movement, like pacing at the back of the classroom while learning.

2. Sensual intensity is an enhanced experience of the senses, including sight, smell, touch, taste, hearing, proprioceptive, and vestibular. Sensory input can result in intense enjoyment of sensory information or a strong dislike for sensations. High sensual intensity children are reactive to sensory input from their environment, like being uncomfortable with tags on clothing or sounds and poor lighting, as well as having strong touch responses, including both seeking out and avoid-

ing physical touch. They may have a limited set of foods they will eat because of texture and taste preferences.

3. Intellectual intensity is an extreme need to seek knowledge and truth, to gain understanding and to analyze information. Thinking is an enjoyable and even playful experience that might include a single-minded pursuit of information or knowledge in areas of extreme interest. Intellectually intense children are seekers of information through various avenues. They may love nonfiction and factual books and rigorous examinations of subject areas, and thrive in extended time to deeply examine an area of interest.

4. Imaginational intensity includes a level of imagination represented by high-level association of images, fantasy thinking, and rich use of metaphor. Those with imaginational intensity have easy flow between truth and fiction, and can easily access their imagination, including both wonderful and awful images. Imaginationally intense children have a love of the unique, creative, and unusual, and may seek out creative outlets, such as art and music, drawing, and storytelling. They sometimes lose focus on other activities when engaged in their creative pursuits and may appear to have an insatiable need to create or explore.

5. Emotional intensity is heightened experience of complex emotions and identification with others' feelings, and can include physical responses to emotional stimuli, such as stomachaches when nervous and obsessive concerns with emotional topics. Emotionally intense people tend to have strong emotional attachments to people, places, and things. They are empathetic, compassionate, and extremely sensitive. Emotionally intense children are highly emotionally responsive to the world. They feel things deeply and tend to express emotions strongly. They may pick up on emotional experiences of those around them and have difficulty separating those from their own emotional experiences. It is not unusual for an emotionally intense child to cry in response to sensitive information at a much older age than their peers, as well as have strong emotional reactions to situations others may see as minor.

Understanding the reactive behaviors that come from intensities as possible superstimulatability of gifted individuals has been explored in both the areas of sensory responses (Duncan et al., 2018a) and emotional processing (Duncan et al., 2018b), pointing toward connections between the brain structure and physiology of the gifted individual and presence of intensity in responses.

Twice-Exceptional Children: Giftedness and Anxiety

Heather sits at her desk and stares at her math test. She has studied for the past 3 days, completed all of the homework, and created her list of equations, and her mind is blank. She had not gotten to sleep until early morning thinking about this test, spinning out her worries of what will happen when she does not pass, creating scenarios of not getting into college, never having a job, and the major impact the Chapter 4 math test is going to have on her life. Her fingernails are bitten to the quick and bleeding in areas. Her vision is blurry, and she feels herself start to hyperventilate, her heart pounding against the wall of her chest. "Here we go again," her mind tells her, as she raises her hand to ask to leave the room. Heather is a gifted child with anxiety. She could be in third grade, 11th grade, or college. Her anxiety and the potential interference of her symptoms on her ability to express her giftedness places her in the category of a twice-exceptional child.

Twice-exceptional (2e) learners are identified as gifted children who have potential for high achievement and display one or more disabilities. One of the identified exceptionalities is emotional/behavioral disorders, including anxiety disorders (National Association for Gifted Children, n.d.). This chapter operationally defines twice-exceptionality as:

> students who demonstrate the potential for high achievement or creative productivity in one or more domains such as math, science, technology, the social arts, visual, spatial, or performing arts or other areas of human productivity AND who manifest one or more disabilities as defined by federal or state eligibility criteria. (Reis et al., 2014. p. 222)

Identification of twice-exceptional students can be complex, with giftedness and disability potentially masking the presence of each other (Reis et al., 2014). Given that at any time, 5% of children and adolescents can be identified with an anxiety disorder and gifted children experience anxiety at the same prevalence as the general population (Eren et al., 2018), it can be anticipated that 5% of gifted children could have an anxiety disorder. Counselors, teachers, and school personnel receive little training in twice-exceptionality and frequently need to seek out continuing education to understand the interplay of giftedness and specific areas of disability (Foley-Nicpon & Assouline, 2015).

Even within that training, the focus is not generally upon anxiety or other emotional and behavioral areas. Students like Heather may get lost in the educational landscape, appearing to be an average student, with achievement outcomes a result of the interplay between the giftedness and anxiety.

Giftedness and Anxiety

Gifted children have many life experiences and characteristics that may contribute to anxiety responses to their environment (Cross & Cross, 2015). Gifted children may have increased environmental pressure to perform because of past optimal outcomes in academic and creative achievements and family focus on success and outcomes. High-achieving schools, which have an emphasis on high standardized test scores and graduates who head to top colleges, have been placed in an at-risk category of having higher rates of behavioral and mental health problems compared with national norms (National Academies of Sciences, Engineering, and Medicine, 2019).

Elliott, a 13-year-old highly gifted young man, captured a link between his giftedness and anxiety in an eloquent and concise way. In a counseling session working through aspects of anxiety, he responded to a query about his anxiety with the phrase, "I don't have anxiety, I have unrelenting forethought" (E. C., personal communication, March 2012). When prodded to explain this sentence, he went on to describe his gifted brain, which echoes the experiences of other gifted individuals. The essence of his explanation was that his brain was constantly thinking through the "what ifs," the next steps, the explanations, and the expectations of parents and others for his life outcomes. Through this process of jumping through various tangential thoughts, he was constantly aware of the joys and pitfalls (both real and imagined) of upcoming situations. He described, in that one phrase, what happens when the firing of the gifted brain, moving at a rapid pace through a variety of depths of information, meets up with emotional and imaginational intensity and identifies the next great worry or problem.

Elliott's experience is consistent with current research that has found a positive correlation between verbal IQ and the tendency to worry and ruminate, both within a group of college students (Penney et al., 2015) and a clinical sample (Coplan et al., 2012). Gifted high school students have also been found to experience higher levels of stress in comparison to nongifted peers (Fouladchang et al., 2010).

Although researchers have looked at anxiety in gifted students since the early 1960s, there is little consensus on whether the prevalence of anxiety among gifted children differs when compared to nongifted students (Eren et al., 2018; Flescher, 1963; Martin et al., 2009). This is not an atypical research outcome when looking at many characteristics and their prevalence in gifted children. The variety of definitions of giftedness, identification of clinical levels of anxiety within research models, and the fact that gifted children are a varied population contribute to this prevalence outcome. Flescher (1963) found no statistical difference in the rate of anxiety when comparing gifted to nongifted students on both a general anxiety and a test anxiety scale. Later studies found lower anxiety among high-IQ students on both anxiety and trait anxiety scales (Reynolds & Bradley, 1983; Scholwinski & Reynolds, 1985) or no difference between high-IQ students with anxiety and prevalence in a national sample of French children (Guénolé et al., 2013). Forsyth (1987) found higher rates of anxiety among gifted girls in a full-time gifted program compared to boys in the same program as well as children from the traditional school experiences. Iranian high school students who attended a full-time high school for gifted children reported lower levels of anxiety compared to students who attended traditional schools (Fouladchang et al., 2010). When looking at children in full-time, specialized programs for gifted, test anxiety was found to be higher for children in those programs than compared to gifted children in regular classrooms (Goetz et al., 2008; Zeidner & Schleyer, 1999). Test anxiety is the worry, fear of failure, and catastrophizing of negative outcomes that occurs before and/or during a testing situation. Although it might be assumed that gifted children would not have test anxiety because of their advanced cognitive skills, there is little research at this point outside of full-time gifted programs to identify increased or decreased prevalence.

A recent study on adults who were part of Mensa, a society for people in the top 2% on tests of intellectual ability, found significantly higher rates of anxiety, as well as many other DSM-5 diagnostic categories and physiological sensitivities (asthma, allergies, environmental sensitivity) in the high-IQ population (Karpinski et al., 2018). This study was of adult Mensa members, who self-identified a diagnosis of anxiety at any point in their lifetime, which was compared with national averages. When the participants were asked if they believed (not formally diagnosed) they had anxiety, the self-report numbers were much higher than the comparison group. This is a narrow population, however, of those who have chosen to belong to Mensa and not a cross section of gifted individuals.

A meta-analysis of four studies found significantly lower rates of anxiety among high-IQ individuals (Martin et al., 2009). One of the studies included in this meta-analysis (Tong & Yewchuk, 1996) found a higher rate of anxiety on a self-concept scale in high school gifted students when compared to nongifted students. Other recent studies not included in the Martin et al. meta-analysis have found no significant difference in anxiety when comparing gifted to nongifted children (e.g., Cernova, 2005; Zeidner & Shani-Zinovich, 2011) and less identified emotional and behavioral risk factors in comparison with nongifted peers (Eklund et al., 2015).

In an attempt to look at the impact of asynchrony on anxiety for gifted children, one study looked at intellectual asynchrony on the Wechsler Intelligence Scale for Children-III (WISC-III; French version) with a group of French gifted children who were referred for socioemotional problems, maladjustment, or school underachievement (Guénolé et al., 2015). Asynchrony, identified as a greater than 15-point difference between verbal and performance scores, was examined in relationship to anxiety. Of the 107 referred gifted children studied, 22 were identified as having anxiety on the Reynolds Manifest Anxiety Scale. Those who were identified with anxiety were not statistically more likely to have asynchrony in their WISC-III subscale scores. The narrow definition of asynchrony, focusing on differences in WISC-III scores, may be a limitation of this study because cognitive differences is only one type of asynchrony experienced by gifted individuals.

The interaction of intensity and anxiety was examined by Harrison and Van Haneghan (2011), comparing middle school and high school gifted students to a nongifted comparison group. Both middle school and high school groups were higher in psychomotor, sensual, intellectual, and imaginational intensity, and the high school group was higher in emotional intensity than the nongifted group. The gifted group was higher on ratings of insomnia and fear of the unknown, and there was a small to moderately statistically significant relationship between intensity (overexcitability) and insomnia, fear of the unknown, and death anxiety. The largest correlation was between imaginational intensity and fear of the unknown, and there was no relationship between intellectual intensity and death anxiety (Harrison & Van Haneghan, 2011). Intensity was not the only factor in anxiety among the gifted group, in that they had higher levels of anxiety even after accounting for the increased levels of intensity among the group.

Mary, a 15-year-old academically talented learner in treatment for anxiety, presented these recent examples from her school day. In three of her sophomore-level classes during group work time, groups were leaving Mary to complete the assignments on her own and walking away while she did the work. When she completed the assigned work (which everyone received the same grade for), she was taunted for actually caring about the outcome of grades and assignments. This was happening daily in multiple classes. Even after appropriate self-advocacy to the teacher and vice principal, this cycle was continuing in her classes and causing significant anxiety and stress on both an ethical and personal level for her. Gifted children may get mixed messages from peers, in that children are told to perform at high levels but are sometimes bullied or ostracized when they do focus on school work (Cross & Cross, 2015).

Based upon prevalence research, gifted children are identified with anxiety at approximately the same rate as the average child (e.g., Eren et al., 2018; Guénolé et al., 2013). Students who are at high-achieving schools or in specialized programs for gifted may experience higher levels of stress (National Academies of Sciences, Engineering, and Medicine, 2019) or test anxiety (Goetz et al., 2008), and gifted characteristics of intensity may be connected to higher levels of anxiety (Harrison & Van Haneghan, 2011). Those who work in educational settings would benefit by identifying the emotional needs of gifted children without believing the myth that gifted children do not have unique social-emotional needs (Peterson, 2009), but instead may need recognition of symptoms of emotional stress or anxiety at least at the same level as the general population.

Perfectionism

Every Wednesday night, Fei sits in front of her spelling work for hours. Wednesday is sentence night, and she crafts each sentence with emphasis on her criteria for correctness—all letters must be formed perfectly, and the sentence must be grammatically correct, of appropriate length, absolutely true, and an honest reflection of her life. Each sentence is labored over, even though she is able to spell and define each word with no difficulty even before the spelling list is distributed, and she receives little reassurance from her parents. She is concerned that the teacher will grade her sentences as wrong unless all of her personal criteria are met.

The impact of perfectionism on the gifted population has been explored in more detail than generalized or specific forms of anxiety. Perfectionism is defined as setting impossibly high standards and striving for flawlessness, combined with excessive self-criticism, an unhealthy concern for others' opinions of one's work, and overgeneralization of failure despite adverse consequences (Van Gemert, 2019). The rigid adherence to high standards and overemphasis placed upon the achievement of those standards has been frequently linked to high intellectual ability (Dixon et al., 2004; Parker, 1997; Shuler, 2000; Speirs Neumeister, 2016). Early research on giftedness and perfectionism focused on different typologies, including healthy, dysfunctional and nonperfectionistic (Parker, 1997), adaptive and maladaptive (Vandiver & Worrell, 2002), and self-oriented, socially prescribed, and other oriented (Hewitt & Flett, 1991). Shuler (2000) found that more than 87% of gifted middle school students she studied scored in perfectionistic clusters. Normal perfectionists (58%) believed their success was due to personal effort, while neurotic perfectionists (29%) fixated on making mistakes, and had a high need for approval from others and limited coping when they made mistakes. There has also been an association between types of perfectionism and mental health symptoms (Dixon et al., 2004). Measuring perfectionism among high school students in a residential program for gifted students, the study found four clusters of students, including three types of perfectionists (mixed adaptive, pervasive, and mixed-maladaptive) and one nonperfectionistic cluster. Mixed adaptive students had high levels of adaptive and low levels of maladaptive dimensions of perfectionism. Pervasive students were high on both adaptive and maladaptive levels. Mixed-maladaptive were high on maladaptive and low on adaptive dimensions of perfectionism. The nonperfectionistic cluster, labeled self-assured, were low on all dimensions of perfectionism. Two of the groups, pervasive and mixed-maladaptive, had a poorer profile of mental health, including somatic complaints, obsessive compulsive tendencies, poorer self-image, lower sense of personal security, and a pattern of dysfunctional coping (Dixon et al., 2004).

Guignard et al. (2012) looked at the relationship of perfectionism and anxiety in French fifth- and sixth-grade children, using typical children and a gifted group. The outcome of the research found differing correlations for each grade, although an overall small association between perfectionism and anxiety. Chan (2007, 2011) looked at positive and negative perfectionism rates among Chinese gifted students in Hong Kong. Positive perfectionism is seen as a realistic striving for excellence, and negative perfectionism is a rigid adherence to high perceived success and high expectations from others. Significantly higher rates of positive perfectionism in comparison to negative perfectionism were found among the Chinese gifted students (Chan, 2007, 2011). The possibility of high standards being a cultural norm for these Chinese students accounts for the high rate of positive perfectionism.

Current research is coalescing the wide variety of typologies to two components of perfectionism to assist in clarifying the healthy/unhealthy and adaptive/maladaptive debate. Positive Strivings is consistent with conscientiousness, positive affect, and internal locus of control, and Evaluative Concerns is consistent with negative affect, neuroticism, and anxiety (Speirs Neumeister, 2016). Positive Striving has been associated with a growth mindset and Evaluative Concerns with a fixed mindset in gifted and advanced students (Mofield & Parker Peters, 2018). Research has also turned to identification of different domains within one person, such as the level of perfectionistic strivings, and perfectionistic concerns in one individual may vary depending upon the area of achievement, such as sports versus math (Fletcher & Speirs Neumeister, 2017).

Components of the gifted child's experience may include an internal, social, or parental demand for perfection and an assumption that perfection may be the expected norm for them. Perfectionism is seen in many gifted individuals, both in their inability to turn in work that does not meet their personal expectations and in spending hours on projects or assignments that are designed to be short or relatively easy. The research is still inconclusive, but perfectionism may be an important puzzle piece in working through connections to anxiety within the gifted children and may be a prominent roadblock in a gifted child's learning journey.

Strategies and Interventions

Tyra, a second-grade student, has been late to school for the last 2 weeks and distracted for most of the day. She walks into the classroom holding tightly to her mother's hand and clinging to her mother when she tries to leave. Two weeks ago, Tyra's mother was in a minor car accident on the way home after dropping off Tyra at school. Now, every morning Tyra imagines her mom in a deadly car crash as she drives away from school. Throughout the school day, she spends her time worrying about her mom and cannot concentrate. At night, she begs her mom not to drive her to school tomorrow in a state of anticipatory anxiety, thinking about the possibilities of what can happen. This fearful event had led to ongoing anxiety that interferes with her daily functioning in class. With integration of services from a number of people, Tyra is a success story. Her teacher recognized her anxiety and also incorporated her knowledge of gifted characteristics in thinking about interventions for Tyra. She identified how Tyra's advanced intellectual skills led her to understand the implications of a car crash, which combined with her imaginational intensity to see images of her mom in a deadly crash over and over in her head. She also saw Tyra's big emotional reaction as a mixture of her emotional intensity and anxiety. Quickly, a team was formed around Tyra. The school social worker met Tyra and her mom at their car every morning and became Tyra's connection person in the morning. A psychologist who specializes in anxiety met with Tyra and her mom to develop coping strategies and teach Tyra to calm her physical reactions to her imagined fears. The psychologist also used higher level educational materials about anxiety, the body's response to fear, and how to take control of cognitions in working with strategies for Tyra. The teacher started incorporating classroom anxiety management techniques into every day, especially at morning meeting time. Within a month, Tyra was back to easing into her school day rather than starting every day with anxiety and stress.

For Tyra and many gifted children, interventions may begin with understanding the advanced cognitive capabilities of the gifted learner, intensity of response to the world, and strong desire to be involved in problem solving. Incorporating all of these areas suggests the need for school-based and counseling strategies that are effective for twice-exceptional gifted learners (Foley-Nicpon & Assouline, 2015).

At this point, little research has been completed looking at interventions and efficacy of treatment specifically with anxious gifted children. Roome and Romney (1985) examined the use of biofeedback and progressive muscle relaxation with a group of 10 gifted children in comparison to a control group of 10 average-ability children. Both biofeedback and relaxation techniques lowered the state anxiety (anxiety connected to an experience) within the gifted groups in comparison with control group. It did not lower trait anxiety (anxiety as a personality characteristic), however, and gifted children were not found to be more anxious to begin with in comparison with the nongifted control group. Mendaglio (2010) focused on applying his theory of giftedness to intervention and treatment based upon his own practical experience over a career of working with gifted children.

More recently, Gaesser (2014) reported on interventions used with gifted children within a clinical setting. In a study comparing cognitive behavioral therapy (CBT) techniques, emotional freedom technique (EFT), and a wait list control group, the effectiveness of each intervention after three sessions was examined. EFT was significantly more effective than the control group in treating anxiety within gifted children, and CBT was not statistically significantly different from control or EFT groups. This is a positive step in moving toward finding specific research-driven interventions that are effective with gifted youth beyond those that are effective with anxious individuals in general.

Given that there are not yet research-based interventions for use with gifted children with anxiety, turning toward anxiety interventions in general helps guide strategies and interventions in the classroom. Many general anxiety resources are available both online and through published materials, and some of these resources are provided in Table 8.2. This list is not exhaustive, but is an attempt to lead educators into possible avenues for greater understanding of anxiety, social-emotional issues, and gifted children.

TABLE 8.2

Resources for Teachers Responding to Anxiety in the Classroom

Type	Resource	Brief Description	Where to Find
Books on Gifted Children and Their Characteristics	*Living With Intensity: Understanding the Sensitivity, Excitability, and the Emotional Development of Gifted Children, Adolescents, and Adults* by Michael Piechowski and Susan Daniels	Parent support information about intensity and how to help intense children	Great Potential Press
	The Smart Teens' Guide to Living With Intensity: How to Get More Out of Life and Learning by Lisa Rivero	Overview and strategies for teens on intensity	Great Potential Press
	Anxiety in the Classroom	Comprehensive website with multiple resources for educators	https://anxietyintheclassroom.org/school-system
Educator Resources on Anxiety	Understanding Anxiety	Australia's school resources for educators	http://understandinganxiety.wayahead.org.au
	Anxiety Canada	Canada's school resources for educators	https://www.anxietycanada.com/resources/educator-resources
Breathing Techniques	Mindfulness Exercises	Scripts for teacher to use in classroom	https://mindfulnessexercises.com/guided-meditation-scripts-for-teachers
	"Sesame Street: Common and Colbie Caillat–'Belly Breathe' With Elmo"	YouTube video for early elementary students with breathing	https://www.youtube.com/watch?v=_mZbzDOpylA

TABLE 8.2, *continued*

Type	Resource	Brief Description	Where to Find
Motivation for Students to Learn About Anxiety	"Just Breathe" by Julie Bayer Salzman & Josh Salzman (Wavecrest Films)"	YouTube video for elementary children on self-control and breathing	https://www.youtube.com/watch?v=RVA2N6tX2cg
	"Overcoming Anxiety | Jonas Kolker | TEDxTheMastersSchool"	One teen's story of anxiety in his life	https://www.youtube.com/watch?v=A1anXJhVamc
What Is Anxiety?	"Fight Flight Freeze - Anxiety Explained for Teens"	YouTube video with overview of Fight Flight Freeze	https://www.youtube.com/watch?v=rpolpKTWrp4
	"OCD and Anxiety Disorders: Crash Course Psychology #29"	YouTube video with teenager-based educational information about anxiety	https://www.youtube.com/watch?v=aX7jnVXXG5o
	The MindUp Curriculum available in grades K–2, 3–5, and 6–8	Mindfulness exercises for the classroom researched and outcome data supported	Scholastic
Curriculum on Mindfulness and Social-Emotional Learning	Mindfulschools.org	Whole-school mindfulness program	https://www.mindfulschools.org/training/mindfulness-fundamentals
	Mindfulness-Based Stress Reduction	Classes through the Center for Mindfulness, Medicine, Healthcare and Society	https://www.umassmed.edu/cfm
	International Foundation for Research and Education on Depression	Free curriculum for teaching social-emotional learning tools	https://hopefulminds.org/curriculum
Books for Students to Assist With Anxiety	*From Worrier to Warrior: A Guide to Conquering Your Fears* by Dan Peters	Elementary-age guide to coping with anxiety with strategies	Great Potential Press
	What to Do When Your Brain Gets Stuck: A Kid's Guide to Overcoming OCD (What-to-Do Guides for Kids) by Dawn Huebner	Elementary-age guide to OCD strategies	Magination Press

TABLE 8.2, *continued*

Type	Resource	Brief Description	Where to Find
Books for Students to Assist With Anxiety, *continued*	*The Shyness and Social Anxiety Workbook: Proven, Step-by-Step Techniques for Overcoming Your Fear* by Martin Anthony and Richard Swinson	Teenage guide to social anxiety strategies	New Harbinger Publications
	Perfectionism: A Practical Guide to Managing Never Good Enough by Lisa Van Gemert	Middle school and older resource for perfectionism	Great Potential Press
	The Anxiety Workbook for Teens: Activities to Help You Deal With Anxiety and Worry by Lisa Schaub	Teenage guide to anxiety strategies	New Harbinger Publications
Books for Parents and Teachers	*The Anxiety Cure for Kids: A Guide for Parents and Children* (2nd ed.) by Elizabeth Dupont Spencer, Robert Dupont, and Caroline Dupont	Parent guide to understanding and helping children with anxiety cope	John Wiley and Sons
	Anxiety-Free Kids: An Interactive Guide for Parents and Children (2nd ed.) by Bonnie Zucker	Parent and elementary-age child joint guide to anxiety	Prufrock Press

Classroom Strategies

Classroom management of social-emotional needs, including anxiety, has become an ever-increasing component within the day of an educator. Developing responses to social-emotional learning needs of students includes knowledge of preventative strategies and classroom-level interventions. Online resources from around the globe are responding to demand with guides for educators on responding in the classroom to anxiety (see Table 8.2). Additionally, the United States Department of Education has created an Office of Safe and Healthy Learners that provides funding through Title IV grants to each state. Mental health training has now become mandatory in New York, Colorado, and Virginia, and many other states have either approved or are developing mental health legislation, or have approved additional mental health workers for schools (Hood, 2019). In Minnesota, suicide prevention training is required for educator license renewal. Teacher response to anxiety includes both education of symptoms and disorders and how to structure classroom experiences and environment to support responding to the needs of anxious children. Table 8.3 provides several classroom management strategies that have been utilized to support the social-emotional needs of gifted children, most specifically around anxiety issues.

One important classroom management strategy for anxiety that can be implemented is teaching students how to create a relaxation response in the body through deep breathing. Gifted children, because of imaginational and emotional intensity in particular, benefit by learning how to respond to big reactions to emotions (Daniels & Piechowski, 2009). All people, however, benefit from learning how to move from a physiological stress response to a more relaxed state, allowing them to begin to gain control of strong emotional reactions, including anxiety.

Breathing techniques must be taught in a nonheightened state and practiced to be effective. Diaphragmatic breathing is more complicated than telling a child to "take a deep breath." The vital components of true relaxation response breathing includes engagement of the diaphragm, or belly breathing; a slow, relaxed pace to the deep breaths; and keeping the shoulders stationary to allow the lungs to fill fully. When inhaling, the belly should extend outward, inflating the lungs and pushing the diaphragm down and out. Exhalation is a long, slow, steady stream of breath pushed by the diaphragm moving up and inward (Harvard Health Publishing, 2018a). Varying pace can be effective, including breathing in and out for counts of 5–8 seconds. Integrating deep breathing and relaxation time-outs during a school day can become second nature to teachers and students. Starting a class session or morning meeting with 5–10

TABLE 8.3
Strategies that Support Social-Emotional Needs

1. **Establish transition routines** for beginning and end of class times (e.g., lights off for first 5 minutes, daily YouTube video, joke of the day, 3 minutes of talk time).

2. **Create a space** in your classroom available for students who need to take time to calm down, move, breathe, pace, etc. Set expectations within your comfort level of how to use the space.

3. **Communicate both in written and visual form** the daily schedule or expectations of what is happening within that class time (this helps keep anxious kids from spending a lot of time worrying about what's next).

4. **Prepare students** for activities, assignments, and tests that are going to be uncomfortable, challenging, new learning, and possibly stir up emotions.

5. **Know** which students have accommodation plans to be able to take breaks when necessary within the classroom or access support people in the building.

6. **Establish signals** with those students who need a fast and easy exit if they have strong anxiety response that needs to be handled out of the classroom.

7. **Create a culture** where your classroom is a place where kids can stay and be emotional in their responses if needed.

8. **Set timer** for a breathing break during a classroom time frame.

9. **Balance** encouraging students to stay in the classroom for small anxiety situations and knowing how to access additional resources within the building for larger panic attacks and crisis situations.

10. **Employ test preparation strategies** that establish a brain readiness to demonstrate knowledge:
    - 2 minutes of quiet reflection, deep breathing, or prayer before a test.
    - Stress dump before a test—encourage students to write down on a piece of paper what they are worried about, crumple those up, and throw in the trash (basketball style shoot-off adds a lightness to the experience before the test).
    - Normalization of what this test actually means to avoid catastrophizing a poor grade or negative outcome.

11. **Provide private praise** to those students who have social anxiety—public praise almost always backfires.

12. **Offer early exposure** (online, posted in the classroom, preview time) to new graphic organizers, questions that will be asked tomorrow, new topics coming up for anxious and introverted students to be able to prep for class.

13. **Respond to opportunities** presented by students to get true feedback on how they feel about the class, life, experience.

14. **Initiate working in small steps**—We are all going to work for 5 minutes, (set an alarm) then stop and ask questions, then work some more.

Note. Strategies were compiled from https://anxietyintheclassroom.org and http://understandinganxiety.wayahead.org.au.

deep, cleansing breaths sets a tone for the day. Teachers have also used alarms set to go off at strategic times on a daily basis as a reminder to integrate breathing practice. Another useful intervention is to create a 2- to 5-minute time before every testing experience in which students practice their deep breathing skills. Imaging studies of the brain have shown that concentration on breathing shows a positive neurological change in the focus and attention areas of the brain (Herrero et al., 2017). Increasing the ability for focus and attention might impact the outcome of tests for all children, and those with test anxiety will directly benefit.

Many schools now integrate mindfulness interventions into their schoolwide experiences, and the data on effectiveness is promising in children and youth interventions, particularly for those children who were already demonstrating psychological symptoms like anxiety (Zoogman et al., 2015). Mindfulness is paying full attention to something in a relaxed, easy way. Mindfulness has been described as a willingness to be open to whatever unfolds and a compassionate curiosity that is free from judgment (Kabat-Zinn, 2003). The ultimate aim of most school-based mindfulness programs is to increase awareness of the influence of thoughts and emotions on speech and behaviors, and thereby enhance the likelihood of making more skillful or appropriate choices (Semple & Lee, 2011). The benefits of mindfulness have been to increase attention focused on immediate experiences and approaching experiences with openness and curiosity, helping students become more responsive, calm, and focused while experiencing less stress and distractions. Numerous curricula have been designed for schoolwide integration of mindful practices, 10 of which have been reviewed for the research support of each program by Semple et al. (2017), providing a starting place for schools and educators to carefully review the interventions that may be used with students. Mindfulness has been suggested as working well with gifted populations (Sharp et al., 2017) to assist in regulating their attention and self-management skills.

A final classroom strategy may be found in applying the biology of anxiety to stressful situations. At some point for all people, the parasympathetic system calms down the acute anxiety response and the physical symptoms of anxiety go down (Godoy et al., 2018). Helping students to "step in" to situations that are causing them anxiety, stay with the situation until the anxiety goes down, and feel successful while staying engaged increases the chance that child will step in again, hopefully with less anxiety the next time. In his TED Talk on anxiety, Kolker (2017) called this experience "embracing the suck." Teachers and parents can help students use this technique, recognize the anxiety and stress in a situation, and as much as possible stay within the anxiety-producing situation to come out the other side.

For children who have a strong flight response to stressful situations, step-ping in to the stress, or embracing the suck, might be through very small steps carried out over time. For example, Josh was a gifted child who had anticipa-tory anxiety about starting anything new. At the start of every school year, sport season, or new activity, the irrational message from his brain was that the new thing would be terrible. He would cry for hours before Meet the Teacher Day or his first soccer practice of the year, even though he had experienced similar events in the past. "Stepping in" to him meant small, incremental steps toward participation, such as sitting in the car through the practice time of the first practice and then on the sidelines for the second. He was more successful at the formal Meet the Teacher Day when he was allowed to set up a premeeting with the teacher, stopping by the classroom for a few minutes at a prearranged time with the teacher and no other students present. Parents and educators found small ways he could step in and stay in experiences until his anxiety went down enough for him to participate more inclusively in the experience.

Effective strategies for anxious gifted learners frequently combine the knowledge of the gifted brain and characteristics with proven interventions for anxiety together into useful tools. Cognitive behavioral therapy is an inter-vention with robust positive outcome research for anxiety (Hofmann et al., 2012). CBT includes the theory that feelings are impacted by the way someone thinks and behaves. Interventions include identification of irrational beliefs, understanding the body reaction to emotional stimulus, and understanding levels of emotional reactions. An important intervention for the gifted child is a thorough and interactive explanation of the physiological components of the anxiety system, responding to their cognitive needs to understand and make sense of the world.

For children under the age of 12, particularly if parents are willing to be active participants in treatment, utilizing a book like *Anxiety-Free Kids* (Zucker, 2016) is helpful. This book has sections for both parents and children that explore the what, why, and what next of anxiety and strategies. A book study with parents/guardians and the child is frequently an effective tool in work-ing with the child's anxiety. Armed with the knowledge of what is happening within their systems, many gifted children can, with the help of their support person, find ways to utilize that information in their own response to anxiety.

When to Refer

The timing of when to refer a child or adolescent for psychological coun-seling to address anxiety is based upon understanding the severity of interference the anxiety has in the youth's life. Worry or fear that is consistently out of proportion to the real or imagined danger, occurs consistently across settings and time for a child, and interferes with their functioning is a sign that a referral would be useful. The most useful rule of thumb is if the anxiety disrupts a child's normal functioning, it is then time to refer to a therapist or psychologist who will help provide treatment options for that child. A psychologist or trained clinician can help that child learn thinking tools, physical calming skills, and tips for confronting the fear or discomfort that comes with anxiety.

School counselors or psychologists may have lists of local professionals who have worked with other children and families from the community. Ideally, a professional who has experience with gifted children would be a possible referral source. Many communities, however, do not have clinicians who understand gifted characteristics. Training on gifted children is not typically integrated into the curriculum for psychology training programs or continuing education, so mental health clinicians who work with gifted children have sought out that population as an additional area of expertise in their clinical practice and are not necessarily easily found within the mental health provider community.

Conclusion

Anxiety is a natural response of the body, which in times of extreme levels of stress or anxiety response out of expectations for a situation, has become categorized as a mental health diagnosis. Anxiety comes in many different forms, all of which can be present in children and adolescents. In fact, anxiety has become a frequently identified mental health need in schools, with up to one third of students identifying worry as a component of their school experience. Anxiety impacts children in their social competence, relationships, and possibly willingness to pursue higher education.

Gifted children are as likely to experience anxiety as any other children. When there is a combination of giftedness and diagnosed anxiety, that child can be identified as a twice-exceptional learner. Specific components of giftedness that may make anxiety more probable have not yet been identified, but perfectionism is a characteristic that seems to have negative outcomes for gifted learners and a correlation with anxiety. Additionally, students in high-performing schools and full-time gifted programs may experience higher levels of stress. Current intervention research is not advanced enough to specifically identify intervention strategies targeted for gifted children with anxiety. However, the knowledge that twice-exceptional students with anxiety are present in the classroom is the first right step toward identification and intervention.

FROM THE EDITORS

Student Vignettes

Astrid

At 14 years old, Astrid is tall, thin, and pale. Dark under-eye circles suggest allergies, sleepless nights, or both. Opening her report card she sees that despite missing 23 of the first 45 days of school, she has received an A in all classes other than physical education for the first quarter. She sighs, knowing she will likely fail physical education because she cannot make up missed class work.

Astrid's migraine headaches result in debilitating nausea and uncontrollable vomiting. Attending school is taxing on "good days" and nearly impossible on all of the others. A 504 plan documents her status as OHI, or other health impaired. Section 504 of the United States Rehabilitation Act prevents discrimination for students with disabilities by ensuring they receive the support they need to thrive in a school setting. Plans are designed to cover any condition that limits daily activities in a major way. Astrid's 504 documents her headaches and anxiety with accommodations that allow frequent absences from school, assignment and homework modifications, test-taking and grading adjustments, and permission to leave the classroom as needed.

On days when Astrid is well enough to attend school, she is nearly overcome by anxiety. She worries about what other students will say to her and the embarrassment of having to rush to the nearest bathroom. Her heart pounds, and her hands feel clammy. She ignores the symptoms as long as she can before calling her mom.

Despite her frequent absences, Astrid finds school easy. She rarely studies for tests and almost always scores in the top percentile. She is bored by the reading assignments and prefers to read her father's old physics and astronomy textbooks. On clear nights, she can be found outside on the balcony looking through her telescope. Her room is littered with sky maps, star charts, and her data collection.

FROM THE EDITORS, *continued*

Discussion Questions

1.   What is Astrid's greatest school challenge? As she moves through the school system, are the challenges she faces likely to increase or decrease? Why, or why not?
2.   How can Astrid's family and school support her academic needs and interests?
3.   What can and should be told to Astrid's teachers and classmates?
4.   What social and emotional supports should the school provide Astrid?
5.   How do the needs of students with OHI and/or anxiety differ from the needs of other twice-exceptional learners?
6.   Should qualified students with frequent absences from school receive gifted services? Why, or why not?

Cory

Each morning, Cory's dad sets the table for breakfast, carefully placing the dishes, silverware, and napkins at precise right angles to match the checkered tablecloth. He knows Cory will enter the kitchen at 7:10 a.m., wash his hands, and then sit down at 7:14 a.m. to eat in silence. He notes his son's small hands, chapped red from excessive washing, are starting to bleed again. He makes a mental note to call in a prescription refill for the salve Cory's pediatrician prescribed to treat contact dermatitis.

At 7:45 a.m., Cory and his dad leave home for the short drive to school. The mature trees and wide sidewalks that originally attracted Cory's parents to the old neighborhood seem to imprison Cory. He rarely ventures outside and prefers spending his time reading or organizing his toys. Cory is terrified of squirrels. Through research, he has learned that squirrels are members of the Sciuridae rodent family, and he dreads the germs that they carry. He fears he would be bitten by a squirrel if he were to play outside or walk to school.

School is difficult for Cory. Although he is intellectually gifted, his classmates perceive his behaviors as odd. They tease him for using hand sanitizer, wiping off his desk, and refusing to share his supplies. They know he avoids touching door knobs, using the bathroom, and going outside.

FROM THE EDITORS, *continued*

Cory's father has been a single parent since his wife lost her battle with cancer 3 years ago. He is concerned about his son's OCD and is in frequent contact with his son's pediatrician, therapist, and teacher. They are all supportive and hope within time that Cory's level of anxiety and his need for reassurance will lessen.

Discussion Questions

1. What information should be shared with Cory's teacher?
2. Should information about Cory, OCD, or other mental health problems be shared with students? Why, or why not?
3. What strategies/intervention may help Cory feel more comfortable in school or other public settings?
4. Should Cory be homeschooled? Explain your answer.

References

Abramovitch, A., Anholt, G., Raveh-Gottfried, S., Hamo, N., & Abramowitz, J. S. (2018, March). Meta-analysis of intelligence quotient (IQ) in obsessive-compulsive disorder. *Neuropsychology Review, 28,* 111–120. https://doi.org/10.1007/s11065-017-9358-0

Akin, C. A. (2005). Academic asynchrony. *Gifted Child Today, 28*(2), 60-66. https://doi.org/10.4219/gct-2005-165

American Psychiatric Association. (1952). *Diagnostic and statistical manual of mental disorders.*

American Psychiatric Association. (2013). *Diagnostic and statistical manual of mental disorders* (5th ed.). https://doi.org/10.1176/appi.books.9780890425596

Bandelow, B., & Michaelis, S. (2015). Epidemiology of anxiety disorders in the 21st century. *Dialogues in Clinical Neuroscience, 17*(3), 327.

Benbow, C. P., & Minor, L. L. (1990). Cognitive profiles of verbally and mathematically precocious students: Implications for identification of the gifted. *Gifted Child Quarterly, 34*(1), 21–26. https://doi.org/10.1177/0016 98629003400105

Bitsko, R. H., Holbrook, J. R., Ghandour, R. M., Blumberg, S. J., Visser, S. N., Perou, R., & Walkup, J. T. (2018). Epidemiology and impact of health care provider-diagnosed anxiety and depression among US children. *Journal of Developmental & Behavioral Pediatrics, 39*(5), 395–403. https://doi.org/ 10.1097/dbp.0000000000000571

Cernova, L. (2005). Aggression and anxiety of intellectually gifted Russian adolescents in Latvia. *PsycEXTRA*.

Chan, D. W. (2007). Positive and negative perfectionism among Chinese gifted students in Hong Kong: Their relationships to general self-efficacy and subjective well-being. *Journal for the Education of the Gifted, 31*(1), 77–102. https://doi.org/10.4219/jeg-2007-512

Chan, D. W. (2011). Perfectionism among Chinese gifted and nongifted students in Hong Kong: The use of the Revised Almost Perfect Scale. *Journal for the Education of the Gifted, 34*(1), 68–98. https://doi.org/10.4219/jeg-2007-512

Columbus Group. (1991, July). *Unpublished transcript of the meeting of the Columbus Group*.

Coplan, J. D., Hodulik, S. G., Mathew, S. J., Mao, X., Hof, P. R., Gorman, J. M., & Shungu, D. C. (2012). The relationship between intelligence and anxiety: An association with subcortical white matter metabolism. *Frontiers in Evolutionary Neuroscience, 3*, 8. https://doi.org/10.3389/fnevo.2011.00008

CrashCourse. (2014, September 1). *OCD and anxiety disorders: Crash course psychology #29* [Video]. YouTube. https://www.youtube.com/watch?v=aX7 jnVXXG5o

Crocq, M. A. (2017). The history of generalized anxiety disorder as a diagnostic category. *Dialogues in Clinical Neuroscience, 19*(2), 107–116.

Cross, J. R., & Cross, T. L. (2015). Clinical and mental health issues in counseling the gifted individual. *Journal of Counseling & Development, 93*(2), 163–172. https://doi.org/10.1002/j.1556-6676.2015.00192.x

Dabrowski, K. (1964). *Positive disintegration*. Little, Brown.

Daniels, S., & Piechowski, M. M. (2009). *Living with intensity: Understanding the sensitivity, excitability, and emotional development of gifted children, adolescents, and adults*. Great Potential Press.

de Lijster, J. M., Dieleman, G. C., Utens, E. M., Dierckx, B., Wierenga, M., Verhulst, F. C., & Legerstee, J. S. (2018, April). Social and academic functioning in adolescents with anxiety disorders: A systematic review. *Journal of Affective Disorders, 230*, 108–117. https://doi.org/10.1016/j.jad.2018.01. 008

Desco, M., Navas-Sanchez, F. J., Sanchez-González, J., Reig, S., Robles, O., Franco, C., Guzman De Villoria, J., Garcia-Barreno, P., & Arango, C. (2011). Mathematically gifted adolescents use more extensive and more bilateral areas of the fronto-parietal network than controls during executive functioning and fluid reasoning tasks. *Neuroimage, 57*(1), 281–292. https://doi.org/10.1016/j.neuroimage.2011.03.063

Dixon, F. A., Lapsley, D. K., & Hanchon, T. A. (2004). An empirical typology of perfectionism in gifted adolescents. *Gifted Child Quarterly, 48*(2), 95–106. https://doi.org/10.1177/001698620404800203

Duncan, S., Goodwin, C., Haase, J., & Wilson, S. (2018a). *Neuroscience of giftedness: Greater sensory sensitivity.* https://www.gro-gifted.org/neuroscience-of-giftedness-greater-sensory-sensitivity

Duncan, S., Goodwin, C., Haase, J., & Wilson, S. (2018b). *Neuroscience of giftedness: Increased brain areas associated with emotional processing.* https://www.gro-gifted.org/neuroscience-of-giftedness-increased-brain-areas-associated-with-emotional-processing

Eklund, K., Tanner, N., Stoll, K., & Anway, L. (2015). Identifying emotional and behavioral risk among gifted and nongifted children: A multi-gate, multi-informant approach. *School Psychology Quarterly, 30*(2), 197–211. https://doi.org/10.1037/spq0000080

Eren, F., Ömerelli Çete, A., Avcil, S., & Baykara, B. (2018). Emotional and behavioral characteristics of gifted children and their families. *Archives of Neuropsychiatry, 55*(2), 105. https://dx.doi.org/10.5152/npa.2017.12731

Flescher, I. (1963). Anxiety and achievement of intellectually gifted and creatively gifted children. *Journal of Psychology, 56*(2), 251–268. https://doi.org/10.1080/00223980.1963.9916644

Fletcher, K. L., & Speirs Neumeister, K. L. (2017). *Perfectionism in school: When achievement is not so perfect.* Momentum Press.

Foley-Nicpon, M., & Assouline, S. G. (2015). Counseling considerations for the twice-exceptional client. *Journal of Counseling & Development, 93*(2), 202–211. https://doi.org/10.1002/j.1556-6676.2015.00196.x

Forsyth, P. (1987). A study of self-concept, anxiety, and security of children in gifted, French immersion, and regular classes. *Canadian Journal of Counselling and Psychotherapy, 21*(2–3). https://cjc-rcc.ucalgary.ca/article/view/59665

Fouladchang, M., Kohgard, A., & Salah, V. (2010). A study of psychological health among students of gifted and nongifted high schools. *Procedia-Social and Behavioral Sciences, 5*, 1220–1225.

Gaesser, A. H. (2014). *Interventions to reduce anxiety for gifted children and adolescents* [Doctoral dissertation]. University of Connecticut.

Ghandour, R. M., Sherman, L. J., Vladutiu, C. J., Ali, M. M., Lynch, S. E., Bitsko, R. H., & Blumberg, S. J. (2019, March). Prevalence and treatment of depression, anxiety, and conduct problems in US children. *The Journal of Pediatrics, 206,* 256–267. https://doi.org/10.1016/j.jpeds.2018.09.021

Godoy, L. D., Rossignoli, M. T., Delfino-Pereira, P., Garcia-Cairasco, N., & de Lima Umeoka, E. H. (2018). A comprehensive overview on stress neurobiology: Basic concepts and clinical implications. *Frontiers in Behavioral Neuroscience, 12,* 127. https://doi.org/10.3389/fnbeh.2018.00127

Goetz, T., Preckel, F., Zeidner, M., & Schleyer, E.. (2008). Big fish in big ponds: A multilevel analysis of test anxiety and achievement in special gifted classes. *Anxiety, Stress & Coping, 21*(2), 185–198. https://doi.org/10.1080/10615800701628827

Guénolé, F., Louis, J., Creveuil, C., Montlahuc, C., Baleyte, J. M., Fourneret, P., & Revol, O. (2013). A cross-sectional study of trait-anxiety in a group of 111 intellectually gifted children. *L'Encephale, 39*(4), 278–283. https://doi.org/10.1016/j.encep.2013.02.001

Guénolé, F., Speranza, M., Louis, J., Fourneret, P., Revol, O., & Baleyte, J. M. (2015). Wechsler profiles in referred children with intellectual giftedness: associations with trait-anxiety, emotional dysregulation, and heterogeneity of Piaget-like reasoning processes. European *Journal of Paediatric Neurology, 19*(4), 402–410. https://doi.org/10.1016/j.ejpn.2015.03.006

Guignard, J.-H., Jacquet, A.-Y., & Lubart, T. I. (2012). Perfectionism and anxiety: A paradox in intellectual giftedness? *PLOS ONE, 7*(7), e41043. https://doi.org/10.1371/journal.pone.0041043

Harrison, G. E., & VanHaneghan, J. P. (2011). The gifted and the shadow of the night: Dabrowski's overexcitabilities and their correlation to insomnia, death anxiety, and fear of the unknown. *Journal for the Education of the Gifted, 34*(4), 669–697. https://doi.org/10.1177/016235321103400407

Harvard Health Publishing. (2018a, April 13). *Relaxation techniques: Breath control helps quell errant stress response.* https://www.health.harvard.edu/mind-and-mood/relaxation-techniques-breath-control-helps-quell-errant-stress-response

Harvard Health Publishing. (2018b, May 1). *Understanding the stress response.* https://www.health.harvard.edu/staying-healthy/understanding-the-stress-response

Herrero, J. L., Khuvis, S., Yeagle, E., Cerf, M., & Mehta, A. D. (2017). Breathing above the brainstem: Volitional control and attentional modulation in humans. *Journal of Neurophysiology, 119*(1), 145–159. https://doi.org/10.1152/jn.00551.2017

Hewitt, P. L., & Flett, G. L. (1991). Perfectionism in the self and social contexts: Conceptualization, assessment, and association with psychopathology. *Journal of Personality and Social Psychology, 60*(3), 456–470. https://doi.org/10.1037/0022-3514.60.3.456

Hofmann, S. G., Asnaani, A., Vonk, I. J. J., Sawyer, A. T., & Fang, A. (2012). The efficacy of cognitive behavioral therapy: A review of meta-analyses. *Cognitive Therapy and Research, 36*(5), 427–440. https://doi.org/10.1007/s10608-012-9476-1

Hood, L. (2019, September 3). *More states requiring mental health education.* https://www.educationdive.com/news/more-states-requiring-mental-health-education/561250

Kabat-Zinn, J. (2003). Mindfulness-based interventions in context: past, present, and future. *Clinical Psychology: Science and Practice 10*(2), 144–156. https://doi.org/10.1093/clipsy.bpg016

Karpinski, R. I., Kolb, A. M. K., Tetreault, N. A., & Borowski, T. B. (2018, January–February). High intelligence: A risk factor for psychological and physiological overexcitabilities. *Intelligence, 66,* 8–23. https://doi.org/10.1016/j.intell.2017.09.001

Kolker, J. (2017, June 2). *Overcoming anxiety* [Video]. YouTube. https://www.youtube.com/watch?v=A1anXJhVamc

Mendaglio, S. (2010). Anxiety in gifted students. In J. C. Cassady (Ed.), *Anxiety in schools: the causes, consequences, and solutions for academic anxieties* (pp. 153–173). Lang.

Martin, L. T., Burns, R. M., & Schonlau, M. (2009). Mental disorders among gifted and nongifted youth: A selected review of the epidemiologic literature. *Gifted Child Quarterly, 54*(1), 31–41. https://doi.org/10.1177/0016986209352684

Minnesota Department of Education. (2019). *Minnesota Student Survey results 2013–2019: Mental health data from 5th, 9th and 11th grade students.* https://education.mn.gov/MDE/dse/health/mss

Mofield, E. L., & Parker Peters, M. (2018). Shifting the perfectionistic mindset: Moving to mindful excellence. *Gifted Child Today, 41*(4), 177–185. https://doi.org/10.1177/1076217518786989

National Academies of Sciences, Engineering, and Medicine. (2019). *Vibrant and healthy kids: Aigning science, practice, and policy to advance health equity.* The National Academies Press. https://doi.org/10.17226/25466

National Association of Gifted Children. (n.d.). *Twice-exceptional students.* https://www.nagc.org/resources-publications/resources-parents/twice-exceptional-students

National Institute of Mental Health. (2017). *Any anxiety order*. https://www.nimh.nih.gov/health/statistics/any-anxiety-disorder.shtml

Parker, W. D. (1997). An empirical typology of perfectionism in academically talented children. *American Educational Research Journal, 34*(3), 545–562. https://doi.org/10.3102/00028312034003545

Penney, A. M., Miedema, V. C., & Mazmanian, D. (2015). Intelligence and emotional disorders: Is the worrying and ruminating mind a more intelligent mind? *Personality and Individual Differences, 74*, 90–93. https://doi.org/10.1016/j.paid.2014.10.005

Peterson, J. S. (2009). Myth 17: Gifted and talented individuals do not have unique social and emotional needs. *Gifted Child Quarterly, 53*(4), 280–282. https://doi.org/10.1177/0016986209346946

Reis, S. M., Baum, S. M., & Burke, E. (2014). An operational definition of twice-exceptional learners: Implications and applications. *Gifted Child Quarterly, 58*(3), 217–230. https://doi.org/10.1177/0016986214534976

Reynolds, C. R., & Bradley, M. (1983). Emotional stability of intellectually superior children versus nongifted peers as estimated by chronic anxiety levels. *School Psychology Review, 12*(2), 190–194.

Roome, J. R., & Romney, D. M. (1985). Reducing anxiety in gifted children by inducing relaxation. *Roeper Review, 7*(3), 177–179. https://doi.org/10.1080/02783198509552888

Rowe, E. W., Dandridge, J., Pawlush, A., Thompson, D. F., & Ferrier, D. E. (2014). Exploratory and confirmatory factor analyses of the WISC-IV with gifted students. *School Psychology Quarterly, 29*(4), 536–552. https://doi.org/10.1037/spq0000009

Scholwinski, E., & Reynolds, C. R. (1985). Dimensions of anxiety among high IQ children. *Gifted Child Quarterly, 29*(3), 125–130. https://doi.org/10.1177/001698628502900305

Semple, R. J., Droutman, V., & Reid, B. A. (2017). Mindfulness goes to school: Things learned (so far) from research and real-world experiences. *Psychology in the Schools, 54*(1), 29–52. https://doi.org/10.1002/pits.21981

Semple, R. J., & Lee, J. (2011). *Mindfulness-based cognitive therapy for anxious children: A manual for treating childhood anxiety*. New Harbinger.

Sharp, J. E., Niemiec, R. M., & Lawrence, C. (2017). Using mindfulness-based strengths practices with gifted populations. *Gifted Education International, 33*(2), 131–144. https://doi.org/10.1177/0261429416641009

Shaw, P., Greenstein, D., Lerch, J., Clasen, L., Lenroot, R., Gogtay, N., Evans, E, Rapport, J., & Giedd, J. (2006). Intellectual ability and cortical development in children and adolescents. *Nature, 440*(7084), 676. https://doi.org/10.1038/nature04513

Shuler, P. A. (2000). Perfectionism and gifted adolescents. *Journal of Secondary Gifted Education, 11*(4), 183–196. https://doi.org/10.4219/jsge-2000-629

Silverman, L. (1997). The construct of asynchronous development. *Peabody Journal of Education, 72*(3/4), 36–58. http://www.jstor.org/stable/1493035

Sousa, D. A. (2009). *How the gifted brain learns* (2nd ed.). Corwin.

Speirs Neumeister, K. L. (2016). Perfectionism in gifted students. In M. Neihart, S. I. Pfeiffer, & T. L. Cross (Eds.), *The social and emotional development of gifted students: What do we know?* (2nd ed., pp. 29–40). Prufrock Press.

Steimer, T. (2002). The biology of fear- and anxiety-related behaviors. *Dialogues in Clinical Neuroscience, 4*(3), 231–249.

Tong, J., & Yewchuk, C. (1996). Self-concept and sex-role orientation in gifted high school students. *Gifted Child Quarterly, 40*(1), 15–23. https://doi.org/10.1177/001698629604000103

Van Gemert, L. (2019). *Perfectionism: A practical guide to managing "never good enough"*. Great Potential Press.

Vandiver, B. J., & Worrell, F. C. (2002). The reliability and validity of scores on the almost perfect scale–revised with academically talented middle school students. *Journal of Advanced Academics, 13*(3), 108–119. https://doi.org/10.4219/jsge-2002-372

Webb, J. T., Amend, E. R., & Beljan, P. (2016). *Misdiagnosis and dual diagnoses of gifted children and adults: ADHD, bipolar, OCD, Asperger's, depression, and other disorders* (2nd ed.). Great Potential Press.

Zeidner, M., & Schleyer, E. J. (1999). Test anxiety in intellectually gifted school students. *Anxiety, Stress and Coping, 12*(2), 163–189. https://doi.org/10.1080/10615809908248328

Zeidner, M., & Shani-Zinovich, I. (2011). Do academically gifted and non-gifted students differ on the Big-Five and adaptive status? Some recent data and conclusions. *Personality and Individual Differences, 51*(5), 566–570. https://doi.org/10.1016/j.paid.2011.05.007

Zoogman, S., Goldberg, S. B., Hoyt, W. T., & Miller, L. (2015, April). Mindfulness interventions with youth: A meta-analysis. *Mindfulness, 6*, 290–302. https://doi.org/10.1007/s12671-013-0260-4

Zucker, B. (2016). *Anxiety-free kids: An interactive guide for parents and children* (2nd ed.). Prufrock Press.

Glossary

Term	Definition
Ability Grouping	Assignment of students by class or group based on observed behavior or performance for the purpose of instruction.
Accelerated Learning	An academic intervention that matches the level, complexity, and pace of the curriculum with the readiness and motivation of the student.
Acceleration	Acceleration is an intervention that allows a student to progress through school at a faster than usual rate and/or younger than typical age. Acceleration may be content- or grade-based.
Accommodation	Changes that allow a person with a disability to participate more fully in learning.
Accountability	Holding students, faculty, administrators, and district personnel responsible for instructional outcomes.
Achievement Test	A test designed to measure what students have already learned, mostly in specific content areas.
Acute Stress Disorder	Categorized by the responses of individuals after exposure to a trauma event, such as threatened death, serious injury, or sexual violence.

Term	Definition
Adaptive Behavior	Skills learned in order to function in everyday life.
Affective Curriculum	A curriculum that focuses on person/social awareness and adjustment, and includes the study of values, attitudes, and self.
Alternative Assessment	A measure of student performance on alternate achievement standards or for a functional life skills curriculum.
Anxiety	Feeling worry, nervousness, or excessive unease about a real or anticipated experience
Aptitude	Developed or undeveloped potential or ability; innate or acquired capacity in a particular area (talent).
Aptitude Test	A test that predicts a student's ability, such as an evaluation of mathematical ability, language proficiency, or abstract reasoning.
Area of Giftedness	The specific set of abilities in which a student performs or shows potential to perform at a remarkably high level of accomplishment (domain).
Array of Learning Experiences	A list of challenging activities or opportunities that fit the unique interests and abilities of advanced-level students.
Artistically Gifted	Possessing outstanding ability in the visual and/or performing arts.
Asperger's Syndrome	A pervasive developmental disorder that involves delays in development of basic skill, including socializing, coordination, and the ability to communicate.
Assessment	The process of documenting, usually in measurable terms, knowledge, skills, and attitudes of an individual learner or learning community.
Assistive Technology	An item, piece of equipment, or product purchased, created, or customized to increase, maintain, or improve functional capability of a student with a disability.
Asynchrony	Disparate rates of intellectual, emotional, and physical growth or development often displayed by gifted children.
At Risk	A student whose economic, physical, emotional, or academic needs go unmet or serve as barriers to talent recognition or development, thus putting them in danger of underachieving or dropping out.
Attending Behavior	A learned behavior in which students are engaged in active listening and appropriate response.
Attention Deficit/ Hyperactivity Disorder (ADHD)	A medical disorder characterized by inattention, an inability to focus, and/or hyperactivity and impulsivity.

Term	Definition
Attention-Deficit Hyperactive Gifted (ADHG)	A designation based on the work of C. Matthew Fugate in which a gifted student with ADHD is recognized for their strengths and creative-thinking ability.
Authentic Assessment	The process of evaluating student learning through the use of student portfolios, performance, or observations in place or in conjunction with more traditional measures of performance, such as tests and written assignments.
Autism Spectrum Disorders (ASD)	A condition that ranges in severity in which an individual's communication and social behavior is markedly different from others.
Automaticity in Math	The ability to easily retrieve basic math facts from long-term memory in addition, subtraction, multiplication, and division without conscious effort (math facts fluency).
Automaticity in Reading	The ability to read words fluidly with the appropriate intonation, tone, stress, and rhythm.
Behavior Management	In special education, responding to, preventing, and deescalating disruptive behavior.
Bloom's Taxonomy	A theoretical framework developed by Benjamin Bloom for determining the degree of rigor in classroom questions and student tasks.
Brainstorming	An activity used to generate many creative ideas that have no right or wrong answers and are accepted without criticism.
Child Find	The responsibility of a school district to locate, identify, and evaluate children with disabilities in its jurisdiction.
Child Study Team	A team that comes together for the purpose of reviewing an individual student's educational progress. May result in recommendation for further assessment, services, or intervention.
Classroom Observation	Observing a student's primary educational setting to see how the student learns and interacts with others.
Classroom Strategy	A technique for instructional, social-emotional management to support student learning within a classroom.
Cluster Grouping	A grouping assignment for students with similar abilities in an otherwise heterogeneous classroom. *Also see Total School Cluster Grouping.*
Cognition	Acquiring knowledge (thinking).
Compacting	Eliminating repetition, minimizing drill, and accelerating instruction in basic skills so that gifted students can move to more challenging material.

Term	Definition
Complexity	Extension of content in, between, and across disciplines through the study of themes, problems, and issues; seeing relationships between and among ideas in/within the topic, discipline, and disciplines; examining relationships in, between, and across disciplines over time and from multiple points of view.
Confident Numeracy	Confidence in the ability to understand, reason with, and apply numerical concepts.
Continuum of Learning Experiences	Articulated intellectual, artistic, creative, and/or leadership activities and opportunities that build upon one another each year a student is in school.
Co-occurring	The presence of one or more conditions, such as giftedness and ADHD.
Creativity	The process of developing new, uncommon, or unique ideas.
Creatively Gifted	Possessing outstanding imagination, thinking ability, innovative or creative reasoning ability, ability in problem solving, and/or high attainment in original or creative thinking.
Criterion-Referenced Testing	An assessment that compares a student's test performance to their mastery of a body of knowledge or specific skill rather than relating scores to the performance of other students.
Critical Thinking	The process of analyzing, reflecting, and applying prior knowledge to discover the best solution to a problem.
Cumulative File	School records maintained by a school or district with information about student performance, including but not limited to test scores, evaluations, student disability, and placement. Parents have the right to see the file at any time.
Curriculum Compacting	After showing a level of proficiency in the basic curriculum, a student is allowed to exchange instructional time for other learning experiences.
Decoding	The process of turning systematic strings of letters into words by stringing together the individual sounds that are mapped on to the letters or letter groups.
Deficit-Based Approach to Education	A needs-driven, problem-focused approach to education in which schools focus on correction of perceived student deficiencies.
Depth	Exploration of content within a discipline to include analyzing from the concrete to the abstract, the familiar to the unfamiliar, the known to the unknown; exploring the discipline by going beyond facts and concepts into generalizations, principles, theories, laws; investigating the layers of experience within a discipline through details, patterns, trends, unanswered questions, and/or ethical considerations.

Term	Definition
Diagnostic and Statistical Manual of Mental Disorders (DSM)	A comprehensive classification system of mental health disorders published by the American Psychiatric Association.
Differentiation	Modifying curriculum and instruction according to content, pacing, and/or product to meet unique student needs in the classroom.
Direct Instruction	An instructional approach to academic subjects that emphasizes the use of carefully sequenced steps, including demonstration, modeling, guided practice, and independent application.
Disorder	A medical term describing a problem or illness affecting an individual's mind or body.
Divergent Thinking	Thinking that results in novel, unique, or creative solutions or answers. Contrasts with convergent thinking.
Diversity	The presence of difference between individuals and among groups, including, but not limited to, age, socioeconomics, education, race and ethnicity, gender, sexual orientation, culture, and religious beliefs.
Dual Diagnosis of the Gifted	The coexistence of giftedness with a specific learning or emotional disorder (co-occuring).
Dyscalculia	A pattern of difficulties characterized by problems processing numerical information, learning arithmetic facts, and performing accurate or fluent calculations.
Dysgraphia	A disorder characterized by difficulties in the acquisition of writing and spelling skills. It is frequently coexistent with dyslexia, as deficits in the ability to identify and manipulate speech sounds, the ability to retain a string of sounds or letters in memory, and the ability to remember the graphemes and words of our language impact accurate and fluent writing and spelling.
Dyslexia	A neurobiological learning disorder that hinders the development of reading skills, and is characterized by deficits in the ability to identify and manipulate speech sounds, the ability to retain a string of sounds or letters in memory, and the ability to remember the graphemes and words of our language.
Early Entrance to Kindergarten or First Grade	When a child who displays academic, social, and emotional readiness begins school at a younger age than most other children.
Ecological Systems Theory	Urie Bronfenbrenner's explanation of how the inherent qualities of a child and their environment interact to influence how they will grow and develop.

Term	Definition
Eligibility	A process of qualifying for a service under one of the federally defined disability categories.
Enrichment	Activities that add or go beyond the existing curriculum and occur in or outside of the classroom.
Evaluation	A critical examination conducted by a professional of the strengths and relative weakness, activities, and behaviors of an individual student.
Evidenced-Based Practice	A practice reflecting best-available information.
Exceptional Learners	Students with an IQ in the bottom or top 3% of the population, or those with other physical or mental differences that affect learning.
Executive Functioning	The cognitive processes that are necessary to direct and control a person's actions.
Executive Functioning Skills	Skills demonstrating what the student in a daily context can do with the innate abilities of the executive function.
Flexible Grouping	An instructional strategy where students are grouped together to receive appropriately challenging instruction. Groups are determined by interest, readiness, or learning profile and may change.
Flexible Pacing	Flexible pacing places students at an appropriate instructional level, allowing them to move forward in the curriculum as they master content and skills.
Fluid Intelligence	Reflects the ability to flexibly reason, induce rules and patterns, problem solve, and manipulate new information.
Formative Assessment	An informal, ongoing method to determine student progress toward a learning goal. Teachers may choose to modify instruction for future lessons based on the results.
Free and Appropriate Education (FAPE)	Special education and related services that are provided at public expense. Services are supervised by the school and must meet state standards.
Generalized Anxiety Disorder (GAD)	Anxiety that is characterized by having worry that occurs on more days than not for a period of 6 months or more.
Gifted and Talented Services	Services and activities not ordinarily provided by the school that are specifically designed to fully develop the capabilities of students who give evidence of high achievement or capability in areas such as intellectual, creative, artistic, or leadership capacity.

Term	Definition
Gifted and Talented Students	The United States government defines gifted and talented students as "Students, children, or youth who give evidence of high achievement capability in areas such as intellectual, creative, artistic, or leadership capacity, or in specific academic fields, and who need services and activities not ordinarily provided by the school in order to fully develop those capabilities."
Gifted in Leadership	Possessing the natural ability to influence others; possessing skills in interpersonal relationships demonstrated, for example, by outstanding ability in such activities as student government.
Gifted in Specific Academic Areas	Possessing superior ability or potential in a specific course of study, such as English language arts/reading, mathematics, science, or social studies.
Grade-Level Acceleration	The practice of assigning a student to a higher grade level than is typical given the student's age full-time for the purpose of meeting the high-achieving or gifted student's unique needs.
Graphic Organizer	A visual representation of organizing thinking and ideas. Graphic organizers are particularly useful for those who organize visual spatially or who need additional scaffolding to engage in a learning task.
Grouping	The practice of grouping or placing students with similar abilities and/or performance together for instruction; has been shown to positively impact student learning gains.
Heterogeneous Classroom	A classroom with students of mixed ability or readiness levels. A teacher is expected to meet the broad range of student needs. Also called an inclusive classroom.
Heterogeneous Grouping	Grouping students by mixed ability.
Holistic Education	A focus on preparing students to meet any challenges they may face in life and in their academic career, including learning about oneself, healthy relationships and positive social behaviors, social and emotional development, and resilience.
Homogenous Grouping	Grouping students by need, ability, or interest to restrict the range of student readiness or needs that a teacher must address.
Identification of Giftedness	The recognition of advanced cognitive and academic aptitudes.
Identification of Students for Services	The assessment of students for specific services and/or programs within a school setting.
IEP Team	A group of qualified individuals who make all decisions related to the instructional program of a child with special needs, including placement and services provided.

Term	Definition
Impairment	Any loss or abnormality of psychological, physiological, or anatomical structure or function.
Imposter Syndrome	Self-doubt caused by not accepting one's success.
Inclusive Classroom	A classroom that contains students of varying ability levels.
Independent Study	A self-directed learning strategy where the teacher acts as guide and the student plays a more active role in designing and managing their own learning.
Individual Education Program (IEP)	A plan that details the support and services a school will provide to meet the individual needs of a student with a disability who qualifies for special education.
Individuals With Disabilities Education Improvement Act (IDEA)	Enacted in 1975 as the Education for all Handicapped Children Act, and subsequently periodically reauthorized, it is a comprehensive federally funded law that governs the education of students with disabilities.
Intellectually Gifted	Possessing superior intelligence, with potential or demonstrated accomplishments in several fields of study; ability to perform complex mental tasks.
Intelligence	The ability to learn, reason, and problem solve.
Intelligence Quotient (IQ)	A numerical representation of intelligence derived from dividing mental age (result from an intelligence test) by the chronological age times 100. Traditionally, an average IQ is considered to be 100.
Intensity/ overexcitability	Heightened physiological experiences as a result of neuronal sensitivities as presented by the research of Kazimierz Dabrowski.
Interest Groups	A group composed of those who share a specific interest of learning.
Interest Inventory	A tool used to help teachers determine the interests of their students in order to provide more motivating and engaged learning.
Interfering Behavior	Behavior that gets in the way of a student's ability to access curriculum and/or participate in the classroom.
Intervention	A set of steps intended to improve student academic outcomes or behaviors.

Term	Definition
Learning Disability (LD)	Disorders that result in learning challenges that are not caused by low intelligence; problems with hearing or vision or lack of educational opportunity. Many children with learning disabilities have difficulties in particular skill areas, such as reading or math.
Learning Preferences	The preferred way(s) in which individuals interact or process new information across cognitive (knowledge), psychomotor (skills), and affective (attitude) domains.
Least Restrictive Environment (LRE)	A setting that provides child-appropriate opportunities to learn alongside nondisabled students, to the greatest extent.
Medical Model of Disability	A disability model that seeks to identify what is wrong with an individual and then provides treatment.
Metacognition	An awareness and understanding of one's thought process.
Modifications	A change in what a student is taught or expected to learn. This term is used in Individualized Education Programs and 504 plans.
Motivation	The process that initiates guides and maintains goal-orientated behaviors.
Multisensory Instruction	Language instruction that incorporates three distinct neurological pathways: visual processing (seeing), auditory processing (hearing), and tactile-kinesthetic processing (feeling).
Neurodiversity	Variations in the human brain regarding sociability, learning, attention, mood, and other mental functions in a nonpathological sense.
Norm-referenced Testing	An assessment that compares an individual's performance to a large group of others who have taken the same assessment.
Numeracy	The ability to understand and apply mathematical concepts to problem solving.
Observational Records	Information about a student's academic performance provided by anyone who works with the student.
Obsessive-Compulsive Disorder (OCD)	An anxiety disorder in which people have recurring, unwanted thoughts, ideas or sensations (obsessions) that make them feel driven to do something repetitively (compulsions).
Occupational Therapy	An intervention that focuses on teaching individuals the skills they need to be independent in their daily activities.
Oppositional Defiant Disorder (ODD)	A pervasive pattern of preoccupation with order, perfectionism, and control at the expense of flexibility.

Term	Definition
Orton-Gillingham Approach to Reading	An approach to reading instruction that centers on multisensory learning and is language-based, multisensory, structured, sequential, cumulative, cognitive, and flexible.
Other Health Impaired (OHI)	A student with chronic health problems that result in limited ability in an educational environment.
Out-of-School Programs	Educational experiences that occur beyond the school day that may provide opportunities for remediation, skill building, interest and/or talent development.
Overexcitabilities (OE)	A term originated by Kazimierz Dabrowski to describe excessive response to stimuli in five psychic domains (psychomotor, sensual, intellectual, imaginational, and emotional), which may occur singly or in combination. Intensity resulting in heightened responses/reactions to everyday stimuli.
Pacing	The speed at which content is presented and instruction delivered. Pacing that matches the student's rate of learning is optimal. Because gifted students are usually able to learn faster, they often need accelerated pacing.
Panic Attack	Sudden onset of fear accompanied by symptoms that include sweating, trembling or shaking, feelings of choking, etc.
Panic Disorder	The presence of recurrent unexpected panic attacks.
Perfectionism	Setting impossibly high standards and striving for flawlessness, combined with excessive self-criticism, an unhealthy concern for others' opinions of one's work, and overgeneralization of failure despite adverse consequences.
Person-First Language	Neutral language in which people are first and a disability second, such as a child with dyslexia and a student with an emotional disorder.
Phoneme	The smallest parts of sound in a spoken word.
Phonemic Awareness	The ability to hear, identify the sequence and number, and manipulate sounds located within each spoken stream.
Placement	The type of setting, classroom or school in which a child is educated. By law, schools in the United States must educate kids with disabilities alongside their nondisabled peers to the maximum extent that is appropriate.
Portfolio Assessment	An alternative or supplement to traditional measures of giftedness, portfolios offer a collection of student work overtime that can help to determine achievement and progress.
Post-Traumatic Stress Disorder	Categorized by the responses of individuals after exposure to a trauma event, such as threatened death, serious injury, or sexual violence.

Term	Definition
Processing Speed	The rate at which an individual is able to make sense and apply information. A measure of cognitive efficiency or cognitive proficiency, not intelligence.
Pull-out Programs and Specialized Programs	Programming options for students that occur in a variety of ways intended to provide additional support and raise student achievement.
Qualitative Measures	Performance indicators that cannot be recorded numerically and that include observations, anecdotal records, checklists, interviews, student products, performances, etc.
Quantitative Measures	Performance indicators that can be expressed in terms of definite numbers or amounts, such as scores on achievement tests.
Reading Comprehension	This process allows students to visualize the item or process represented by the printed words, and it relies solely upon the accurate identification and pronunciation of the sequential strings of graphemes and phonemes presented.
Reading Fluency	The ability to read a sentence with ease, accuracy and understanding.
Referral	An action that directs a student or family to access consultation or additional resources.
Remediation	Instruction provided to students to increase performance and achieve expected competency in core areas such as reading and math.
Researched-Based	Facts that are accumulated by research.
School Psychologist	A licensed professional who assists in the identification of students' intellectual, social and emotional needs.
School Suspension	A consequence of inappropriate behavior in which a student is not allowed on campus for a prescribed length of time.
Scientifically Based	A research finding that can be replicated.
Section 504	A federal law that requires a school district to provide a free and appropriate public education to each child with a disability in the district.
Self-Monitoring	The ability to observe yourself and know if you are doing an activity according to a standard. For example, knowing if you do or do not understand what you are reading, or whether your tone of voice is appropriate for the circumstances.
Separation Anxiety Disorder	Excessive fear or anxiety concerning separation from those to whom the individual is attached.
Social Model of Disability	A model defining a disability as emerging from the social environment around an individual; focuses on issues related to barriers, attitudes, and exclusion.

Term	Definition
Specific Phobia	The fear or anxiety around a specific object or situation.
Stealth Dyscalculia	A math-based difficulty that may remain undetected due to strong compensation mechanisms with verbal, fluid reasoning and working memory strengths.
Social and Emotional Needs	Gifted and talented students may have affective needs that include heightened or unusual sensitivity to self-awareness, emotions, and expectations of themselves or others, and a sense of justice, moral judgment, or altruism.
Social Anxiety Disorder (SAD)	The marked fear about one or more social situations in which the individual is exposed to possible scrutiny by others.
Sound/ Symbolism Correspondence	The act of connecting the symbols used in the written language with the corresponding sounds that they represent in the spoken language.
Special Education	Specially designed instruction, provided at no cost to parents, to meet the unique needs of a child with a disability. It can include specialized activities in gym, music and arts education and specialized instruction in the classroom, home or other settings.
Specific Learning Disability (SLD)	A disorder unrelated to intelligence, motivation, effort, or other known causes of low achievement that causes a student to struggle in certain areas of learning, such as reading, writing or doing math.
Standardized Tests	Objective measures of student achievement on academic or proficiency standards that require all test takers to answer the same questions and are scored in a consistent manner, making it possible to compare relative performance of individual students to groups of students.
Strength-Based Approach to Learning	Asset-based, opportunity-focused approach to education in which inherent capacities by students are nurtured.
Student Advocate	An individual who works on behalf of students to provide resources and referrals that address student needs within a school setting.
Subject Acceleration	The process of moving a student through content-specific curriculum at a faster rate than age-mates.
Summative Assessment	Occurs at the end of a unit of study to determine student mastery of specific learning goals.
Syndrome	A medical term describing a group of symptoms that commonly occur together or condition characterized by specific symptoms.
Talent Development	Advancing or developing student potential or demonstrated talent in a particular area.

Term	Definition
Telescope Curriculum	To cover the same amount of materials or activities in less time, allowing more time for enrichment activities and projects that better suit the interests, needs, and readiness levels of gifted students.
Testing Accommodations	Modifications made to tests or testing conditions that allow students to demonstrate their knowledge and skills in a testing situation.
Tiered Assignments	A differentiated instructional strategy in which all students work toward the same goal, but activities are geared toward each student's level of understanding.
Total School Cluster Grouping (TSCG)	The Total School Cluster Grouping Model (TSCG) is a specific, research-based, total-school application of cluster grouping combined with differentiation, focused on meeting the needs of students identified as gifted, while also improving teaching, learning, and achievement of all students.
Twice-Exceptional (2e) Learners	Learners who are identified as gifted children who have potential for high achievement and give evidence of one or more disabilities. Twice-exceptional learners may qualify for gifted program services as well as special education services.
Underlearning	A situation wherein the student's developmental potential is not actualized as a result of a mismatch between the educational opportunities provided and the student's educational needs.
Universal Design for Learning (UDL)	A framework intended to optimize teaching and learning for all based on scientific research on how people learn.
Universal Screening	A practice in which all students in a target grade or grades are administered an initial assessment to determine eligibility for services.
Visual Processing Disorder (VPD)	The process for interpreting visual information. Students with visual processing issues may have difficulty recognizing differences between two shapes or finding specific information on a page or screen.
Whole Child Education	A model in which parents, families, and communities are seen as critical partners in student learning. Whole Child education honors creativity, confidence, and collaboration.
Whole-Grade Acceleration	Assigning a student full-time to a higher grade than typical for the purpose of meeting the high-achieving or gifted student's unique needs (grade acceleration, grade skipping).
Working Memory	The ability to store and manage information in one's mind for a short period of time

About the Editors

C. Matthew Fugate, Ph.D., is an assistant professor of educational psychology and assistant chair of Urban Education at the University of Houston-Downtown. He earned his doctorate in gifted education at Purdue University. Prior to this, Matthew worked as an elementary teacher in the Houston Independent School District, where he also served as a gifted coordinator and magnet coordinator. During this time, Matthew earned his master's in educational psychology with a concentration in gifted education from the University of Connecticut. His research has examined the relationship between working memory and levels of creativity in gifted students who also have characteristics related to Attention Deficit/Hyperactivity Disorder (ADHD). He has also examined the coping mechanisms of twice-exceptional girls in secondary school as they navigate both their academic studies and interpersonal relationships. Matthew was also part of a team that looked at the benefits of the Total School Cluster Grouping Model, a Jacob K. Javits grant-funded project. He has presented to parents, teachers, and schools across the United States and internationally on topics such as creativity, curriculum compacting, identification, twice-exceptionality, underserved populations, and Total School Cluster

295

Grouping. Matthew serves on the board of the Texas Association for the Gifted and Talented (TAGT)and as chair of the Special Populations Network for the National Association for Gifted Children (NAGC). Additionally, he serves as a reviewer for several journals and is the associate editor of *Teaching for High Potential*. He has published several articles, book chapters, and books related to his work.

Wendy A. Behrens, M.A. Ed., a graduate of Bradley University and Hamline University, is the Gifted and Talented Education Specialist for the Minnesota Department of Education, where she advises educators, administrators, parents, and policymakers. Prior to her service to the state, Wendy worked as a district K–12 gifted services coordinator and a consultant for the Science Museum of Minnesota. In 2009, her vision for professional learning led to the creation of the Hormel Foundation Gifted and Talented Education Symposium, an annual event attracting attendees from around the country and the world. Recently, Wendy was the director of Project North Star, a Jacob K. Javits grant designed to elevate the identification and programming approaches provided for disadvantaged and underserved rural populations. Her current Javits grant work, Universal Plus, focuses on creating a two-step process for equitably identifying computer talent. Wendy is a past-president of the Council of State Directors of Programs for the Gifted. In 2013, she received the President's Award from NAGC. Wendy is an active member of and has held leadership roles in NAGC, the Council of Exceptional Children, The Association for the Gifted, and World Council on Gifted Children. Additionally, Wendy serves on several education-related advisory councils and the *Gifted Child Today* editorial board. She has published several books, chapters, and articles related to the education of gifted learners and frequently presents to national and international audiences on comprehensive service design, acceleration, underserved populations, and policies that support highly able learners.

For 17 years, **Cecelia Boswell, Ed.D.,** taught migrant and gifted students in a rural school. During that time, she was a finalist for Texas Migrant Teacher of the Year. After public school, Cecelia began work for a Texas Education Service Center (ESC) as the Director of Gifted Education and State Director of AP/IB Projects. She received the award for Gifted Advocate of the Year and, upon completion of her doctorate, the National Rural Education Association's award for Dissertation of the Year. She founded Austin Creek Education Systems, developed curriculum for the Texas and Florida Departments of Education, led research projects for International Baccalaureate, and audited gifted programs across the state. During this time, she served on the board and as president of TAGT. Cecelia next became the Executive Director of Advanced Academics in an urban school. While there, she developed a middle school academy for gifted learners. She was awarded the Texas Administrator of the Year by TAGT and was elected to the board and became president for Council for Exceptional Children, The Association for the Gifted. Cecelia has published in juried journals and written teacher guides for children's novels. She has coauthored five books on gifted education. Cecelia has also conducted a rural research study with a colleague, and an article is in press. Currently, she works with a school district's efforts to revamp services for the gifted students, facilitates online classes, contracts with TAGT, and presents sessions for teachers of the gifted.

About the Authors

Susan M. Baum, Ph.D., is the director of the 2e Center for Research and Professional Development at Bridges Academy, a school for twice-exceptional students, and provost of the Bridges Graduate School of Cognitive Diversity in Education. She is the author of more than 20 books, chapters, and research monographs, as well as more than 30 articles primarily focusing on understanding and nurturing the needs of special populations of underachieving gifted students, including the award-winning third edition of her seminal work, *To Be Gifted and Learning Disabled*. Her research and experience in the field of twice-exceptional education have earned her much recognition. She was named the recipient of the 2010 the Lifetime Achievement Award granted by the Weinfeld Group, the 2011 Connecticut Association for the Gifted's Friend of the Gifted Award, the 2015 Distinguished Professional Alumni Award from the Neag School of Education, the Lifetime Achievement Award from the Association for the Education of Gifted Underachieving Students and the *2e Newsletter* in 2017, and the 2019 Alexinia Baldwin Award from National Association for Gifted Students.

Professor Emeritus from The College of New Rochelle, Dr. Baum is widely published in the areas of differentiated instruction, twice-exceptional students, primary-aged gifted students, and social and emotional factors affecting gifted students. A popular speaker and workshop presenter, she has traveled worldwide teaching about creativity, education of the gifted and talented, and twice-exceptionality. She currently is a frequent presenter at Bright and Quirky—an online summit for supporting twice-exceptionality.

Dr. Baum has served on the Board of Directors of the National Association for Gifted Students and Smart Kids With 2e, and is the past president and founder of the Association for the Education of Gifted Underachieving Students.

Teresa Argo Boatman is a licensed psychologist in private practice in Plymouth, MN. She specializes in assessment of gifted children as well as interventions with families and children. Her clinical work focuses on helping children, adults, and families find solutions in their real-world situations. Teresa is the current president of the Minnesota Council for the Gifted and Talented and has worked for more than 20 years with families and school districts in the Midwest on educational choices and emotional health for children and adults.

Anne E. Boatman is a graduate of the University of Rochester with a Bachelor's of Science in Brain & Cognitive Science. Her degree focus is in neurobiology and neuropsychology. Her research focus is broadly in adolescent mental health and specficially on the risk and resilience factors around suicide.

Stephen H. Chou, Psy.D., is a supervising clinical psychologist in private practice in both California and Colorado, and the Director of Training and Research at the Summit Center. Stephen is a former director of the board of directors of Supporting the Emotional Needs of the Gifted (SENG). He is also a former adjunct professor with the University of Denver and a former adjunct professor at Alliant International University–California School of Professional Psychology in San Francisco, CA, and Hong Kong, supervising clinical psychologist at the Chinatown Child Development Center through the Department of Public Health with the City and County of San Francisco. He was executive director of the Big Sibling Program. Stephen practices from a developmental, strength-based, and multicultural stance through individual and family counseling, as well as intellectual, educational, behavioral, emotional, and neuropsychological assessments with children, families, and adults, especially with those who are gifted, talented, twice-exceptional, and multi-exceptional. Stephen also presents at state, national, and international conferences on a variety of topics in giftedness/2e.

Walter Edward Dunson, Ph.D., B.C.A.S.E., is a board-certified advocate in special education, senior literacy therapist, author, and professor. He is the executive director and founder of Cardinal Reading Strategies and has 24 years of experience working with students in the areas of language-based learning and language acquisition.

Formerly, he served as a literature instructor, a reading lab coordinator, and curriculum developer at The Briarwood School, a school for dyslexics in Houston, TX, and he served as a language training instructor at The Kildonan School, a school for dyslexics in Amenia, NY.

Walter is a strong proponent of evidence-based reading research, a former member of the board of directors of the International Dyslexia Association (Houston Branch), and the author of *School Success for Kids With Dyslexia and Other Reading Difficulties* and *The English Code*. He has appeared as a guest on NPR and Project Baltimore, and he has presented on the importance of evidence-based reading instruction before the Maryland State Board of Education, the Maryland Higher Education Commission, the Maryland House of Delegates, and the Maryland Senate. Walter also served as an adjunct professor in Loyola University Maryland's Graduate School of Education, where he taught structured literacy skills to public and private school educators. He is a former member of the Maryland State Department of Education Elementary Literacy Work Group, a committee chartered to revise the four reading courses at the college/university level that teachers must complete in order to obtain state certification.

Claire E. Hughes, Ph.D., is an associate professor of Education and Teacher Preparation at the College of Coastal Georgia. Previously, she was faculty director of the Special Needs and Inclusion program at Canterbury Christ Church University in England, and a Fulbright Scholar to Greece. She is active in the National Association for Gifted Children, The Association for the Gifted (CEC-TAG) and Teacher Education Divisions (CEC-TED) of the Council for Exceptional Children. She is author of numerous books and chapters, and her research areas include twice-exceptional children—particularly gifted children with autism, positivistic views of exceptionality, and international education. A member of a team that won the 2018 Times Higher Education Award for International Impact, she is passionate about working with teachers around the world on developing abilities and talents in all children through Universal Design for Learning, higher order thinking, creativity, and differentiated instruction.

Nancy Knop, Ph.D., ET/P, is an educational therapist practicing in San Francisco. She works with children and adolescents to provide prescriptive remediation for challenges and background gaps in math and other subjects, specializing in work with 2e students. Nancy taught science for 23 years to grades 7–12 at Head Royce School in Oakland and served as department chair for 5 years. She holds a B.S. degree from the University of Connecticut, a Ph.D. from University of California, Berkeley, and a graduate-level certificate in Educational Therapy from UC Berkeley Extension. Registered at the professional level with the Association of Educational Therapists, she has practiced as an educational therapist for 15 years, including several years at Summit Center. Nancy writes and speaks locally and nationally, interpreting primary research about the biology of learning, including brain development, the neurobiology of math and language learning, the role of vision, the importance of gesture, and the essential nature of sleep and other environmental influences that relate to learning and learning differences.

Robin M. Schader holds a Ph.D. in Educational Psychology from the University of Connecticut, specializing in Gifted and Talented Education, with a focus on talent development and the role of parents. She worked as a research professor at the University of Connecticut and, for 10 years, was the Parent Resource Advisor for the National Association for Gifted Children (NAGC), writing a regular column in *Parenting for High Potential.* She has been invited to speak at numerous state and national conferences, including NAGC, National PTA, National HeadStart, and the National Association for the Education of Young Children (NAEYC). Before graduate school, she founded and directed Music House, a nonprofit "home away from home" for exceptionally talented precollege music students from around the world who had outgrown the teaching available in their communities and needed to live near the San Francisco Conservatory of Music to pursue high-level training. Having served on the boards of both public and private institutions, she is currently a trustee of Bridges Academy, a school for twice-exceptional students, as well as on the executive board of the 2e Center for Research and Professional Development. Robin is the mother of three children—now grown and parents themselves—who each continue to contribute generously to her education as parent.

Drs. Eleonoor van Gerven studied at the Radboud University Nijmegen and got a double degree in educational sociology and philosophy and history of education. She is executive director of Slim! Educatief, a teacher-educating institute for continuous professional development. She specialized in gifted education and the systemic change and solution focused approach. She developed the postgraduate teacher education Specialist in Gifted Education and the postmaster teacher education Specialist in Educating Twice-Exceptional Students, which are both accredited by the Dutch Association for Higher Education. Eleonoor has written 13 books on (gifted) education and almost 100 articles on this topic. Her current international research focuses on the competencies for specialists in gifted education and the impact of Dublin Descriptors on teacher education courses aiming for continuous professional development regarding gifted education.

In 2014, Eleonoor won a Mensa award for her lifelong contribution to Dutch Education. In September 2019, she received an honourable live membership of the Dutch Association for SEN Coordinators and the Dutch Association of Specialists in Gifted Education as a reward for her careerlong contribution to the education of gifted children.